Härdle • Kleinow • Stahl
Applied Quantitative Finance

Springer
Berlin
Heidelberg
New York
Barcelona
Hong Kong
London
Milan
Paris
Tokyo

W. Härdle • T. Kleinow • G. Stahl

Applied
Quantitative Finance

Theory and Computational Tools

 Springer

Wolfgang Härdle
Torsten Kleinow
Humboldt-Universität zu Berlin
Institut für Statistik und Ökonometrie
CASE-Center for Applied Statistics and Economics
10178 Berlin, Germany
e-mail: haerdle/kleinow@wiwi.hu-berlin.de

Gerhard Stahl
Bundesanstalt für Finanzdienstleistungsaufsicht
Graurheindorfer Str. 108
53117 Bonn, Germany
e-mail: gstahl@bakred.bund.de

Cover art: Detail of "Portrait of the Franciscan monk Luca Pacioli, humanist and mathematician (1445-1517)" by Jacopo de Barbari, Museo di Capodimonte, Naples, Italy

---

This book is also available as e-book on www.i-xplore.de .
Use the licence code at the end of the book to download the e-book.

CIP-Data applied for
Die Deutsche Bibliothek - CIP-Einheitsaufnahme

Härdle, Wolfgang:
Applied quantitative finance: theory and computational tools / W. Härdle; T. Kleinow; G. Stahl. - Berlin; Heidelberg; New York; Barcelona; Hong Kong; London; Milan; Paris; Tokyo: Springer, 2002
ISBN 3-540-43460-7

ISBN 3-540-43460-7 Springer-Verlag Berlin Heidelberg New York

---

Mathematics Subject Classification (2000): 62-07, 62P05, 68N15, 91B28, 91B84

Springer-Verlag Berlin Heidelberg New York
a member of BertelsmannSpringer Science+Business Media GmbH

http://www.springer.de

© Springer-Verlag Berlin Heidelberg 2002
Printed in Germany

Cover design: *design & production GmbH*, Heidelberg
Typesetting by the authors using a MD*book macro package
Printed on acid-free paper   SPIN 10874956   40/3142ck-5 4 3 2 1 0

Contents

II Credit Risk   85

4 Rating Migrations   87

Steffi Höse, Stefan Huschens and Robert Wania

III Implied Volatility 125

IV Econometrics 219

10 Multivariate Volatility Models 221

Matthias R. Fengler and Helmut Herwartz

11 Statistical Process Control 237

Sven Knoth

12 An Empirical Likelihood Goodness-of-Fit Test for Diffusions 259

Song Xi Chen, Wolfgang Härdle and Torsten Kleinow

13 A simple state space model of house prices   283

Rainer Schulz and Axel Werwatz

14 Long Memory Effects Trading Strategy 309

Oliver Jim Blaskowitz and Peter Schmidt

15 Locally time homogeneous time series modeling 323

Danilo Mercurio

Preface

This book is designed for students and researchers who want to develop professional skill in modern quantitative applications in finance. The Center for Applied Statistics and Economics (CASE) course at Humboldt-Universität zu Berlin that forms the basis for this book is offered to interested students who have had some experience with probability, statistics and software applications but have not had advanced courses in mathematical finance. Although the course assumes only a modest background it moves quickly between different fields of applications and in the end, the reader can expect to have theoretical and computational tools that are deep enough and rich enough to be relied on throughout future professional careers.

The text is readable for the graduate student in financial engineering as well as for the inexperienced newcomer to quantitative finance who wants to get a grip on modern statistical tools in financial data analysis. The experienced reader with a bright knowledge of mathematical finance will probably skip some sections but will hopefully enjoy the various computational tools of the presented techniques. A graduate student might think that some of the econometric techniques are well known. The mathematics of risk management and volatility dynamics will certainly introduce him into the rich realm of quantitative financial data analysis.

The computer inexperienced user of this e-book is softly introduced into the interactive book concept and will certainly enjoy the various practical examples. The e-book is designed as an interactive document: a stream of text and information with various hints and links to additional tools and features. Our e-book design offers also a complete PDF and HTML file with links to world wide computing servers. The reader of this book may therefore without download or purchase of software use all the presented examples and methods via the enclosed license code number with a local XploRe Quantlet Server (XQS). Such XQ Servers may also be installed in a department or addressed freely on the web, click to www.xplore-stat.de and www.quantlet.com.

"Applied Quantitative Finance" consists of four main parts: Value at Risk, Credit Risk, Implied Volatility and Econometrics. In the first part Jaschke and Jiang treat the Approximation of the Value at Risk in conditional Gaussian Models and Rank and Siegl show how the VaR can be calculated using copulas.

The second part starts with an analysis of rating migration probabilities by Höse, Huschens and Wania. Frisch and Knöchlein quantify the risk of yield spread changes via historical simulations. This part is completed by an analysis of the sensitivity of risk measures to changes in the dependency structure between single positions of a portfolio by Kiesel and Kleinow.

The third part is devoted to the analysis of implied volatilities and their dynamics. Fengler, Härdle and Schmidt start with an analysis of the implied volatility surface and show how common PCA can be applied to model the dynamics of the surface. In the next two chapters the authors estimate the risk neutral state price density from observed option prices and the corresponding implied volatilities. While Härdle and Zheng apply implied binomial trees to estimate the SPD, the method by Huynh, Kervella and Zheng is based on a local polynomial estimation of the implied volatility and its derivatives. Blaskowitz and Schmidt use the proposed methods to develop trading strategies based on the comparison of the historical SPD and the one implied by option prices.

Recently developed econometric methods are presented in the last part of the book. Fengler and Herwartz introduce a multivariate volatility model and apply it to exchange rates. Methods used to monitor sequentially observed data are treated by Knoth. Chen, Härdle and Kleinow apply the empirical likelihood concept to develop a test about a parametric diffusion model. Schulz and Werwatz estimate a state space model of Berlin house prices that can be used to construct a time series of the price of a standard house. The influence of long memory effects on financial time series is analyzed by Blaskowitz and Schmidt. Mercurio propose a methodology to identify time intervals of homogeneity for time series. The pricing of exotic options via a simulation approach is introduced by Lüssem and Schumacher The chapter by Franke, Holzberger and Müller is devoted to a nonparametric estimation approach of GARCH models. The book closes with a chapter of Aydınlı, who introduces a technology to connect standard software with the XploRe server in order to have access to quantlets developed in this book.

We gratefully acknowledge the support of Deutsche Forschungsgemeinschaft, SFB 373 Quantifikation und Simulation Ökonomischer Prozesse. A book of this kind would not have been possible without the help of many friends, colleagues and students. For the technical production of the e-book platform we would like to thank Jörg Feuerhake, Zdeněk Hlávka, Sigbert Klinke, Heiko Lehmann and Rodrigo Witzel.

W. Härdle, T. Kleinow and G. Stahl

Berlin and Bonn, June 2002

Contributors

Gökhan Aydınlı Humboldt-Universität zu Berlin, CASE, Center for Applied Statistics and Economics

Oliver Jim Blaskowitz Humboldt-Universität zu Berlin, CASE, Center for Applied Statistics and Economics

Song Xi Chen The National University of Singapore, Dept. of Statistics and Applied Probability

Matthias R. Fengler Humboldt-Universität zu Berlin, CASE, Center for Applied Statistics and Economics

Jürgen Franke Universität Kaiserslautern

Christoph Frisch Landesbank Rheinland-Pfalz, Risikoüberwachung

Wolfgang Härdle Humboldt-Universität zu Berlin, CASE, Center for Applied Statistics and Economics

Helmut Herwartz Humboldt-Universität zu Berlin, CASE, Center for Applied Statistics and Economics

Harriet Holzberger IKB Deutsche Industriebank AG

Steffi Höse Technische Universität Dresden

Stefan Huschens Technische Universität Dresden

Kim Huynh Queen's Economics Department, Queen's University

Stefan R. Jaschke Weierstrass Institute for Applied Analysis and Stochastics

Yuze Jiang Queen's School of Business, Queen's University

Pierre Kervella Humboldt-Universität zu Berlin, CASE, Center for Applied Statistics and Economics

Rüdiger Kiesel London School of Economics, Department of Statistics

Torsten Kleinow Humboldt-Universität zu Berlin, CASE, Center for Applied Statistics and Economics

Germar Knöchlein Landesbank Rheinland-Pfalz, Risikoüberwachung

Sven Knoth European University Viadrina Frankfurt (Oder)

Jens Lüssem Landesbank Kiel

Danilo Mercurio Humboldt-Universität zu Berlin, CASE, Center for Applied Statistics and Economics

Marlene Müller Humboldt-Universität zu Berlin, CASE, Center for Applied Statistics and Economics

Jörn Rank Andersen, Financial and Commodity Risk Consulting

Peter Schmidt Humboldt-Universität zu Berlin, CASE, Center for Applied Statistics and Economics

Rainer Schulz Humboldt-Universität zu Berlin, CASE, Center for Applied Statistics and Economics

Jürgen Schumacher University of Bonn, Department of Computer Science

Thomas Siegl BHF Bank

Robert Wania Technische Universität Dresden

Axel Werwatz Humboldt-Universität zu Berlin, CASE, Center for Applied Statistics and Economics

Jun Zheng Department of Probability and Statistics, School of Mathematical Sciences, Peking University, 100871, Beijing, P.R. China

Frequently Used Notation

$x \overset{\text{def}}{=} \ldots$ x is defined as ...
$\mathbb{R}$ real numbers
$\overline{\mathbb{R}} \overset{\text{def}}{=} \mathbb{R} \cup \{\infty, \infty\}$
$A^\top$ transpose of matrix A
$X \sim D$ the random variable X has distribution D
$E[X]$ expected value of random variable X
$\text{Var}(X)$ variance of random variable X
$\text{Std}(X)$ standard deviation of random variable X
$\text{Cov}(X, Y)$ covariance of two random variables X and Y
$N(\mu, \Sigma)$ normal distribution with expectation μ and covariance matrix Σ, a similar notation is used if Σ is the correlation matrix
cdf denotes the cumulative distribution function
pdf denotes the probability density function
$P[A]$ or $P(A)$ probability of a set A
$\mathbf{1}$ indicator function
$(F \circ G)(x) \overset{\text{def}}{=} F\{G(x)\}$ for functions F and G
$\alpha_n = \mathcal{O}(\beta_n)$ iff $\frac{\alpha_n}{\beta_n} \longrightarrow$ constant, as $n \longrightarrow \infty$
$\alpha_n = o(\beta_n)$ iff $\frac{\alpha_n}{\beta_n} \longrightarrow 0$, as $n \longrightarrow \infty$
$\mathcal{F}_t$ is the information set generated by all information available at time t

Let A_n and B_n be sequences of random variables.
$A_n = \mathcal{O}_p(B_n)$ iff $\forall \varepsilon > 0 \, \exists M, \, \exists N$ such that $P[|A_n/B_n| > M] < \varepsilon, \, \forall n > N$.
$A_n = o_p(B_n)$ iff $\forall \varepsilon > 0 \, : \, \lim_{n \to \infty} P[|A_n/B_n| > \varepsilon] = 0$.

Part I

Value at Risk

1 Approximating Value at Risk in Conditional Gaussian Models

Stefan R. Jaschke and Yuze Jiang

1.1 Introduction

1.1.1 The Practical Need

Financial institutions are facing the important task of estimating and controlling their exposure to market risk, which is caused by changes in prices of equities, commodities, exchange rates and interest rates. A new chapter of risk management was opened when the Basel Committee on Banking Supervision proposed that banks may use internal models for estimating their market risk (Basel Committee on Banking Supervision, 1995). Its implementation into national laws around 1998 allowed banks to not only compete in the innovation of financial products but also in the innovation of risk management methodology. Measurement of market risk has focused on a metric called Value at Risk (VaR). VaR quantifies the maximal amount that may be lost in a portfolio over a given period of time, at a certain confidence level. Statistically speaking, the VaR of a portfolio is the quantile of the distribution of that portfolio's loss over a specified time interval, at a given probability level.

The implementation of a firm-wide risk management system is a tremendous job. The biggest challenge for many institutions is to implement interfaces to all the different front-office systems, back-office systems and databases (potentially running on different operating systems and being distributed all over the world), in order to get the portfolio positions and historical market data into a centralized risk management framework. This is a software engineering problem. The second challenge is to use the computed VaR numbers to actually *control* risk and to build an atmosphere where the risk management system is accepted by all participants. This is an organizational and social problem. The methodological question how risk should be modeled and approximated is – in terms of the cost of implementation – a smaller one. In terms of importance, however, it is a crucial question. A non-adequate VaR-methodology can jeopardize all the other efforts to build a risk management system. See (Jorion, 2000) for more on the general aspects of risk management in financial institutions.

1.1.2   Statistical Modeling for VaR

VaR methodologies can be classified in terms of *statistical modeling decisions* and *approximation decisions*. Once the statistical model and the estimation procedure is specified, it is a purely numerical problem to compute or approximate the Value at Risk. The modeling decisions are:

1. *Which risk factors to include.* This mainly depends on a banks' business (portfolio). But it may also depend on the availability of historical data. If data for a certain contract is not available or the quality is not sufficient, a related risk factor with better historical data may be used. For smaller stock portfolios it is customary to include each stock itself as a risk factor. For larger stock portfolios, only country or sector indexes are taken as the risk factors (Longerstaey, 1996). Bonds and interest rate derivatives are commonly assumed to depend on a fixed set of interest rates at key maturities. The value of options is usually assumed to depend on implied volatility (at certain key strikes and maturities) as well as on everything the underlying depends on.

2. *How to model security prices as functions of risk factors, which is usually called "the mapping".* If X_t^i denotes the log return of stock i over the time interval $[t-1, t]$, i.e., $X_t^i = \log(S_t^i) - \log(S_{t-1}^i)$, then the change in the value of a portfolio containing one stock i is

$$\Delta S_t^i = S_{t-1}^i (e^{X_t^i} - 1),$$

where S_t^i denotes the price of stock i at time t. Bonds are first decomposed into a portfolio of zero bonds. Zero bonds are assumed to depend on the two key interest rates with the closest maturities. How to do the interpolation is actually not as trivial as it may seem, as demonstrated by Mina and Ulmer (1999). Similar issues arise in the interpolation of implied volatilities.

3. *What stochastic properties to assume for the dynamics of the risk factors X_t.* The basic benchmark model for stocks is to assume that logarithmic stock returns are joint normal (cross-sectionally) and independent in time. Similar assumptions for other risk factors are that changes in the logarithm of zero-bond yields, changes in log exchange rates, and changes in the logarithm of implied volatilities are all independent in time and joint normally distributed.

4. *How to estimate the model parameters from the historical data.* The usual statistical approach is to define the model and then look for estimators that have certain optimality criteria. In the basic benchmark model the minimal-variance unbiased estimator of the covariance matrix Σ of risk factors X_t is the "rectangular moving average"

$$\hat{\Sigma} = \frac{1}{T-1} \sum_{t=1}^{T} (X_t - \mu)(X_t - \mu)^{\top}$$

(with $\mu \overset{\text{def}}{=} E[X_t]$). An alternative route is to first specify an estimator and then look for a model in which that estimator has certain optimality properties. The exponential moving average

$$\hat{\Sigma}_T = (e^{\lambda} - 1) \sum_{t=-\infty}^{T-1} e^{-\lambda(T-t)}(X_t - \mu)(X_t - \mu)^{\top}$$

can be interpreted as an efficient estimator of the conditional covariance matrix Σ_T of the vector of risk factors X_T, given the information up to time $T-1$ in a very specific GARCH model.

While there is a plethora of analyses of alternative statistical models for market risks (see Barry Schachter's Gloriamundi web site), mainly two classes of models for market risk have been used in practice:

1. iid-models, i.e., the risk factors X_t are assumed to be independent in time, but the distribution of X_t is not necessarily Gaussian. Apart from some less common models involving hyperbolic distributions (Breckling, Eberlein and Kokic, 2000), most approaches either estimate the distribution

of X_t completely non-parametrically and run under the name "histori-cal simulation", or they estimate the tail using generalized Pareto dis-tributions (Embrechts, Klüppelberg and Mikosch, 1997, "extreme value theory").

2. conditional Gaussian models, i.e., the risk factors X_t are assumed to be joint normal, conditional on the information up to time $t - 1$.

Both model classes can account for unconditional "fat tails".

1.1.3   VaR Approximations

In this paper we consider certain approximations of VaR in the conditional Gaussian class of models. We assume that the conditional expectation of X_t, μ_t, is zero and its conditional covariance matrix Σ_t is estimated and given at time $t - 1$. The change in the portfolio value over the time interval $[t - 1, t]$ is then

$$\Delta V_t(X_t) = \sum_{i=1}^{n} w_i \Delta S_t^i(X_t),$$

where the w_i are the portfolio weights and ΔS_t^i is the function that "maps" the risk factor vector X_t to a change in the value of the i-th security value over the time interval $[t - 1, t]$, given all the information at time $t - 1$. These functions are usually nonlinear, even for stocks (see above). In the following, we will drop the time index and denote by ΔV the change in the portfolio's value over the next time interval and by X the corresponding vector of risk factors.

The only general method to compute quantiles of the distribution of ΔV is Monte Carlo simulation. From discussion with practitioners "full valuation Monte Carlo" appears to be practically infeasible for portfolios with securi-ties whose mapping functions are first, extremely costly to compute – like for certain path-dependent options whose valuation itself relies on Monte-Carlo simulation – and second, computed inside complex closed-source front-office systems, which cannot be easily substituted or adapted in their accuracy/speed trade-offs. Quadratic approximations to the portfolio's value as a function of the risk factors

$$\Delta V(X) \approx \Delta^\top X + \frac{1}{2} X^\top \Gamma X, \tag{1.1}$$

have become the industry standard since its use in RiskMetrics (Longerstaey, 1996). (Δ and Γ are the aggregated first and second derivatives of the indi-vidual mapping functions ΔS^i w.r.t. the risk factors X. The first version of

RiskMetrics in 1994 considered only the first derivative of the value function, the "delta". Without loss of generality, we assume that the constant term in the Taylor expansion (1.1), the "theta", is zero.)

1.1.4   Pros and Cons of Delta-Gamma Approximations

Both assumptions of the Delta-Gamma-Normal approach – Gaussian innovations and a reasonably good quadratic approximation of the value function V – have been questioned. Simple examples of portfolios with options can be constructed to show that quadratic approximations to the value function can lead to very large errors in the computation of VaR (Britton-Jones and Schaefer, 1999). The Taylor-approximation (1.1) holds only *locally* and is questionable from the outset for the purpose of modeling *extreme* events. Moreover, the conditional Gaussian framework does not allow to model joint extremal events, as described by Embrechts, McNeil and Straumann (1999). The Gaussian dependence structure, the copula, assigns too small probabilities to joint extremal events compared to some empirical observations.

Despite these valid critiques of the Delta-Gamma-Normal model, there are good reasons for banks to implement it alongside other models. (1) The statistical assumption of conditional Gaussian risk factors can explain a wide range of "stylized facts" about asset returns like unconditional fat tails and autocorrelation in realized volatility. Parsimonious multivariate conditional Gaussian models for dimensions like 500-2000 are challenging enough to be the subject of ongoing statistical research, Engle (2000). (2) First and second derivatives of financial products w.r.t. underlying market variables (= deltas and gammas) and other "sensitivities" are widely implemented in front office systems and routinely used by traders. Derivatives w.r.t. possibly different risk factors used by central risk management are easily computed by applying the chain rule of differentiation. So it is tempting to stay in the framework and language of the trading desks and express portfolio value changes in terms of deltas and gammas. (3) For many actual portfolios the delta-gamma approximation may serve as a good control-variate within variance-reduced Monte-Carlo methods, if it is not a sufficiently good approximation itself. Finally (4), is it extremely risky for a senior risk manager to ignore delta-gamma models if his friendly consultant tells him that 99% of the competitors have it implemented.

Several methods have been proposed to compute a quantile of the distribution defined by the model (1.1), among them Monte Carlo simulation (Pritsker, 1996), Johnson transformations (Zangari, 1996a; Longerstaey, 1996), Cornish-

Fisher expansions (Zangari, 1996b; Fallon, 1996), the Solomon-Stephens approximation (Britton-Jones and Schaefer, 1999), moment-based approximations motivated by the theory of estimating functions (Li, 1999), saddle-point approximations (Rogers and Zane, 1999), and Fourier-inversion (Rouvinez, 1997; Albanese, Jackson and Wiberg, 2000). Pichler and Selitsch (1999) compare five different VaR-methods: Johnson transformations, Delta-Normal, and Cornish-Fisher-approximations up to the second, fourth and sixth moment. The sixth-order Cornish-Fisher-approximation compares well against the other techniques and is the final recommendation. Mina and Ulmer (1999) also compare Johnson transformations, Fourier inversion, Cornish-Fisher approximations, and partial Monte Carlo. (If the true value function $\Delta V(X)$ in Monte Carlo simulation is used, this is called "full Monte Carlo". If its quadratic approximation is used, this is called "partial Monte Carlo".) Johnson transformations are concluded to be "not a robust choice". Cornish-Fisher is "extremely fast" compared to partial Monte Carlo and Fourier inversion, but not as robust, as it gives "unacceptable results" in one of the four sample portfolios.

The main three methods used in practice seem to be Cornish-Fisher expansions, Fourier inversion, and partial Monte Carlo, whose implementation in XploRe will be presented in this paper. What makes the Normal-Delta-Gamma model especially tractable is that the characteristic function of the probability distribution, i.e. the Fourier transform of the probability density, of the quadratic form (1.1) is known analytically. Such general properties are presented in section 1.2. Sections 1.3, 1.4, and 1.5 discuss the Cornish-Fisher, Fourier inversion, and partial Monte Carlo techniques, respectively.

1.2   General Properties of Delta-Gamma-Normal Models

The change in the portfolio value, ΔV, can be expressed as a sum of independent random variables that are quadratic functions of standard normal random variables Y_i by means of the solution of the generalized eigenvalue problem

$$CC^\top = \Sigma,$$
$$C^\top \Gamma C = \Lambda.$$

This implies

$$\Delta V = \sum_{i=1}^{m} (\delta_i Y_i + \frac{1}{2} \lambda_i Y_i^2) \tag{1.2}$$

$$= \sum_{i=1}^{m} \left\{ \frac{1}{2} \lambda_i \left(\frac{\delta_i}{\lambda_i} + Y_i \right)^2 - \frac{\delta_i^2}{2\lambda_i} \right\}$$

with $X = CY$, $\delta = C^\top \Delta$ and $\Lambda = \mathrm{diag}(\lambda_1, \ldots, \lambda_m)$. Packages like LAPACK (Anderson, Bai, Bischof, Blackford, Demmel, Dongarra, Croz, Greenbaum, Hammarling, McKenney and Sorensen, 1999) contain routines directly for the generalized eigenvalue problem. Otherwise C and Λ can be computed in two steps:

1. Compute some matrix B with $BB^\top = \Sigma$. If Σ is positive definite, the fastest method is Cholesky decomposition. Otherwise an eigenvalue decomposition can be used.

2. Solve the (standard) symmetric eigenvalue problem for the matrix $B^\top \Gamma B$:

$$Q^\top B^\top \Gamma B Q = \Lambda$$

with $Q^{-1} = Q^\top$ and set $C \overset{\mathrm{def}}{=} BQ$.

The decomposition is implemented in the quantlet

```
npar= VaRDGdecomp(par)
```
> uses a generalized eigen value decomposition to do a suitable coordinate change. `par` is a list containing `Delta`, `Gamma`, `Sigma` on input. `npar` is the same list, containing additionally B, `delta`, and `lambda` on output.

The characteristic function of a non-central χ_1^2 variate $((Z+a)^2$, with standard normal $Z)$ is known analytically:

$$\mathrm{E} e^{it(Z+a)^2} = (1 - 2it)^{-1/2} \exp \left(\frac{a^2 it}{1 - 2it} \right).$$

This implies the characteristic function for ΔV

$$\mathrm{E} e^{it\Delta V} = \prod_j \frac{1}{\sqrt{1 - i\lambda_j t}} \exp\{ -\frac{1}{2} \delta_j^2 t^2 / (1 - i\lambda_j t) \}, \tag{1.3}$$

which can be re-expressed in terms of Γ and B

$$\mathrm{E}e^{it\Delta V} = \det(I - itB^\top\Gamma B)^{-1/2}\exp\{-\frac{1}{2}t^2\Delta^\top B(I - itB^\top\Gamma B)^{-1}B^\top\Delta\}, \quad (1.4)$$

or in terms of Γ and Σ

$$\mathrm{E}e^{it\Delta V} = \det(I - it\Gamma\Sigma)^{-1/2}\exp\{-\frac{1}{2}t^2\Delta^\top\Sigma(I - it\Gamma\Sigma)^{-1}\Delta\}. \quad (1.5)$$

Numerical Fourier-inversion of (1.3) can be used to compute an approximation to the cumulative distribution function (cdf) F of ΔV. (The α-quantile is computed by root-finding in $F(x) = \alpha$.) The cost of the Fourier-inversion is $\mathcal{O}(N\log N)$, the cost of the function evaluations is $\mathcal{O}(mN)$, and the cost of the eigenvalue decomposition is $\mathcal{O}(m^3)$. The cost of the eigenvalue decomposition dominates the other two terms for accuracies of one or two decimal digits and the usual number of risk factors of more than a hundred. Instead of a full spectral decomposition, one can also just reduce $B^\top\Gamma B$ to tridiagonal form $B^\top\Gamma B = QTQ^\top$. ($T$ is tridiagonal and Q is orthogonal.) Then the evaluation of the characteristic function in (1.4) involves the solution of a linear system with the matrix $I - itT$, which costs only $\mathcal{O}(m)$ operations. An alternative route is to reduce $\Gamma\Sigma$ to Hessenberg form $\Gamma\Sigma = QHQ^\top$ or do a Schur decomposition $\Gamma\Sigma = QRQ^\top$. (H is Hessenberg and Q is orthogonal. Since $\Gamma\Sigma$ has the same eigenvalues as $B^\top\Gamma B$ and they are all real, R is actually triangular instead of quasi-triangular in the general case, Anderson et al. (1999). The evaluation of (1.5) becomes $\mathcal{O}(m^2)$, since it involves the solution of a linear system with the matrix $I - itH$ or $I - itR$, respectively. Reduction to tridiagonal, Hessenberg, or Schur form is also $\mathcal{O}(m^3)$, so the asymptotics in the number of risk factors m remain the same in all cases. The critical N, above which the complete spectral decomposition + fast evaluation via (1.3) is faster than the reduction to tridiagonal or Hessenberg form + slower evaluation via (1.4) or (1.5) remains to be determined empirically for given m on a specific machine.

The computation of the cumulant generating function and the characteristic function from the diagonalized form is implemented in the following quantlets:

```
z= VaRcgfDG(t,par)
```
   Computes the cumulant generating function (cgf) for the class of quadratic forms of Gaussian vectors.

```
z= VaRcharfDG(t,par)
```
   Computes the characteristic function for the class of quadratic forms of Gaussian vectors.

t is the complex argument and **par** the parameter list generated by VaRDGdecomp.

The advantage of the Cornish-Fisher approximation is that it is based on the cumulants, which can be computed without any matrix decomposition:

$$\kappa_1 = \frac{1}{2}\sum_i \lambda_i \qquad\qquad = \frac{1}{2}\,\mathrm{tr}(\Gamma\Sigma),$$

$$\kappa_r = \frac{1}{2}\sum_i \{(r-1)!\lambda_i^r + r!\delta_i^2 \lambda_i^{r-2}\} = \frac{1}{2}(r-1)!\,\mathrm{tr}((\Gamma\Sigma)^r)$$

$$+ \frac{1}{2}r!\Delta^\top\Sigma(\Gamma\Sigma)^{r-2}\Delta$$

$(r \geq 2)$. Although the cost of computing the cumulants needed for the Cornish-Fisher approximation is also $\mathcal{O}(m^3)$, this method can be faster than the eigenvalue decomposition for small orders of approximation and relatively small numbers of risk factors.

The computation of all cumulants up to a certain order directly from $\Gamma\Sigma$ is implemented in the quantlet **VaRcumulantsDG**, while the computation of a single cumulant from the diagonal decomposition is provided by **VaRcumulantDG**:

```
vec= VaRcumulantsDG(n,par)
```
   Computes the first n cumulants for the class of quadratic forms of Gaussian vectors. The list **par** contains at least **Gamma** and **Sigma**.

```
z= VaRcumulantDG(n,par)
```
   Computes the n-th cumulant for the class of quadratic forms of Gaussian vectors. The parameter list **par** is to be generated with VaRDGdecomp.

Partial Monte-Carlo (or partial Quasi-Monte-Carlo) costs $\mathcal{O}(m^2)$ operations per sample. (If Γ is sparse, it may cost even less.) The number of samples needed is a function of the desired accuracy. It is clear from the asymptotic costs of the three methods that partial Monte Carlo will be preferable for sufficiently large m.

While Fourier-inversion and Partial Monte-Carlo can in principal achieve any desired accuracy, the Cornish-Fisher approximations provide only a limited accuracy, as shown in the next section.

1.3   Cornish-Fisher Approximations

1.3.1   Derivation

The Cornish-Fisher expansion can be derived in two steps. Let Φ denote some base distribution and ϕ its density function. The generalized Cornish-Fisher expansion (Hill and Davis, 1968) aims to approximate an α-quantile of F in terms of the α-quantile of Φ, i.e., the concatenated function $F^{-1} \circ \Phi$. The key to a series expansion of $F^{-1} \circ \Phi$ in terms of derivatives of F and Φ is Lagrange's inversion theorem. It states that if a function $s \mapsto t$ is implicitly defined by

$$t = c + s \cdot h(t) \tag{1.6}$$

and h is analytic in c, then an analytic function $f(t)$ can be developed into a power series in a neighborhood of $s = 0$ $(t = c)$:

$$f(t) = f(c) + \sum_{r=1}^{\infty} \frac{s^r}{r!} D^{r-1}[f' \cdot h^r](c), \tag{1.7}$$

where D denotes the differentation operator. For a given probability $c = \alpha$, $f = \Phi^{-1}$, and $h = (\Phi - F) \circ \Phi^{-1}$ this yields

$$\Phi^{-1}(t) = \Phi^{-1}(\alpha) + \sum_{r=1}^{\infty} (-1)^r \frac{s^r}{r!} D^{r-1}[((F - \Phi)^r/\phi) \circ \Phi^{-1}](\alpha). \tag{1.8}$$

Setting $s = 1$ in (1.6) implies $\Phi^{-1}(t) = F^{-1}(\alpha)$ and with the notations $x = F^{-1}(\alpha)$, $z = \Phi^{-1}(\alpha)$ (1.8) becomes the formal expansion

$$x = z + \sum_{r=1}^{\infty} (-1)^r \frac{1}{r!} D^{r-1}[((F - \Phi)^r/\phi) \circ \Phi^{-1}](\Phi(z)).$$

With $a = (F - \Phi)/\phi$ this can be written as

$$x = z + \sum_{r=1}^{\infty} (-1)^r \frac{1}{r!} D_{(r-1)}[a^r](z) \tag{1.9}$$

with $D_{(r)} = (D + \frac{\phi'}{\phi})(D + 2\frac{\phi'}{\phi}) \ldots (D + r\frac{\phi'}{\phi})$ and $D_{(0)}$ being the identity operator.

(1.9) is the generalized Cornish-Fisher expansion. The second step is to choose a specific base distribution Φ and a series expansion for a. The classical Cornish-Fisher expansion is recovered if Φ is the standard normal distribution, a is (formally) expanded into the Gram-Charlier series, and the terms are re-ordered as described below.

The idea of the Gram-Charlier series is to develop the ratio of the moment generating function of the considered random variable ($M(t) = \mathrm{E}e^{t\Delta V}$) and the moment generating function of the standard normal distribution ($e^{t^2/2}$) into a power series at 0:

$$M(t)e^{-t^2/2} = \sum_{k=0}^{\infty} c_k t^k. \tag{1.10}$$

(c_k are the Gram-Charlier coefficients. They can be derived from the moments by multiplying the power series for the two terms on the left hand side.) Componentwise Fourier inversion yields the corresponding series for the probability density

$$f(x) = \sum_{k=0}^{\infty} c_k (-1)^k \phi^{(k)}(x) \tag{1.11}$$

and for the cumulative distribution function (cdf)

$$F(x) = \Phi(x) - \sum_{k=1}^{\infty} c_k (-1)^{k-1} \phi^{(k-1)}(x). \tag{1.12}$$

(ϕ und Φ are now the standard normal density and cdf. The derivatives of the standard normal density are $(-1)^k \phi^{(k)}(x) = \phi(x)H_k(x)$, where the Hermite polynomials H_k form an orthogonal basis in the Hilbert space $L^2(\mathbb{R}, \phi)$ of the square integrable functions on $\mathbb{R}$ w.r.t. the weight function ϕ. The Gram-Charlier coefficients can thus be interpreted as the Fourier coefficients of the function $f(x)/\phi(x)$ in the Hilbert space $L^2(\mathbb{R}, \phi)$ with the basis $\{H_k\}$ $f(x)/\phi(x) = \sum_{k=0}^{\infty} c_k H_k(x)$.) Plugging (1.12) into (1.9) gives the formal Cornish-Fisher expansion, which is re-grouped as motivated by the central limit theorem.

Assume that ΔV is already normalized ($\kappa_1 = 0$, $\kappa_2 = 1$) and consider the normalized sum of independent random variables ΔV_i with the distribution F, $S_n = \frac{1}{\sqrt{n}} \sum_{i=1}^{n} \Delta V_i$. The moment generating function of the random variable S_n is

$$M_n(t) = M(t/\sqrt{n})^n = e^{t^2/2} (\sum_{k=0}^{\infty} c_k t^k n^{-k/2})^n.$$

Multiplying out the last term shows that the k-th Gram-Charlier coefficient $c_k(n)$ of S_n is a polynomial expression in $n^{-1/2}$, involving the coefficients c_i up to $i = k$. If the terms in the formal Cornish-Fisher expansion

$$x = z + \sum_{r=1}^{\infty} (-1)^r \frac{1}{r!} D_{(r-1)} \left[\left(-\sum_{k=1}^{\infty} c_k(n) H_{k-1} \right)^r \right] (z) \qquad (1.13)$$

are sorted and grouped with respect to powers of $n^{-1/2}$, the classical Cornish-Fisher series

$$x = z + \sum_{k=1}^{\infty} n^{-k/2} \xi_k(z) \qquad (1.14)$$

results. (The Cornish-Fisher approximation for ΔV results from setting $n = 1$ in the re-grouped series (1.14).)

It is a relatively tedious process to express the adjustment terms ξ_k correpond-ing to a certain power $n^{-k/2}$ in the Cornish-Fisher expansion (1.14) directly in terms of the cumulants κ_r, see (Hill and Davis, 1968). Lee developed a recurrence formula for the k-th adjustment term ξ_k in the Cornish-Fisher ex-pansion, which is implemented in the algorithm AS269 (Lee and Lin, 1992; Lee and Lin, 1993). (We write the recurrence formula here, because it is incorrect in (Lee and Lin, 1992).)

$$\xi_k(H) = a_k H^{*(k+1)} - \sum_{j=1}^{k-1} \frac{j}{k} (\xi_{k-j}(H) - \xi_{k-j}) * (\xi_j - a_j H^{*(j+1)}) * H, \quad (1.15)$$

with $a_k = \frac{\kappa_{k+2}}{(k+2)!}$. $\xi_k(H)$ is a formal polynomial expression in H with the usual algebraic relations between the summation "+" and the "multiplication" "*". Once $\xi_k(H)$ is multiplied out in *-powers of H, each H^{*k} is to be interpreted as the Hermite polynomial H_k and then the whole term becomes a polynomial in z with the "normal" multiplication ".". ξ_k denotes the scalar that results when the "normal" polynomial $\xi_k(H)$ is evaluated at the fixed quantile z, while $\xi_k(H)$ denotes the expression in the $(+, *)$-algebra.

This formula is implemented by the quantlet

```
q = CornishFisher (z, n, cum)
    Cornish-Fisher expansion for arbitrary orders for the standard
    normal quantile z, order of approximation n, and the vector of
    cumulants cum.
```

The following example prints the Cornish-Fisher approximation for increasing
orders for z=2.3 and cum=1:N:

Q XFGcofi.xpl

```
Contents of r

[1,]      2    4.2527
[2,]      3    5.3252
[3,]      4    5.0684
[4,]      5    5.2169
[5,]      6    5.1299
[6,]      7    5.1415
[7,]      8     5.255
```

1.3.2 Properties

The qualitative properties of the Cornish-Fisher expansion are:

+ If F_m is a sequence of distributions converging to the standard normal distribution Φ, the Edgeworth- and Cornish-Fisher approximations present better approximations (asymptotically for $m \to \infty$) than the normal approximation itself.

− The approximated functions $\tilde{F}$ and $\tilde{F}^{-1} \circ \Phi$ are not necessarily monotone.

− $\tilde{F}$ has the "wrong tail behavior", i.e., the Cornish-Fisher approximation for α-quantiles becomes less and less reliable for $\alpha \to 0$ (or $\alpha \to 1$).

− The Edgeworth- and Cornish-Fisher approximations do not necessarily improve (converge) for a fixed F and increasing order of approximation, k.

For more on the qualitative properties of the Cornish-Fisher approximation see (Jaschke, 2001). It contains also an empirical analysis of the error of the Cornish-Fisher approximation to the 99%-VaR in real-world examples as well as its worst-case error on a certain class of one- and two-dimensional delta-gamma-normal models:

+ The error for the 99%-VaR on the real-world examples - which turned out to be remarkably close to normal - was about $10^{-6}\sigma$, which is more than sufficient. (The error was normalized with respect to the portfolio's standard deviation, σ.)

− The (lower bound on the) worst-case error for the one- and two-dimensional problems was about 1.0σ, which corresponds to a relative error of up to 100%.

In summary, the Cornish-Fisher expansion can be a quick approximation with sufficient accuracy in many practical situations, but it should not be used unchecked because of its bad worst-case behavior.

1.4   Fourier Inversion

1.4.1   Error Types in Approximating the Quantile through Fourier Inversion

Let f denote a continuous, absolutely integrable function and $\phi(t) = \int_{-\infty}^{\infty} e^{itx} f(x)dx$ its Fourier transform. Then, the inversion formula

$$f(x) = \frac{1}{2\pi} \int_{-\infty}^{\infty} e^{-itx} \phi(t)dt \qquad (1.16)$$

holds.

The key to an error analysis of trapezoidal, equidistant approximations to the integral (1.16)

$$\tilde{f}(x, \Delta_t, t) \stackrel{\text{def}}{=} \frac{\Delta_t}{2\pi} \sum_{k=-\infty}^{\infty} \phi(t + k\Delta_t) e^{-i(t+k\Delta_t)x} \qquad (1.17)$$

is the Poisson summation formula

$$\tilde{f}(x, \Delta_t, t) = \sum_{j=-\infty}^{\infty} f(x + \frac{2\pi}{\Delta_t}j)e^{2\pi itj/\Delta_t}, \qquad (1.18)$$

see (Abate and Whitt, 1992, p.22). If $f(x)$ is approximated by $\tilde{f}(x, \Delta_t, 0)$, the residual

$$e_a(x, \Delta_t, 0) = \sum_{j \neq 0} f(x + \frac{2\pi}{\Delta_t}j) \qquad (1.19)$$

is called the *aliasing error*, since different "pieces" of f are aliased into the window $(-\pi/\Delta_t, \pi/\Delta_t)$. Another suitable choice is $t = \Delta_t/2$:

$$\tilde{f}(x, \Delta_t, \Delta_t/2) = \sum_{j=-\infty}^{\infty} f(x + \frac{2\pi}{\Delta_t}j)(-1)^j. \qquad (1.20)$$

If f is nonnegative, $\tilde{f}(x, \Delta_t, 0) \geq f(x)$. If $f(x)$ is decreasing in $|x|$ for $|x| > \pi/\Delta_t$, then $\tilde{f}(x, \Delta_t, \Delta_t/2) \leq f(x)$ holds for $|x| < \pi/\Delta_t$. The aliasing error can be controlled by letting Δ_t tend to 0. It decreases only slowly when f has "heavy tails", or equivalently, when ϕ has non-smooth features.

It is practical to first decide on Δ_t to control the aliasing error and then decide on the cut-off in the sum (1.17):

$$\tilde{\tilde{f}}(x, T, \Delta_t, t) = \frac{\Delta_t}{2\pi} \sum_{|t+k\Delta_t| \leq T}^{\backprime} \phi(t + k\Delta_t)e^{-i(t+k\Delta_t)x}. \qquad (1.21)$$

Call $e_t(x, T, \Delta_t, t) \stackrel{\text{def}}{=} \tilde{\tilde{f}}(x, T, \Delta_t, t) - \tilde{f}(x, \Delta_t, t)$ the *truncation error*.

For practical purposes, the truncation error $e_t(x, T, \Delta_t, t)$ essentially depends only on (x, T) and the decision on how to choose T and Δ_t can be decoupled. $e_t(x, T, \Delta_t, t)$ converges to

$$e_t(x, T) \stackrel{\text{def}}{=} \frac{1}{2\pi} \int_{-T}^{T} e^{-itx} \phi(t)dt - f(x) \qquad (1.22)$$

for $\Delta_t \downarrow 0$. Using $\frac{1}{2\pi} \int_{-\pi}^{\pi} e^{-itx}dt = \frac{\sin(\pi x)}{\pi x} \stackrel{\text{def}}{=} \mathrm{sinc}(x)$ and the convolution theorem, one gets

$$\frac{1}{2\pi} \int_{-\pi/\Delta_x}^{\pi/\Delta_x} e^{-itx} \phi(t)dt = \int_{-\infty}^{\infty} f(y\Delta_x) \, \mathrm{sinc}(x/\Delta_x - y)dy, \qquad (1.23)$$

which provides an explicit expression for the truncation error $e_t(x, T)$ in terms of f. It decreases only slowly with $T \uparrow \infty$ ($\Delta_x \downarrow 0$) if f does not have infinitely many derivatives, or equivalently, ϕ has "power tails". The following lemma leads to the asymptotics of the truncation error in this case.

LEMMA 1.1 *If $\lim_{t \to \infty} \alpha(t) = 1$, $\nu > 0$, and $\int_T^\infty \alpha(t) t^{-\nu} e^{it} dt$ exists and is finite for some T, then*

$$\int_T^\infty \alpha(t) t^{-\nu} e^{itx} dt \sim \begin{cases} 1\nu - 1T^{-\nu+1} & \text{if } x = 0 \\ \frac{i}{x} T^{-\nu} e^{ixT} & \text{if } x \neq 0 \end{cases} \tag{1.24}$$

for $T \to \infty$.

PROOF:
Under the given conditions, both the left and the right hand side converge to 0, so l'Hospital's rule is applicable to the ratio of the left and right hand sides.   □

THEOREM 1.1 *If the asymptotic behavior of a Fourier transform ϕ of a function f can be described as*

$$\phi(t) = w|t|^{-\nu} e^{ib \, \text{sign}(t) + ix_* t} \alpha(t) \tag{1.25}$$

with $\lim_{t \to \infty} \alpha(t) = 1$, then the truncation error (1.22)

$$e_t(x, T) = -\frac{1}{\pi} \Re \left\{ \int_T^\infty \phi(t) e^{-itx} dt \right\}$$

where $\Re$ denotes the real part, has the asymptotic behavior

$$\sim \begin{cases} wT^{-\nu+1} \pi (1 - \nu) \cos(b) & \text{if } x = x_* \\ -\frac{wT^{-\nu}}{\pi(x_* - x)} \cos(b + \frac{\pi}{2} + (x_* - x)T) & \text{if } x \neq x_* \end{cases} \tag{1.26}$$

for $T \to \infty$ at all points x where $\frac{1}{2\pi} \int_{-T}^T \phi(t) e^{-itx}$ converges to $f(x)$. (If in the first case $\cos(b) = 0$, this shall mean that $\lim_{T \to \infty} e_t(x; T) T^{\nu - 1} = 0$.)

PROOF:
The previous lemma is applicable for all points x where the Fourier inversion integral converges. $\square$

The theorem completely characterizes the truncation error for those cases, where f has a "critical point of non-smoothness" and has a higher degree of smoothness everywhere else. The truncation error decreases one power faster away from the critical point than at the critical point. Its amplitude is inversely proportional to the distance from the critical point.

Let $\tilde{F}$ be a (continuous) approximation to a (differentiable) cdf F with $f = F' > 0$. Denote by $\epsilon \geq |\tilde{F}(x) - F(x)|$ a known error-bound for the cdf. Any solution $\tilde{q}(x)$ to $\tilde{F}(\tilde{q}(x)) = F(x)$ may be considered an approximation to the true $F(x)$-quantile x. Call $e_q(x) = \tilde{q}(x) - x$ the *quantile error*. Obviously, the quantile error can be bounded by

$$|e_q(x)| \leq \frac{\epsilon}{\inf_{y \in U} f(y)}, \tag{1.27}$$

where U is a suitable neighborhood of x. Given a sequence of approximations $\tilde{F}_\epsilon$ with $\sup_x |\tilde{F}_\epsilon(x) - F(x)| = \epsilon \to 0$,

$$e_q(x) \sim \frac{F(x) - \tilde{F}_\epsilon(x)}{f(x)} \qquad (\epsilon \to 0) \tag{1.28}$$

holds.

FFT-based Fourier inversion yields approximations for the cdf F on equidistant Δ_x-spaced grids. Depending on the smoothness of F, linear or higher-order interpolations may be used. Any monotone interpolation of $\{F(x_0 + \Delta_x j)\}_j$ yields a quantile approximation whose *interpolation error* can be bounded by Δ_x. This bound can be improved if an *upper* bound on the density f in a suitable neighborhood of the true quantile is known.

1.4.2   Tail Behavior

If $\lambda_j = 0$ for some j, then $|\phi(t)| = \mathcal{O}(e^{-\delta_j^2 t^2/2})$. In the following, we assume that $|\lambda_i| > 0$ for all i. The norm of $\phi(t)$ has the form

$$|\phi(t)| = \prod_{i=1}^{m}(1 + \lambda_i^2 t^2)^{-1/4}\exp\left\{-\frac{\delta_i^2 t^2/2}{1 + \lambda_i^2 t^2}\right\}, \tag{1.29}$$

$$|\phi(t)| \sim w_*|t|^{-m/2} \quad |t| \to \infty \tag{1.30}$$

with

$$w_* \stackrel{\text{def}}{=} \prod_{i=1}^{m}|\lambda_i|^{-1/2}\exp\left\{-\frac{1}{2}(\delta_i/\lambda_i)^2\right\}. \tag{1.31}$$

The arg has the form

$$\arg\phi(t) = \theta t + \sum_{i=1}^{m}\left\{\frac{1}{2}\arctan(\lambda_i t) - \frac{1}{2}\delta_i^2 t^2\frac{\lambda_i t}{1 + \lambda_i^2 t^2}\right\}, \tag{1.32}$$

$$\arg\phi(t) \sim \theta t + \sum_{i=1}^{m}\left\{\frac{\pi}{4}\text{sign}(\lambda_i t) - \frac{\delta_i^2 t}{2\lambda_i}\right)\right\} \tag{1.33}$$

(for $|t| \to \infty$). This motivates the following approximation for ϕ:

$$\tilde{\phi}(t) \stackrel{\text{def}}{=} w_*|t|^{-m/2}\exp\left\{i\frac{\pi}{4}m_*\text{sign}(t) + ix_* t\right\} \tag{1.34}$$

with

$$m_* \stackrel{\text{def}}{=} \sum_{i=1}^{m}\text{sign}(\lambda_i), \tag{1.35}$$

$$x_* \stackrel{\text{def}}{=} \theta - \frac{1}{2}\sum_{i=1}^{m}\frac{\delta_i^2}{\lambda_i}. \tag{1.36}$$

x_* is the location and w_* the "weight" of the singularity. The multivariate delta-gamma-distribution is C^∞ except at x_*, where the highest continuous derivative of the cdf is of order $[(m - 1)/2]$.

Note that

$$\alpha(t) \stackrel{\text{def}}{=} \phi(t)/\tilde{\phi}(t) = \prod_{j}(1 - (i\lambda_j t)^{-1})^{-1/2}\exp\{\frac{1}{2}\frac{\delta_j^2}{\lambda_j^2}(1 - i\lambda_j t)^{-1}\} \tag{1.37}$$

and α meets the assumptions of theorem 1.1.

1.4.3   Inversion of the cdf minus the Gaussian Approximation

Assume that F is a cdf with mean μ and standard deviation σ, then

$$F(x) - \Phi(x; \mu, \sigma) = \frac{1}{2\pi} \int_{-\infty}^{\infty} e^{-ixt} \frac{i}{t} (\phi(t) - e^{i\mu t - \sigma^2 t^2/2}) \, dt \qquad (1.38)$$

holds, where $\Phi(.; \mu, \sigma)$ is the normal cdf with mean μ and standard deviation σ and $e^{i\mu t - \sigma^2 t^2/2}$ its characteristic function. (Integrating the inversion formula (1.16) w.r.t. x and applying Fubini's theorem leads to (1.38).) Applying the Fourier inversion to $F(x) - \Phi(x; \mu, \sigma)$ instead of $F(x)$ solves the (numerical) problem that $\frac{i}{t}\phi(t)$ has a pole at 0. Alternative distributions with known Fourier transform may be chosen if they better approximate the distribution F under consideration.

The moments of the delta-gamma-distribution can be derived from (1.3) and (1.5):

$$\mu = \sum_i (\theta_i + \frac{1}{2}\lambda_i) = \theta^\top \mathbf{1} + \frac{1}{2}\operatorname{tr}(\Gamma\Sigma)$$

and

$$\sigma^2 = \sum_i (\delta_i^2 + \frac{1}{2}\lambda_i^2) = \Delta^\top \Sigma \Delta + \frac{1}{2}\operatorname{tr}((\Gamma\Sigma)^2).$$

Let $\psi(t) \stackrel{\text{def}}{=} \frac{i}{t}(\phi(t) - e^{i\mu t - \sigma^2 t^2/2})$. Since $\psi(-t) = \overline{\psi(t)}$, the truncated sum (1.21) can for $t = \Delta_t/2$ and $T = (K - \frac{1}{2})\Delta_t$ be written as

$$\tilde{F}(x_j; T, \Delta_t, t) - \Phi(x_j) = \frac{\Delta_t}{\pi} \Re \left(\sum_{k=0}^{K-1} \psi((k + \frac{1}{2})\Delta_t) e^{-i((k+\frac{1}{2})\Delta_t)x_j} \right),$$

which can comfortably be computed by a FFT with modulus $N \geq K$:

$$= \frac{\Delta_t}{\pi} \Re \left(e^{-i\frac{\Delta_t}{2}x_j} \sum_{k=0}^{K-1} \psi((k + \frac{1}{2})\Delta_t) e^{-ik\Delta_t x_0} e^{-2\pi ikj/N} \right), \qquad (1.39)$$

with $\Delta_x \Delta_t = \frac{2\pi}{N}$ and the last $N - K$ components of the input vector to the FFT are padded with zeros.

The *aliasing error* of the approximation (1.20) applied to $F - N$ is

$$e_a(x, \Delta_t, \Delta_t/2) = \sum_{j \neq 0} \left[F(x + \frac{2\pi}{\Delta_t}j) - \Phi(x + \frac{2\pi}{\Delta_t}j) \right] (-1)^j. \qquad (1.40)$$

The cases $(\lambda, \delta, \theta) = (\pm\sqrt{2}, 0, \mp\sqrt{2}/2)$ are the ones with the fattest tails and are thus candidates for the worst case for (1.40), asymptotically for $\Delta_t \to 0$. In these cases, (1.40) is eventually an alternating sequence of decreasing absolute value and thus

$$F(-\pi/\Delta_t) + 1 - F(\pi/\Delta_t) \leq \sqrt{\frac{2}{\pi e}} e^{-\frac{1}{2}\sqrt{2}\pi/\Delta_t} \tag{1.41}$$

is an asymptotic bound for the aliasing error.

The *truncation error* (1.22) applied to $F - N$ is

$$e_t(x;T) = -\frac{1}{\pi}\Re\left\{\int_T^\infty \frac{i}{t}\big(\phi(t) - e^{i\mu t - \sigma^2 t^2/2}\big)dt\right\}. \tag{1.42}$$

The Gaussian part plays no role asymptotically for $T \to \infty$ and Theorem 1.1 applies with $\nu = m/2 + 1$.

The *quantile error* for a given parameter ϑ is

$$\tilde{q}(\vartheta) - q(\vartheta) \sim -\frac{e_a^\vartheta(q(\vartheta); \Delta_t) + e_t^\vartheta(q(\vartheta); T)}{f^\vartheta(q(\vartheta))}, \tag{1.43}$$

asymptotically for $T \to \infty$ and $\Delta_t \to 0$. ($q(\vartheta)$ denotes the true 1%-quantile for the triplet $\vartheta = (\theta, \Delta, \Gamma)$.) The problem is now to find the right trade-off between "aliasing error" and "truncation error", i.e., to choose Δ_t optimally for a given K.

Empirical observation of the one- and two-factor cases shows that $(\lambda, \delta, \theta) = (-\sqrt{2}, 0, \sqrt{2}/2)$ has the smallest density (≈ 0.008) at the 1%-quantile. Since $(\lambda, \delta, \theta) = (-\sqrt{2}, 0, \sqrt{2}/2)$ is the case with the maximal "aliasing error" as well, it is the only candidate for the worst case of the ratio of the "aliasing error" over the density (at the 1%-quantile).

The question which ϑ is the worst case for the ratio of the "truncation error" over the density (at the 1%-quantile) is not as clear-cut. Empirical observation shows that the case $(\lambda, \delta, \theta) = (-\sqrt{2}, 0, \sqrt{2}/2)$ is also the worst case for this ratio over a range of parameters in one- and two-factor problems. This leads to the following heuristic to choose Δ_t for a given K ($T = (K - 0.5)\Delta_t$). Choose Δ_t such as to minimize the sum of the aliasing and truncation errors for the case $(\lambda, \delta, \theta) = (-\sqrt{2}, 0, \sqrt{2}/2)$, as approximated by the bounds (1.41) and

$$\limsup_{T\to\infty} |e_t(x, T)|T^{3/2} = \frac{w}{\pi|x_* - x|} \tag{1.44}$$

with $w = 2^{-1/4}$, $x_* = \sqrt{2}/2$, and the 1%-quantile $x \approx -3.98$. (Note that this is suitable only for intermediate K, leading to accuracies of 1 to 4 digits in the quantile. For higher K, other cases become the worst case for the ratio of the truncation error over the density at the quantile.)

Since $F - N$ has a kink in the case $m = 1$, $\lambda \neq 0$, higher-order interpolations are futile in non-adaptive methods and $\Delta_x = \frac{2\pi}{N\Delta_t}$ is a suitable upper bound for the interpolation error. By experimentation, $N \approx 4K$ suffices to keep the interpolation error comparatively small.

$K = 2^6$ evaluations of ϕ ($N = 2^8$) suffice to ensure an accuracy of 1 digit in the approximation of the 1%-quantile over a sample of one- and two-factor cases. $K = 2^9$ function evaluations are needed for two digits accuracy. The XploRe implementation of the Fourier inversion is split up as follows:

---

z= VaRcharfDGF2(t,par)

    implements the function $\psi(t) \overset{\text{def}}{=} \frac{i}{t}(\phi(t) - e^{i\mu t - \sigma^2 t^2/2})$ for the complex argument t and the parameter list par.

z= VaRcorrfDGF2(x,par)

    implements the correction term $\Phi(x, \mu, \sigma^2)$ for the argument x and the parameter list par.

vec= gFourierInversion(N,K,dt,t0,x0,charf,par)

    implements a generic Fourier inversion like in (1.39). charf is a string naming the function to be substituted for ψ in (1.39). par is the parameter list passed to charf.

---

gFourierInversion can be applied to VaRcharfDG, giving the density, or to VaRcharfDGF2, giving the cdf minus the Gaussian approximation. The three auxiliary functions are used by

---

```
l= VaRcdfDG(par,N,K,dt)
```
   to approximate the cumulative distribution function (cdf) of the
   distribution from the class of quadratic forms of Gaussian vectors
   with parameter list `par`. The output is a list of two vectors x and
   y, containing the cdf-approximation on a grid given by x.

```
q= cdf2quant(a,l)
```
   approximates the a-quantile from the list l, as returned from
   VaRcdfDG.

```
q= VaRqDG(a,par,N,K,dt)
```
   calls `VaRcdfDG` and `cdf2quant` to approximate an a-quantile for
   the distribution of the class of quadratic forms of Gaussian vectors
   that is defined by the parameter list `par`.

The following example plots the 1%-quantile for a one-parametric family of the
class of quadratic forms of one- and two-dimensional Gaussian vectors:

Q XFGqDGtest.xpl

1.5   Variance Reduction Techniques in Monte-Carlo Simulation

1.5.1   Monte-Carlo Sampling Method

The partial Monte-Carlo method is a Monte-Carlo simulation that is performed
by generating underlying prices given the statistical model and then valuing
them using the simple delta-gamma approximation. We denote X as a vector
of risk factors, ΔV as the change in portfolio value resulting from X, L as
$-\Delta V$, α as a confidence level and l as a loss threshold.

We also let

- Δ = first order derivative with regard to risk factors

- Γ = second order derivative with regard to risk factors

- Σ_X = covariance matrix of risk factors

Equation 1.1 defines the class of Delta-Gamma normal methods. The detailed procedures to implement the partial Monte-Carlo method are as follows

1. Generate N scenarios by simulating risk factors $X_1, ..., X_N$ according to Σ_X;

2. Revalue the portfolio and determine the loss in the portfolio values $L_1, ..., L_N$ using the simple delta-gamma approximation;

3. Calculate the fraction of scenarios in which losses exceed l:

$$N^{-1} \sum_{i=1}^{N} \mathbf{1}(L_i > l), \tag{1.45}$$

where $\mathbf{1}(L_i > l) = 1$ if $L_i > l$ and 0 otherwise.

The partial Monte-Carlo method is flexible and easy to implement. It provides the accurate estimation of the VaR when the loss function is approximately quadratic. However, one drawback is that for a large number of risk factors, it requires a large number of replications and takes a long computational time. According to Boyle, Broadie and Glasserman (1998), the convergence rate of the Monte-Carlo estimate is $1/\sqrt{N}$. Different variance reduction techniques have been developed to increase the precision and speed up the process. In the next section, we will give a brief overview of different types of variance reduction techniques, Boyle et al. (1998).

1. *Antithetic Method*

   We assume $W_i = f(z_i)$, where $z_i \in \mathbb{R}^m$ are independent samples from the standard normal distribution. In our case, the function f is defined as

   $$f(z_i) = I(L_i > l) = I[-\sum_{i=1}^{m}(\delta_i z_i + \frac{1}{2}\lambda_i z_i^2) > l]. \tag{1.46}$$

   Based on N replications, an unbiased estimator of the $\mu = E(W)$ is given by

   $$\hat{\mu} = \frac{1}{N} \sum_{i=1}^{N} W_i = \frac{1}{N} \sum_{i=1}^{N} f(z_i). \tag{1.47}$$

In this context, the method of antithetic variates is based on the observation that if z_i has a standard normal distribution, then so does $-z_i$. Similarly, each

$$\tilde{\mu} = \frac{1}{N} \sum_{i=1}^{N} f(-z_i) \tag{1.48}$$

is also an unbiased estimator of μ. Therefore,

$$\hat{\mu}_{AV} = \frac{\hat{\mu} + \tilde{\mu}}{2} \tag{1.49}$$

is an unbiased estimator of μ as well.

The intuition behind the antithetic method is that the random inputs obtained from the collection of antithetic pairs $(z_i, -z_i)$ are more regularly distributed than a collection of $2N$ independent samples. In particular, the sample mean over the antithetic pairs always equals the population mean of 0, whereas the mean over finitely many independent samples is almost surely different from 0.

2. *Control Variates*

The basic idea of control variates is to replace the evaluation of an unknown expectation with the evaluation of the difference between the unknown quantity and another expectation whose value is known. The standard Monte-Carlo estimate of $\mu = E[W_i] = E[f(z_i)]$ is $\frac{1}{N} \sum_{i=1}^{N} W_i$. Suppose we know $\tilde{\mu} = E[g(z_i)]$. The method of control variates uses the known error

$$\frac{1}{N} \sum_{i=1}^{N} \tilde{W}_i - \tilde{\mu} \tag{1.50}$$

to reduce the unknown error

$$\frac{1}{N} \sum_{i=1}^{N} W_i - \mu. \tag{1.51}$$

The controlled estimator has the form

$$\frac{1}{N} \sum_{i=1}^{N} W_i - \beta \left(\frac{1}{N} \sum_{i=1}^{N} \tilde{W}_i - \tilde{\mu} \right). \tag{1.52}$$

Since the term in parentheses has expectation zero, equation (1.52) provides an unbiased estimator of μ as long as β is independent. In practice, if the function $g(z_i)$ provides a close approximation of $f(z_i)$, we usually set $\beta = 1$ to simplify the calculation.

3. *Moment Matching Method*

Let $z_i, i = 1, ..., n$, denote an independent standard normal random vector used to drive a simulation. The sample moments will not exactly match those of the standard normal. The idea of moment matching is to transform the z_i to match a finite number of the moments of the underlying population. For example, the first and second moment of the normal random number can be matched by defining

$$\tilde{z}_i = (z_i - \tilde{z})\frac{\sigma_z}{s_z} + \mu_z, i = 1, ...n \qquad (1.53)$$

where $\tilde{z}$ is the sample mean of the z_i, σ_z is the population standard deviation, s_z is the sample standard deviation of z_i, and μ_z is the population mean.

The moment matching method can be extended to match covariance and higher moments as well.

4. *Stratified Sampling*

Like many variance reduction techniques, stratified sampling seeks to make the inputs to simulation more regular than the random inputs. In stratified sampling, rather than drawing z_i randomly and independent from a given distribution, the method ensures that fixed fractions of the samples fall within specified ranges. For example, we want to generate N m-dimensional normal random vectors for simulation input. The empirical distribution of an independent sample $(z_1, \ldots, z_N)$ will look only roughly like the true normal density; the rare events - which are important for calculating the VaR - will inevitably be underrepresented. Stratified sampling can be used to ensure that exactly one observation z_i^k lies between the $(i-1)/N$ and i/N quantiles $(i = 1, ..., N)$ of the k-th marginal distribution for each of the m components. One way to implement that is to generate Nm independent uniform random numbers u_i^k on $[0, 1]$ $(k = 1, \ldots, m, i = 1, \ldots, N)$ and set

$$\tilde{z}_i^k = \Phi^{-1}[(i + u_i^k - 1)/N], i = 1, ..., N \qquad (1.54)$$

where Φ^{-1} is the inverse of the standard normal cdf. (In order to achieve satisfactory sampling results, we need a good numerical procedure to calculate Φ^{-1}.) An alternative is to apply the stratification only to the most important components (directions), usually associated to the eigenvalues of largest absolute value.

5. *Latin Hypercube Sampling*

   The Latin Hypercube Sampling method was first introduced by McKay, Beckman and Conover (1979). In the Latin Hypercube Sampling method, the range of probable values for each component u_i^k is divided into N segments of equal probability. Thus, the m-dimensional space, consisting of k parameters, is partitioned into N^m cells, each having equal probability. For example, for the case of dimension $m = 2$ and $N = 10$ segments, the parameter space is divided into 10×10 cells. The next step is to choose 10 cells from the 10×10 cells. First, the uniform random numbers are generated to calculate the cell number. The cell number indicates the segment number the sample belongs to, with respect to each of the parameters. For example, a cell number (1,8) indicates that the sample lies in the segment 1 with respect to first parameter, segment 10 with respect to second parameter. At each successive step, a random sample is generated, and is accepted only if it does not agree with any previous sample on any of the segment numbers.

6. *Importance sampling*

   The technique builds on the observation that an expectation under one probability measure can be expressed as an expectation under another through the use of a likelihood ratio. The intuition behind the method is to generate more samples from the region that is more important to the practical problem at hand. In next the section, we will give a detailed description of calculating VaR by the partial Monte-Carlo method with importance sampling.

1.5.2   Partial Monte-Carlo with Importance Sampling

In the basic partial Monte-Carlo method, the problem of sampling changes in market risk factors X_i is transformed into a problem of sampling the vector z of underlying standard normal random variables. In importance sampling, we will change the distribution of z from $N(0, I)$ to $N(\mu, \Sigma)$. The key steps proposed by Glasserman, Heidelberger and Shahabuddin (2000) are to calculate

$$P(L > l) = E_{\mu,\Sigma}[\theta(z)I(L > l)] \tag{1.55}$$

Expectation is taken with z sampled from $N(\mu, \Sigma)$ rather than its original distribution $N(0, I)$. To correct for this change of distribution, we weight the loss indictor $I(L > l)$ by the likelihood ratio

$$\theta(z) = |\Sigma|^{1/2} e^{-\frac{1}{2}\mu^{\top}\Sigma^{-1}\mu} e^{-\frac{1}{2}[z^{\top}(I-\Sigma^{-1})z - 2\mu^{\top}\Sigma^{-1}z]}, \tag{1.56}$$

which is simply the ratio of $N[0, I]$ and $N[\mu, \Sigma]$ densities evaluated at z.

The next task is to choose μ and Σ so that the Monte-Carlo estimator will have minimum variance. The key to reducing the variance is making the likelihood ratio small when $L > l$. Equivalently, μ and Σ should be chosen in the way to make $L > l$ more likely under $N(\mu, \Sigma)$ than under $N(0, I)$. The steps of the algorithm are following:

1. *Decomposition Process*

   We follow the decomposition steps described in the section 1.2 and find the cumulant generating function of L given by

   $$\kappa(\omega) = \sum_{i=1}^{m} \frac{1}{2} \left[\frac{(\omega\delta_i)^2}{1 - \omega\lambda_i} - \log(1 - \omega\lambda_i) \right] \tag{1.57}$$

2. *Transform $N(0, I)$ to $N(\mu, \Sigma)$*

   If we take the first derivative of $\kappa(\omega)$ with respect to ω, we will get:

   $$\frac{d}{d\omega}\kappa(\omega) = E_{\mu(\omega),\Sigma(\omega)}[L] = l \tag{1.58}$$

   where $\Sigma(\omega) = (I - \omega\Lambda)^{-1}$ and $\mu(\omega) = \omega\Sigma(\omega)\delta$. Since our objective is to estimate $P(L > l)$, we will choose ω to be the solution of equation (1.58). The loss exceeding scenarios $(L > l)$, which were previously rare under $N(0, I)$, are typical under $N(\mu, \Sigma)$, since the expected value of the approximate value L is now l. According to Glasserman et al. (2000), the effectiveness of this importance sampling procedure is not very sensitive to the choice of ω.

   After we get $N(\mu(\omega), \Sigma(\omega))$, we can follow the same steps in the basic partial Monte-Carlo simulation to calculate the VaR. The only difference is that the fraction of scenarios in which losses exceed l is calculated by:

   $$\frac{1}{N} \sum_{i=1}^{N} [\exp(-\omega L_i + \kappa(\omega)) I(L_i > l)] \tag{1.59}$$

An important feature of this method is that it can be easily added to an existing implementation of partial Monte-Carlo simulation. The importance sampling algorithm differs only in how it generates scenarios and in how it weights scenarios as in equation (1.59).

1.5.3   XploRe Examples

VaRMC = VaRestMC (VaRdelta, VaRgamma, VaRcovmatrix,
    smethod, opt)
    Partial Monte-Carlo method to calculate VaR based on Delta-
    Gamma Approximation.

The function VaRestMC uses the different types of variance reduction to calculate the VaR by the partial Monte-Carlo simulation. We employ the variance reduction techniques of moment matching, Latin Hypercube Sampling and importance sampling. The output is the estimated VaR. In order to test the efficiency of different Monte-Carlo sampling methods, we collect data from the MD*BASE and construct a portfolio consisting of three German stocks (Bayer, Deutsche Bank, Deutsche Telekom) and corresponding 156 options on these underlying stocks with maturity ranging from 18 to 211 days on May 29, 1999. The total portfolio value is 62,476 EUR. The covariance matrix for the stocks is provided as well. Using the Black-Scholes model, we also construct the aggregate delta and aggregate gamma as the input to the Quantlet. By choosing the importance sampling method, 0.01 confidence level, 1 days forecast horizon and 1,000 times of simulation, the result of the estimation is as follows.

Q XFGVaRMC.xpl

Contents of VaRMC

[1,]   771.73

It tells us that we expect the loss to exceed 771.73 EUR or 1.24% of portfolio value with less than 1% probability in 1 day. However, the key question of the empirical example is that how much variance reduction is achieved by the different sampling methods. We run each of the four sampling methods 1,000 times and estimated the standard error of the estimated VaR for each sampling method. The table (1.1) summarizes the results.

	Estimated VaR	Standard Error	Variance Reduction
Plain-Vanilla	735.75	36.96	0%
Moment Matching	734.92	36.23	1.96%
Latin Hypercube	757.83	21.32	42.31%
Importance Sampling	761.75	5.66	84.68%

Table 1.1. Variance Reduction of Estimated VaR for German Stock Option Portfolio

As we see from the table (1.1), the standard error of the importance sampling is 84.68% less than those of plain-vanilla sampling and it demonstrates that approximately 42 times more scenarios would have to be generated using the plain-vanilla method to achieve the same precision obtained by importance sampling based on Delta-Gamma approximation. These results clearly indicate the great potential speed-up of estimation of the VaR by using the importance sampling method. This is why we set the importance sampling as the default sampling method in the function VaRestMC. However, the Latin Hypercube sampling method also achieved 42.31% of variance reduction. One advantage of the Latin Hypercube sampling method is that the decomposition process is not necessary. Especially when the number of risk factors (m) is large, the decomposition ($\mathcal{O}(m^3)$) dominates the sampling ($\mathcal{O}(m)$) and summation $O(1)$ in terms of computational time. In this case, Latin Hypercube sampling may offer the better performance in terms of precision for a given computational time.

Bibliography

Abate, J. and Whitt, W. (1992). The Fourier-series method for inverting transforms of probability distributions, *Queuing Systems Theory and Applications* **10**: 5–88.

Albanese, C., Jackson, K. and Wiberg, P. (2000). Fast convolution method for VaR and VaR gradients, http://www.math-point.com/fconv.ps.

Anderson, E., Bai, Z., Bischof, C., Blackford, S., Demmel, J., Dongarra, J., Croz, J. D., Greenbaum, A., Hammarling, S., McKenney, A. and

Sorensen, D. (1999). *LAPACK Users' Guide*, third edn, SIAM. `http://www.netlib.org/lapack/lug/`.

Basel Committee on Banking Supervision (1995). An internal model-based approach to market risk capital requirements, `http://www.bis.org/publ/bcbsc224.pdf`.

Boyle, P., Broadie, M. and Glasserman, P. (1998). Monte Carlo methods for security pricing, *Journal of Economic Dynamics and Control* **3**: 1267–1321.

Breckling, J., Eberlein, E. and Kokic, P. (2000). A tailored suit for risk management: Hyperbolic model, *in* J. Franke, W. Härdle and G. Stahl (eds), *Measuring Risk in Complex Stochastic Systems*, Vol. 147 of *Lecture Notes in Statistics*, Springer, New York, chapter 12, pp. 198–202.

Britton-Jones, M. and Schaefer, S. (1999). Non-linear Value-at-Risk, *European Finance Review* **2**: 161–187.

Embrechts, P., Klüppelberg, C. and Mikosch, T. (1997). *Modelling extremal events*, Springer-Verlag, Berlin.

Embrechts, P., McNeil, A. and Straumann, D. (1999). Correlation and dependence in risk management: Properties and pitfalls, `http://www.math.ethz.ch/~strauman/preprints/pitfalls.ps`.

Engle, R. (2000). Dynamic conditional correlation - a simple class of multivariate GARCH models, `http://weber.ucsd.edu/~mbacci/engle/`.

Fallon, W. (1996). Calculating Value at Risk, `http://wrdsenet.wharton.upenn.edu/fic/wfic/papers/96/9649.pdf`. Wharton Financial Institutions Center Working Paper 96-49.

Glasserman, P., Heidelberger, P. and Shahabuddin, P. (2000). Efficient monte carlo methods for value at risk, `http://www.research.ibm.com/people/b/berger/papers/RC21723.pdf`. IBM Research Paper RC21723.

Hill, G. W. and Davis, A. W. (1968). Generalized asymptotic expansions of Cornish-Fisher type, *Ann. Math. Statist.* **39**: 1264–1273.

Jaschke, S. (2001). The Cornish-Fisher-expansion in the context of delta-gamma-normal approximations, `http://www.jaschke-net.de/papers/CoFi.pdf`. Discussion Paper 54, Sonderforschungsbereich 373, Humboldt-Universität zu Berlin.

Jorion, P. (2000). *Value at Risk: The New Benchmark for Managing Financial Risk*, McGraw-Hill, New York.

Lee, Y. S. and Lin, T. K. (1992). Higher-order Cornish Fisher expansion, *Applied Statistics* **41**: 233–240.

Lee, Y. S. and Lin, T. K. (1993). Correction to algorithm AS269 : Higher-order Cornish Fisher expansion, *Applied Statistics* **42**: 268–269.

Li, D. (1999). Value at Risk based on the volatility, skewness and kurtosis, http://www.riskmetrics.com/research/working/var4mm.pdf. Risk-Metrics Group.

Longerstaey, J. (1996). RiskMetrics technical document, *Technical Report fourth edition*, J.P.Morgan. originally from http://www.jpmorgan.com/RiskManagement/RiskMetrics/, now http://www.riskmetrics.com.

McKay, M. D., Beckman, R. J. and Conover, W. J. (1979). A comparison of three methods for selecting values of input variables in the analysis of output from a computer code, *Technometrics* **21**(2): 239–245.

Mina, J. and Ulmer, A. (1999). Delta-gamma four ways, http://www.riskmetrics.com.

Pichler, S. and Selitsch, K. (1999). A comparison of analytical VaR methodologies for portfolios that include options, http://www.tuwien.ac.at/E330/Research/paper-var.pdf. Working Paper TU Wien.

Pritsker, M. (1996). Evaluating Value at Risk methodologies: Accuracy versus computational time, http://wrdsenet.wharton.upenn.edu/fic/wfic/papers/96/9648.pdf. Wharton Financial Institutions Center Working Paper 96-48.

Rogers, L. and Zane, O. (1999). Saddle-point approximations to option prices, *Annals of Applied Probability* **9**(2): 493–503. http://www.bath.ac.uk/~maslcgr/papers/.

Rouvinez, C. (1997). Going greek with VaR, *Risk* **10**(2): 57–65.

Zangari, P. (1996a). How accurate is the delta-gamma methodology?, *RiskMetrics Monitor* **1996**(third quarter): 12–29.

Zangari, P. (1996b). A VaR methodology for portfolios that include options, *RiskMetrics Monitor* **1996**(first quarter): 4–12.

2 Applications of Copulas for the Calculation of Value-at-Risk

Jörn Rank and Thomas Siegl

We will focus on the computation of the Value-at-Risk (VaR) from the perspective of the dependency structure between the risk factors. Apart from historical simulation, most VaR methods assume a multivariate normal distribution of the risk factors. Therefore, the dependence structure between different risk factors is defined by the correlation between those factors. It is shown in Embrechts, McNeil and Straumann (1999) that the concept of correlation entails several pitfalls. The authors therefore propose the use of *copulas* to quantify dependence.

For a good overview of copula techniques we refer to Nelsen (1999). Copulas can be used to describe the dependence between two or more random variables with arbitrary marginal distributions. In rough terms, a copula is a function $C : [0,1]^n \to [0,1]$ with certain special properties. The joint multidimensional cumulative distribution can be written as

$$
\begin{aligned}
\mathrm{P}(X_1 \leq x_1, \ldots, X_n \leq x_n) &= C\left(\mathrm{P}(X_1 \leq x_1), \ldots, \mathrm{P}(X_n \leq x_n)\right) \\
&= C\left(F_1(x_1), \ldots, F_n(x_n)\right),
\end{aligned}
$$

where $F_1, \ldots, F_n$ denote the cumulative distribution functions of the n random variables $X_1, \ldots, X_n$. In general, a copula C depends on one or more copula parameters $p_1, \ldots, p_k$ that determine the dependence between the random variables $X_1, \ldots, X_n$. In this sense, the correlation $\rho(X_i, X_j)$ can be seen as a parameter of the so-called Gaussian copula.

Here we demonstrate the process of deriving the VaR of a portfolio using the copula method with XploRe, beginning with the estimation of the selection of the copula itself, estimation of the copula parameters and the computation of the VaR. Backtesting of the results is performed to show the validity and relative quality of the results. We will focus on the case of a portfolio containing two market risk factors only, the FX rates USD/EUR and GBP/EUR. Copulas in more dimensions exist, but the selection of suitable n-dimensional copulas is still quite limited. While the case of two risk factors is still important for applications, e.g. spread trading, it is also the case that can be best described.

As we want to concentrate our attention on the modelling of the dependency structure, rather than on the modelling of the marginal distributions, we restrict our analysis to normal marginal densities. On the basis of our backtesting results, we find that the copula method produces more accurate results than "correlation dependence".

2.1　Copulas

In this section we summarize the basic results without proof that are necessary to understand the concept of copulas. Then, we present the most important properties of copulas that are needed for applications in finance. In doing so, we will follow the notation used in Nelsen (1999).

2.1.1　Definition

DEFINITION 2.1 *A 2-dimensional copula is a function* $C : [0,1]^2 \rightarrow [0,1]$ *with the following properties:*

1. *For every* $u \in [0,1]$
$$C(0, u) = C(u, 0) = 0 . \tag{2.1}$$

2. *For every* $u \in [0,1]$
$$C(u, 1) = u \quad and \quad C(1, u) = u . \tag{2.2}$$

3. *For every* $(u_1, u_2), (v_1, v_2) \in [0,1] \times [0,1]$ *with* $u_1 \leq v_1$ *and* $u_2 \leq v_2$:
$$C(v_1, v_2) - C(v_1, u_2) - C(u_1, v_2) + C(u_1, u_2) \geq 0 . \tag{2.3}$$

A function that fulfills property 1 is also said to be *grounded*. Property 3 is the two-dimensional analogue of a nondecreasing one-dimensional function. A function with this feature is therefore called *2-increasing*.

The usage of the name "copula" for the function C is explained by the following theorem.

2.1.2 Sklar's Theorem

The *distribution function* of a random variable R is a function F that assigns all $r \in \overline{\mathbb{R}}$ a probability $F(r) = \mathrm{P}(R \leq r)$. In addition, the *joint distribution function* of two random variables R_1, R_2 is a function H that assigns all $r_1, r_2 \in \mathbb{R}$ a probability $H(r_1, r_2) = \mathrm{P}(R_1 \leq r_1, R_2 \leq r_2)$.

THEOREM 2.1 (Sklar's theorem) *Let H be a joint distribution function with margins F_1 and F_2. Then there exists a copula C with*

$$H(x_1, x_2) = C(F_1(x_1), F_2(x_2)) \tag{2.4}$$

for every $x_1, x_2 \in \overline{\mathbb{R}}$. If F_1 and F_2 are continuous, then C is unique. Otherwise, C is uniquely determined on Range $F_1 \times$ Range F_2. On the other hand, if C is a copula and F_1 and F_2 are distribution functions, then the function H defined by (2.4) is a joint distribution function with margins F_1 and F_2.

It is shown in Nelsen (1999) that H has margins F_1 and F_2 that are given by $F_1(x_1) \stackrel{\text{def}}{=} H(x_1, +\infty)$ and $F_2(x_2) \stackrel{\text{def}}{=} H(+\infty, x_2)$, respectively. Furthermore, F_1 and F_2 themselves are distribution functions. With Sklar's Theorem, the use of the name "copula" becomes obvious. It was chosen by Sklar (1996) to describe "a function that links a multidimensional distribution to its one-dimensional margins" and appeared in mathematical literature for the first time in Sklar (1959).

2.1.3 Examples of Copulas

Product Copula The structure of independence is especially important for applications.

DEFINITION 2.2 *Two random variables R_1 and R_2 are independent if and only if the product of their distribution functions F_1 and F_2 equals their joint distribution function H,*

$$H(r_1, r_2) = F_1(r_1) \cdot F_2(r_2) \quad \text{for all} \quad r_1, r_2 \in \overline{\mathbb{R}}. \tag{2.5}$$

Thus, we obtain the independence copula $C = \Pi$ by

$$\Pi(u_1, \ldots, u_n) = \prod_{i=1}^{n} u_i,$$

which becomes obvious from the following theorem:

THEOREM 2.2 *Let R_1 and R_2 be random variables with continuous distribution functions F_1 and F_2 and joint distribution function H. Then R_1 and R_2 are independent if and only if $C_{R_1 R_2} = \Pi$.*

From Sklar's Theorem we know that there exists a unique copula C with

$$P(R_1 \leq r_1, R_2 \leq r_2) = H(r_1, r_2) = C(F_1(r_1), F_2(r_2)). \qquad (2.6)$$

Independence can be seen using Equation (2.4) for the joint distribution function H and the definition of Π,

$$H(r_1, r_2) = C(F_1(r_1), F_2(r_2)) = F_1(r_1) \cdot F_2(r_2) . \qquad (2.7)$$

Gaussian Copula   The second important copula that we want to investigate is the *Gaussian* or *normal copula*,

$$C_\rho^{\text{Gauss}}(u, v) \stackrel{\text{def}}{=} \int_{-\infty}^{\Phi_1^{-1}(u)} \int_{-\infty}^{\Phi_2^{-1}(v)} f_\rho(r_1, r_2) dr_2 dr_1 , \qquad (2.8)$$

see Embrechts, McNeil and Straumann (1999). In (2.8), f_ρ denotes the bivariate normal density function with correlation ρ for $n = 2$. The functions Φ_1, Φ_2 in (2.8) refer to the corresponding one-dimensional, cumulated normal density functions of the margins.

In the case of vanishing correlation, $\rho = 0$, the Gaussian copula becomes

$$
\begin{aligned}
C_0^{\text{Gauss}}(u, v) &= \int_{-\infty}^{\Phi_1^{-1}(u)} f_1(r_1) dr_1 \int_{-\infty}^{\Phi_2^{-1}(v)} f_2(r_2) dr_2 \\
&= u\,v \\
&= \Pi(u, v) \quad \text{if} \quad \rho = 0 .
\end{aligned}
\qquad (2.9)
$$

Result (2.9) is a direct consequence of Theorem 2.2.

As $\Phi_1(r_1), \Phi_2(r_2) \in [0, 1]$, one can replace u, v in (2.8) by $\Phi_1(r_1), \Phi_2(r_2)$. If one considers r_1, r_2 in a probabilistic sense, i.e. r_1 and r_2 being values of two random variables R_1 and R_2, one obtains from (2.8)

$$C_\rho^{\text{Gauss}}(\Phi_1(r_1), \Phi_2(r_2)) = P(R_1 \leq r_1, R_2 \leq r_2) . \qquad (2.10)$$

In other words: $C_\rho^{\text{Gauss}}(\Phi_1(r_1), \Phi_2(r_2))$ is the binormal cumulated probability function.

Gumbel-Hougaard Copula Next, we consider the *Gumbel-Hougaard* family of copulas, see Hutchinson (1990). A discussion in Nelsen (1999) shows that C_θ is suited to describe bivariate extreme value distributions. It is given by the function

$$C_\theta(u, v) \stackrel{\text{def}}{=} \exp\left\{ - \left[(-\ln u)^\theta + (-\ln v)^\theta \right]^{1/\theta} \right\} . \tag{2.11}$$

The parameter θ may take all values in the interval $[1, \infty)$.

For $\theta = 1$, expression (2.11) reduces to the product copula, i.e. $C_1(u, v) = \Pi(u, v) = u\,v$. For $\theta \to \infty$ one finds for the Gumbel-Hougaard copula

$$C_\theta(u, v) \stackrel{\theta \to \infty}{\longrightarrow} \min(u, v) \stackrel{\text{def}}{=} M(u, v).$$

It can be shown that M is also a copula. Furthermore, for any given copula C one has $C(u, v) \leq M(u, v)$, and M is called the *Fréchet-Hoeffding upper bound*. The two-dimensional function $W(u, v) \stackrel{\text{def}}{=} \max(u + v - 1, 0)$ defines a copula with $W(u, v) \leq C(u, v)$ for any other copula C. W is called the *Fréchet-Hoeffding lower bound*.

2.1.4 Further Important Properties of Copulas

In this section we focus on the properties of copulas. The theorem we will present next establishes the continuity of copulas via a Lipschitz condition on $[0, 1] \times [0, 1]$:

THEOREM 2.3 *Let C be a copula. Then for every $u_1, u_2, v_1, v_2 \in [0, 1]$:*

$$|C(u_2, v_2) - C(u_1, v_1)| \leq |u_2 - u_1| + |v_2 - v_1| . \tag{2.12}$$

From (2.12) it follows that every copula C is uniformly continuous on its domain. A further important property of copulas concerns the partial derivatives of a copula with respect to its variables:

THEOREM 2.4 *Let C be a copula. For every $u \in [0, 1]$, the partial derivative $\partial C / \partial v$ exists for almost every $v \in [0, 1]$. For such u and v one has*

$$0 \leq \frac{\partial}{\partial v} C(u, v) \leq 1 . \tag{2.13}$$

The analogous statement is true for the partial derivative $\partial C / \partial u$.

In addition, the functions $u \to C_v(u) \stackrel{\text{def}}{=} \partial C(u, v) / \partial v$ and $v \to C_u(v) \stackrel{\text{def}}{=} \partial C(u, v) / \partial u$ are defined and nondecreasing almost everywhere on [0,1].

To give an example of this theorem, we consider the partial derivative of the Gumbel-Hougaard copula (2.11) with respect to u,

$$C_{\theta,u}(v) = \frac{\partial}{\partial u} C_\theta(u,v) = \exp\left\{-\left[(-\ln u)^\theta + (-\ln v)^\theta\right]^{1/\theta}\right\} \times$$

$$\left[(-\ln u)^\theta + (-\ln v)^\theta\right]^{-\frac{\theta-1}{\theta}} \frac{(-\ln u)^{\theta-1}}{u}. \quad (2.14)$$

Note that for $u \in (0,1)$ and for all $\theta \in \mathbb{R}$ where $\theta > 1$, $C_{\theta,u}$ is a strictly increasing function of v. Therefore the inverse function $C_{\theta,u}^{-1}$ is well defined. However, as one might guess from (2.14), $C_{\theta,u}^{-1}$ can not be calculated analytically so that some kind of numerical algorithm has to be used for this task. As C_θ is symmetric in u and v, the partial derivative of C_θ with respect to v shows an identical behaviour for the same set of parameters.

We will end this section with a statement on the behaviour of copulas under strictly monotone transformations of random variables.

THEOREM 2.5 *Let R_1 and R_2 be random variables with continuous distribution functions and with copula $C_{R_1 R_2}$. If α_1 and α_2 are strictly increasing functions on Range R_1 and Range R_2, then $C_{\alpha_1(R_1)\alpha_2(R_2)} = C_{R_1 R_2}$. In other words: $C_{R_1 R_2}$ is invariant under strictly increasing transformations of R_1 and R_2.*

2.2 Computing Value-at-Risk with Copulas

Now that we have given the most important properties of copulas, we turn to the practical question of how to compute the Value-at-Risk of a portfolio using copulas. The following steps need to be performed:

2.2.1 Selecting the Marginal Distributions

The copula method works with any given marginal distribution, i.e. it does not restrict the choice of margins. However, we will use normal margins for simplicity and in order to allow a comparison with standard VaR methods.

2.2.2 Selecting a Copula

A wide variety of copulas exists, mainly for the two dimensional case (Nelsen (1999)). In our numerical tests, we will use some of the copulas presented in Table 4.1 of Nelsen (1999) in our experiments for comparison which are implemented in the function

```
C = VaRcopula(uv,theta,0,copula)
```
       returns $C_\theta(u,v)$ for copula `copula` with parameter $\theta = $ `theta`. `uv` is a $n \times 2$ vector of coordinates, where the copula is calculated.

For easy reference the implemented copulas are given in Table 2.1.

2.2.3 Estimating the Copula Parameters

After selecting a copula we fit the copula to a time series

$$s = s^{(1)}, \ldots, s^{(T)} \text{ with } s^{(t)} = (s_1^{(t)}, \ldots, s_n^{(t)})$$

for $t \in 1, \ldots, T$. For simplicity we assume that the $s^{(t)}$ are realizations of i.i.d. random variables $S^{(t)}$. The first step will be to determine the parameters of the marginal distributions. In the numerical example we will use the normal distribution $N(0, \sigma_i^2)$, and estimate the volatility σ_i using an equally weighted volatility estimator $\hat{\sigma}_i^2 = \frac{1}{T-1} \sum_{t=2}^{T} (r_i^{(t)})^2$ of the returns $r_i^{(t)} = \log(s_i^{(t)}/s_i^{(t-1)})$ for simplicity. The marginal distributions of the risk factors are then log-normal. The remaining task is to estimate the copula parameters. In the XploRe `VaR` quantlib this is done by the function

```
res = VaRfitcopula(history,copula,method)
```
       fits the `copula` to the `history` using fitting function `method`. The result `res` is a list containing the estimates of the copula parameter together with there standard deviations.

Least Square Fit The main idea of the least square fit is that the cumulative distribution function $F_\theta^{(C)}(x)$ defined by the copula C should fit the sample

#	$C_\theta(u,v) =$	$\theta \in$
1	$\max\left([u^{-\theta} + v^{-\theta} - 1]^{-1/\theta}, 0\right)$	$[-1, \infty)\setminus\{0\}$
2	$\max\left(1 - [(1-u)^\theta + (1-v)^\theta - 1]^{1/\theta}, 0\right)$	$[1, \infty)$
3	$\frac{uv}{1 - \theta(1-u)(1-v)}$	$[-1, 1)$
4	$\exp\left(-[(-\ln u)^\theta + (-\ln v)^\theta]^{1/\theta}\right)$	$[1, \infty)$
5	$-\frac{1}{\theta}\ln\left(1 + \frac{(e^{-\theta u}-1)(e^{-\theta v}-1)}{e^{-\theta}-1}\right)$	$(-\infty, \infty)\setminus\{0\}$
6	$1 - \left[(1-u)^\theta + (1-v)^\theta - (1-u)^\theta(1-v)^\theta\right]^{1/\theta}$	$[1, \infty)$
7	$\max\left[\theta uv + (1-\theta)(u+v-1), 0\right]$	$(0, 1]$
8	$\max\left[\frac{\theta^2 uv - (1-u)(1-v)}{\theta^2 - (\theta-1)^2(1-u)(1-v)}, 0\right]$	$(0, 1]$
9	$uv\exp(-\theta \ln u \ln v)$	$(0, 1]$
10	$uv/\left[1 + (1-u^\theta)(1-v^\theta)\right]^{1/\theta}$	$(0, 1]$
11	$\max\left(\left[u^\theta v^\theta - 2(1-u^\theta)(1-v^\theta)\right]^{1/\theta}, 0\right)$	$(0, 1/2]$
12	$\left(1 + \left[(u^{-1}-1)^\theta + (v^{-1}-1)^\theta\right]^{1/\theta}\right)^{-1}$	$[1, \infty)$
13	$\exp\left(1 - \left[(1-\ln u)^\theta + (1-\ln v)^\theta - 1\right]^{1/\theta}\right)$	$(0, \infty)$
14	$\left(1 + \left[(u^{-1/\theta}-1)^\theta + (v^{-1/\theta}-1)^\theta\right]^{1/\theta}\right)^{-\theta}$	$[1, \infty)$
15	$\max\left(\left\{1 - \left[(1-u^{1/\theta})^\theta + (1-v^{1/\theta})^\theta\right]^{1/\theta}\right\}^\theta, 0\right)$	$[1, \infty)$
16	$\frac{1}{2}\left(S + \sqrt{S^2 + 4\theta}\right)$	$[0, \infty)$
	$\hookrightarrow S = u + v - 1 - \theta\left(\frac{1}{u} + \frac{1}{v} - 1\right)$	
21	$1 - \left(1 - \left\{\max(S(u) + S(v) - 1, 0)\right\}^\theta\right)^{\frac{1}{\theta}}$	$[1, \infty)$
	$\hookrightarrow S(u) = \left[1 - (1-u)^\theta\right]^{1/\theta}$	

Table 2.1. Copulas implemented in the VaR quantlib.

distribution function $S(x) = \frac{1}{T}\sum_{t=1}^{T} \mathbf{1}(s_1^{(t)} \leq x_1, \ldots, s_n^{(t)} \leq x_n)$ as close as possible in the mean square sense. The function $\mathbf{1}(A)$ is the indicator function of the event A. In order to solve the least square problem on a computer, a discretization of the support of $F_\theta^{(C)}$ is needed, for which the sample set $s^{(t)}$

seems to be well suited. The copula parameter estimators are therefore the solution of the following minimization problem:

$$\min \sum_{t=1}^{T} \left(F_{\theta}^{(c)}(s^{(t)}) - S(s^{(t)}) + \frac{1}{2T} \right)^2 \text{ subject to } \theta \in D_C.$$

using the Newton method on the first derivative (method = 1). The addition of $\frac{1}{2T}$ avoids problems that result from the $\frac{1}{T}$ jumps at the sample points. While this method is inherently numerically stable, it will produce unsatisfactory results when applied to risk management problems, because the minimization will fit the copula best where there are the most datapoints, and not necessarily at the extreme ends of the distribution. While this can be somewhat rectified by weighting schemes, the maximum likelihood method does this directly.

Maximum Likelihood The likelihood function of a probability density function $f_{\theta}^{(C)}(x)$ evaluated for a time series s is given by $l(\theta) = \prod_{t=1}^{T} f_{\theta}^{(C)}(s^t)$. The maximum likelihood method states that the copula parameters at which l reaches its maximum are good estimators of the "real" copula parameters. Instead of the likelihood function, it is customary to maximize the log-likelihood function

$$\max \sum_{t=1}^{T} \log \left(f_{\theta}^{(C)}(x^{(t)}) \right) \text{ s.t. } \theta \in D_C.$$

Maximization can be performed on the copula function itself by the Newton method on the first derivative (method=2) or by an interval search (method=3). The true maximum likelihood method is implemented in method=4 using an interval search. Depending on the given copula it may not be possible to maximize the likelihood function (i.e. if $f_{\theta}^{(C)}(s^{(t)})) = 0$ for some t and all θ. In this case the least square fit may be used as a fallback.

2.2.4 Generating Scenarios - Monte Carlo Value-at-Risk

Assume now that the copula C has been selected. For risk management purposes, we are interested in the Value-at-Risk of a position. While analytical methods for the computation of the Value-at-Risk exist for the multivariate normal distribution (i.e. for the Gaussian copula), we will in general have to use numerical simulations for the computation of the VaR. To that end, we need to generate pairs of random variables $(X_1, X_2) \sim F^{(C)}$, which form scenarios of possible changes of the risk factor. The Monte Carlo method generates a number N of such scenarios, and evaluates the present value change of a portfolio under each scenario. The sample $\alpha-$quantile is then the one period Value-at-Risk with confidence α.

Our first task is to generate pairs (u, v) of observations of $U(0, 1)$ distributed random variables U and V whose joint distribution function is $C(u, v)$. To reach this goal we use the method of conditional distributions. Let c_u denote the conditional distribution function for the random variable V at a given value u of U,

$$c_u(v) \stackrel{\text{def}}{=} P(V \leq v, U = u) . \tag{2.15}$$

From (2.6) we have

$$c_u(v) = \lim_{\Delta u \to 0} \frac{C(u + \Delta u, v) - C(u, v)}{\Delta u} = \frac{\partial}{\partial u} C(u, v) = C_u(v) , \tag{2.16}$$

where C_u is the partial derivative of the copula. From Theorem 2.4 we know that $c_u(v)$ is nondecreasing and exists for almost all $v \in [0, 1]$.

For the sake of simplicity, we assume from now on that c_u is strictly increasing and exists for all $v \in [0, 1]$. If these conditions are not fulfilled, one has to replace the term "inverse" in the remaining part of this section by "quasi-inverse", see Nelsen (1999).

With result (2.16) at hand we can now use the method of variable transformation to generate the desired pair (u, v) of pseudo random numbers (PRN). The algorithm consists of the following two steps:

- Generate two independent uniform PRNs $u, w \in [0, 1]$. u is already the first number we are looking for.

- Compute the inverse function of c_u. In general, it will depend on the parameters of the copula and on u, which can be seen, in this context, as an additional parameter of c_u. Set $v = c_u^{-1}(w)$ to obtain the second PRN.

It may happen that the inverse function cannot be calculated analytically. In this case one has to use a numerical algorithm to determine v. This situation occurs for example when Gumbel-Hougaard copulas are used.

```
v = VaRcopula(uv,theta,-1,copula)
```
    returns inverse $v = c_u^{-1}$ such that $res = c_u(u, v)$ for copula `copula`
with parameter $\theta =$ `theta`. `uv` is a $n \times 2$ vector of coordinates,
where the copula is calculated.

Finally we determine $x_1 = \Phi_1^{-1}(u)$ and $x_2 = \Phi_2^{-1}(v)$ to obtain one pair (x_1, x_2) of random variables with the desired copula dependence structure. For a Monte Carlo simulation, this procedure is performed N times to yield a sample $X = (x^{(1)}, \ldots, x^{(N)})$.

```
X = VaRsimcopula(N, sigma_1, sigma_2, theta, copula)
```
    returns a sample of size `N` for the copula `copula` with parameter
$\theta =$ `theta` and normal distributions with standard deviations
$\sigma_1 =$ `sigma_1`, $\sigma_2 =$ `sigma_2`.

If we assume a linear position a with holdings $a_1, \ldots, a_n$ in each of the risk factors, the change in portfolio value is approximately $\sum_{i=1}^{n} a_i \cdot x_i$. Using a first order approximation, this yields a sample Value-at-Risk with confidence level α.

```
VaR = VaRestMCcopula(history,a,copula,opt)
```
    fits the copula `copula` to the history `history` and returns the
N-sample Monte Carlo Value-at-Risk with confidence level $\alpha =$
`alpha` for position `a`. N and `alpha` are contained in list `opt`.

2.3 Examples

In this section we show possible applications for the Gumbel-Hougaard copula, i.e. for `copula` $= 4$. First we try to visualize $C_4(u, v)$ in Figure 2.1.

Q XFGaccvar1.xpl

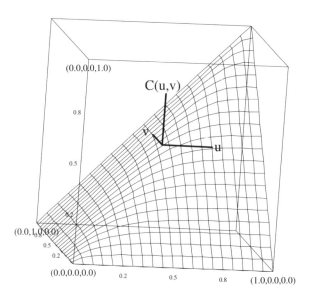

Figure 2.1. Plot of $C_4(u, v)$ for $\theta = 3$

In the next Figure 2.2 we show an example of copula sampling for fixed parameters $\sigma_1 = 1$, $\sigma_2 = 1$, $\theta = 3$ for copulas numbered 4, 5, 6, and 12, see Table 2.1.

Q XFGaccvar2.xpl

In order to investigate the connection between the Gaussian and Copula based dependency structure we plot θ against correlation ρ in Figure 2.3. We assume that `tmin` and `tmax` hold the minimum respectively maximum possible θ values. Those can also be obtained by `tmin=VaRcopula(0,0,0,8,copula)` and `tmax=VaRcopula(0,0,0,9,copula)`. Care has to be taken that the values are finite, so we have set the maximum absolute θ bound to 10.

Q XFGaccvar3.xpl

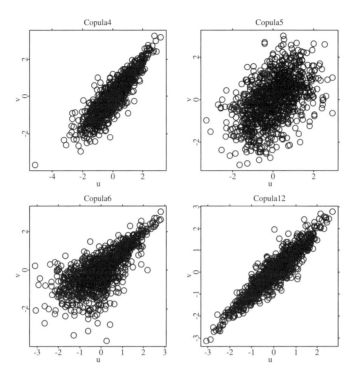

Figure 2.2. 10000-sample output for $\sigma_1 = 1$, $\sigma_2 = 1$, $\theta = 3$

2.4   Results

To judge the effectiveness of a Value-at-Risk model, it is common to use back-testing. A simple approach is to compare the predicted and empirical number of outliers, where the actual loss exceeds the VaR. We implement this test in a two risk factor model using real life time series, the FX rates USD/EUR and GBP/EUR, respectively their DEM counterparts before the introduction of the Euro. Our backtesting investigation is based on a time series ranging from 2 Jan. 1991 until 9 Mar. 2000 and simple linear portfolios $i = 1, \ldots, 4$:

$$\text{Value}(a_i, t)[EUR] = a_{i,1} \times \text{USD}_t - a_{i,2} \times \text{GBP}_t . \qquad (2.17)$$

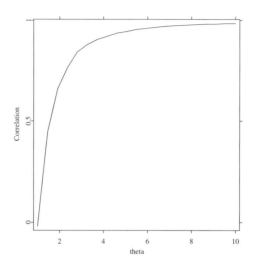

Figure 2.3. Plot of θ against correlation ρ for C_4.

The Value-at-Risk is computed with confidence level $1-\alpha_i$ ($\alpha_1 = 0.1$, $\alpha_2 = 0.05$, and $\alpha_3 = 0.01$) based on a time series for the statistical estimators of length $T = 250$ business days. The actual next day value change of the portfolio is compared to the VaR estimate. If the portfolio loss exceeds the VaR estimate, an outlier has occurred. This procedure is repeated for each day in the time series.

The prediction error as the absolute difference of the relative number of outliers $\hat{\alpha}$ to the predicted number α is averaged over different portfolios and confidence levels. The average over the portfolios ($a_1 = (-3, -2)$ $a_2 = (+3, -2)$ $a_3 = (-3, +2)$ $a_4 = (+3, +2)$) uses equal weights, while the average over the confidence levels i emphasizes the tails by a weighting scheme w_i ($w_1 = 1$, $w_2 = 5$, $w_3 = 10$). Based on the result, an overall error and a relative ranking of the different methods is obtained (see Table 2.2).

As benchmark methods for Value-at-Risk we use the variance-covariance (vcv) method and historical simulation (his), for details see Deutsch and Eller (1999). The variance covariance method is an analytical method which uses a multivariate normal distribution. The historical simulation method not only includes the empirical copula, but also empirical marginal distributions. For the copula VaR methods, the margins are assumed to be normal, the only difference between the copula VaR's is due to different dependence structures (see Table 2.1). Mainly as a consequence of non-normal margins, the historical simulation has the best backtest results. However, even assuming normal margins, certain copulas (5, 12–14) give better backtest results than the traditional variance-covariance method.

$\alpha=$	$a=$	his	vcv	Copula as in Table 2.1																
				1	2	3	4	5	6	7	8	9	10	11	12	13	14	15	16	21
.10	a_1	.103	.084	.111	.074	.100	.086	.080	.086	.129	.101	.128	.129	.249	.090	.087	.084	.073	.104	.080
.05	a_1	.053	.045	.066	.037	.059	.041	.044	.040	.079	.062	.076	.079	.171	.052	.051	.046	.038	.061	.041
.01	a_1	.015	.019	.027	.013	.027	.017	.020	.016	.032	.027	.033	.034	.075	.020	.022	.018	.015	.027	.018
.10	a_2	.092	.078	.066	.064	.057	.076	.086	.062	.031	.049	.031	.031	.011	.086	.080	.092	.085	.065	.070
.05	a_2	.052	.044	.045	.023	.033	.041	.049	.031	.012	.024	.012	.013	.003	.051	.046	.054	.049	.039	.032
.01	a_2	.010	.011	.016	.002	.007	.008	.009	.006	.002	.002	.002	.002	.001	.015	.010	.018	.025	.011	.005
.10	a_3	.099	.086	.126	.086	.064	.088	.096	.073	.032	.054	.033	.031	.016	.094	.086	.105	.133	.070	.086
.05	a_3	.045	.048	.093	.047	.032	.052	.050	.040	.017	.026	.017	.016	.009	.049	.047	.058	.101	.034	.050
.01	a_3	.009	.018	.069	.018	.012	.018	.016	.012	.007	.009	.006	.006	.002	.018	.015	.018	.073	.013	.020
.10	a_4	.103	.090	.174	.147	.094	.095	.086	.103	.127	.094	.129	.127	.257	.085	.085	.085	.136	.088	.111
.05	a_4	.052	.058	.139	.131	.056	.060	.058	.071	.084	.068	.084	.085	.228	.053	.054	.051	.114	.053	.098
.01	a_4	.011	.020	.098	.108	.017	.025	.025	.035	.042	.056	.041	.042	.176	.016	.017	.016	.087	.015	.071
.10	Avg	.014	.062	.145	.123	.085	.055	.052	.082	.193	.104	.194	.194	.478	.045	.061	.045	.110	.082	.075
.05	Avg	.011	.021	.154	.124	.051	.030	.016	.060	.134	.080	.132	.136	.387	.006	.012	.017	.127	.041	.075
.01	Avg	.007	.029	.169	.117	.028	.031	.032	.036	.065	.071	.065	.067	.249	.029	.025	.029	.160	.026	.083
Avg	Avg	.009	.028	.163	.120	.039	.032	.028	.047	.095	.076	.094	.096	.306	.022	.023	.026	.147	.034	.080
Rank		1	6	18	16	9	7	5	10	14	11	13	15	19	2	3	4	17	8	12

Table 2.2. Relative number of backtest outliers $\hat{\alpha}$ for the VaR with confidence $1 - \alpha$, weighted average error $|\hat{\alpha} - \alpha|$ and error ranking.
Q XFGaccvar4.xpl

Bibliography

H.-P. Deutsch, R. Eller (1999). *Derivatives and Internal Models*. Macmillan Press.

T. P. Hutchinson, C. D. Lai (1990). *Continuous Bivariate Distributions, Emphasising Applications*. Rumsby Scientific Publishing, Adelaide.

P. Embrechts, A. McNeil, D. Straumann (1999). *Correlation: Pitfalls and Alternatives*. RISK, May, pages 69-71.

P. Embrechts, A. McNeil, D. Straumann (1999). *Correlation and Dependence in Risk Management: Properties and Pitfalls*. Preprint ETH Zürich.

R. B. Nelsen (1999). *An Introduction to Copulas.* Springer, New York.

A. Sklar (1959). *Fonctions de répartition à n dimensions et leurs marges.* Publ. Inst. Statist. Univ. Paris 8, pages 229-231.

A. Sklar (1996). *Random Variables, Distribution Functions, and Copulas – a Personal Look Backward and Forward* published in *Distributions with Fixed Marginals and Related Topics,* edited by L. Rüschendorf, B. Schweizer, and M.D. Taylor, Institute of Mathematical Statistics, Hayward, CA, pages 1-14.

3 Quantification of Spread Risk by Means of Historical Simulation

Christoph Frisch and Germar Knöchlein

3.1 Introduction

Modeling spread risk for interest rate products, i.e., changes of the yield difference between a yield curve characterizing a class of equally risky assets and a riskless benchmark curve, is a challenge for any financial institution seeking to estimate the amount of economic capital utilized by trading and treasury activities. With the help of standard tools this contribution investigates some of the characteristic features of yield spread time series available from commercial data providers. From the properties of these time series it becomes obvious that the application of the parametric variance-covariance-approach for estimating idiosyncratic interest rate risk should be called into question. Instead we apply the non-parametric technique of historical simulation to synthetic zero-bonds of different riskiness, in order to quantify general market risk and spread risk of the bond. The quality of value-at-risk predictions is checked by a backtesting procedure based on a mark-to-model profit/loss calculation for the zero-bond market values. From the backtesting results we derive conclusions for the implementation of internal risk models within financial institutions.

3.2 Risk Categories – a Definition of Terms

For the analysis of obligor-specific and market-sector-specific influence on bond price risk we make use of the following subdivision of "price risk", Gaumert (1999), Bundesaufsichtsamt für das Kreditwesen (2001).

1. General market risk: This risk category comprises price changes of a financial instrument, which are caused by changes of the general market situation. General market conditions in the interest rate sector are characterized by the shape and the moves of benchmark yield curves, which are usually constructed from several benchmark instruments. The benchmark instruments are chosen in such a way so that they allow for a representative view on present market conditions in a particular market sector.

2. Residual risk: Residual risk characterizes the fact that the actual price of a given financial instrument can change in a way different from the changes of the market benchmark (however, abrupt changes which are caused by events in the sphere of the obligor are excluded from this risk category). These price changes cannot be accounted for by the volatility of the market benchmark. Residual risk is contained in the day-to-day price variation of a given instrument relative to the market benchmark and, thus, can be observed continuously in time. Residual risk is also called *idiosyncratic risk*.

3. Event risk: Abrupt price changes of a given financial instrument relative to the benchmark, which significantly exceed the continuously observable price changes due to the latter two risk categories, are called event risk. Such price jumps are usually caused by events in the sphere of the obligor. They are observed infrequently and irregularly.

Residual risk and event risk form the two components of so-called specific price risk or *specific risk* — a term used in documents on banking regulation, Bank for International Settlements (1998a), Bank for International Settlements (1998b) — and characterize the contribution of the individual risk of a given financial instrument to its overall risk.

The distinction between general market risk and residual risk is not unique but depends on the choice of the benchmark curve, which is used in the analysis of general market risk: The market for interest rate products in a given currency has a substructure (market-sectors), which is reflected by product-specific (swaps, bonds, etc.), industry-specific (bank, financial institution, retail company, etc.) and rating-specific (AAA, AA, A, BBB, etc.) yield curves. For the most liquid markets (USD, EUR, JPY), data for these sub-markets is available from commercial data providers like Bloomberg. Moreover, there are additional influencing factors like collateral, financial restrictions etc., which give rise to further variants of the yield curves mentioned above. Presently, however, hardly any standardized data on these factors is available from data providers.

The larger the universe of benchmark curves a bank uses for modeling its interest risk, the smaller is the residual risk. A bank, which e.g. only uses product-specific yield curves but neglects the influence of industry- and rating-specific effects in modelling its general market risk, can expect specific price risk to be significantly larger than in a bank which includes these influences in modeling general market risk. The difference is due to the consideration of product-, industry- and rating-specific spreads over the benchmark curve for (almost) riskless government bonds. This leads to the question, whether the risk of a spread change, the *spread risk*, should be interpreted as part of the general market risk or as part of the specific risk. The uncertainty is due to the fact that it is hard to define what a market-sector is. The definition of benchmark curves for the analysis of general market risk depends, however, critically on the market sectors identified.

We will not further pursue this question in the following but will instead investigate some properties of this spread risk and draw conclusions for modeling spread risk within internal risk models. We restrict ourselves to the continuous changes of the yield curves and the spreads, respectively, and do not discuss event risk. In this contribution different methods for the quantification of the risk of a fictive USD zero bond are analyzed. Our investigation is based on time series of daily market yields of US treasury bonds and US bonds (banks and industry) of different credit quality (rating) and time to maturity.

3.3 Descriptive Statistics of Yield Spread Time Series

Before we start modeling the interest rate and spread risk we will investigate some of the descriptive statistics of the spread time series. Our investigations are based on commercially available yield curve histories. The Bloomberg dataset we use in this investigation consists of daily yield data for US treasury bonds as well as for bonds issued by banks and financial institutions with ratings AAA, AA+/AA, A+, A, A− (we use the Standard & Poor's naming convention) and for corporate/industry bonds with ratings AAA, AA, AA−, A+, A, A−, BBB+, BBB, BBB−, BB+, BB, BB−, B+, B, B−. The data we use for the industry sector covers the time interval from March 09 1992 to June 08 2000 and corresponds to 2147 observations. The data for banks/financial institutions covers the interval from March 09 1992 to September 14 1999 and corresponds to 1955 observations. We use yields for 3 and 6 month (3M, 6M) as well as 1, 2, 3, 4, 5, 7, and 10 year maturities (1Y, 2Y, 3Y, 4Y, 5Y, 7Y, 10Y). Each yield curve is based on information on the prices of a set of representative bonds with different maturities. The yield curve, of course, depends on the choice of bonds. Yields are option-adjusted but not corrected for coupon payments. The yields for the chosen maturities are constructed by Bloomberg's interpolation algorithm for yield curves. We use the USD treasury curve as a benchmark for riskless rates and calculate yield spreads relative to the benchmark curve for the different rating categories and the two industries. We correct the data history for obvious flaws using complementary information from other data sources. Some parts of our analysis in this section can be compared with the results given in Kiesel, Perraudin and Taylor (1999).

3.3.1   Data Analysis with XploRe

We store the time series of the different yield curves in individual files. The file names, the corresponding industries and ratings and the names of the matrices used in the XploRe code are listed in Table 3.2. Each file contains data for the maturities 3M to 10Y in columns 4 to 12. XploRe creates matrices from the data listed in column 4 of Table 3.2 and produces summary statistics for the different yield curves. As example files the data sets for US treasury and industry bonds with rating AAA are provided. The output of the `summarize` command for the INAAA curve is given in Table 3.1.

```
Contents of summ
```

	Minimum	Maximum	Mean	Median	Std.Error
3M	3.13	6.93	5.0952	5.44	0.95896
6M	3.28	7.16	5.2646	5.58	0.98476
1Y	3.59	7.79	5.5148	5.75	0.95457
2Y	4.03	8.05	5.8175	5.95	0.86897
3Y	4.4	8.14	6.0431	6.1	0.79523
4Y	4.65	8.21	6.2141	6.23	0.74613
5Y	4.61	8.26	6.3466	6.36	0.72282
7Y	4.75	8.3	6.5246	6.52	0.69877
10Y	4.87	8.36	6.6962	6.7	0.69854

Table   3.1.   Output   of   `summarize`   for   the   INAAA   curve.
Q XFGsummary.xpl

The long term means are of particular interest. Therefore, we summarize them in Table 3.3. In order to get an impression of the development of the treasury

Industry	Rating	File Name	Matrix Name
Government	riskless	USTF	USTF
Industry	AAA	INAAA	INAAA
Industry	AA	INAA2.DAT	INAA2
Industry	AA-	INAA3.DAT	INAA3
Industry	A+	INA1.DAT	INA1
Industry	A	INA2.DAT	INA2
Industry	A-	INA3.DAT	INA3
Industry	BBB+	INBBB1.DAT	INBBB1
Industry	BBB	INBBB2.DAT	INBBB2
Industry	BBB-	INBBB3.DAT	INBBB3
Industry	BB+	INBB1.DAT	INBB1
Industry	BB	INBB2.DAT	INBB2
Industry	BB-	INBB3.DAT	INBB3
Industry	B+	INB1.DAT	INB1
Industry	B	INB2.DAT	INB2
Industry	B-	INB3.DAT	INB3
Bank	AAA	BNAAA.DAT	BNAAA
Bank	AA+/AA	BNAA12.DAT	BNAA12
Bank	A+	BNA1.DAT	BNA1
Bank	A	BNA2.DAT	BNA2
Bank	A-	BNA3.DAT	BNA3

Table 3.2. Data variables

yields in time, we plot the time series for the USTF 3M, 1Y, 2Y, 5Y, and 10Y yields. The results are displayed in Figure 3.1, **Q** XFGtreasury.xpl. The averaged yields within the observation period are displayed in Figure 3.2 for USTF, INAAA, INBBB2, INBB2 and INB2, **Q** XFGyields.xpl.

In the next step we calculate spreads relative to the treasury curve by subtracting the treasury curve from the rating-specific yield curves and store them to variables SINAAA, SINAA2, etc. For illustrative purposes we display time series of the 1Y, 2Y, 3Y, 5Y, 7Y, and 10Y spreads for the curves INAAA, INA2, INBBB2, INBB2, INB2 in Figure 3.3, **Q** XFGseries.xpl.

We run the summary statistics to obtain information on the mean spreads. Our results, which can also be obtained with the mean command, are collected in Table 3.4, **Q** XFGmeans.xpl.

Curve	3M	6M	1Y	2Y	3Y	4Y	5Y	7Y	10Y
USTF	4.73	4.92	5.16	5.50	5.71	5.89	6.00	6.19	6.33
INAAA	5.10	5.26	5.51	5.82	6.04	6.21	6.35	6.52	6.70
INAA2	5.19	5.37	5.59	5.87	6.08	6.26	6.39	6.59	6.76
INAA3	5.25	-	5.64	5.92	6.13	6.30	6.43	6.63	6.81
INA1	5.32	5.50	5.71	5.99	6.20	6.38	6.51	6.73	6.90
INA2	5.37	5.55	5.76	6.03	6.27	6.47	6.61	6.83	7.00
INA3	-	-	5.84	6.12	6.34	6.54	6.69	6.91	7.09
INBBB1	5.54	5.73	5.94	6.21	6.44	6.63	6.78	7.02	7.19
INBBB2	5.65	5.83	6.03	6.31	6.54	6.72	6.86	7.10	7.27
INBBB3	5.83	5.98	6.19	6.45	6.69	6.88	7.03	7.29	7.52
INBB1	6.33	6.48	6.67	6.92	7.13	7.29	7.44	7.71	7.97
INBB2	6.56	6.74	6.95	7.24	7.50	7.74	7.97	8.34	8.69
INBB3	6.98	7.17	7.41	7.71	7.99	8.23	8.46	8.79	9.06
INB1	7.32	7.53	7.79	8.09	8.35	8.61	8.82	9.13	9.39
INB2	7.80	7.96	8.21	8.54	8.83	9.12	9.37	9.68	9.96
INB3	8.47	8.69	8.97	9.33	9.60	9.89	10.13	10.45	10.74
BNAAA	5.05	5.22	5.45	5.76	5.99	6.20	6.36	6.60	6.79
BNAA12	5.14	5.30	5.52	5.83	6.06	6.27	6.45	6.68	6.87
BNA1	5.22	5.41	5.63	5.94	6.19	6.39	6.55	6.80	7.00
BNA2	5.28	5.47	5.68	5.99	6.24	6.45	6.61	6.88	7.07
BNA3	5.36	5.54	5.76	6.07	6.32	6.52	6.68	6.94	7.13

Table 3.3. Long term mean for different USD yield curves

Now we calculate the 1-day spread changes from the observed yields and store them to variables DASIN01AAA, etc. We run the descriptive routine to calculate the first four moments of the distribution of absolute spread changes. Volatility as well as skewness and kurtosis for selected curves are displayed in Tables 3.5, 3.6 and 3.7.

Q XFGchange.xpl

For the variable DASIN01AAA[,12] (the 10 year AAA spreads) we demonstrate the output of the descriptive command in Table 3.8.

Finally we calculate 1-day relative spread changes and run the descriptive command. The results for the estimates of volatility, skewness and kurtosis are summarized in Tables 3.9, 3.10 and 3.11.   **Q** XFGrelchange.xpl

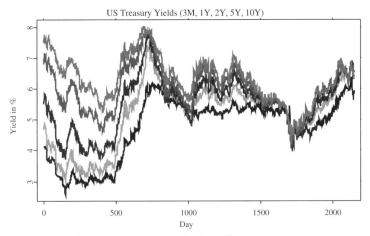

Figure 3.1. US Treasury Yields. Q XFGtreasury.xpl

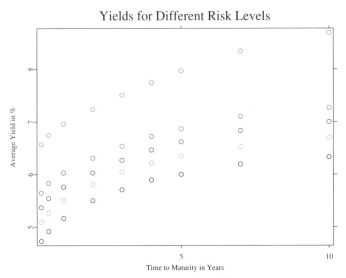

Figure 3.2. Averaged Yields. Q XFGyields.xpl

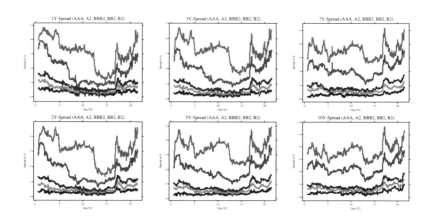

Figure 3.3. Credit Spreads. ⬛ XFGseries.xpl

3.3.2   Discussion of Results

Time Development of Yields and Spreads: The time development of US treasury yields displayed in Figure 3.1 indicates that the yield curve was steeper at the beginning of the observation period and flattened in the second half. However, an inverse shape of the yield curve occurred hardly ever. The long term average of the US treasury yield curve, the lowest curve in Figure 3.2, also has an upward sloping shape.

The time development of the spreads over US treasury yields displayed in Figure 3.3 is different for different credit qualities. While there is a large variation of spreads for the speculative grades, the variation in the investment grade sector is much smaller. A remarkable feature is the significant spread increase for all credit qualities in the last quarter of the observation period which coincides with the emerging market crises in the late 90s. The term structure of the long term averages of the rating-specific yield curves is also normal. The spreads over the benchmark curve increase with decreasing credit quality.

Mean Spread: The term structure of the long term averages of the rating-specific yield curves, which is displayed in Figure 3.3, is normal (see also Table 3.4). The spreads over the benchmark curve increase with decreasing credit quality. For long maturities the mean spreads are larger than for intermediate maturities as expected. However, for short maturities the mean spreads are

Curve	3M	6M	1Y	2Y	3Y	4Y	5Y	7Y	10Y
INAAA	36	35	35	31	33	31	35	33	37
INAA2	45	45	43	37	37	36	40	39	44
INAA3	52	-	48	42	42	40	44	44	49
INA1	58	58	55	49	49	49	52	53	57
INA2	63	63	60	53	56	57	62	64	68
INA3	-	-	68	62	63	64	69	72	76
INBBB1	81	82	78	71	72	74	79	83	86
INBBB2	91	91	87	80	82	82	87	90	94
INBBB3	110	106	103	95	98	98	104	110	119
INBB1	160	156	151	142	141	140	145	151	164
INBB2	183	182	179	173	179	185	197	215	236
INBB3	225	225	225	221	228	233	247	259	273
INB1	259	261	263	259	264	271	282	294	306
INB2	306	304	305	304	311	322	336	348	363
INB3	373	377	380	382	389	400	413	425	441
BNAAA	41	39	38	33	35	35	41	43	47
BNAA12	50	47	45	40	42	42	49	52	56
BNA1	57	59	57	52	54	54	59	64	68
BNA2	64	65	62	57	59	60	65	71	75
BNA3	72	72	70	65	67	67	72	76	81

Table 3.4. Mean spread in basis points p.a.

larger compared with intermediate maturities.

Volatility: The results for the volatility for absolute 1-day spread changes in basis points p.a. are listed in Table 3.5. From short to intermediate maturities the volatilities decrease. For long maturities a slight volatility increase can be observed compared to intermediate maturities. For equal maturities volatility is constant over the investment grade ratings, while for worse credit qualities a significant increase in absolute volatility can be observed. Volatility for relative spread changes is much larger for short maturities than for intermediate and long maturities. As in the case of absolute spread changes, a slight volatility increase exists for the transition from intermediate to long maturities. Since absolute spreads increase more strongly with decreasing credit quality than absolute spread volatility, relative spread volatility decreases with decreasing credit quality (see Table 3.9).

Skewness: The results for absolute 1-day changes (see Table 3.6) are all close to zero, which indicates that the distribution of changes is almost symmetric. The corresponding distribution of relative changes should have a positive skewness,

Curve	3M	6M	1Y	2Y	3Y	4Y	5Y	7Y	10Y
INAAA	4.1	3.5	3.3	2.3	2.4	2.2	2.1	2.2	2.5
INAA2	4.0	3.5	3.3	2.3	2.4	2.2	2.2	2.2	2.5
INAA3	4.0	-	3.3	2.2	2.3	2.2	2.2	2.2	2.5
INA1	4.0	3.7	3.3	2.3	2.4	2.2	2.2	2.2	2.6
INA2	4.1	3.7	3.3	2.4	2.4	2.1	2.2	2.3	2.5
INA3	-	-	3.4	2.4	2.4	2.2	2.2	2.3	2.6
INBBB1	4.2	3.6	3.2	2.3	2.3	2.2	2.1	2.3	2.6
INBBB2	4.0	3.5	3.4	2.3	2.4	2.1	2.2	2.3	2.6
INBBB3	4.2	3.6	3.5	2.4	2.5	2.2	2.3	2.5	2.9
INBB1	4.8	4.4	4.1	3.3	3.3	3.1	3.1	3.9	3.4
INBB2	4.9	4.6	4.5	3.8	3.8	3.8	3.7	4.3	4.0
INBB3	5.5	5.1	4.9	4.3	4.4	4.2	4.1	4.7	4.3
INB1	6.0	5.2	4.9	4.5	4.5	4.4	4.4	4.9	4.6
INB2	5.6	5.2	5.2	4.8	4.9	4.8	4.8	5.3	4.9
INB3	5.8	6.1	6.4	5.1	5.2	5.1	5.1	5.7	5.3
BNAAA	3.9	3.5	3.3	2.5	2.5	2.3	2.2	2.3	2.6
BNAA12	5.4	3.6	3.3	2.4	2.3	2.2	2.1	2.3	2.6
BNA1	4.1	3.7	3.2	2.1	2.2	2.1	2.0	2.2	2.6
BNA2	3.8	3.5	3.1	2.3	2.2	2.0	2.1	2.2	2.5
BNA3	3.8	3.5	3.2	2.2	2.2	2.1	2.1	2.2	2.5

Table 3.5. volatility for absolute spread changes in basis points p.a.

Curve	3M	6M	1Y	2Y	3Y	4Y	5Y	10Y
INAAA	0.1	0.0	-0.1	0.6	0.5	0.0	-0.5	0.6
INAA2	0.0	-0.2	0.0	0.4	0.5	-0.1	-0.2	0.3
INA2	0.0	-0.3	0.1	0.2	0.4	0.1	-0.1	0.4
INBBB2	0.2	0.0	0.2	1.0	1.1	0.5	0.5	0.9
INBB2	-0.2	-0.5	-0.4	-0.3	0.3	0.5	0.4	-0.3

Table 3.6. Skewness for absolute 1-day spread changes (in σ^3).

which is indeed the conclusion from the results in Table 3.10.

Kurtosis: The absolute 1-day changes lead to a kurtosis, which is significantly larger than 3 (see Table 3.6). Thus, the distribution of absolute changes is leptokurtic. There is no significant dependence on credit quality or maturity. The distribution of relative 1-day changes is also leptokurtic (see Table 3.10). The deviation from normality increases with decreasing credit quality and decreasing maturity.

Curve	3M	6M	1Y	2Y	3Y	4Y	5Y	10Y
INAAA	12.7	6.0	8.1	10.1	16.8	9.1	11.2	12.8
INAA2	10.5	6.4	7.8	10.1	15.8	7.8	9.5	10.0
INA2	13.5	8.5	9.2	12.3	18.2	8.2	9.4	9.8
INBBB2	13.7	7.0	9.9	14.5	21.8	10.5	13.9	14.7
INBB2	11.2	13.0	11.0	15.8	12.3	13.2	11.0	11.3

Table 3.7. Kurtosis for absolute spread changes (in σ^4).

```
===========================================================
Variable 10Y
===========================================================

Mean          0.000354147
Std.Error     0.0253712     Variance      0.000643697

Minimum           -0.18     Maximum              0.2
Range              0.38

Lowest cases                Highest cases
    1284:         -0.18          1246:         0.14
    1572:         -0.14          1283:         0.14
    1241:         -0.13          2110:         0.19
    1857:         -0.11          1062:         0.19
     598:          -0.1          2056:          0.2

Median                0
25% Quartile      -0.01     75% Quartile         0.01

Skewness       0.609321     Kurtosis         9.83974

Observations                    2146
Distinct observations             75

Total number of {-Inf,Inf,NaN}     0
===========================================================
```

Table 3.8. Output of descriptive for the 10 years AAA spread.

We visualize symmetry and leptokursis of the distribution of absolute spread changes for the INAAA 10Y data in Figure 3.4, where we plot the empirical distribution of absolute spreads around the mean spread in an averaged shifted histogram and the normal distribution with the variance estimated from historical data.

Q XFGdist.xpl

Curve	3M	6M	1Y	2Y	3Y	4Y	5Y	7Y	10Y
INAAA	36.0	19.2	15.5	8.9	8.4	8.0	6.4	7.8	10.4
INAA2	23.5	13.1	11.2	7.2	7.4	6.4	5.8	6.2	7.6
INAA3	13.4	-	9.0	5.8	6.2	5.3	5.0	5.8	6.4
INA1	13.9	9.2	7.7	5.7	5.6	4.7	4.5	4.6	5.7
INA2	11.5	8.1	7.1	5.1	4.9	4.3	4.0	4.0	4.5
INA3	-	-	6.4	4.6	4.3	3.8	3.5	3.5	4.1
INBBB1	8.1	6.0	5.4	3.9	3.7	3.3	3.0	3.2	3.8
INBBB2	7.0	5.3	5.0	3.3	3.3	2.9	2.8	2.9	3.3
INBBB3	5.7	4.7	4.4	3.2	3.0	2.7	2.5	2.6	2.9
INBB1	4.3	3.8	3.4	2.5	2.4	2.2	2.1	2.5	2.2
INBB2	3.7	3.3	3.0	2.2	2.1	2.0	1.8	2.0	1.7
INBB3	3.2	2.8	2.5	2.0	1.9	1.8	1.6	1.8	1.5
INB1	3.0	2.4	2.1	1.7	1.7	1.6	1.5	1.6	1.5
INB2	2.3	2.1	1.9	1.6	1.6	1.5	1.4	1.5	1.3
INB3	1.8	2.2	2.3	1.3	1.3	1.2	1.2	1.3	1.1
BNAAA	37.0	36.6	16.9	9.8	9.0	8.2	6.1	5.9	6.5
BNAA12	22.8	9.7	8.3	7.0	6.3	5.8	4.6	4.8	5.5
BNA1	36.6	10.1	7.9	5.6	4.8	4.4	3.8	3.9	4.4
BNA2	17.8	8.0	6.6	4.5	4.1	3.6	3.4	3.3	3.7
BNA3	9.9	6.9	5.6	3.7	3.6	3.3	3.1	3.1	3.4

Table 3.9. Volatility for relative spread changes in %

Curve	3M	6M	1Y	2Y	3Y	4Y	5Y	10Y
INAAA	2.3	4.6	4.3	2.2	2.3	2.1	0.6	4.6
INAA2	5.4	2.6	3.7	1.6	2.0	0.6	0.8	1.8
INA2	7.6	1.5	1.2	0.9	1.6	0.8	0.9	0.8
INBBB2	5.5	0.7	0.8	0.8	1.4	0.8	0.7	0.8
INBB2	0.8	0.4	0.6	0.3	0.4	0.5	0.3	-0.2

Table 3.10. Skewness for relative spread changes (in σ^3).

We note that by construction the area below both curves is normalized to one. We calculate the 1%, 10%, 90% and 99% quantiles of the spread distribution with the `quantile` command. Those quantiles are popular in market risk management. For the data used to generate Figure 3.4 the results are 0.30%, 0.35%, 0.40%, and 0.45%, respectively. The corresponding quantiles of the plotted normal distribution are 0.31%, 0.34%, 0.41%, 0.43%. The differences are less obvious than the difference in the shape of the distributions. However, in a portfolio with different financial instruments, which is exposed to different

Curve	3M	6M	1Y	2Y	3Y	4Y	5Y	10Y
INAAA	200.7	54.1	60.1	27.8	28.3	33.9	16.8	69.3
INAA2	185.3	29.5	60.5	22.1	27.4	11.0	17.5	23.0
INA2	131.1	22.1	18.0	13.9	26.5	16.4	18.5	13.9
INBBB2	107.1	13.9	16.9	12.0	20.0	14.0	16.6	16.7
INBB2	16.3	11.9	12.9	12.4	11.0	10.1	10.2	12.0

Table 3.11. Kurtosis for relative spread changes (in σ^4).

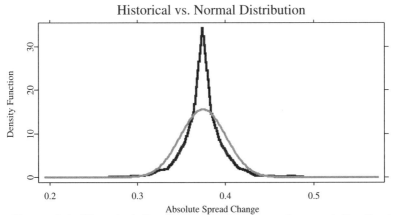

Figure 3.4. Historical distribution and estimated normal distribution.
Q XFGdist.xpl

risk factors with different correlations, the difference in the shape of the distribution can play an important role. That is why a simple variance-covariance approach, J.P. Morgan (1996) and Kiesel et al. (1999), seems not adequate to capture spread risk.

3.4 Historical Simulation and Value at Risk

We investigate the behavior of a fictive zero-bond of a given credit quality with principal 1 USD, which matures after T years. In all simulations $t = 0$ denotes the beginning and $t = T$ the end of the lifetime of the zero-bond. The starting point of the simulation is denoted by t_0, the end by t_1. The observation period, i.e., the time window investigated, consists of $N \geq 1$ trading days and the holding period of $h \geq 1$ trading days. The confidence level for the VaR is $\alpha \in [0,1]$. At each point in time $0 \leq t \leq t_1$ the risky yields $R_i(t)$ (full yield curve) and the riskless treasury yields $B_i(t)$ (benchmark curve) for any time to maturity $0 < T_1 < \cdots < T_n$ are contained in our data set for $1 \leq i \leq n$, where n is the number of different maturities. The corresponding spreads are defined by $S_i(t) = R_i(t) - B_i(t)$ for $1 \leq i \leq n$.

In the following subsections 3.4.1 to 3.4.5 we specify different variants of the historical simulation method which we use for estimating the distribution of losses from the zero-bond position. The estimate for the distribution of losses can then be used to calculate the quantile-based risk measure Value-at-Risk. The variants differ in the choice of risk factors, i.e., in our case the components of the historical yield time series. In Section 3.6 we describe how the VaR estimation is carried out with XploRe commands provided that the loss distribution has been estimated by means of one of the methods introduced and can be used as an input variable.

3.4.1   Risk Factor: Full Yield

1. Basic Historical Simulation:

We consider a historical simulation, where the risk factors are given by the full yield curve, $R_i(t)$ for $i = 1, \ldots, n$. The yield $R(t, T - t)$ at time $t_0 \leq t \leq t_1$ for the remaining time to maturity $T - t$ is determined by means of linear interpolation from the adjacent values $R_i(t) = R(t, T_i)$ and $R_{i+1}(t) = R(t, T_{i+1})$ with $T_i \leq T - t < T_{i+1}$ (for reasons of simplicity we do not consider remaining times to maturity $T - t < T_1$ and $T - t > T_n$):

$$R(t, T - t) = \frac{[T_{i+1} - (T - t)]R_i(t) + [(T - t) - T_i]R_{i+1}(t)}{T_{i+1} - T_i} . \qquad (3.1)$$

The present value of the bond $PV(t)$ at time t can be obtained by discounting,

$$PV(t) = \frac{1}{[1 + R(t, T - t)]^{T-t}}, \qquad t_0 \leq t \leq t_1. \qquad (3.2)$$

In the historical simulation the relative risk factor changes

$$\Delta_i^{(k)}(t) = \frac{R_i(t - k/N) - R_i(t - (k + h)/N)}{R_i(t - (k + h)/N)}, \qquad 0 \leq k \leq N - 1, \qquad (3.3)$$

are calculated for $t_0 \leq t \leq t_1$ and each $1 \leq i \leq n$. Thus, for each scenario k we obtain a new fictive yield curve at time $t + h$, which can be determined from the observed yields and the risk factor changes,

$$R_i^{(k)}(t + h) = R_i(t)\left[1 + \Delta_i^{(k)}(t)\right], \qquad 1 \leq i \leq n, \tag{3.4}$$

by means of linear interpolation. This procedure implies that the distribution of risk factor changes is stationary between $t - (N - 1 + h)/N$ and t. Each scenario corresponds to a drawing from an identical and independent distribution, which can be related to an i.i.d. random variable $\varepsilon_i(t)$ with variance one via

$$\Delta_i(t) = \sigma_i \varepsilon_i(t). \tag{3.5}$$

This assumption implies homoscedasticity of the volatility of the risk factors, i.e., a constant volatility level within the observation period. If this were not the case, different drawings would originate from different underlying distributions. Consequently, a sequence of historically observed risk factor changes could not be used for estimating the future loss distribution.

In analogy to (3.1) for time $t + h$ and remaining time to maturity $T - t$ one obtains

$$R^{(k)}(t + h, T - t) = \frac{[T_{i+1} - (T - t)]R_i^{(k)}(t) + [(T - t) - T_i]R_{i+1}^{(k)}(t)}{T_{i+1} - T_i}$$

for the yield. With (3.2) we obtain a new fictive present value at time $t + h$:

$$PV^{(k)}(t + h) = \frac{1}{\left[1 + R^{(k)}(t + h, T - t)\right]^{T-t}}. \tag{3.6}$$

In this equation we neglected the effect of the shortening of the time to maturity in the transition from t to $t + h$ on the present value. Such an approximation should be refined for financial instruments whose time to maturity/time to expiration is of the order of h, which is not relevant for the constellations investigated in the following.

Now the fictive present value $PV^{(k)}(t + h)$ is compared with the present value for unchanged yield $R(t + h, T - t) = R(t, T - t)$ for each scenario k (here the remaining time to maturity is not changed, either).

$$PV(t + h) = \frac{1}{\{1 + R(t + h, T - t)\}^{T-t}}. \tag{3.7}$$

The loss occurring is

$$L^{(k)}(t+h) = PV(t+h) - PV^{(k)}(t+h) \qquad 0 \le k \le N-1, \tag{3.8}$$

i.e., losses in the economic sense are positive while profits are negative. The VaR is the loss which is not exceeded with a probability α and is estimated as the $[(1-\alpha)N + 1]$-th-largest value in the set

$$\{L^{(k)}(t+h) \mid 0 \le k \le N-1\}.$$

This is the $(1-\alpha)$-quantile of the corresponding empirical distribution.

2. Mean Adjustment:

A refined historical simulation includes an adjustment for the average of those relative changes in the observation period which are used for generating the scenarios according to (3.3). If for fixed $1 \le i \le n$ the average of relative changes $\Delta_i^{(k)}(t)$ is different from 0, a trend is projected from the past to the future in the generation of fictive yields in (3.4). Thus the relative changes are corrected for the mean by replacing the relative change $\Delta_i^{(k)}(t)$ with $\Delta_i^{(k)}(t) - \overline{\Delta}_i(t)$ for $1 \le i \le n$ in (3.4):

$$\overline{\Delta}_i(t) = \frac{1}{N} \sum_{k=0}^{N-1} \Delta_i^{(k)}(t), \tag{3.9}$$

This mean correction is presented in Hull (1998).

3. Volatility Updating:

An important variant of historical simulation uses volatility updating Hull (1998). At each point in time t the exponentially weighted volatility of relative historical changes is estimated for $t_0 \le t \le t_1$ by

$$\sigma_i^2(t) = (1-\gamma) \sum_{k=0}^{N-1} \gamma^k \{\Delta_i^{(k)}(t)\}^2, \qquad 1 \le i \le n. \tag{3.10}$$

The parameter $\gamma \in [0,1]$ is a decay factor, which must be calibrated to generate a best fit to empirical data. The recursion formula

$$\sigma_i^2(t) = (1-\gamma)\sigma_i^2(t - 1/N) + \gamma\{\Delta_i^{(0)}(t)\}^2, \qquad 1 \le i \le n, \tag{3.11}$$

is valid for $t_0 \le t \le t_1$. The idea of volatility updating consists in adjusting the historical risk factor changes to the present volatility level. This is achieved by a renormalization of the relative risk factor changes from (3.3) with the corresponding estimation of volatility for the observation day and a multiplication with the estimate for the volatility valid at time t. Thus, we calculate the quantity

$$\delta_i^{(k)}(t) = \sigma_i(t) \cdot \frac{\Delta_i^{(k)}(t)}{\sigma_i(t - (k+h)/N)}, \qquad 0 \le k \le N - 1. \qquad (3.12)$$

In a situation, where risk factor volatility is heteroscedastic and, thus, the process of risk factor changes is not stationary, volatility updating cures this violation of the assumptions made in basic historical simulation, because the process of re-scaled risk factor changes $\Delta_i(t)/\sigma_i(t)$ is stationary. For each k these renormalized relative changes are used in analogy to (3.4) for the determination of fictive scenarios:

$$R_i^{(k)}(t+h) = R_i(t)\{1 + \delta_i^{(k)}(t)\}, \qquad 1 \le i \le n, \qquad (3.13)$$

The other considerations concerning the VaR calculation in historical simulation remain unchanged.

4. Volatility Updating and Mean Adjustment:

Within the volatility updating framework, we can also apply a correction for the average change according to 3.4.1(2). For this purpose, we calculate the average

$$\bar{\delta}_i(t) = \frac{1}{N} \sum_{k=0}^{N-1} \delta_i^{(k)}(t), \qquad (3.14)$$

and use the adjusted relative risk factor change $\delta_i^{(k)}(t) - \bar{\delta}_i(t)$ instead of $\delta_i^{(k)}(t)$ in (3.13).

3.4.2 Risk Factor: Benchmark

In this subsection the risk factors are relative changes of the benchmark curve instead of the full yield curve. This restriction is adequate for quantifying general market risk, when there is no need to include spread risk. The risk factors are the yields $B_i(t)$ for $i = 1, \ldots, n$. The yield $B(t, T - t)$ at time t for remaining time to maturity $T - t$ is calculated similarly to (3.1) from adjacent values by linear interpolation,

$$B(t, T - t) = \frac{\{T_{i+1} - (T - t)\}B_i(t) + \{(T - t) - T_i\}B_{i+1}(t)}{T_{i+1} - T_i}. \tag{3.15}$$

The generation of scenarios and the interpolation of the fictive benchmark curve is carried out in analogy to the procedure for the full yield curve. We use

$$\Delta_i^{(k)}(t) = \frac{B_i\big(t - k/N\big) - B_i\big(t - (k+h)/N\big)}{B_i\big(t - (k+h)/N\big)}, \quad 0 \le k \le N - 1, \tag{3.16}$$

and

$$B_i^{(k)}(t + h) = B_i(t)\big[1 + \Delta_i^{(k)}(t)\big], \qquad 1 \le i \le n. \tag{3.17}$$

Linear interpolation yields

$$B^{(k)}(t + h, T - t) = \frac{\{T_{i+1} - (T - t)\}B_i^{(k)}(t) + \{(T - t) - T_i\}B_{i+1}^{(k)}(t)}{T_{i+1} - T_i}.$$

In the determination of the fictive full yield we now assume that the spread remains unchanged within the holding period. Thus, for the k-th scenario we obtain the representation

$$R^{(k)}(t + h, T - t) = B^{(k)}(t + h, T - t) + S(t, T - t), \tag{3.18}$$

which is used for the calculation of a new fictive present value and the corresponding loss. With this choice of risk factors we can introduce an adjustment for the average relative changes or/and volatility updating in complete analogy to the four variants described in the preceding subsection.

3.4.3   Risk Factor: Spread over Benchmark Yield

When we take the view that risk is only caused by spread changes but not by changes of the benchmark curve, we investigate the behavior of the spread risk factors $S_i(t)$ for $i = 1, \ldots, n$. The spread $S(t, T - t)$ at time t for time to maturity $T - t$ is again obtained by linear interpolation. We now use

$$\Delta_i^{(k)}(t) = \frac{S_i\big(t - k/N\big) - S_i\big(t - (k+h)/N\big)}{S_i\big(t - (k+h)/N\big)}, \quad 0 \le k \le N - 1, \tag{3.19}$$

and

$$S_i^{(k)}(t+h) = S_i(t)\big\{1 + \Delta_i^{(k)}(t)\big\}, \qquad 1 \le i \le n. \tag{3.20}$$

Here, linear interpolation yields

$$S^{(k)}(t+h, T-t) = \frac{\{T_{i+1} - (T-t)\}S_i^{(k)}(t) + \{(T-t) - T_i\}S_{i+1}^{(k)}(t)}{T_{i+1} - T_i}.$$

Thus, in the determination of the fictive full yield the benchmark curve is considered deterministic and the spread stochastic. This constellation is the opposite of the constellation in the preceding subsection. For the k-th scenario one obtains

$$R^{(k)}(t+h, T-t) = B(t, T-t) + S^{(k)}(t+h, T-t). \tag{3.21}$$

In this context we can also work with adjustment for average relative spread changes and volatility updating.

3.4.4 Conservative Approach

In the conservative approach we assume full correlation between risk from the benchmark curve and risk from the spread changes. In this worst case scenario we add (ordered) losses, which are calculated as in the two preceding sections from each scenario. From this loss distribution the VaR is determined.

3.4.5 Simultaneous Simulation

Finally, we consider simultaneous relative changes of the benchmark curve and the spreads. For this purpose (3.18) and (3.21) are replaced with

$$R^{(k)}(t+h, T-t) = B^{(k)}(t+h, T-t) + S^{(k)}(t, T-t), \tag{3.22}$$

where, again, corrections for average risk factor changes or/and volatility updating can be added. We note that the use of relative risk factor changes is the reason for different results of the variants in subsection 3.4.1 and this subsection.

3.5   Mark-to-Model Backtesting

A backtesting procedure compares the VaR prediction with the observed loss. In a mark-to-model backtesting the observed loss is determined by calculation of the present value before and after consideration of the actually observed risk factor changes. For $t_0 \leq t \leq t_1$ the present value at time $t+h$ is calculated with the yield $R(t + h, T - t)$, which is obtained from observed data for $R_i(t + h)$ by linear interpolation, according to

$$PV(t) = \frac{1}{\{1 + R(t + h, T - t)\}^{T-t}}. \tag{3.23}$$

This corresponds to a loss $L(t) = PV(t) - PV(t + h)$, where, again, the shortening of the time to maturity is not taken into account.

The different frameworks for the VaR estimation can easily be integrated into the backtesting procedure. When we, e.g., only consider changes of the benchmark curve, $R(t+h, T-t)$ in (3.23) is replaced with $B(t+h, T-t) + S(t, T-t)$. On an average $(1 - \alpha) \cdot 100$ per cent of the observed losses in a given time interval should exceed the corresponding VaR (outliers). Thus, the percentage of observed losses is a measure for the predictive power of historical simulation.

3.6   VaR Estimation and Backtesting with XploRe

In this section we explain, how a VaR can be calculated and a backtesting can be implemented with the help of XploRe routines. We present numerical results for the different yield curves. The VaR estimation is carried out with the help of the `VaRest` command. The `VaRest` command calculates a VaR for historical simulation, if one specifies the method parameter as "EDF" (empirical distribution function). However, one has to be careful when specifying the sequence of asset returns which are used as input for the estimation procedure. If one calculates zero-bond returns from relative risk factor changes (interest rates or spreads) the complete empirical distribution of the profits and losses must be estimated anew for each day from the N relative risk factor changes, because the profit/loss observations are not identical with the risk factor changes.

For each day the N profit/loss observations generated with one of the methods described in subsections 3.4.1 to 3.4.5 are stored to a new row in an array `PL`. The actual profit and loss data from a mark-to-model calculation for holding period h are stored to a one-column-vector MMPL. It is not possible to use a continuous sequence of profit/loss data with overlapping time windows for the VaR estimation. Instead the VaRest command must be called separately for each day. The consequence is that the data the VaRest command operates on consists of a row of $N + 1$ numbers: N profit/loss values contained in the vector (PL[t,])', which has one column and N rows followed by the actual mark-to-model profit or loss MMPL[t,1] within holding period h in the last row. The procedure is implemented in the quantlet XFGpl which can be downloaded from quantlet download page of this book.

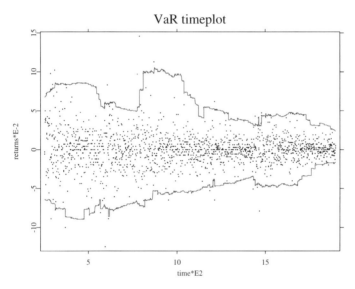

Figure 3.5. VaR time plot basic historical simulation.
◘ XFGtimeseries.xpl

The result is displayed for the INAAA curve in Figures. 3.5 (basic historical simulation) and 3.6 (historical simulation with volatility updating). The time plots allow for a quick detection of violations of the VaR prediction. A striking feature in the basic historical simulation with the full yield curve as risk factor is the platform-shaped VaR prediction, while with volatility updating the VaR prediction decays exponentially after the occurrence of peak events in the market data. This is a consequence of the exponentially weighted historical

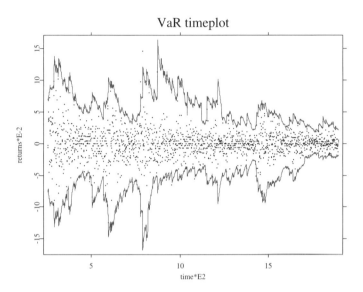

Figure 3.6. VaR time plot historical simulation with volatility updating.
Q XFGtimeseries2.xpl

volatility in the scenarios. The peak VaR values are much larger for volatility updating than for the basic historical simulation.

In order to find out, which framework for VaR estimation has the best predictive power, we count the number of violations of the VaR prediction and divide it by the number of actually observed losses. We use the 99% quantile, for which we would expect an violation rate of 1% for an optimal VaR estimator. The history used for the drawings of the scenarios consists of $N = 250$ days, and the holding period is $h = 1$ day. For the volatility updating we use a decay factor of $\gamma = 0.94$, J.P. Morgan (1996). For the simulation we assume that the synthetic zero-bond has a remaining time to maturity of 10 years at the beginning of the simulations. For the calculation of the first scenario of a basic historical simulation $N + h - 1$ observations are required. A historical simulation with volatility updating requires $2(N + h - 1)$ observations preceding the trading day the first scenario refers to. In order to allow for a comparison between different methods for the VaR calculation, the beginning of the simulations is $t_0 = [2(N + h - 1)/N]$. With these simulation parameters we obtain 1646

observations for a zero-bond in the industry sector and 1454 observations for a
zero-bond in the banking sector.

In Tables 3.12 to 3.14 we list the percentage of violations for all yield curves
and the four variants of historical simulation V1 to V4 (V1 = Basic Historical
Simulation; V2 = Basic Historical Simulation with Mean Adjustment; V3 =
Historical Simulation with Mean Adjustment; V4 = Historical Simulation with
Volatility Updating and Mean Adjustment). In the last row we display the
average of the violations of all curves. Table 3.12 contains the results for the
simulation with relative changes of the full yield curves and of the yield spreads
over the benchmark curve as risk factors. In Table 3.13 the risk factors are
changes of the benchmark curves. The violations in the conservative approach
and in the simultaneous simulation of relative spread and benchmark changes
are listed in Table 3.14.

Q XFGexc.xpl

3.7 P-P Plots

The evaluation of the predictive power across all possible confidence levels
$\alpha \in [0, 1]$ can be carried out with the help of a transformation of the empirical
distribution $\{L^{(k)} \mid 0 \leq k \leq N - 1\}$. If F is the true distribution function
of the loss L within the holding period h, then the random quantity $F(L)$ is
(approximately) uniformly distributed on $[0, 1]$. Therefore we check the values
$F_e\big[L(t)\big]$ for $t_0 \leq t \leq t_1$, where F_e is the empirical distribution. If the prediction
quality of the model is adequate, these values should not differ significantly from
a sample with size $250\,(t_1 - t_0 + 1)$ from a uniform distribution on $[0, 1]$.

The P-P plot of the transformed distribution against the uniform distribution
(which represents the distribution function of the transformed empirical distribution) should therefore be located as closely to the main diagonal as possible.
The mean squared deviation from the uniform distribution (MSD) summed
over all quantile levels can serve as an indicator of the predictive power of a
quantile-based risk measure like VaR. The **Q** XFGpp.xpl quantlet creates a P-P
plot and calculates the MSD indicator.

Curve	Full yield				Spread curve			
	V1	V2	V3	V4	V1	V2	V3	V4
INAAA	1,34	1,34	1,09	1,28	1,34	1,34	1,34	1,34
INAA2	1,34	1,22	1,22	1,22	1,46	1,52	1,22	1,22
INAA3	1,15	1,22	1,15	1,15	1,09	1,09	0,85	0,91
INA1	1,09	1,09	1,46	1,52	1,40	1,46	1,03	1,09
INA2	1,28	1,28	1,28	1,28	1,15	1,15	0,91	0,91
INA3	1,22	1,22	1,15	1,22	1,15	1,22	1,09	1,15
INBBB1	1,28	1,22	1,09	1,15	1,46	1,46	1,40	1,40
INBBB2	1,09	1,15	0,91	0,91	1,28	1,28	0,91	0,91
INBBB3	1,15	1,15	1,09	1,09	1,34	1,34	1,46	1,52
INBB1	1,34	1,28	1,03	1,03	1,28	1,28	0,97	0,97
INBB2	1,22	1,22	1,22	1,34	1,22	1,22	1,09	1,09
INBB3	1,34	1,28	1,28	1,22	1,09	1,28	1,09	1,09
INB1	1,40	1,40	1,34	1,34	1,52	1,46	1,09	1,03
INB2	1,52	1,46	1,28	1,28	1,34	1,40	1,15	1,15
INB3	1,40	1,40	1,15	1,15	1,46	1,34	1,09	1,15
BNAAA	1,24	1,38	1,10	1,10	0,89	0,89	1,03	1,31
BNAA1/2	1,38	1,24	1,31	1,31	1,03	1,10	1,38	1,38
BNA1	1,03	1,03	1,10	1,17	1,03	1,10	1,24	1,24
BNA2	1,24	1,31	1,24	1,17	0,76	0,83	1,03	1,03
BNA3	1,31	1,24	1,17	1,10	1,03	1,10	1,24	1,17
Average	**1,27**	**1,25**	**1,18**	**1,20**	**1,22**	**1,24**	**1,13**	**1,15**

Table 3.12. Violations full yield and spread curve (in %)

Curve	V1	V2	V3	V4
INAAA, INAA2, INAA3, INA1, INA2, INA3, INBBB1, INBBB2, INBBB3, INBB1, INBB2, INBB3, INB1, INB2, INB3	1,52	1,28	1,22	1,15
BNAAA, BNAA1/2, BNA1, BNA2, BNA3	1,72	1,44	1,17	1,10
Average	**1,57**	**1,32**	**1,20**	**1,14**

Table 3.13. Violations benchmark curve (in %)

3.8 Q-Q Plots

With a quantile plot (Q-Q plot) it is possible to visualize whether an ordered sample is distributed according to a given distribution function. If, e.g., a sample is normally distributed, the plot of the empirical quantiles vs. the

	conservative approach				simultaneous simulation			
Curve	**V1**	**V2**	**V3**	**V4**	**V1**	**V2**	**V3**	**V4**
INAAA	0,24	0,24	0,30	0,30	1,22	1,28	0,97	1,03
INAA2	0,24	0,30	0,36	0,30	1,22	1,28	1,03	1,15
INAA3	0,43	0,36	0,30	0,30	1,22	1,15	1,09	1,09
INA1	0,36	0,43	0,55	0,55	1,03	1,03	1,03	1,09
INA2	0,49	0,43	0,49	0,49	1,34	1,28	0,97	0,97
INA3	0,30	0,36	0,30	0,30	1,22	1,15	1,09	1,09
INBBB1	0,43	0,49	0,36	0,36	1,09	1,09	1,03	1,03
INBBB2	0,49	0,49	0,30	0,30	1,03	1,03	0,85	0,79
INBBB3	0,30	0,30	0,36	0,36	1,15	1,22	1,03	1,03
INBB1	0,36	0,30	0,43	0,43	1,34	1,34	1,03	0,97
INBB2	0,43	0,36	0,43	0,43	1,40	1,34	1,15	1,09
INBB3	0,30	0,30	0,36	0,36	1,15	1,15	0,91	0,91
INB1	0,43	0,43	0,43	0,43	1,34	1,34	0,91	0,97
INB2	0,30	0,30	0,30	0,30	1,34	1,34	0,97	1,03
INB3	0,30	0,30	0,36	0,30	1,46	1,40	1,22	1,22
BNAAA	0,62	0,62	0,48	0,48	1,31	1,31	1,10	1,03
BNAA1/2	0,55	0,55	0,55	0,48	1,24	1,31	1,10	1,17
BNA1	0,62	0,62	0,55	0,55	0,96	1,03	1,10	1,17
BNA2	0,55	0,62	0,69	0,69	0,89	1,96	1,03	1,03
BNA3	0,55	0,55	0,28	0,28	1,38	1,31	1,03	1,10
Average	**0,41**	**0,42**	**0,41**	**0,40**	**1,22**	**1,22**	**1,03**	**1,05**

Table 3.14. Violations in the conservative approach and simultaneous simulation(in %)

quantiles of a normal distribution should result in an approximately linear plot. Q-Q plots vs. a normal distribution can be generated with the following command:

```
VaRqqplot(matrix(N,1)|MMPL,VaR,opt)
```

3.9   Discussion of Simulation Results

In Figure 3.7 the P-P plots for the historical simulation with the full yield curve (INAAA) as risk factor are displayed for the different variants of the simulation. From the P-P plots it is apparent that mean adjustment significantly improves the predictive power in particular for intermediate confidence levels (i.e., for small risk factor changes).

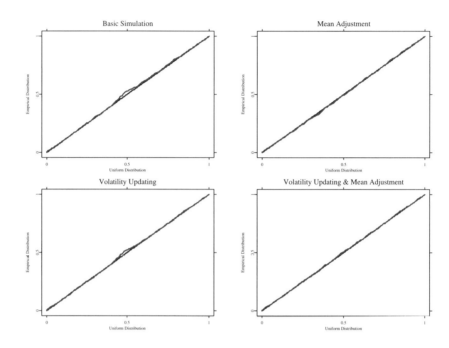

Figure 3.7. P-P Plots variants of the simulation. ⊡ XFGpp.xpl

Figure 3.8 displays the P-P plots for the same data set and the basic historical simulation with different choices of risk factors. A striking feature is the poor predictive power for a model with the spread as risk factor. Moreover, the over-estimation of the risk in the conservative approach is clearly reflected by a sine-shaped function, which is superposed on the ideal diagonal function.

In Figs. 3.9 and 3.10 we show the Q-Q plots for basic historic simulation and volatility updating using the INAAA data set and the full yield curve as risk factors. A striking feature of all Q-Q plots is the deviation from linearity (and, thus, normality) for extreme quantiles. This observation corresponds to the leptokurtic distributions of time series of market data changes (e.g. spread changes as discussed in section 3.3.2).

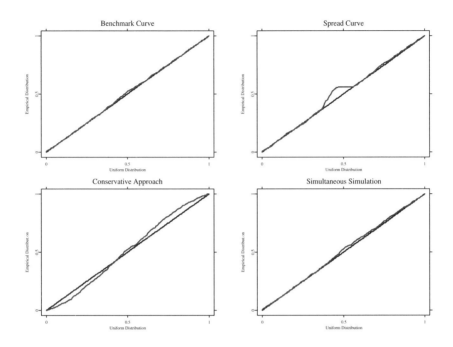

Figure 3.8. P-P Plots choice of risk factors. ⌕ XFGpp.xpl

3.9.1 Risk Factor: Full Yield

The results in Table 3.12 indicate a small under-estimation of the actually observed losses. While volatility updating leads to a reduction of violations, this effect is not clearly recognizable for the mean adjustment. The positive results for volatility updating are also reflected in the corresponding mean squared deviations in Table 3.15. Compared with the basic simulation, the model quality can be improved. There is also a positive effect of the mean adjustment.

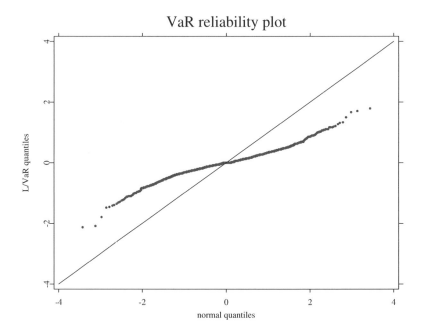

Figure 3.9. Q-Q Plot for basic historical simulation.

3.9.2   Risk Factor: Benchmark

The results for the number of violations in Table 3.13 and the mean squared deviations in Table 3.16 are comparable to the analysis, where risk factors are changes of the full yield. Since the same relative changes are applied for all yield curves, the results are the same for all yield curves. Again, the application of volatility updating improves the predictive power and mean adjustment also has a positive effect.

3.9.3   Risk Factor: Spread over Benchmark Yield

The number of violations (see Table 3.12) is comparable to the latter two variants. Volatility updating leads to better results, while the effect of mean

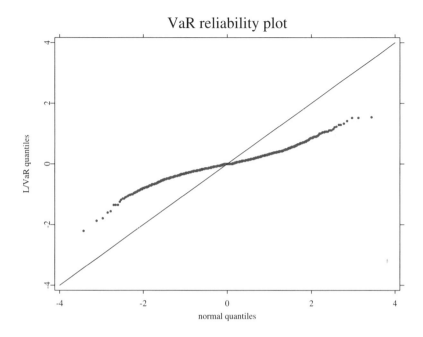

Figure 3.10. Q-Q plot for volatility updating.

adjustment is only marginal. However, the mean squared deviations (see Table 3.15) in the P-P plots are significantly larger than in the case, where the risk factors are contained in the benchmark curve. This can be traced back to a partly poor predictive power for intermediate confidence levels (see Figure 3.8). Mean adjustment leads to larger errors in the P-P plots.

3.9.4   Conservative Approach

From Table 3.14 the conclusion can be drawn, that the conservative approach significantly over-estimates the risk for all credit qualities. Table 3.17 indicates the poor predictive power of the conservative approach over the full range of confidence levels.

	full yield				spread curve			
Curve	**V1**	**V2**	**V3**	**V4**	**V1**	**V2**	**V3**	**V4**
INAAA	0,87	0,28	0,50	0,14	8,13	22,19	8,14	16,15
INAA2	0,45	0,36	0,32	0,16	6,96	21,41	7,25	15,62
INAA3	0,54	0,41	0,43	0,23	7,91	21,98	7,97	15,89
INA1	0,71	0,27	0,41	0,13	7,90	15,32	8,10	8,39
INA2	0,50	0,39	0,42	0,17	9,16	15,15	9,51	6,19
INA3	0,81	0,24	0,58	0,24	9,53	12,96	9,61	7,09
INBBB1	0,71	0,29	0,54	0,13	9,59	15,71	9,65	11,13
INBBB2	0,33	0,34	0,26	0,12	11,82	14,58	11,59	10,72
INBBB3	0,35	0,59	0,40	0,34	7,52	11,49	7,78	6,32
INBB1	0,31	0,95	0,26	0,28	4,14	4,57	3,90	1,61
INBB2	0,52	0,49	0,36	0,19	6,03	3,63	5,89	2,12
INBB3	0,53	0,41	0,36	0,17	3,11	3,65	3,09	1,67
INB1	0,51	0,29	0,38	0,15	3,59	1,92	2,85	1,16
INB2	0,51	0,48	0,31	0,22	4,29	2,31	3,41	1,42
INB3	0,72	0,38	0,32	0,16	3,70	2,10	2,99	3,02
BNAAA	0,59	0,19	0,48	0,56	10,13	17,64	9,74	11,10
BNAA1/2	0,54	0,21	0,45	0,46	5,43	13,40	5,73	7,50
BNA1	0,31	0,12	0,29	0,25	8,65	17,19	8,09	8,21
BNA2	0,65	0,19	0,57	0,59	6,52	12,52	6,95	6,45
BNA3	0,31	0,19	0,32	0,29	6,62	9,62	6,59	3,80
Average	**0,54**	**0,35**	**0,40**	**0,25**	**7,04**	**11,97**	**6,94**	**7,28**

Table 3.15.   MSD P-P Plot for the full yield and the spread curve($\times 10\,000$)

The mean squared deviations are the worst of all approaches. Volatility updating and/or mean adjustment does not lead to any significant improvements.

3.9.5   Simultaneous Simulation

From Tables 3.14 and 3.17 it is apparent that simultaneous simulation leads to much better results than the model with risk factors from the full yield curve, when volatility updating is included. Again, the effect of mean adjustment does not in general lead to a significant improvement. These results lead to the conclusion that general market risk and spread risk should be modeled independently, i.e., that the yield curve of an instrument exposed to credit risk should be modeled with two risk factors: benchmark changes and spread changes.

Curve	V1	V2	V3	V4
INAAA, INAA2, INAA3	0,49	0,23	0,26	0,12
INA1	0,48	0,23	0,26	0,12
INA2, INA3, INBBB1, INBBB2, INBBB3, INBB1, INBB2	0,49	0,23	0,26	0,12
INBB3	0,47	0,23	0,25	0,12
INB1	0,49	0,23	0,26	0,12
INB2	0,47	0,23	0,25	0,12
INB3	0,48	0,23	0,26	0,12
BNAAA, BNAA1/2	0,42	0,18	0,25	0,33
BNA1	0,41	0,18	0,23	0,33
BNA2	0,42	0,18	0,25	0,33
BNA3	0,41	0,18	0,24	0,33
Average	**0,47**	**0,22**	**0,25**	**0,17**

Table 3.16. MSD P-P-Plot benchmark curve ($\times 10\,000$)

3.10   XploRe for Internal Risk Models

In this contribution it is demonstrated that XploRe can be used as a tool in the analysis of time series of market data and empirical loss distributions. The focus of this contribution is on the analysis of spread risk. Yield spreads are an indicator of an obligor's credit risk. The distributions of spread changes are leptokurtic with typical fat tails, which makes the application of conventional variance-covariance risk models problematic. That is why in this contribution we prefer the analysis of spread risk by means of historical simulation. Since it is not a priori clear, how spread risk should be integrated in a risk model for interest rate products and how it can be separated from general market risk, we investigate several possibilities, which include modelling the full yield curve (i.e., consideration of only one risk factor category, which covers both benchmark and spread risk) as well as separately modelling spread risk and benchmark risk. The aggregation of both risk categories is carried out in a conservative way (addition of the risk measure for both risk categories) as well as coherently (simultaneous simulation of spread and benchmark risk). Moreover, in addition to the basic historical simulation method we add additional features like mean adjustment and volatility updating. Risk is quantified by means of a quantile-based risk measure in this contribution - the VaR. We demonstrate the differences between the different methods by calculating the VaR for a fictive zero-bond.

Curve	conservative approach				simultaneous simulation			
	V1	V2	V3	V4	V1	V2	V3	V4
INAAA	14,94	14,56	14,00	13,88	1,52	0,64	0,75	0,40
INAA2	13,65	13,51	14,29	14,31	0,79	0,38	0,40	0,23
INAA3	14,34	13,99	13,66	13,44	0,79	0,32	0,49	0,27
INA1	15,39	15,60	15,60	15,60	0,95	0,40	0,52	0,29
INA2	13,95	14,20	14,32	14,10	0,71	0,55	0,50	0,39
INA3	14,73	14,95	14,45	14,53	0,94	0,30	0,59	0,35
INBBB1	13,94	14,59	14,05	14,10	1,00	0,33	0,43	0,17
INBBB2	13,74	13,91	13,67	13,73	0,64	0,52	0,45	0,29
INBBB3	13,68	14,24	14,10	14,09	0,36	0,78	0,31	0,31
INBB1	19,19	20,68	18,93	19,40	0,73	1,37	0,52	0,70
INBB2	13,21	14,17	14,79	15,15	0,30	0,82	0,35	0,51
INBB3	15,19	16,47	15,40	15,67	0,55	0,65	0,15	0,21
INB1	15,47	15,64	15,29	15,51	0,53	0,44	0,19	0,26
INB2	14,47	14,93	15,46	15,77	0,24	0,55	0,24	0,24
INB3	14,78	14,67	16,77	17,03	0,38	0,44	0,27	0,22
BNAAA	14,80	15,30	16,30	16,64	1,13	0,33	0,99	0,96
BNAA1/2	13,06	13,45	14,97	15,43	0,73	0,16	0,57	0,50
BNA1	11,95	11,83	12,84	13,08	0,52	0,26	0,44	0,41
BNA2	13,04	12,58	14,31	14,56	0,78	0,13	0,51	0,58
BNA3	12,99	12,70	15,19	15,42	0,34	0,18	0,58	0,70
Average	**14,33**	**14,60**	**14,92**	**15,07**	**0,70**	**0,48**	**0,46**	**0,40**

Table 3.17. MSD P-P Plot for the conservative approach and the simultaneous simulation($\times 10\,000$)

The numerical results indicate, that the conservative approach over-estimates the risk of our fictive position, while the simulation results for the full yield as single risk factor are quite convincing. The best result, however, is delivered by a combination of simultaneous simulation of spread and benchmark risk and volatility updating, which compensates for non-stationarity in the risk factor time series. The conclusion from this contribution for model-builders in the banking community is, that it should be checked, whether the full yield curve or the simultaneous simulation with volatility updating yield satisfactory results for the portfolio considered.

Bibliography

Bank for International Settlements (1998a). Amendment to the Capital Accord to incorporate market risks, www.bis.org. (January 1996, updated to April 1998).

Bank for International Settlements (1998b). Overview of the Amendment to the Capital Accord to incorporate market risk, www.bis.org. (January 1996, updated to April 1998).

Bundesaufsichtsamt für das Kreditwesen (2001). Grundsatz I/Modellierung des besonderen Kursrisikos, Rundschreiben 1/2001, www.bakred.de.

Gaumert, U. (1999).   *Zur Diskussion um die Modellierung besonderer Kursrisiken in VaR-Modellen, Handbuch Bankenaufsicht und Interne Risikosteuerungsmodelle*, Schäffer-Poeschel.

Hull, J. C. (1998). Integrating Volatility Updating into the Historical Simulation Method for Value at Risk, *Journal of Risk* .

J.P. Morgan (1996). RiskMetrics, *Technical report*, J.P. Morgan, New York.

Kiesel, R., Perraudin, W. and Taylor, A. (1999). The Structure of Credit Risk. Working Paper, London School of Economics.

Part II

Credit Risk

4 Rating Migrations

Steffi Höse, Stefan Huschens and Robert Wania

The bond rating is one of the most important indicators of a corporation's credit quality and therefore its default probability. It was first developed by Moody's in 1914 and by Poor's Corporation in 1922 and it is generally assigned by external agencies to publicly traded debts. Apart from the external ratings by independent rating agencies, there are internal ratings by banks and other financial institutions, Basel Committee on Banking Supervision (2001). External rating data by agencies are available for many years, in contrast to internal ratings. Their short history in most cases does not exceed 5–10 years. Both types of ratings are usually recorded on an ordinal scale and labeled alphabetically or numerically. For the construction of a rating system see Crouhy, Galai, and Mark (2001).

A change in a rating reflects the assessment that the company's credit quality has improved (upgrade) or deteriorated (downgrade). Analyzing these rating migrations including default is one of the preliminaries for credit risk models in order to measure future credit loss. In such models, the matrix of rating transition probabilities, the so called transition matrix, plays a crucial role. It allows to calculate the joint distribution of future ratings for borrowers that compose a portfolio, Gupton, Finger, and Bhatia (1997). An element of a transition matrix gives the probability that an obligor with a certain initial rating migrates to another rating by the risk horizon. For the econometric analysis of transition data see Lancaster (1990).

In a study by Jarrow, Lando, and Turnbull (1997) rating transitions were modeled as a time-homogeneous Markov chain, so future rating changes are not affected by the rating history (Markov property). The probability of changing from one rating to another is constant over time (homogeneous), which is assumed solely for simplicity of estimation. Empirical evidence indicates that transition probabilities are time-varying. Nickell, Perraudin, and Varotto (2000) show that different transition matrices are identified across various factors such as the obligor's domicile and industry and the stage of business cycle.

Rating migrations are reviewed from a statistical point of view throughout this chapter using XploRe. The way from the observed data to the estimated one-year transition probabilities is shown and estimates for the standard deviations of the transition rates are given. In further extension, dependent rating migrations are discussed. In particular, the modeling by a threshold normal model is presented.

Time stability of transition matrices is one of the major issues for credit risk estimation. Therefore, a chi-square test of homogeneity for the estimated rating transition probabilities is applied. The test is illustrated by an example and is compared to a simpler approach using standard errors. Further, assuming time stability, multi-period rating transitions are discussed. An estimator for multi-period transition matrices is given and its distribution is approximated by bootstrapping. Finally, the change of the composition of a credit portfolio caused by rating migrations is considered. The expected composition and its variance is calculated for independent migrations.

4.1   Rating Transition Probabilities

In this section, the way from raw data to estimated rating transition probabilities is described. First, migration events of the same kind are counted. The resulting migration counts are transformed into migration rates, which are used as estimates for the unknown transition probabilities. These estimates are complemented with estimated standard errors for two cases, for independence and for a special correlation structure.

4.1.1   From Credit Events to Migration Counts

We assume that credits or credit obligors are rated in d categories ranging from 1, the best rating category, to the category d containing defaulted credits. The raw data consist of a collection of *migration events*. The n observed migration events form a $n \times 2$ matrix with rows

$$(e_{i1}, e_{i2}) \in \{1, \ldots, d-1\} \times \{1, \ldots, d\}, \quad i = 1, \ldots, n.$$

Thereby, e_{i1} characterizes the rating of i-th credit at the beginning and e_{i2} the rating at the end of the risk horizon, which is usually one year. Subsequently, migration events of the same kind are aggregated in a $(d-1) \times d$ matrix $\mathbf{C}$ of *migration counts*, where the generic element

$$c_{jk} \overset{\text{def}}{=} \sum_{i=1}^{n} \mathbf{1}\{(e_{i1}, e_{i2}) = (j, k)\}$$

is the number of migration events from j to k. Clearly, their total sum is

$$\sum_{j=1}^{d-1} \sum_{k=1}^{d} c_{jk} = n.$$

4.1.2   Estimating Rating Transition Probabilities

We assume that each observation e_{i2} is a realization of a random variable $\tilde{e}_{i2}$ with conditional probability distribution

$$p_{jk} = \mathrm{P}(\tilde{e}_{i2} = k | \tilde{e}_{i1} = j), \quad \sum_{k=1}^{d} p_{jk} = 1,$$

where p_{jk} is the probability that a credit migrates from an initial rating j to rating k. These probabilities are the so called *rating transition (or migration) probabilities*. Note that the indicator variable $\mathbf{1}\{\tilde{e}_{i2} = k\}$ conditional on $\tilde{e}_{i1} = j$ is a Bernoulli distributed random variable with success parameter p_{jk},

$$\mathbf{1}\{\tilde{e}_{i2} = k\} \mid \tilde{e}_{i1} = j \sim \mathrm{Ber}(p_{jk}). \tag{4.1}$$

In order to estimate these rating transition probabilities we define the number of migrations starting from rating j as

$$n_j \overset{\text{def}}{=} \sum_{k=1}^{d} c_{jk}, \quad j = 1, \dots, d-1 \tag{4.2}$$

and assume $n_j > 0$ for $j = 1, \dots, d-1$. Thus, $(n_1, \dots, n_{d-1})$ is the composition of the portfolio at the beginning of the period and

$$\left(\sum_{j=1}^{d-1} c_{j1}, \dots, \sum_{j=1}^{d-1} c_{jd} \right) \tag{4.3}$$

is the composition of the portfolio at the end of the period, where the last element is the *number of defaulted credits*. The observed *migration rate* from j to k,

$$\hat{p}_{jk} \stackrel{\text{def}}{=} \frac{c_{jk}}{n_j},\tag{4.4}$$

is the natural estimate of the unknown transition probability p_{jk}.

If the migration events are independent, i. e., the variables $\tilde{e}_{12}, \ldots, \tilde{e}_{n2}$ are stochastically independent, c_{jk} is the observed value of the binomially distributed random variable

$$\tilde{c}_{jk} \sim \mathrm{B}(n_j, p_{jk}),$$

and therefore the standard deviation of $\hat{p}_{jk}$ is

$$\sigma_{jk} = \sqrt{\frac{p_{jk}(1 - p_{jk})}{n_j}},$$

which may be estimated by

$$\hat{\sigma}_{jk} = \sqrt{\frac{\hat{p}_{jk}(1 - \hat{p}_{jk})}{n_j}}.\tag{4.5}$$

The estimated standard errors must be carefully interpreted, because they are based on the assumption of independence.

4.1.3   Dependent Migrations

The case of dependent rating migrations raises new problems. In this context, $\tilde{c}_{jk}$ is distributed as sum of n_j correlated Bernoulli variables, see (4.1), indicating for each credit with initial rating j a migration to k by 1. If these Bernoulli variables are pairwise correlated with correlation ρ_{jk}, then the variance σ_{jk}^2 of the unbiased estimator $\hat{p}_{jk}$ for p_{jk} is (Huschens and Locarek-Junge, 2000, p. 44)

$$\sigma_{jk}^2 = \frac{p_{jk}(1 - p_{jk})}{n_j} + \frac{n_j - 1}{n_j}\rho_{jk}p_{jk}(1 - p_{jk}).$$

The limit

$$\lim_{n_j \to \infty} \sigma_{jk}^2 = \rho_{jk}p_{jk}(1 - p_{jk})$$

shows that the sequence $\hat{p}_{jk}$ does not obey a law of large numbers for $\rho_{jk} > 0$. Generally, the failing of convergence in quadratic mean does not imply the failing of convergence in probability. But in this case all moments of higher order exist since the random variable $\hat{p}_{jk}$ is bounded and so the convergence in probability implies the convergence in quadratic mean. For $\rho_{jk} = 0$ the law of large numbers holds. Negative correlations can only be obtained for finite n_j. The lower boundary for the correlation is given by $\rho_{jk} \geq -\frac{1}{n_j - 1}$, which converges to zero when the number of credits n_j grows to infinity.

The law of large numbers fails also if the correlations are different with either a common positive lower bound, or non vanishing positive average correlation or constant correlation blocks with positive correlations in each block (Finger, 1998, p. 5). This failing of the law of large numbers may not surprise a time series statistician, who is familiar with mixing conditions to ensure mean ergodicity of stochastic processes (Davidson, 1994, chapter 14). In statistical words, in the case of non-zero correlation the relative frequency is not a consistent estimator of the Bernoulli parameter.

The parameters ρ_{jk} may be modeled in consistent way in the framework of a *threshold normal model* with a single parameter ρ (Basel Committee on Banking Supervision, 2001; Gupton et al., 1997; Kim, 1999). This model specifies a special dependence structure based on a standard multinormal distribution for a vector $(R_1, \ldots, R_n)$ with equicorrelation matrix (Mardia, Kent, and Bibby, 1979, p. 461), where R_i $(i = 1, \ldots, n)$ is the standardized asset return and n is the number of obligors. The parameter $\rho > 0$ may be interpreted as a mean asset return correlation. In this model each pair of variables $(X, Y) = (R_i, R_{i'})$ with $i, i' = 1, \ldots, n$ and $i \neq i'$ is bivariate normally distributed with density function

$$\varphi(x, y; \rho) = \frac{1}{2\pi\sqrt{1-\rho^2}} \exp\left(-\frac{x^2 - 2\rho xy + y^2}{2(1-\rho^2)}\right).$$

The probability $P[(X, Y) \in (a, b)^2]$ is given by

$$\beta(a, b; \rho) = \int_a^b \int_a^b \varphi(x, y; \rho)\, dx\, dy. \tag{4.6}$$

Thresholds for rating j are derived from $p_{j1}, \ldots, p_{j,d-1}$ by

$$z_{j0} \stackrel{\text{def}}{=} -\infty, \ z_{j1} \stackrel{\text{def}}{=} \Phi^{-1}(p_{j1}), \ z_{j2} \stackrel{\text{def}}{=} \Phi^{-1}(p_{j1} + p_{j2}), \ldots, z_{jd} \stackrel{\text{def}}{=} +\infty,$$

where Φ is the distribution function of the standardized normal distribution and Φ^{-1} it's inverse. Each credit in category j is characterized by a normally distributed variable Z which determines the migration events by

$$p_{jk} = P(Z \in (z_{j,k-1}, z_{jk})) = \Phi(z_{jk}) - \Phi(z_{j,k-1}).$$

The *simultaneous* transition probabilities of two credits i and i' from category j to k are given by

$$p_{jj:kk} = \mathrm{P}(\tilde{e}_{i2} = \tilde{e}_{i'2} = k | \tilde{e}_{i1} = \tilde{e}_{i'1} = j) = \beta(z_{j,k-1}, z_{jk}; \rho),$$

i.e., the probability of simultaneous default is

$$p_{jj:dd} = \beta(z_{j,d-1}, z_{jd}; \rho).$$

For a detailed example see Saunders (1999, pp. 122-125). In the special case of independence we have $p_{jj:kk} = p_{jk}^2$. Defining a migration from j to k as success we obtain correlated Bernoulli variables with common success parameter p_{jk}, with probability $p_{jj:kk}$ of a simultaneous success, and with the *migration correlation*

$$\rho_{jk} = \frac{p_{jj:kk} - p_{jk}^2}{p_{jk}(1 - p_{jk})}.$$

Note that $\rho_{jk} = 0$ if $\rho = 0$.

Given $\rho \geq 0$ we can estimate the migration correlation $\rho_{jk} \geq 0$ by the restricted Maximum-Likelihood estimator

$$\hat{\rho}_{jk} = \max \left\{ 0; \frac{\beta(\hat{z}_{j,k-1}, \hat{z}_{jk}; \rho) - \hat{p}_{jk}^2}{\hat{p}_{jk}(1 - \hat{p}_{jk})} \right\} \tag{4.7}$$

with

$$\hat{z}_{jk} = \Phi^{-1} \left(\sum_{i=1}^{k} \hat{p}_{ji} \right). \tag{4.8}$$

The estimate

$$\hat{\sigma}_{jk} = \sqrt{\frac{\hat{p}_{jk}(1 - \hat{p}_{jk})}{n_j} + \frac{n_j - 1}{n_j} \hat{\rho}_{jk} \hat{p}_{jk}(1 - \hat{p}_{jk})} \tag{4.9}$$

of the standard deviation

$$\sigma_{jk} = \sqrt{\frac{p_{jk}(1 - p_{jk})}{n_j} + \frac{n_j - 1}{n_j} \rho_{jk} p_{jk}(1 - p_{jk})}$$

is used. The estimator in (4.9) generalizes (4.5), which results in the special case $\rho = 0$.

4.1.4 Computation and Quantlets

```
counts = VaRRatMigCount (d, e)
    computes migration counts from migration events
```

The quantlet `VaRRatMigCount` can be used to compute migration counts from migration events, where `d` is the number of categories including default and `e` is the $n \times 2$ data matrix containing n migration events. The result is assigned to the variable `counts`, which is the $(d-1) \times d$ matrix of migration counts.

Q XFGRatMig1.xpl

```
b = VaRRatMigRate (c, rho, s)
    computes migration rates and related estimated standard errors
```

The quantlet `VaRRatMigRate` computes migration rates and related estimated standard errors for m periods from an input matrix of migration counts and a given correlation parameter. Here, `c` is a $(d-1) \times d \times m$ array of m-period migration counts and `rho` is a non-negative correlation parameter as used in (4.6). For `rho = 0` the independent case is computed.

The calculation uses stochastic integration in order to determine the probability β from (4.6). The accuracy of the applied Monte Carlo procedure is controlled by the input parameter `s`. For $s > 0$ the sample size is at least $n \geq (2s)^{-2}$. This guarantees that the user-specified value `s` is an upper bound for the standard deviation of the Monte Carlo estimator for β. Note that with increasing accuracy (i. e. decreasing `s`) the computational effort increases proportional to n.

The result is assigned to the variable `b`, which is a list containing:

- `b.nstart`
  the $(d-1) \times 1 \times m$ array of portfolio weights before migration

- `b.nend`
  the $d \times 1 \times m$ array portfolio weights after migration

- `b.etp`
  the $(d-1) \times d \times m$ array of estimated transition probabilities

- `b.etv`
  the $(d-1) \times (d-1) \times m$ array of estimated threshold values

- `b.emc`
  the $(d-1) \times d \times m$ array of estimated migration correlations

- `b.esd`
  the $(d-1) \times d \times m$ array of estimated standard deviations

The matrices `b.nstart` and `b.nend` have components given by (4.2) and (4.3). The matrices `b.etp`, `b.emc`, and `b.esd` contain the $\hat{p}_{jk}$, $\hat{\rho}_{jk}$, and $\hat{\sigma}_{jk}$ from (4.4), (4.7), and (4.9) for $j = 1, \ldots, d-1$ and $k = 1, \ldots, d$. The estimates $\hat{\rho}_{jk}$ are given only for $\hat{p}_{jk} > 0$. The matrix `b.etv` contains the $\hat{z}_{jk}$ from (4.8) for $j, k = 1, \ldots, d-1$. Note that $z_{j0} = -\infty$ and $z_{jd} = +\infty$.

Q XFGRatMig2.xpl

4.2   Analyzing the Time-Stability of Transition Probabilities

4.2.1   Aggregation over Periods

We assume that migration data are given for m periods. This data consist in m matrices of migration counts $\mathbf{C}(t)$ for $t = 1, \ldots, m$ each of type $(d-1) \times d$. The generic element $c_{jk}(t)$ of the matrix $\mathbf{C}(t)$ is the number of migrations from j to k in period t. These matrices may be computed from m data sets of migration events.

An obvious question in this context is whether the transition probabilities can be assumed to be constant in time or not. A first approach to analyze the time-stability of transition probabilities is to compare the estimated transition probabilities per period for m periods with estimates from pooled data.

The *aggregated migration counts* from m periods are

$$c_{jk}^{+} \stackrel{\text{def}}{=} \sum_{t=1}^{m} c_{jk}(t) \tag{4.10}$$

which are combined in the matrix

$$\mathbf{C}^+ \stackrel{\text{def}}{=} \sum_{t=1}^{m} \mathbf{C}(t)$$

of type $(d-1) \times d$. The migration rates computed per period

$$\hat{p}_{jk}(t) \stackrel{\text{def}}{=} \frac{c_{jk}(t)}{n_j(t)}, \quad t = 1, \ldots, m \tag{4.11}$$

with

$$n_j(t) \stackrel{\text{def}}{=} \sum_{k=1}^{d} c_{jk}(t)$$

have to be compared with the migration rates from the pooled data. Based on the aggregated migration counts the estimated transition probabilities

$$\hat{p}_{jk}^+ \stackrel{\text{def}}{=} \frac{c_{jk}^+}{n_j^+} \tag{4.12}$$

with

$$n_j^+ \stackrel{\text{def}}{=} \sum_{k=1}^{d} c_{jk}^+ = \sum_{t=1}^{m} n_j(t), \quad j = 1, \ldots, d-1$$

can be computed.

4.2.2   Are the Transition Probabilities Stationary?

Under the assumption of *independence* for the migration events the vector of migration counts $(c_{j1}(t), \ldots c_{jd}(t))$ starting from j is in each period t a realization from a multinomial distributed random vector

$$(\tilde{c}_{j1}(t), \ldots, \tilde{c}_{jd}(t)) \sim \text{Mult}(n_j(t); p_{j1}(t), \ldots, p_{jd}(t)),$$

where $p_{jk}(t)$ denotes the transition probability from j to k in period t. For fixed $j \in \{1, \ldots, d-1\}$ the hypothesis of homogeneity

$$H_0 : p_{j1}(1) = \ldots = p_{j1}(m), p_{j2}(1) = \ldots = p_{j2}(m), \ldots, p_{jd}(1) = \ldots = p_{jd}(m)$$

may be tested with the statistic

$$X_j^2 = \sum_{k=1}^{d} \sum_{t=1}^{m} \frac{\left[\tilde{c}_{jk}(t) - n_j(t)\hat{p}_{jk}^+ \right]^2}{n_j(t)\hat{p}_{jk}^+}. \tag{4.13}$$

This statistic is asymptotically χ^2-distributed with $(d-1)(m-1)$ degrees of freedom under H_0. H_0 is rejected with approximative level α if the statistic computed from the data is greater than the $(1-\alpha)$-quantile of the χ^2-distribution with $(d-1)(m-1)$ degrees of freedom.

The combined hypothesis of homogeneity

$$H_0 : p_{jk}(t) = p_{jk}(m), \quad t = 1, \ldots, m-1, \quad j = 1, \ldots, d-1, \quad k = 1, \ldots, d$$

means that the matrix of transition probabilities is constant over time. Therefore, the combined null hypothesis may equivalently be formulated as

$$H_0 : \mathbf{P}(1) = \mathbf{P}(2) = \ldots = \mathbf{P}(m),$$

where $\mathbf{P}(t)$ denotes the transition matrix at t with generic element $p_{jk}(t)$. This hypothesis may be tested using the statistic

$$X^2 = \sum_{j=1}^{d-1} X_j^2, \tag{4.14}$$

which is under H_0 asymptotically χ^2-distributed with $(d-1)^2(m-1)$ degrees of freedom. The combined null hypothesis is rejected with approximative level α if the computed statistic is greater than the $(1-\alpha)$-quantile of the χ^2-distribution with $(d-1)^2(m-1)$ degrees of freedom (Bishop, Fienberg, and Holland, 1975, p. 265).

This approach creates two problems. Firstly, the two tests are based on the assumption of independence. Secondly, the test statistics are only asymptotically χ^2-distributed. This means that sufficiently large sample sizes are required. A rule of thumb given in the literature is $n_j(t)\hat{p}_{jk}^+ \geq 5$ for all j and k which is hardly fulfilled in the context of credit migrations.

The two χ^2-statistics in (4.13) and (4.14) are of the Pearson type. Two other frequently used and asymptotically equivalent statistics are the corresponding χ^2-statistics of the Neyman type

$$Y_j^2 = \sum_{k=1}^{d} \sum_{t=1}^{m} \frac{\left[\tilde{c}_{jk}(t) - n_j(t)\hat{p}_{jk}^+\right]^2}{\tilde{c}_{jk}(t)}, \quad Y^2 = \sum_{j=1}^{d-1} Y_j^2$$

and the χ^2-statistics

$$G_j^2 = 2 \sum_{k=1}^{d} \sum_{t=1}^{m} \tilde{c}_{jk}(t) \ln \left[\frac{\tilde{c}_{jk}(t)}{n_j(t)\hat{p}_{jk}^+} \right], \quad G^2 = \sum_{j=1}^{d-1} G_j^2,$$

which results from Wilks log-likelihood ratio.

Considering the strong assumptions on which these test procedures are based on, one may prefer a simpler approach complementing the point estimates $\hat{p}_{jk}(t)$ by estimated standard errors

$$\hat{\sigma}_{jk}(t) = \sqrt{\frac{\hat{p}_{jk}(t)(1 - \hat{p}_{jk}(t))}{n_j(t)}}$$

for each period $t \in \{1, \ldots, m\}$. For correlated migrations the estimated standard deviation is computed analogously to (4.9). This may graphically be visualized by showing

$$\hat{p}_{jk}^+, \quad \hat{p}_{jk}(t), \quad \hat{p}_{jk}(t) \pm 2\hat{\sigma}_{jk}(t), \quad t = 1, \ldots, m \tag{4.15}$$

simultaneously for $j = 1, \ldots, d-1$ and $k = 1, \ldots, d$.

4.2.3 Computation and Quantlets

The quantlet **Q** XFGRatMig3.xpl computes aggregated migration counts, estimated transition probabilities and χ^2-statistics. The call is `out = XFGRatMig3(c, rho, s)`, where `c` is a $(d-1) \times d \times m$ array of counts for m periods and `rho` is a non-negative correlation parameter. For `rho = 0` the independent case is computed, compare Section 4.1.4. The last input parameter `s` controls the accuracy of the computation, see Section 4.1.4.

The result is assigned to the variable `out`, which is a list containing:

- `out.cagg`
  the $(d-1) \times d$ matrix with aggregated counts

- `out.etpagg`
  the $(d-1) \times d$ matrix with estimated aggregated transition probabilities

- `out.esdagg`
  the $(d-1) \times d$ matrix with estimated aggregated standard deviations

- `out.etp`
  the $(d-1) \times d \times m$ array with estimated transition probabilities per period

- `out.esd`
  the $(d-1) \times d \times m$ array with estimated standard deviations per period

- `out.chi`
  the $3 \times d$ matrix with χ^2-statistics, degrees of freedom and p-values

The matrices `out.cagg`, `out.etpagg` and `out.etp` have components given by (4.10), (4.12) and (4.11). The elements of `out.esdagg` and `out.esd` result by replacing $\hat{p}_{jk}$ in (4.9) by $\hat{p}_{jk}^+$ or $\hat{p}_{jk}(t)$, respectively. The matrix `out.chi` contains in the first row the statistics from (4.13) for $j = 1, \ldots, d-1$ and (4.14). The second and third row gives the corresponding degrees of freedom and p-values.

The quantlet ◨ `XFGRatMig4.xpl` (`XFGRatMig4(etp, esd, etpagg)`) graphs migration rates per period with estimated standard deviations and migration rates from pooled data. The inputs are:

- `etp`
  the $(d-1) \times d \times m$ array with estimated transition probabilities per period

- `esd`
  the $(d-1) \times d \times m$ array with estimated standard deviations per period

- `etpagg`
  the $(d-1) \times d$ matrix with estimated aggregated transition probabilities

The output consists of $(d-1)d$ graphics for $j = 1, \ldots, d-1$ and $k = 1, \ldots, d$. Each graphic shows $t = 1, \ldots, m$ at the x-axis versus the four variables from (4.15) at the y-axis.

4.2.4 Examples with Graphical Presentation

The following examples are based on transition matrices given by Nickell et al. (2000, pp. 208, 213). The data set covers long-term bonds rated by Moody's in the period 1970–1997. Instead of the original matrices of type 8×9 we use condensed matrices of type 3×4 by combining the original data in the $d = 4$ basic rating categories A, B, C, and D, where D stands for the category of defaulted credits.

The aggregated data for the full period from 1970 to 1997 are

$$
\mathbf{C} = \begin{bmatrix} 21726 & 790 & 0 & 0 \\ 639 & 21484 & 139 & 421 \\ 0 & 44 & 307 & 82 \end{bmatrix}, \quad \hat{\mathbf{P}} = \begin{bmatrix} 0.965 & 0.035 & 0 & 0 \\ 0.028 & 0.947 & 0.006 & 0.019 \\ 0 & 0.102 & 0.709 & 0.189 \end{bmatrix},
$$

where $\mathbf{C}$ is the matrix of migration counts and $\hat{\mathbf{P}}$ is the corresponding matrix of estimated transition probabilities. These matrices may be compared with corresponding matrices for three alternative states of the business cycles:

$$
\mathbf{C}(1) = \begin{bmatrix} 7434 & 277 & 0 & 0 \\ 273 & 7306 & 62 & 187 \\ 0 & 15 & 94 & 33 \end{bmatrix}, \quad \hat{\mathbf{P}}(1) = \begin{bmatrix} 0.964 & 0.036 & 0 & 0 \\ 0.035 & 0.933 & 0.008 & 0.024 \\ 0 & 0.106 & 0.662 & 0.232 \end{bmatrix},
$$

for the *through* of the business cycle,

$$
\mathbf{C}(2) = \begin{bmatrix} 7125 & 305 & 0 & 0 \\ 177 & 6626 & 35 & 147 \\ 0 & 15 & 92 & 24 \end{bmatrix}, \quad \hat{\mathbf{P}}(2) = \begin{bmatrix} 0.959 & 0.041 & 0 & 0 \\ 0.025 & 0.949 & 0.005 & 0.021 \\ 0 & 0.115 & 0.702 & 0.183 \end{bmatrix},
$$

for the *normal* phase of the business cycle, and

$$
\mathbf{C}(3) = \begin{bmatrix} 7167 & 208 & 0 & 0 \\ 189 & 7552 & 42 & 87 \\ 0 & 14 & 121 & 25 \end{bmatrix}, \quad \hat{\mathbf{P}}(3) = \begin{bmatrix} 0.972 & 0.028 & 0 & 0 \\ 0.024 & 0.960 & 0.005 & 0.011 \\ 0 & 0.088 & 0.756 & 0.156 \end{bmatrix},
$$

for the *peak* of the business cycle. The three categories depend on whether real GDP growth in the country was in the upper, middle or lower third of the growth rates recorded in the sample period (Nickell et al., 2000, Sec. 2.4).

In the following we use these matrices for illustrative purposes *as if* data from $m = 3$ periods are given. Figure 4.1 gives a graphical presentation for $d = 4$ rating categories and $m = 3$ periods.

In order to illustrate the testing procedures presented in Section 4.2.2 in the following the hypothesis is tested that the data from the three periods came from the same theoretical transition probabilities. Clearly, from the construction of the three periods we may expect, that the test rejects the null hypothesis. The three χ^2-statistics with $6 = 3(3 - 1)$ degrees of freedom for testing the equality of the rows of the transition matrices have p-values 0.994, > 0.9999, and 0.303. Thus, the null hypothesis must be clearly rejected for the first two rows at any usual level of confidence while the test for the last row suffers from the limited sample size. Nevertheless, the χ^2-statistic for the simultaneous test of the equality of the transition matrices has $18 = 3^2 \cdot (3 - 1)$ degrees of freedom and a p-value > 0.9999. Consequently, the null hypothesis must be rejected at any usual level of confidence.

Q XFGRatMig3.xpl

A second example is given by comparing the matrix $\hat{\mathbf{P}}$ based on the whole data with the matrix $\hat{\mathbf{P}}(2)$ based on the data of the *normal* phase of the business

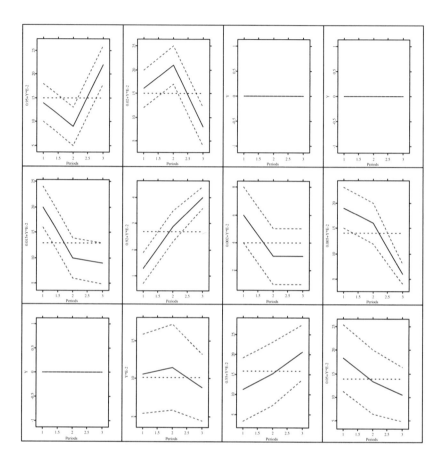

Figure 4.1. Example for ⧠ XFGRatMig4.xpl

cycle. In this case a test possibly may not indicate that differences between
$\mathbf{P}$ and $\mathbf{P}(2)$ are significant. Indeed, the χ^2-statistics for testing the equality
of the rows of the transition matrices with 3 degrees of freedom have p-values
0.85, 0.82, and 0.02. The statistic of the simultaneous test with 9 degrees of
freedom has a p-value of 0.69.

4.3   Multi-Period Transitions

In the multi-period case, transitions in credit ratings are also characterized by rating transition matrices. The m-period transition matrix is labeled $\mathbf{P}^{(m)}$. Its generic element $p_{jk}^{(m)}$ gives the rating transition probability from rating j to k over the $m \geq 1$ periods. For the sake of simplicity the one-period transition matrix $\mathbf{P}^{(1)}$ is shortly denoted by $\mathbf{P}$ in the following. This transition matrix is considered to be of type $d \times d$. The last row contains $(0, 0, \dots, 0, 1)$ expressing the absorbing default state. Multi-period transition matrices can be constructed from one-period transition matrices under the assumption of the Markov property.

4.3.1   Time Homogeneous Markov Chain

Let $\{X(t)\}_{t \geq 0}$ be a discrete-time stochastic process with countable state space. It is called a *first-order Markov chain* if

$$P\left[(X(t+1) = x(t+1)|X(t) = x(t), \dots, X(0) = x(0)\right]$$
$$= P\left[X(t+1) = x(t+1)|X(t) = x(t)\right] \quad (4.16)$$

whenever both sides are well-defined. Further, the process is called a *homogeneous first-order Markov chain* if the right-hand side of (4.16) is independent of t (Brémaud, 1999).

Transferred to rating transitions, homogeneity and the Markov property imply constant one-period transition matrices $\mathbf{P}$ independent of the time t, i. e. $\mathbf{P}$ obeys time-stability. Then the one-period $d \times d$ transition matrix $\mathbf{P}$ contains the non-negative rating transition probabilities

$$p_{jk} = P(X(t+1) = k|X(t) = j).$$

They fulfill the conditions

$$\sum_{k=1}^{d} p_{jk} = 1$$

and

$$(p_{d1}, p_{d2}, \dots, p_{dd}) = (0, \dots, 0, 1).$$

The latter reflects the absorbing boundary of the transition matrix $\mathbf{P}$.

The two-period transition matrix is then calculated by ordinary matrix multiplication, $\mathbf{P}^{(2)} = \mathbf{PP}$. Qualitatively, the composition of the portfolio after one period undergoes the same transitions again. Extended for m periods this reads as

$$\mathbf{P}^{(m)} = \mathbf{P}^{(m-1)}\mathbf{P} = \mathbf{P}^m$$

with non-negative elements

$$p_{jk}^{(m)} = \sum_{i=1}^{d} p_{ji}^{(m-1)} p_{ik}.$$

The recursive scheme can also be applied for non-homogeneous transitions, i.e. for one-period transition matrices being not equal, which is the general case.

4.3.2   Bootstrapping Markov Chains

The one-period transition matrix $\mathbf{P}$ is unknown and must be estimated. The estimator $\hat{\mathbf{P}}$ is associated with estimation errors which consequently influence the estimated multi-period transition matrices. The traditional approach to quantify this influence turns out to be tedious since it is difficult to obtain the distribution of $(\hat{\mathbf{P}} - \mathbf{P})$, which could characterize the estimation errors. Furthermore, the distribution of $(\hat{\mathbf{P}}^{(m)} - \mathbf{P}^{(m)})$, with

$$\hat{\mathbf{P}}^{(m)} \stackrel{\text{def}}{=} \hat{\mathbf{P}}^m, \tag{4.17}$$

has to be discussed in order to address the sensitivity of the estimated transition matrix in the multi-period case. It might be more promising to apply resampling methods like the bootstrap combined with Monte Carlo sampling. For a representative review of resampling techniques see Efron and Tibshirani (1993) and Shao and Tu (1995), for bootstrapping Markov chains see Athreya and Fuh (1992) and Härdle, Horowitz, and Kreiss (2001).

Assuming a *homogeneous first-order Markov chain* $\{X(t)\}_{t \geq 0}$, the rating transitions are generated from the unknown transition matrix $\mathbf{P}$. In the spirit of the *bootstrap method*, the unknown transition matrix $\mathbf{P}$ is substituted by the estimated transition matrix $\hat{\mathbf{P}}$, containing transition rates. This then allows to draw a bootstrap sample from the multinomial distribution assuming *independent* rating migrations,

$$(\tilde{c}_{j1}^*, \ldots, \tilde{c}_{jd}^*) \sim \text{Mult}(n_j; \hat{p}_{j1}, \ldots, \hat{p}_{jd}), \tag{4.18}$$

for all initial rating categories $j = 1, \ldots, d-1$. Here, $\tilde{c}^*_{jk}$ denotes the bootstrap random variable of migration counts from j to k in one period and $\hat{p}_{jk}$ is the estimated one-period transition probability (transition rate) from j to k.

Then the bootstrap sample $\{c^*_{jk}\}_{j=1,\ldots,d-1,k=1,\ldots,d}$ is used to estimate a bootstrap transition matrix $\hat{\mathbf{P}}^*$ with generic elements $\hat{p}^*_{jk}$ according

$$\hat{p}^*_{jk} = \frac{c^*_{jk}}{n_j}. \tag{4.19}$$

Obviously, defaulted credits can not upgrade. Therefore, the bootstrap is not necessary for obtaining the last row of $\hat{\mathbf{P}}^*$, which is $(\hat{p}^*_{d1}, \ldots, \hat{p}^*_{dd}) = (0, \ldots, 0, 1)$. Then matrix multiplication gives the m-period transition matrix estimated from the bootstrap sample,

$$\hat{\mathbf{P}}^{*(m)} = \hat{\mathbf{P}}^{*m},$$

with generic elements $\hat{p}^{*(m)}_{jk}$.

We can now access the distribution of $\hat{\mathbf{P}}^{*(m)}$ by *Monte Carlo sampling*, e. g. B samples are drawn and labeled $\hat{\mathbf{P}}^{*(m)}_b$ for $b = 1, \ldots, B$. Then the distribution of $\hat{\mathbf{P}}^{*(m)}$ estimates the distribution of $\hat{\mathbf{P}}^{(m)}$. This is justified since the consistency of this bootstrap estimator has been proven by Basawa, Green, McCormick, and Taylor (1990). In order to characterize the distribution of $\hat{\mathbf{P}}^{*(m)}$, the standard deviation Std $\left(\hat{p}^{*(m)}_{jk}\right)$ which is the bootstrap estimator of Std $\left(\hat{p}^{(m)}_{jk}\right)$, is estimated by

$$\widehat{\mathrm{Std}}\left(\hat{p}^{*(m)}_{jk}\right) = \sqrt{\frac{1}{B-1} \sum_{b=1}^{B} \left[\hat{p}^{*(m)}_{jk,b} - \hat{\mathrm{E}}\left(\hat{p}^{*(m)}_{jk}\right)\right]^2} \tag{4.20}$$

with

$$\hat{\mathrm{E}}\left(\hat{p}^{*(m)}_{jk}\right) = \frac{1}{B} \sum_{b=1}^{B} \hat{p}^{*(m)}_{jk,b}$$

for all $j = 1, \ldots, d-1$ and $k = 1, \ldots, d$. Here, $\hat{p}^{*(m)}_{jk,b}$ is the generic element of the b-th m-period bootstrap sample $\hat{\mathbf{P}}^{*(m)}_b$. So (4.20) estimates the unknown standard deviation of the m-period transition rate Std $\left(\hat{p}^{(m)}_{jk}\right)$ using B Monte Carlo samples.

4.3.3   Computation and Quantlets

For time homogeneity, the m-period rating transition matrices are obtained by the quantlet **Q** XFGRatMig5.xpl (q = XFGRatMig5(p, m)). It computes all $t = 1, 2, \ldots, $m multi-period transition matrices given the one-period $d \times d$ matrix p. Note that the output q is a $d \times d \times m$ array, which can be directly visualized by **Q** XFGRatMig6.xpl (XFGRatMig6(q)) returning a graphical output. To visualize t-period transition matrices each with d^2 elements for $t = 1, \ldots, m$, we plot d^2 aggregated values

$$j - 1 + \sum_{l=1}^{k} p_{jl}^{(t)}, \quad j, k = 1, \ldots, d \tag{4.21}$$

for all $t = 1, \ldots, m$ periods simultaneously.

A typical example is shown in Figure 4.2 for the one-year transition matrix given in Nickell et al. (2000, p. 208), which uses Moody's unsecured bond ratings between 31/12/1970 and 31/12/1997. According (4.21), aggregated values are plotted for $t = 1, \ldots, 10$. Thereby, the transition matrix is condensed for simplicity to 4×4 with only 4 basic rating categories, see the example in Section 4.2.4. Again, the last category stands for defaulted credits. Estimation errors are neglected in Figure 4.2.

```
out = VaRRatMigRateM (counts, m, B)
      bootstraps m-period transition probabilities
```

Bootstrapping is performed by the quantlet VaRRatMigRateM. It takes as input counts, the $(d - 1) \times d$ matrix of migration counts, from which the bootstrap sample is generated. Further, m denotes the number of periods and B the number of generated bootstrap samples. The result is assigned to the variable out, which is a list of the following output:

- out.btm
  the $(d-1) \times d \times B$ array of bootstrapped m-period transition probabilities

- out.etm
  the $(d - 1) \times d$ matrix of m-period transition rates

- out.stm
  the $(d - 1) \times d$ matrix of estimated standard deviations of the m-period transition rates

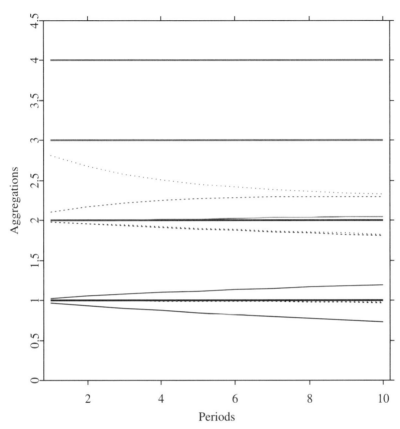

Figure 4.2. Example for XFGRatMig6.xpl:
Aggregated values of multi-period transition matrices.

The components of the matrices `out.btm` are calculated according (4.18) and
(4.19). The matrices `out.etm` and `out.stm` have components given by (4.17)
and (4.20).

From j	To k							n_j
	1	2	3	4	5	6	Default	
1	0.51	0.40	0.09	0.00	0.00	0.00	0.00	35
2	0.08	0.62	0.19	0.08	0.02	0.01	0.00	103
3	0.00	0.08	0.69	0.17	0.06	0.00	0.00	226
4	0.01	0.01	0.10	0.64	0.21	0.03	0.00	222
5	0.00	0.01	0.02	0.19	0.66	0.12	0.00	137
6	0.00	0.00	0.00	0.02	0.16	0.70	0.12	58
Default	0.00	0.00	0.00	0.00	0.00	0.00	1.00	0

Table 4.1. German rating transition matrix ($d = 7$) and the number of migrations starting from rating $j = 1, \ldots, d$

4.3.4 Rating Transitions of German Bank Borrowers

In the following the bootstrapping is illustrated in an example. As estimator $\hat{\mathbf{P}}$ we use the 7×7 rating transition matrix of small and medium-sized *German bank borrowers* from Machauer and Weber (1998, p. 1375), shown in Table 4.1. The data cover the period from January 1992 to December 1996.

With the quantlet VaRRatMigRateM the m-period transition probabilities are estimated by $\hat{p}_{jk}^{(m)}$ and the bootstrap estimators of their standard deviations are calculated. This calculations are done for 1, 5 and 10 periods and B = 1000 Monte Carlo steps. A part of the resulting output is summarized in Table 4.2, only default probabilities are considered. Note that the probabilities in Table 4.1 are rounded and the following computations are based on integer migration counts $c_{jk} \approx n_j p_{jk}$.

Q XFGRatMig7.xpl

4.3.5 Portfolio Migration

Based on the techniques presented in the last sections we can now tackle the problem of portfolio migration, i. e. we can assess the distribution of $n(t)$ credits over the d rating categories and its evolution over periods $t \in \{1, \ldots m\}$. Here, a *stationary* transition matrix $\mathbf{P}$ is assumed. The randomly changing number of credits in category j at time t is labeled by $\tilde{n}_j(t)$ and allows to define non-

From j	$\hat{p}_{jd}^{(1)}$	$\widehat{Std}\left(\hat{p}_{jd}^{*(1)}\right)$	$\hat{p}_{jd}^{(5)}$	$\widehat{Std}\left(\hat{p}_{jd}^{*(5)}\right)$	$\hat{p}_{jd}^{(10)}$	$\widehat{Std}\left(\hat{p}_{jd}^{*(10)}\right)$
1	0.00	0.000	0.004	0.003	0.037	0.015
2	0.00	0.000	0.011	0.007	0.057	0.022
3	0.00	0.000	0.012	0.005	0.070	0.025
4	0.00	0.000	0.038	0.015	0.122	0.041
5	0.00	0.000	0.079	0.031	0.181	0.061
6	0.12	0.042	0.354	0.106	0.465	0.123

Table 4.2. Estimated m-period default probabilities and the bootstrap estimator of their standard deviations for $m = 1, 5, 10$ periods

negative *portfolio weights*

$$\tilde{w}_j(t) \stackrel{\text{def}}{=} \frac{\tilde{n}_j(t)}{n(t)}, \quad j = 1, \ldots, d,$$

which are also random variables. They can be related to migration counts $\tilde{c}_{jk}(t)$ of period t by

$$\tilde{w}_k(t+1) = \frac{1}{n(t)} \sum_{j=1}^{d} \tilde{c}_{jk}(t) \tag{4.22}$$

counting all migrations going from any category to the rating category k. Given the weights $\tilde{w}_j(t) = w_j(t)$ at t, the migration counts $\tilde{c}_{jk}(t)$ are binomially distributed

$$\tilde{c}_{jk}(t)|\tilde{w}_j(t) = w_j(t) \sim B\left(n(t)\,w_j(t), p_{jk}\right). \tag{4.23}$$

The non-negative weights are aggregated in a row vector

$$\tilde{w}(t) = (\tilde{w}_1(t), \ldots, \tilde{w}_d(t))$$

and sum up to one

$$\sum_{j=1}^{d} w_j(t) = 1.$$

In the case of *independent* rating migrations, the expected portfolio weights at $t+1$ given the weights at t result from (4.22) and (4.23) as

$$E[\tilde{w}(t+1)|\tilde{w}(t) = w(t)] = w(t)\mathbf{P}$$

and the conditional covariance matrix $V[\tilde{w}(t+1)|\tilde{w}(t) = w(t)]$ has elements

$$
v_{kl} \stackrel{\text{def}}{=} \begin{cases} \frac{1}{n(t)} \sum_{j=1}^{d} w_j(t) p_{jk}(1 - p_{jk}) & k = l \\[2mm] & \text{for} \\[2mm] -\frac{1}{n(t)} \sum_{j=1}^{d} w_j(t) p_{jk} p_{jl} & k \neq l. \end{cases} \tag{4.24}
$$

For m periods the multi-period transition matrix $\mathbf{P}^{(m)} = \mathbf{P}^m$ has to be used, see Section 4.3.1. Hence, (4.22) and (4.23) are modified to

$$
\tilde{w}_k(t+m) = \frac{1}{n(t)} \sum_{j=1}^{d} \tilde{c}_{jk}^{(m)}(t)
$$

and

$$
\tilde{c}_{jk}^{(m)}(t)|\tilde{w}_j(t) = w_j(t) \sim \mathrm{B}\left(n(t)\, w_j(t), p_{jk}^{(m)}\right).
$$

Here, $c_{jk}^{(m)}(t)$ denotes the number of credits migrating from j to k over m periods starting in t. The conditional mean of the portfolio weights is now given by

$$
\mathrm{E}[\tilde{w}(t+m)|\tilde{w}(t) = w(t)] = w(t)\mathbf{P}^{(m)}
$$

and the elements of the conditional covariance matrix $V[\tilde{w}(t+m)|\tilde{w}(t) = w(t)]$ result by replacing p_{jk} and p_{jl} in (4.24) by $p_{jk}^{(m)}$ and $p_{jl}^{(m)}$.

Bibliography

Athreya, K. B. and Fuh, C. D. (1992). Bootstrapping Markov chains, *in* R. LePage and L. Billard (eds), *Exploring the Limits of Bootstrap*, Wiley, New York, pp. 49–64.

Basawa, I. V., Green, T. A., McCormick, W. P., and Taylor, R. L. (1990). Asymptotic bootstrap validity for finite Markov chains, *Communications in Statistics A* **19**: 1493–1510.

Basel Committee on Banking Supervision (2001). The Internal Ratings-Based Approach. Consultative Document.

Bishop, Y. M. M., Fienberg, S. E., and Holland, P. W. (1975). *Discrete Multivariate Analysis: Theory and Practice*, MIT Press, Cambridge.

Brémaud, P. (1999). *Markov Chains: Gibbs Fields, Monte Carlo Simulation, and Queues*, Springer, New York.

Crouhy, M., Galai, D., and Mark, R. (2001). Prototype risk rating system, *Journal of Banking & Finance* **25**: 47–95.

Davidson, J. (1994). *Stochastic Limit Theory*, Oxford University Press, Oxford.

Efron, B. and Tibshirani, R. J. (1993). *An Introduction to the Bootstrap*, Chapman & Hall, New York.

Finger, C. C. (1998). Extended "constant correlations" in CreditManager 2.0, *CreditMetrics Monitor* pp. 5–8. 3rd Quarter.

Gupton, G. M., Finger, C. C., and Bhatia, M. (1997). CreditMetrics - Technical Document, J.P. Morgan.

Härdle, W., Horowitz, J., and Kreiss, J. P. (2001). Bootstrap Methods for Time Series, SFB Discussion Paper, 59.

Huschens, S. and Locarek-Junge, H. (2000). Konzeptionelle und statistische Grundlagen der portfolioorientierten Kreditrisikomessung, *in* A. Oehler (ed.), *Kreditrisikomanagement - Portfoliomodelle und Derivate*, Schäffer-Poeschel Verlag, Stuttgart, pp. 25–50.

Jarrow, R. A., Lando, D., and Turnbull, S. M. (1997). A Markov model for the term structure of credit risk spreads, *The Review of Financial Studies* **10**(2): 481–523.

Kim, J. (1999). Conditioning the transition matrix, *Risk: Credit Risk Special Report*, October: 37–40.

Lancaster, T. (1990). *The Econometric Analysis of Transition Data*, Cambridge University Press.

Machauer, A. and Weber, M. (1998). Bank behavior based on internal credit ratings of borrowers, *Journal of Banking & Finance* **22**: 1355–1383.

Mardia, K. V., Kent, J. T., and Bibby, J. M. (1979). *Multivariate Analysis*, Academic Press, London.

Nickell, P., Perraudin, W., and Varotto, S. (2000). Stability of rating transitions, *Journal of Banking & Finance* **24**: 203–227.

Saunders, A. (1999). *Credit Risk Measurement: New Approaches to Value at Risk and Other Paradigms*, Wiley, New York.

Shao, J. and Tu, D. (1995). *The Jackknife and Bootstrap*, Springer, New York.

5 Sensitivity analysis of credit portfolio models

Rüdiger Kiesel and Torsten Kleinow

To assess the riskiness of credit-risky portfolios is one of the most challenging tasks in contemporary finance. The decision by the Basel Committee for Banking Supervision to allow sophisticated banks to use their own internal credit portfolio risk models has further highlighted the importance of a critical evaluation of such models. A crucial input for a model of credit-risky portfolios is the dependence structure of the underlying obligors. We study two widely used approaches, namely a factor structure and the direct specification of a copula, within the framework of a default-based credit risk model. Using the powerful simulation tools of XploRe we generate portfolio default distributions and study the sensitivity of commonly used risk measures with respect to the approach in modelling the dependence structure of the portfolio.

5.1 Introduction

Understanding the principal components of portfolio credit risk and their interaction is of considerable importance. Investment banks use risk-adjusted capital ratios such as risk-adjusted return on capital (RAROC) to allocate economic capital and measure performance of business units and trading desks. The current attempt by the Basel Committee for Banking Supervision in its Basel II proposals to develop an appropriate framework for a global financial regulation system emphasizes the need for an accurate understanding of credit risk; see BIS (2001). Thus bankers, regulators and academics have put considerable effort into attempts to study and model the contribution of various ingredients of credit risk to overall credit portfolio risk. A key development has been the introduction of credit portfolio models to obtain portfolio loss distributions either analytically or by simulation. These models can roughly be classified as based on credit rating systems, on Merton's contingent claim approach or on actuarial techniques; see Crouhy, Galai and Mark (2001) for exact description and discussion of the various models.

However, each model contains parameters that effect the risk measures produced, but which, because of a lack of suitable data, must be set on a judgemental basis. There are several empirical studies investigating these effects: Gordy (2000) and Koyluoglu and Hickmann (1998) show that parametrisation of various models can be harmonized, but use only default-driven versions (a related study with more emphasis on the mathematical side of the models is Frey and McNeil (2001)). Crouhy, Galai and Mark (2000) compare models on benchmark portfolio and find that the highest VaR estimate is 50 per cent larger than the lowest. Finally, Nickell, Perraudin and Varotto (1998) find that models yield too many exceptions by analyzing VaRs for portfolios over rolling twelve-month periods.

Despite these shortcomings credit risk portfolio models are regarded as valuable tools to measure the relative riskiness of credit risky portfolios – not least since measures such as e.g. the spread over default-free interest rate or default probabilities calculated from long runs of historical data suffer from other intrinsic drawbacks – and are established as benchmark tools in measuring credit risk.

The calculation of risk capital based on the internal rating approach, currently favored by the Basel Supervisors Committee, can be subsumed within the class of ratings-based models. To implement such an approach an accurate understanding of various relevant portfolio characteristics within such a model is required and, in particular, the sensitivity of the risk measures to changes in input parameters needs to be evaluated. However, few studies have attempted to investigate aspects of portfolio risk based on rating-based credit risk models thoroughly. In Carey (1998) the default experience and loss distribution for privately placed US bonds is discussed. VaRs for portfolios of public bonds, using a bootstrap-like approach, are calculated in Carey (2000). While these two papers utilize a "default-mode" (abstracting from changes in portfolio value due to changes in credit standing), Kiesel, Perraudin and Taylor (1999) employ a "mark-to-market" model and stress the importance of stochastic changes in credit spreads associated with market values – an aspect also highlighted in Hirtle, Levonian, Saidenberg, Walter and Wright (2001).

The aim of this chapter is to contribute to the understanding of the performance of rating-based credit portfolio models. Our emphasis is on comparing the effect of the different approaches to modelling the dependence structure of the individual obligors within a credit-risky portfolio. We use a default-mode model (which can easily be extended) to investigate the effect of changing dependence structure within the portfolio. We start in Section 5.2 by reviewing the construction of a rating-based credit portfolio risk model. In Section 5.3 we discuss approaches to modelling dependence within the portfolio. In Section 5.4 we comment on the implementation in XploRe and present results from our simulations.

5.2   Construction of portfolio credit risk models

To construct a credit risk model we have to consider *individual risk elements* such as

(1i) *Default Probability:* the probability that the obligor or counterparty will default on its contractual obligations to repay its debt,

(2i) *Recovery Rates:* the extent to which the face value of an obligation can be recovered once the obligor has defaulted,

(3i) *Credit Migration:* the extent to which the credit quality of the obligor or counterparty improves or deteriorates;

and *portfolio risk elements*

(1p) *Default and Credit Quality Correlation:* the degree to which the default or credit quality of one obligor is related to the default or credit quality of another,

(2p) *Risk Contribution and Credit Concentration:* the extent to which an individual instrument or the presence of an obligor in the portfolio contributes to the totality of risk in the overall portfolio.

From the above building blocks a rating-based credit risk model is generated by

(1m) the definition of the possible states for each obligor's credit quality, and a description of how likely obligors are to be in any of these states at the horizon date, i.e. specification of rating classes and of the corresponding matrix of transition probabilities (relating to (1i) and (3i)).

(2m) quantifying the interaction and correlation between credit migrations of different obligors (relating to (1p)).

(3m) the re-evaluation of exposures in all possible credit states, which in case of default corresponds to (2i) above; however, for non-default states a mark-to-market or mark-to-model (for individual assets) procedure is required.

During this study we will focus on the effects of default dependence modelling. Furthermore, we assume that on default we are faced with a zero recovery rate. Thus, only aspects (1i) and (1p) are of importance in our context and only two rating classes – default and non-default – are needed. A general discussion of further aspects can be found in any of the books Caouette, Altman and Narayanan (1998), Ong (1999), Jorion (2000) and Crouhy et al. (2001). For practical purposes we emphasize the importance of a proper mark-to-market methodology (as pointed out in Kiesel et al. (1999)). However, to study the effects of dependence modelling more precisely, we feel a simple portfolio risk model is sufficient.

As the basis for comparison we use Value at Risk (VaR) – the loss which will be exceeded on some given fractions of occasions (the confidence level) if a portfolio is held for a particular time (the holding period).

5.3   Dependence modelling

To formalize the ratings-based approach, we characterize each exposure $j \in \{1, \ldots, n\}$ by a four-dimensional stochastic vector

$$(S_j, k_j, l_j, \pi(j, k_j, l_j)),$$

where for obligor j

(1) S_j is the driving stochastic process for defaults and rating migrations,

(2) k_j, l_j represent the initial and end-of-period rating category,

(3) $\pi(.)$ represents the credit loss (end-of-period exposure value).

In this context S_j (which is, with reference to the Merton model, often interpreted as a proxy of the obligor's underlying equity) is used to obtain the end-of-period state of the obligor. If we assume N rating classes, we obtain cut-off points $-\infty = z_{k,0}, z_{k,1}, z_{k,2}, \ldots, z_{k,N-1}, z_{k,N} = \infty$ using the matrix of transition probabilities together with a distributional assumption on S_j. Then, obligor j changes from rating k to rating l if the variable S_j falls in the range $[z_{k,l-1}, z_{kl}]$. Our default-mode framework implies two rating classes, default resp. no-default, labeled as 1 resp. 0 (and thus only a single cut-off point obtained from the probability of default). Furthermore, interpreting $\pi(\bullet)$ as the individual loss function, $\pi(j,0,0) = 0$ (no default) and according to our zero recovery assumption $\pi(j,0,1) = 1$. To illustrate the methodology we plot in Figure 5.1 two simulated drivers S_1 and S_2 together with the corresponding cut-off points $z_{1,1}$ and $z_{2,1}$.

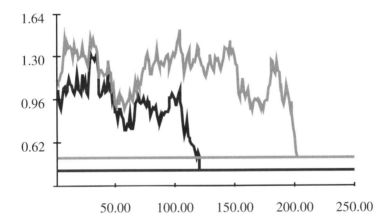

Figure 5.1. Two simulated driver S_j and the corresponding cut-off points for default. Q XFGSCP01.xpl

5.3.1 Factor modelling

In a typical credit portfolio model dependencies of individual obligors are modelled via dependencies of the underlying latent variables $S = (S_1, \ldots, S_n)^\top$. In the typical portfolio analysis the vector S is embedded in a factor model, which allows for easy analysis of correlation, the typical measure of dependence. One assumes that the underlying variables S_j are driven by a vector of common factors. Typically, this vector is assumed to be normally distributed (see e.g. JP Morgan (1997)). Thus, with $Z \sim N(0, \Sigma)$ a p-dimensional normal vector and $\epsilon = (\epsilon_1, \ldots, \epsilon_n)^\top$ independent normally distributed random variables, independent also from Z, we define

$$S_j = \sum_{i=1}^{p} a_{ji} Z_i + \sigma_j \epsilon_j, \quad j = 1, \ldots n. \tag{5.1}$$

Here a_{ji} describes the exposure of obligor j to factor i, i.e. the so-called factor loading, and σ_j is the volatility of the idiosyncratic risk contribution. In such a framework one can easily interfere default correlation from the correlation of the underlying drivers S_j. To do so, we define default indicators

$$Y_j = \mathbf{1}(S_j \leq D_j),$$

where D_j is the cut-off point for default of obligor j. The individual default probabilities are

$$\pi_j = P(Y_j = 1) = P(S_j \leq D_j),$$

and the joint default probability is

$$\pi_{ij} = P(Y_i = 1, Y_j = 1) = P(S_i \leq D_i, S_j \leq D_j).$$

If we denote by $\rho_{ij} = Corr(S_i, S_j)$ the correlation of the underlying latent variables and by $\rho_{ij}^D = Corr(Y_i, Y_j)$ the default correlation of obligors i and j, then we obtain for the default correlation the simple formula

$$\rho_{ij}^D = \frac{\pi_{ij} - \pi_i \pi_j}{\sqrt{\pi_i \pi_j (1 - \pi_i)(1 - \pi_j)}}. \tag{5.2}$$

Under the assumption that (S_i, S_j) are bivariate normal, we obtain for the joint default probability

$$\pi_{ij} = \int_{-\infty}^{D_i} \int_{-\infty}^{D_j} \varphi(u, v; \rho_{ij}) du dv,$$

where $\varphi(u, v; \rho)$ is bivariate normal density with correlation coefficient ρ. Thus, asset (factor) correlation influences default correlation by entering in joint default probability. Within the Gaussian framework we can easily evaluate the above quantities, see (5.1). We see, that under our modelling assumption default correlation is of an order of magnitude smaller than asset correlation (which is also supported by empirical evidence).

Asset correlation	Default correlation
0.1	0.0094
0.2	0.0241
0.3	0.0461

Table 5.1. Effect of asset correlation on default correlation

5.3.2 Copula modelling

As an alternative approach to the factor assumption, we can model each of the underlying variables independently and subsequently use a copula to generate the dependence structure. (For basic facts on copulae we refer the reader to Chapter 2 and the references given there.)

So, suppose we have specified the individual distributions F_j of the variables S_j and a copula C for the dependence structure. Then, for any subgroup of obligors $\{j_1, \ldots, j_m\}$, we have for the joint default probability

$$P\left(Y_{j_1} = 1, \ldots, Y_{j_m} = 1\right)$$

$$= P\left(S_{j_1} \leq D_{j_1}, \ldots, S_{j_m} \leq D_{j_m}\right)$$

$$= C_{j_1, \ldots, j_m}\left\{F_{j_1}(D_{j_1}), \ldots, F_{j_m}(D_{j_m})\right\},$$

where we denote by $C_{j_1, \ldots, j_m}$ the m-dimensional margin of C. In particular, the joint default probability of two obligors is now

$$\pi_{ij} = C_{i,j}\left\{F_i(D_i), F_j(D_j)\right\}.$$

To study the effect of different copulae on default correlation, we use the following examples of copulae (further details on these copulae can be found in Embrechts, Lindskog and McNeil (2001)).

1. Gaussian copula:

$$C_R^{Gauss}(u) = \Phi_R^n(\Phi^{-1}(u_1), \ldots, \Phi^{-1}(u_n)).$$

Here Φ_R^n denotes the joint distribution function of the n-variate normal with linear correlation matrix R, and Φ^{-1} the inverse of the distribution function of the univariate standard normal.

2. t-copula:

$$C_{\nu,R}^t(u) = t_{\nu,R}^n(t_\nu^{-1}(u_1), \ldots, t_\nu^{-1}(u_n)),$$

where $t_{\nu,R}^n$ denotes the distribution function of an n-variate t-distributed random vector with parameter $\nu > 2$ and linear correlation matrix R. Furthermore, t_ν is the univariate t-distribution function with parameter ν.

3. Gumbel copula:

$$C_\theta^{Gumbel}(u) = \exp\left\{-[(-\log u_1)^\theta + \ldots + (-\log u_n)^\theta]^{1/\theta}\right\},$$

where $\theta \in [1,\infty)$. This class of copulae is a sub-class of the class of Archimedean copulae. Furthermore, Gumbel copulae have applications in multivariate extreme-value theory.

In Table 5.2 joint default probabilities of two obligors are reported using three types of obligors with individual default probabilities roughly corresponding to rating classes A,B,C. We assume that underlying variables S are univariate normally distributed and model the joint dependence structure using the above copulae.

Copula	Default probability		
	class A ($\times 10^{-6}$)	class B ($\times 10^{-4}$)	class C ($\times 10^{-4}$)
Gaussian	6.89	3.38	52.45
C_{10}^t	46.55	7.88	71.03
C_4^t	134.80	15.35	97.96
Gumbel, C_2	57.20	14.84	144.56
Gumbel, C_4	270.60	41.84	283.67

Table 5.2. Copulae and default probabilities

The computation shows that t and Gumbel copulae have higher joint default probabilities than the Gaussian copula (with obvious implication for default correlation, see equation (5.2)). To explain the reason for this we need the concept of tail dependence:

DEFINITION 5.1 *Let X and Y be continuous random variables with distribution functions F and G. The coefficient of upper tail dependence of X and Y is*

$$\lim_{u \to 1} P[Y > G^{-1}(u)|X > F^{-1}(u)] = \lambda_U \tag{5.3}$$

provided that the limit $\lambda_U \in [0,1]$ exists. If $\lambda_U \in (0,1]$, X and Y are said to be asymptotically dependent in the upper tail; if $\lambda_U = 0$, X and Y are said to be asymptotically independent in the upper tail.

For continuous distributions F and G one can replace (5.3) by a version involving the bivariate copula directly:

$$\lim_{u \to 1} \frac{1 - 2u + C(u,u)}{1 - u} = \lambda_U. \tag{5.4}$$

Lower tail dependence, which is more relevant to our current purpose, is defined in a similar way. Indeed, if

$$\lim_{u \to 0} \frac{C(u,u)}{u} = \lambda_L \tag{5.5}$$

exists, then C exhibits lower tail dependence if $\lambda_L \in (0,1]$, and lower tail independence if $\lambda_L = 0$.

It can be shown that random variables linked by Gaussian copulae have no tail-dependence, while the use of t_ν and the Gumbel copulae results in tail-dependence. In fact, in case of the t_ν copula, we have increasing tail dependence with decreasing parameter ν, while for the Gumbel family tail dependence increases with increasing parameter θ.

5.4   Simulations

The purpose here is to generate portfolios with given marginals (normal) and the above copulae. We focus on the Gaussian and t-copula case.

5.4.1   Random sample generation

For the generation of an n-variate Normal with linear correlation matrix R, $(x_1, \ldots, x_n)^\top \sim N(0, R)$, we apply the quantlet **gennorm**. To obtain realizations from a Gaussian copula we simply have to transform the marginals:

- Set $u_i = \Phi(x_i)$, $i = 1, \ldots, n$.

- $(u_1, \ldots, u_n)^\top \sim C_R^{Gauss}$.

To generate random variates from the t-copula $C_{\nu,R}^t$ we recall that if the random vector X admits the stochastic representation

$$X = \mu + \sqrt{\frac{\nu}{Z}}Y \quad \text{(in distribution)}, \tag{5.6}$$

with $\mu \in \mathbb{R}^n$, $Z \sim \chi_\nu^2$ and $Y \sim \mathrm{N}(0,\Sigma)$, where Z and Y are independent, then X is t_ν distributed with mean μ and covariance matrix $\frac{\nu}{\nu-2}\Sigma$. Here we assume as above, that $\nu > 2$. While the stochastic representation (5.6) is still valid, the interpretation of the parameters has to change for $\nu \leq 2$. Thus, the following algorithm can be used (this is Algorithm 5.2 in Embrechts et al. (2001)):

- Simulate $x = (x_1,\ldots,x_n)^\top \sim \mathrm{N}(0,R)$ using `gennorm`.

- Simulate a random variate z from χ_ν^2 independent of $y_1,\ldots,y_n$.

- Set $x = \sqrt{\frac{\nu}{z}}$.

- Set $u_i = t_\nu(x_i),\ \ i = 1,\ldots,n$.

- $(u_1,\ldots,u_n)^\top \sim C_{\nu,R}^t$.

Having obtained the t-copula $C_{\nu,R}^t$, we only need to replace the u_i with $\Phi^{-1}(u_i)$ in order to have a multivariate distribution with t-copula and normal marginals.

The implementation of these algorithms in XploRe is very straightforward. Indeed, using the quantlet `normal` we can generate normally distributed random variables. Naturally all the distribution functions needed are also implemented, `cdfn`, `cdft` etc.

5.4.2 Portfolio results

We simulate standard portfolios of size 500 with all obligors belonging to one rating class. We use three rating classes, named A,B,C with default probabilities $0.005, 0.05, 0.15$ roughly corresponding to default probabilities from standard rating classes, Ong (1999), p. 77.

For our first simulation exercise we assume that the underlying variables S_j are normally distributed within a single factor framework, i.e. $p = 1$ in (5.1). The factor loadings a_{j1} in (5.1) are constant and chosen so that the correlation for the underlying latent variables S_j is $\rho = 0.2$, which is a standard baseline value for credit portfolio simulations, Kiesel et al. (1999). To generate different degrees of tail correlation, we link the individual assets together using a Gaussian, a t_{10} and a t_4-copula as implemented in VaRcredN and VaRcredTcop.

```
out = VaRcredN (d, p, rho, opt)
    simulates the default distribution for a portfolio of d homogeneous
    obligors assuming a Gaussian copula.

out = VaRcredTcop (d, p, rho, df, opt)
    simulates the default distribution for a portfolio of d homogeneous
    obligors assuming a t-copula with df degrees of freedom.
```

The default driver S_j are normal for all obligors j in both quantlets. p denotes the default probability π_j of an individual obligor and rho is the asset correlation ρ. opt is an optional list parameter consisting of opt.alpha, the significance level for VaR estimation and opt.nsimu, the number of simulations. Both quantlets return a list containing the mean, the variance and the opt.alpha-quantile of the portfolio default distribution.

		VaR	
Portfolio	Copula	$\alpha = 0.95$	$\alpha = 0.99$
A	Normal	10	22
	t_{10}	14	49
	t_4	10	71
B	Normal	77	119
	t_{10}	95	178
	t_4	121	219
C	Normal	182	240
	t_{10}	198	268
	t_4	223	306

Table 5.3. Effect of different copulae **Q** XFGSCP02.xpl

The most striking observation from Table 5.3 is the effect tail-dependence has on the high quantiles of highly-rated portfolios: the 99%-quantile for the t_4-copula is more than 3-times larger than the corresponding quantile for the Gaussian copula. The same effect can be observed for lower rated portfolios although not quite with a similar magnitude.

To assess the effects of increased correlation within parts of the portfolio, we change the factor loading within parts of our portfolio. We assume a second factor, i.e. $p = 2$ in (5.1), for a sub-portfolio of 100 obligors increasing the correlation of the latent variables S_j within the sub-portfolio to 0.5. In the simulation below, the quantlets VaRcredN2 and VaRcredTcop2 are used.

---

out = VaRcredN2 (d1, d2, p, rho1, rho2, opt)
    simulates the default distribution for a portfolio consisting of two homogeneous subportfolios using a Gaussian copula.

out = VaRcredTcop2 (d1, d2, p, rho1, rho2, df, opt)
    simulates the default distribution for a portfolio consisting of two homogeneous subportfolios using a *t*-copula with df degrees of freedom.

The number of obligors in the first (second) subportfolio is d1 (d2). rho1 (rho2) is the asset correlation generated by the first (second) factor. The other parameters correspond to the parameters in VaRcredN and VaRcredTcop.

Such a correlation cluster might be generated by a sector or regional exposure for a real portfolio. Again, degrees of tail correlation are generated by using a Gaussian, a t_{10} and a t_4-copula. As expected the results in Table 5.4 show a slight increase in the quantiles due to the increased correlation within the portfolio. However, comparing the two tables we see that the sensitivity of the portfolio loss quantiles is far higher with regard to the underlying copula – and its corresponding tail dependence – than to the correlation within the portfolio.

Our simulation results indicate that the degree of tail dependence of the underlying copula plays a major role as a credit risk characteristicum. Thus, while analysis of the driving factors for the underlying variables (obligor equity, macroeconomic variables, ..) remains an important aspect in modelling credit risky portfolio, the copula linking the underlying variables together is of crucial importance especially for portfolios of highly rated obligors.

| | | VaR | |
Portfolio	Copula	$\alpha = 0.95$	$\alpha = 0.99$
A	Normal	10	61
	t_{10}	9	61
	t_4	5	60
B	Normal	161	318
	t_{10}	157	344
	t_4	176	360
C	Normal	338	421
	t_{10}	342	426
	t_4	350	432

Table 5.4. Effect of correlation cluster **Q** XFGSCP03.xpl

Bibliography

BIS (2001). Overview of the new Basel capital accord, *Technical report*, Basel Committee on Banking Supervision.

Caouette, J., Altman, E. and Narayanan, P. (1998). *Managing Credit Risk, The Next Great Financial Challenge, Wiley Frontiers in Finance*, Vol. Wiley Frontiers in Finance, Wiley & Sons, Inc, New York.

Carey, M. (1998). Credit risk in private debt portfolios, *Journal of Finance* **53**(4): 1363–1387.

Carey, M. (2000). Dimensions of credit risk and their relationship to economic capital requirements. Preprint, Federal Reserve Board.

Crouhy, M., Galai, D. and Mark, R. (2000). A comparative analysis of current credit risk models, *Journal of Banking and Finance* **24**(1-2): 59–117.

Crouhy, M., Galai, D. and Mark, R. (2001). *Risk management*, McGraw Hill.

Embrechts, P., Lindskog, F. and McNeil, A. (2001). Modelling dependence with copulas and applications to risk management. Working paper, ETH Zürich.

Frey, R. and McNeil, A. (2001). Modelling dependent defaults. Working paper, ETH Zürich.

Gordy, M. (2000). A comparative anatomy of credit risk models, *Journal of Banking and Finance* **24**: 119–149.

Hirtle, B., Levonian, M., Saidenberg, M., Walter, S. and Wright, D. (2001). Using credit risk models for regulartory capital: Issues and options, *FRBNY Economic Policy Review* **6**(2): 1–18.

Jorion, P. (2000). *Value at Risk*, 2nd. edn, McGraw-Hill, New York.

JP Morgan (1997). *Creditmetrics-Technical Document*, JP Morgan, New York.

Kiesel, R., Perraudin, W. and Taylor, A. (1999). The structure of credit risk. Preprint, Birkbeck College.

Koyluoglu, H. and Hickmann, A. (1998). A generalized framework for credit portfolio models. Working Paper, Oliver, Wyman & Company.

Nickell, P., Perraudin, W. and Varotto, S. (1998). Ratings-versus equity-based credit risk models: An empirical investigation. unpublished Bank of England mimeo.

Ong, M. (1999). *Internal Credit Risk Models. Capital Allocation and Performance Measurement*, Risk Books, London.

Part III

Implied Volatility

6 The Analysis of Implied Volatilities

Matthias R. Fengler, Wolfgang Härdle and Peter Schmidt

The analysis of volatility in financial markets has become a first rank issue in modern financial theory and practice: Whether in risk management, portfolio hedging, or option pricing, we need to have a precise notion of the market's expectation of volatility. Much research has been done on the analysis of realized historic volatilities, Roll (1977) and references therein. However, since it seems unsettling to draw conclusions from past to expected market behavior, the focus shifted to implied volatilities, Dumas, Fleming and Whaley (1998). To derive implied volatilities the Black and Scholes (BS) formula is solved for the constant volatility parameter σ using observed option prices. This is a more natural approach as the option value is decisively determined by the market's assessment of current and future volatility. Hence implied volatility may be used as an indicator for market expectations over the remaining lifetime of the option.

It is well known that the volatilities implied by observed market prices exhibit a pattern that is far different from the flat constant one used in the BS formula. Instead of finding a constant volatility across strikes, implied volatility appears to be non flat, a stylized fact which has been called "smile" effect. In this chapter we illustrate how implied volatilites can be analyzed. We focus first on a static and visual investigation of implied volatilities, then we concentrate on a dynamic analysis with two variants of principal components and interpret the results in the context of risk management.

6.1   Introduction

Implied volatilities are the focus of interest both in volatility trading and in risk management. As common practice traders directly trade the so called "vega", i.e. the sensitivity of their portfolios with respect to volatility changes. In order to establish vega trades market professionals use delta-gamma neutral hedging strategies which are insensitive to changes in the underlying and to time decay, Taleb (1997). To accomplish this, traders depend on reliable estimates of implied volatilities and - most importantly - their dynamics.

One of the key issues in option risk management is the measurement of the inherent volatility risk, the so called "vega" exposure. Analytically, the "vega" is the first derivative of the BS formula with respect to the volatility parameter σ, and can be interpreted as a sensitivity of the option value with respect to changes in (implied) volatility. When considering portfolios composed out of a large number of different options, a reduction of the risk factor space can be very useful for assessing the riskiness of the current position. Härdle and Schmidt (2002) outline a procedure for using principal components analysis (PCA) to determine the maximum loss of option portfolios bearing vega exposure. They decompose the term structure of DAX implied volatilities "at the money" (ATM) into orthogonal factors. The maximum loss, which is defined directly in the risk factor space, is then modeled by the first two factors.

Our study on DAX options is organized as follows: First, we show how to derive and to estimate implied volatilities and the implied volatility surface. A data decription follows. In section 6.3.2, we perfom a standard PCA on the covariance matrix of VDAX returns to identify the dominant factor components driving term structure movements of ATM DAX options. Section 6.3.3 introduces a common principal components approach that enables us to model not only ATM term structure movements of implied volatilities but the dynamics of the "smile" as well.

6.2   The Implied Volatility Surface

6.2.1   Calculating the Implied Volatility

The BS formula for the price C_t of a European call at time t is given by

$$C_t = S_t \Phi(d_1) - Ke^{-r\tau} \Phi(d_2), \tag{6.1}$$

$$d_1 = \frac{\ln(S_t/K) + (r + \frac{1}{2}\sigma^2)\tau}{\sigma\sqrt{\tau}}, \tag{6.2}$$

$$d_2 = d_1 - \sigma\sqrt{\tau}, \tag{6.3}$$

where Φ denotes the cumulative distribution function of a standard normal random variable. r denotes the risk-free interest rate, S the price of the underlying, $\tau = T - t$ the time to maturity and K the strike price. For ATM options the equality $K = S_t$ holds.

The only parameter in the Black and Scholes formula that cannot be observed directly is the actual volatility of the underlying price process. However, we may study the volatility which is implied by option prices observed in the markets, the so called implied volatility: implied volatility is defined as the parameter $\hat{\sigma}$ that yields the actually observed market price of a particular option when substituted into the BS formula. The implied volatility of a European put with the same strike and maturity can be deduced from the "put-call parity"

$$C_t - P_t = S_t - Ke^{-r\tau}.$$

XploRe offers a fast and convenient numerical way to invert the BS formula in order to recover $\hat{\sigma}$ from the market prices of C_t or P_t.

```
y = ImplVola(x{, IVmethod})
      calculates implied volatilities.
```

As numerical procedures both a bisectional method and a Newton-Raphson algorithm are available. They are selected by the option IVmethod, which can either be the bisection method IVmethod="bisect" or the default Newton-Raphson. Within arbitrage bounds on the other input parameters there exists a unique solution, since the BS formula is globally concave in σ. The input vector x contains the data in an $n \times 6$ dimensional matrix, where the first column contains the underlying asset prices S, the second the strikes K, the third the interest rates r [on a yearly basis], the fourth maturities τ [in scale of years], the fifth the observed option prices C_t and P_t. The sixth column contains the type of the option, where 0 abbreviates a put and 1 a call. For example, the command ImplVola(100~120~0.05~0.5~1.94~1) yields the implied volatility of a European call at strike $K = 120$ with maturity τ of half a year, where the interest rate is assumed to be $r = 5\%$, the price of the underlying asset $S = 100$ and the option price $C_t = 1.94$: the result is $\hat{\sigma} = 24.94\%$. One may verify this result by using XploRe:

```
opc = BlackScholes(S, K, r, sigma, tau, task)
```

which calculates European option prices according to the Black and Scholes model, when no dividend is assumed. The first 5 input parameters follow the notation in this paper, and task specifies whether one desires to know a call price, task=1, or a put price, task=0. Indeed, for $\sigma = 24.94\%$ we reproduce the assumed option call price of $C_t = 1.94$.   **Q** XFGiv00.xpl

Now we present a more complex example using option data from the German and Swiss Futures Exchange (EUREX). The data set volsurfdata2 contains the full set of option prices (settlement prices) as observed on January 4th, 1999. The first column contains the settlement price S of the DAX, the second the strike price K of the option, the third the interest rate r, the fourth time to maturity τ, the fifth the option prices C_t or P_t and the last column finally the type of option, either 0, i.e. a put, or 1, i.e. a call. Hence the data set is already in the form as required by the quantlet ImplVola. We may therefore use the following code to calculate the implied volatilities:

```
library ("finance")
x=read("volsurfdata2.dat")        ; read the data
x=paf(x,x[,4]>0.14&&x[,4]<0.22)   ; select 2 months maturity
y=ImplVola(x,"bisect")            ; calculate ImplVola
sort(x[,2]~y)                     ; sort data according to strikes
```

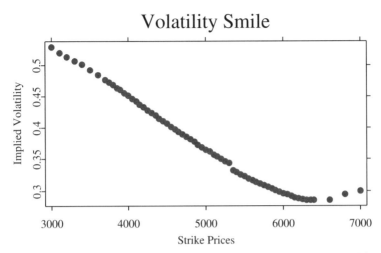

Figure 6.1. Implied volatility "smile" as observed on January 4th, 1999

Q XFGiv01.xpl

In Figure 6.1 we display the output for the strike dimension. The deviation from the BS model is clearly visible: implied volatilities form a convex "smile" in strikes. One finds a curved shape also across different maturities. In combination with the strike dimension this yields a surface with pronounced curvature (Figure 6.2). The discontinuity of the ATM position is related to tax effects exerting different influences on puts and calls, Hafner and Wallmeier (2001). In our case this effect is not so important, since we smooth the observations and calculate the returns of the implied volatility time series before applying the PCA.

6.2.2 Surface smoothing

Calculation of implied volatilities at different strikes *and* maturities yields a surface. The quantlet `volsurf` estimates the implied volatility surface on a specified grid using a bi-dimensional kernel smoothing procedure. A Nadaraya-Watson estimator with a quartic kernel is employed, Aït-Sahalia, and Lo (1998), Aït-Sahalia and Lo (2000), Härdle (1990), Härdle, Müller, Sperlich, and Werwatz (2002).

More technically, given a partition of explanatory variables $(x_1, x_2) = (K, \tau)$, i.e. of strikes and maturities, the two-dimensional Nadaraya-Watson kernel estimator is

$$\hat{\sigma}(x_1, x_2) = \frac{\sum_{i=1}^{n} K_1\left(\frac{x_1 - x_{1i}}{h_1}\right) K_2\left(\frac{x_2 - x_{2i}}{h_2}\right) \hat{\sigma}_i}{\sum_{i=1}^{n} K_1\left(\frac{x_1 - x_{1i}}{h_1}\right) K_2\left(\frac{x_2 - x_{2i}}{h_2}\right)}, \quad (6.4)$$

where $\hat{\sigma}_i$ is the volatility implied by the observed option prices C_{ti} or P_{ti}. K_1 and K_2 are univariate kernel functions, and h_1 and h_2 are bandwidths. The order 2 quartic kernel is given by

$$K_i(u) = \frac{15}{16} \left(1 - u^2\right)^2 \mathbf{1}(|u| \leq 1).$$

The basic structure of `volsurf` is given by

```
{IVsurf, IVpoints} = volsurf(x, stepwidth, firstXF,
     lastXF, firstMat, lastMat, metric, bandwidth, p,
     {IVmethod})
```

As input parameters we first have the $n \times 6$ matrix **x** which has been explained in section 6.2.1. The remaining parameters concern the surface: `stepwidth` is a 2×1 vector determining the stepwidth in the grid of the surface; the first entry relates to the strike dimension, the second to the dimension across time to maturity. `firstXF, lastXF, firstMat, lastMat` are scalar constants giving the lowest limit and the highest limit in the strike dimension, and the lowest and the highest limit of time to maturity in the volatility surface. The option `metric` gives the choice whether to compute the surface in a moneyness or in a strike metric. Setting `metric = 0` will generate a surface computed in a moneyness metric K/F, i.e. strike divided by the (implied) forward price of the underlying, where the forward price is computed by $F_t = S_t e^{r\tau}$. If `metric = 1`, the surface is computed in the original strike dimension in terms of K. `bandwidth` is a 2×1 vector determining the width of the bins for the kernel estimator. `p` determines whether for computation a simple Nadaraya-Watson estimator, `p = 0`, or a local polynomial regression, `p` $\neq$ `0`, is used. The last and optional parameter `IVmethod` has the same meaning as in the

ImplVola quantlet. It tells XploRe which method to use for calculating the implied volatilities, default again is Newton-Raphson.

The output are two variables.   IVsurf is an $N \times 3$ matrix containing the coordinates of the points computed for the implied volatility surface, where the first column contains the values of the strike dimension, the second those of time to maturity, the third estimated implied volatilities. N is the number of grid points. IVpoints is a $M \times 3$ matrix containing the coordinates of the M options used to estimate the surface. As before, the first column contains the values for the strike dimension, the second the maturity, the third the implied volatilities.

Before presenting an example we briefly introduce a graphical tool for display-ing the volatility surface. The following quantlet plots the implied surface:

```
volsurfplot(IVsurf, IVpoints, {AdjustToSurface})
```

As input parameters we have the output of volsurf, i.e. the volatility sur-face IVsurf, and the original observations IVpoints. An optional parame-ter AdjustToSurface determines whether the surface plot is shown based on the surface data given in IVsurf, or on the basis of the original observations IVpoints. This option might be useful in a situation where one has estimated a smaller part of the surface than would be possible given the data. By default, or AdjustToSurface = 1, the graph is adjusted according to the estimated surface.

Q XFGiv02.xpl

Q XFGiv02.xpl computes an implied volatility surface with the Nadaraya-Watson estimator and displays it (Figure 6.2). The parameters are determined in order to suit the example best, then volsurfplot is used to create the graphic. The output matrix IVsurf contains now all surface values on a grid at the given stepwidth. Doing this for a sequential number of dates produces a *time series* $\{\hat{\sigma}_t\}$ of implied volatility surfaces. Empirical evidence shows that this surface changes its shape and characteristics as time goes on. This is what we analyze in the subsequent sections.

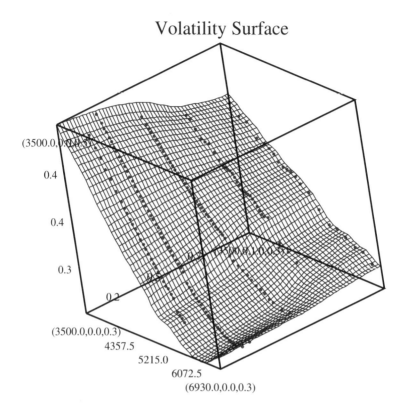

Figure 6.2. Implied volatility surface as observed on January 4th, 1999

Q XFGiv02.xpl

6.3   Dynamic Analysis

6.3.1   Data description

Options on the DAX are the most actively traded contracts at the derivatives exchange EUREX. Contracts of various strikes and maturities constitute a liquid market at any specific time. This liquidity yields a rich basket of implied volatilities for many pairs (K, τ). One subject of our research concerning the dynamics of term structure movements is implied volatility as measured by the German VDAX subindices available from Deutsche Börse AG (http://deutsche-boerse.com/)

These indices, representing different option maturities, measure volatility implied in ATM European calls and puts. The VDAX calculations are based on the BS formula. For a detailed discussion on VDAX calculations we refer to Redelberger (1994). Term structures for ATM DAX options can be derived from VDAX subindices for any given trading day since 18 March 1996. On that day, EUREX started trading in long term options. Shapes of the term structure on subsequent trading days are shown in Figure 6.3.

If we compare the volatility structure of 27 October 1997 (blue line) with that of 28 October 1997 (green line), we easily recognize an overnight upward shift in the levels of implied volatilities. Moreover, it displays an inversion as short term volatilities are higher than long term ones. Only a couple of weeks later, on 17 November (cyan line) and 20 November (red line), the term structure had normalized at lower levels and showed its typical shape again. Evidently, during the market tumble in fall 1997, the ATM term structure shifted and changed its shape considerably over time.

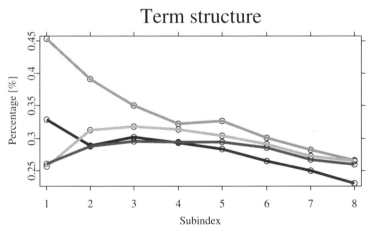

Figure 6.3. Term Structure of VDAX Subindices

XFGiv03.xpl

As an option approaches its expiry date T, time to maturity $\tau = T - t$ is declining with each trading day. Hence, in order to analyze the dynamic structure of implied volatility surfaces, we need to calibrate τ as time t passes. To accomplish this calibration we linearly interpolate between neighboring VDAX subindices. For example, to recover the implied volatility $\hat{\sigma}$ at a fixed τ, we use the subindices at τ_- and τ_+ where $\tau_- \leq \tau \leq \tau_+$, i.e. we compute $\hat{\sigma}_t(\tau)$ with fixed maturities of $\tau \in \{30, 60, 90, 180, 270, 360, 540, 720\}$ calendar days by

$$\hat{\sigma}_t(\tau) = \hat{\sigma}_t(\tau_-)\left[1 - \frac{\tau - \tau_-}{\tau_+ - \tau_-}\right] + \hat{\sigma}_t(\tau_+)\left[\frac{\tau - \tau_-}{\tau_+ - \tau_-}\right] \tag{6.5}$$

Proceeding this way we obtain 8 time series of fixed maturity. Each time series is a weighted average of two neighboring maturities and contains $n = 440$ data points of implied volatilities.

6.3.2   PCA of ATM Implied Volatilities

The data set for the analysis of variations of implied volatilities is a collection of term structures as given in Figure 6.3. In order to identify common factors we use Principal Components Analysis (PCA). Changes in the term structure can be decomposed by PCA into a set of orthogonal factors.

Define $X_c = (x_{tj})$ as the $T \times J$ matrix of centered first differences of ATM implied volatilities for subindex $j = 1, ..., J$ in time $t = 1, ..., T$, where in our case $J = 8$ and $T = 440$. The sample covariance matrix $S = T^{-1}X_c^\top X_c$ can be decomposed by the spectral decomposition into

$$S = \Gamma \Lambda \Gamma^\top, \tag{6.6}$$

where Γ is the 8×8 matrix of eigenvectors and Λ the 8×8 diagonal matrix of eigenvalues λ_j of S. Time series of principal components are obtained by $Y = X_c \Gamma$.

A measure of how well the PCs explain variation of the underlying data is given by the relative proportion ζ_l of the sum of the first l eigenvalues to the overall sum of eigenvalues:

$$\zeta_l = \frac{\sum_{j=1}^{l} \lambda_j}{\sum_{j=1}^{8} \lambda_j} = \frac{\sum_{j=1}^{l} Var(y_j)}{\sum_{j=1}^{8} Var(y_j)} \qquad \text{for} \qquad l < 8 \tag{6.7}$$

The quantlet **Q** XFGiv04.xpl uses the VDAX data to estimate the proportion of variance ζ_l explained by the first l PCs.

Q XFGiv04.xpl

As the result shows the first PC captures around 70% of the total data variability. The second PC captures an additional 13%. The third PC explains a considerably smaller amount of total variation. Thus, the two dominant PCs together explain around 83% of the total variance in implied ATM volatilities for DAX options. Taking only the first two factors, i.e. those capturing around 83% in the data, the time series of implied ATM volatilities can therefore be represented by a factor model of reduced dimension:

$$x_{tj} = \gamma_{j1} y_{t1} + \gamma_{j2} y_{t2} + \epsilon_t, \tag{6.8}$$

where γ_{jk} denotes the jkth element of $\Gamma = (\gamma_{jk})$, y_{tk} is taken from the matrix of principal components Y, and ϵ_t denotes white noise. The γ_j are in fact the sensitivities of the implied volatility time series to shocks on the principal components. As is evident from Figure 6.4, a shock on the first factor tends to affect all maturities in a similar manner, causing a non-parallel shift of the term structure. A shock in the second factor has a strong negative impact on the front maturity but a positive impact on the longer ones, thus causing a change of curvature in the term structure of implied volatilities.

6.3.3 Common PCA of the Implied Volatility Surface

Implied volatilities calculated for different strikes and maturities constitute a surface. The principle component analysis as outlined above, does not take this structure into account, since only one slice of the surface, the term structure of ATM options are used. In this section we present a technique that allows us to analyze several slices of the surface *simultaneously*. Since options naturally fall into maturity groups, one could analyze several slices of the surface taken at different maturities. What we propose to do is a principal component analysis of these different groups. Enlarging the basis of analysis will lead to a better understanding of the dynamics of the surface. Moreover, from a statistical point of view, estimating PCs simultaneously in different groups will result in a joint dimension reducing transformation. This multi-group PCA, the so called common principle components analysis (CPCA), yields the joint eigenstructure across groups.

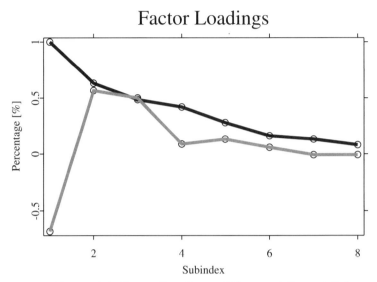

Figure 6.4. Factor Loadings of First and Second PC

⌕ XFGiv05.xpl

In addition to traditional PCA, the basic assumption of CPCA is that the space spanned by the eigenvectors is identical *across* several groups, whereas variances associated with the components are allowed to vary. This approach permits us to analyze a p variate random vector in k groups, say k maturities of implied volatilities jointly, Fengler, Härdle and Villa (2001).

More formally, the hypothesis of common principle components can be stated in the following way, Flury (1988):

$$H_{CPC} : \Psi_i = \Gamma \Lambda_i \Gamma^\top, \qquad i = 1, ..., k$$

where the Ψ_i are positive definite $p \times p$ population covariance matrices, $\Gamma = (\gamma_1, ..., \gamma_p)$ is an orthogonal $p \times p$ transformation matrix and $\Lambda_i = \mathrm{diag}(\lambda_{i1}, ..., \lambda_{ip})$ is the matrix of eigenvalues. Moreover, assume that all λ_i are distinct.

Let S be the (unbiased) sample covariance matrix of an underlying p-variate normal distribution $N_p(\mu, \Psi)$ with sample size n. Then the distribution of nS is Wishart, Muirhead (1982), p. 86, with $n-1$ degrees of freedom:

$$nS \sim \mathcal{W}_p(\Psi, n-1)$$

The density of the Wishart distribution is given by

$$f(S) \quad = \quad \frac{1}{\Gamma_p(\frac{n-1}{2})|\Psi|^{(n-1)/2}} \left(\frac{n-1}{2}\right)^{\frac{p(n-1)}{2}}$$
$$\exp\left\{\operatorname{tr}\left(-\frac{n-1}{2}\Psi^{-1}S\right)\right\}|S|^{(n-p-2)/2}, \qquad (6.9)$$

where

$$\Gamma_p(x) = \pi^{p(p-1)/4} \prod_{i=1}^{p} \Gamma\left\{x - \frac{1}{2}(i-1)\right\}$$

is the multivariate gamma function, Muirhead (1982). Hence for given Wishart matrices S_i with sample size n_i the likelihood function can be written as

$$L(\Psi_1, ..., \Psi_k) = C\prod_{i=1}^{k}\exp\left\{\operatorname{tr}\left(-\frac{1}{2}(n_i-1)\Psi_i^{-1}S_i\right)\right\}|\Psi_i|^{-\frac{1}{2}(n_i-1)} \qquad (6.10)$$

where C is a constant not depending on the parameters Ψ_i. Maximizing the likelihood is equivalent to minimizing the function

$$g(\Psi_1, ..., \Psi_k) = \sum_{i=1}^{k}(n_i-1)\left\{\ln|\Psi_i| + \operatorname{tr}(\Psi_i^{-1}S_i)\right\}.$$

Assuming that H_{CPC} holds, i.e. in replacing Ψ_i by $\Gamma\Lambda_i\Gamma^\top$, one gets after some manipulations

$$g(\Gamma, \Lambda_1, ..., \Lambda_k) = \sum_{i=1}^{k}(n_i-1)\sum_{j=1}^{p}\left(\ln\lambda_{ij} + \frac{\gamma_j^\top S_i\gamma_j}{\lambda_{ij}}\right).$$

As we know from section 6.3.2, the vectors γ_j in Γ need to be orthogonal. We achieve orthogonality of the vectors γ_j via the Lagrange method, i.e. we impose the p constraints $\gamma_j^\top \gamma_j = 1$ using the Lagrange multiplyers μ_j, and the remaining $p(p-1)/2$ constraints $\gamma_h^\top \gamma_j = 0$ for $(h \neq j)$ using the multiplyer μ_{hj}. This yields

$$g^*(\Gamma, \Lambda_1, ..., \Lambda_k) = g(\cdot) - \sum_{j=1}^{p} \mu_j(\gamma_j^\top \gamma_j - 1) - 2 \sum_{h<j}^{p} \mu_{hj}\gamma_h^\top \gamma_j.$$

Taking partial derivatives with respect to all λ_{im} and γ_m, it can be shown (Flury, 1988) that the solution of the CPC model is given by the generalized system of characteristic equations

$$\gamma_m^\top \left(\sum_{i=1}^{k}(n_i - 1)\frac{\lambda_{im} - \lambda_{ij}}{\lambda_{im}\lambda_{ij}}S_i \right) \gamma_j = 0, \qquad m, j = 1, ..., p, \quad m \neq j. \quad (6.11)$$

This has to be solved using

$$\lambda_{im} = \gamma_m^\top S\gamma_m, \qquad i = 1, ..., k, \quad m = 1, ..., p$$

under the constraints

$$\gamma_m^\top \gamma_J = \begin{cases} 0 & m \neq j \\ 1 & m = j \end{cases}.$$

Flury (1988) proves existence and uniqueness of the maximum of the likelihood function, and Flury and Gautschi (1988) provide a numerical algorithm, which has been implemented in the quantlet CPC.

CPC-Analysis

A number of quantlets are designed for an analysis of covariance matrices, amongst them the CPC quantlet:

```
{B, betaerror, lambda, lambdaerror, psi} = CPC(A,N)
       estimates a common principle components model.
```

As input variables we need a $p \times p \times k$ array A, produced from k $p \times p$ co-variance matrices, and a $k \times 1$ vector of weights N. Weights are the number of observations in each of the k groups.

The quantlet produces the $p \times p$ common transformation matrix B, and the $p \times p$ matrix of asymptotic standard errors betaerror. Next, eigenvalues lambda and corresponding standard errors lamdbaerror are given in a vector array of $1 \times p \times k$. Estimated population covariances psi are also provided. As an example we provide the data sets volsurf01, volsurf02 and volsurf03 that have been used in Fengler, Härdle and Villa (2001) to estimate common principle components for the implied volatility surfaces of the DAX 1999. The data has been generated by smoothing a surface day by day as spelled out in section 6.2.2 on a specified grid. Next, the estimated grid points have been grouped into maturities of $\tau = 1$, $\tau = 2$ and $\tau = 3$ months and transformed into a vector of time series of the "smile", i.e. each element of the vector belongs to a distinct moneyness ranging from 0.85 to 1.10.

Q XFGiv06.xpl

We plot the first three eigenvectors in a parallel coordinate plot in Figure 6.5. The basic structure of the first three eigenvectors is not altered. We find a shift, a slope and a twist structure. This structure is *common* to all maturity groups, i.e. when exploiting PCA as a dimension reducing tool, the same transformation applies to each group! However, from comparing the size of eigenvalues among groups, i.e. ZZ.lambda, we find that variability is dropping across groups as we move from the front contracts to long term contracts.

Before drawing conclusions we should convince ourselves that the CPC model is truly a good description of the data. This can be done by using a likelihood ratio test. The likelihood ratio statistic for comparing a restricted (the CPC) model against the unrestricted model (the model where all covariances are treated separately) is given by

$$T_{(n_1,n_2,...,n_k)} = -2 \ln \frac{L(\widehat{\Psi}_1, ..., \widehat{\Psi}_k)}{L(S_1, ..., S_k)}.$$

Inserting from the likelihood function we find that this is equivalent to

$$T_{(n_1,n_2,...,n_k)} = \sum_{i=1}^{k} (n_i - 1) \frac{\det \widehat{\Psi}_i}{\det S_i},$$

Common Coordinate Plot: First three Eigenvectors

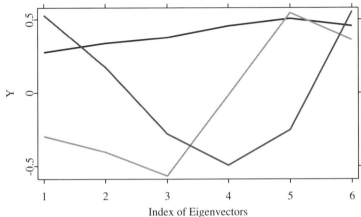

Figure 6.5. Factor loadings of the first (blue), the second (green), and the third PC (red)

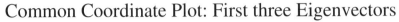 XFGiv06.xpl

which is χ^2 distributed as $\min(n_i)$ tends to infinity with

$$k\left\{\frac{1}{2}p(p-1)+1\right\} - \left\{\frac{1}{2}p(p-1)+kp\right\} = \frac{1}{2}(k-1)p(p-1)$$

degrees of freedom. In the quantlet **Q** XFGiv06.xpl this test is included.

Q XFGiv06.xpl

The calculations yield $T_{(n_1,n_2,...,n_k)} = 31.836$, which corresponds to the p-value $p = 0.37512$ for the $\chi^2(30)$ distribution. Hence we cannot reject the CPC model against the unrelated model, where PCA is applied to each maturity separately.

Using the methods in section 6.3.2, we can estimate the amount of variability ζ_l explained by the first l principle components: again a few number of factors, up to three at the most, is capable of capturing a large amount of total variability present in the data. Since the model now captures variability both in strike *and* maturity dimension, this can be a suitable starting point for a simplified

VaR calculation for delta-gamma neutral option portfolios using Monte Carlo methods, and is hence a valuable insight for risk management.

Bibliography

Aït-Sahalia, Y. and Lo, A. W. (1998). Nonparametric Estimation of State-Price Densities Implicit in Financial Assets, *Journal of Finance* Vol. LIII, 2, pp. 499–547.

Aït-Sahalia, Y. and Lo, A. W. (2000). Nonparametric Risk management and implied risk aversion, *Journal of Econometrics* **94**, pp. 9–51.

Dumas, B., Fleming, J. and Whaley, R. E. (1998). Implied Volatility Functions: Empirical Tests, *Journal of Finance* Vol. LIII, 6, pp. 2059–2106.

Fengler, M. R., Härdle, W. and Villa, Chr. (2001). *The Dynamics of Implied Volatilities: A Common Principal Components Approach*, SfB 373 Discussion Paper No. 2001/38, HU Berlin.

Flury, B. (1988). *Common Principle Components Analysis and Related Multivariate Models*, Wiley Series in Probability and Mathematical Statistics, John Wiley & Sons, New York.

Flury, B. and Gautschi, W. (1986). An Algorithm for simultaneous orthogonal transformation of several positive definite symmetric matrices to nearly diagonal form *SIAM Journal on Scientific and Statistical Computing*,**7**, pp. 169–184.

Härdle, W.(1990). *Applied Nonparametric Regression*, Econometric Society Monographs **19**, Cambridge University Press.

Härdle, W., Müller, M., Sperlich, S. and Werwartz, A. (2002). *Non- and Semiparametric Modelling*, Springer, e-book http://www.xplore-stat.de

Härdle, W. and Schmidt, P. (2002). Common Factors Governing VDAX Movements and the Maximum Loss, *Financial Markets and Portfolio Management*, forthcoming.

Hafner, R. and Wallmeier, M. (2001). The Dynamics of DAX Implied Volatilities, *International Quarterly Journal of Finance*,**1**, 1, pp. 1–27.

Muirhead, R. J. (1982). *Aspects of Multivariate Statistics*, Wiley Series in Probability and Mathematical Statistics, John Wiley & Sons, New York.

Redelberger, T. (1994). *Grundlagen und Konstruktion des VDAX-Volatilitäts-index der Deutsche Börse AG*, Deutsche Börse AG, Frankfurt am Main.

Roll, R. (1977). A Critique of the Asset Pricing Theory's Tests: Part I, *Journal of Financial Economics*,**4**, pp. 129–176.

Taleb, N. (1997). *Dynamic Hedging: Managing Vanilla and Exotic Options*, John Wiley & Sons, New York.

Villa, C. and Sylla, A. (2000). *Measuring implied surface risk using PCA* in Franke, J., Härdle, W. and Stahl, G.: *Measuring Risk in Complex Stochastic Systems*, LNS 147, Springer Verlag, New York, pp. 131–147.

7 How Precise Are Price Distributions Predicted by Implied Binomial Trees?

Wolfgang Härdle and Jun Zheng

In recent years, especially after the 1987 market crash, it became clear that the prices of the underlying asset do not exactly follow the Geometric Brownian Motion (GBM) model of Black and Scholes. The GBM model with constant volatility leads to a log-normal price distribution at any expiration date: All options on the underlying must have the same Black-Scholes (BS) implied volatility, and the Cox-Ross-Rubinstein (CRR) binomial tree makes use of this fact via the construction of constant transition probability from one node to the corresponding node at the next level in the tree. In contrast, the implied binomial tree (IBT) method simply constructs a numerical procedure consistent with the volatility smile. The empirical fact that the market implied volatilities decrease with the strike level, and increase with the time to maturity of options is better reflected by this construction. The algorithm of the IBT is a data adaptive modification of the CRR method.

An implied tree should satisfy the following principles:

- It must correctly reproduce the volatility smile.

- negative node transition probabilities are not allowed.

- The branching process must be risk neutral (forward price of the asset equals to the conditional expected value of it) at each step .

The last two conditions also eliminate arbitrage opportunities.

The basic purpose of the IBT is its use in hedging and calculations of implied probability distributions (or state price density (SPD)) and volatility surfaces.

Besides these practical issues, the IBT may evaluate the future stock price distributions according to the BS implied volatility surfaces which are calculated from currently observed daily market option prices.

We describe the construction of the IBT and analyze the precision of the predicted implied price distributions. In Section 7.1, a detailed outline of the IBT algorithm for a liquid European-style option is given. We follow first the Derman and Kani (1994) algorithm, discuss its possible shortcomings, and then present the Barle and Cakici (1998) construction. This method is characterized by a normalization of the central nodes according to the forward price. Next, we study the properties of the IBT via Monte-Carlo simulations and comparison with simulated conditional density from a diffusion process with a non-constant volatility. In Section 7.3, we apply the IBT to a DAX index data set containing the underlying asset price, strike price, interest rate, time to maturity, and call or put option price from the MD*BASE database (included in XploRe), and compare SPD estimated by historical index price data with those predicted by the IBT. Conclusions and discussions on practical issues are presented in the last section.

7.1   Implied Binomial Trees

A well known model for financial option pricing is a GBM with constant volatility, it has a log-normal price distribution with density,

$$
p(S_t, S_T, r, \tau, \sigma) = \frac{1}{S_T \sqrt{2\pi\sigma^2\tau}} \exp\left[-\frac{\left\{ \ln\left(\frac{S_T}{S_t}\right) - (r - \frac{\sigma^2}{2})\tau \right\}^2}{2\sigma^2\tau} \right], \quad (7.1)
$$

at any option expiration T, where S_t is the stock price at time t, r is the riskless interest rate, $\tau = T - t$ is time to maturity, and σ the volatility. The model also has the characteristic that all options on the underlying must have the same BS implied volatility.

However, the market implied volatilities of stock index options often show "the volatility smile", which decreases with the strike level, and increases with the time to maturity τ. There are various proposed extensions of this GBM model to account for "the volatility smile". One approach is to incorporate a stochastic volatility factor, Hull and White (1987); another allows for discontinuous jumps in the stock price, Merton (1976). However, these extensions cause several practical difficulties. For example, they violate the risk-neutral condition.

The IBT technique proposed by Rubinstein (1994), Derman and Kani (1994), Dupire (1994), and Barle and Cakici (1998) account for this phenomenon. These papers assume the stock prices in the future are generated by a modified random walk where the underlying asset has a variable volatility that depends on both stock price and time. Since the implied binomial trees allow for non-constant volatility $\sigma = \sigma(S_t, t)$, they are in fact modifications of the original Cox, Ross and Rubinstein (1979) binomial trees. The IBT construction uses the observable market option prices in order to estimate the implied distribution. It is therefore nonparametric in nature. Alternative approaches may be based on the kernel method, Aït-Sahalia, and Lo (1998), nonparametric constrained least squares, Härdle and Yatchew (2001), and curve-fitting methods, Jackwerth and Rubinstein (1996).

The CRR binomial tree is the discrete implementation of the GBM process

$$\frac{dS_t}{S_t} = \mu dt + \sigma dZ_t, \tag{7.2}$$

where Z_t is a standard Wiener process, and μ and σ are constants. Similarly, the IBT can be viewed as a discretization of the following model in which the generalized volatility parameter is allowed to be a function of time and the underlying price,

$$\frac{dS_t}{S_t} = \mu_t dt + \sigma(S_t, t) dZ_t, \tag{7.3}$$

where $\sigma(S_t, t)$ is the instantaneous local volatility function. The aim of the IBT is to construct a discrete approximation of the model on the basis of the observed option prices yielding the variable volatility $\sigma(S_t, t)$. In addition, the IBT may reflect a non-constant drift μ_t.

7.1.1 The Derman and Kani (D & K) algorithm

In the implied binomial tree framework, stock prices, transition probabilities, and Arrow-Debreu prices (discounted risk-neutral probabilities, see Chapter 8) at each node are calculated iteratively level by level.

Suppose we want to build an IBT on the time interval $[0, T]$ with equally spaced levels, $\triangle t$ apart. At $t = 0, S_0 = S$, is the current price of the underlying, and there are n nodes at the nth level of the tree. Let $s_{n,i}$ be the stock price of the ith node at the nth level, $s_{1,1} = S$ and $F_{n,i} = e^{r \triangle t} s_{n,i}$ the forward price at level $n + 1$ of $s_{n,i}$ at level n, and $p_{n,i}$ the transition probability of making

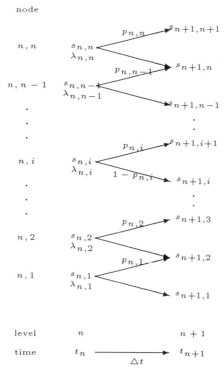

Figure 7.1. Construction of an implied binomial tree

a transition from node (n, i) to node $(n + 1, i + 1)$. Figure 7.1 illustrates the construction of an IBT.

We assume the forward price $F_{n,i}$ satisfies the risk-neutral condition:

$$F_{n,i} = p_{n,i} s_{n+1,i+1} + (1 - p_{n,i}) s_{n+1,i}. \tag{7.4}$$

Thus the transition probability can be obtained from the following equation:

$$p_{n,i} = \frac{F_{n,i} - s_{n+1,i}}{s_{n+1,i+1} - s_{n+1,i}}. \tag{7.5}$$

The Arrow-Debreu price $\lambda_{n,i}$, is the price of an option that pays 1 unit payoff in one and only one state i at nth level, and otherwise pays 0. In general,

Arrow-Debreu prices can be obtained by the iterative formula, where $\lambda_{1,1} = 1$ as a definition.

$$
\begin{cases}
\lambda_{n+1,1} = & e^{-r\triangle t}\left\{(1 - p_{n,1})\lambda_{n,1}\right\}, \\
\lambda_{n+1,i+1} = & e^{-r\triangle t}\left\{\lambda_{n,i}p_{n,i} + \lambda_{n,i+1}(1 - p_{n,i+1})\right\}, \quad 2 \le i \le n, \\
\lambda_{n+1,n+1} = & e^{-r\triangle t}\left\{\lambda_{n,n}p_{n,n}\right\}.
\end{cases}
\tag{7.6}
$$

We give an example to illustrate the calculation of Arrow-Debreu prices in a CRR Binomial tree. Suppose that the current value of the underlying $S = 100$, time to maturity $T = 2$ years, $\triangle t = 1$ year, constant volatility $\sigma = 10\%$, and riskless interest rate $r = 0.03$, and $\tau = T$. The Arrow-Debreu price tree can be calculated from the stock price tree:

```
stock price
                           122.15
               110.52
   100.00                  100.00
               90.48
                           81.88


Arrow-Debreu price

                           0.37
               0.61
   1.00                    0.44
               0.36
                           0.13
```

For example, using the CRR method, $s_{2,1} = s_{1,1}e^{-\sigma\triangle t} = 100 \times e^{-0.1} = 90.48$, and $s_{2,2} = s_{1,1}e^{\sigma\triangle t} = 110.52$, the transition probability $p_{1,1} = 0.61$ is obtained by the formula (7.5), then according to the formula (7.6), $\lambda_{2,1} = e^{-r\triangle t}(1 - p_{1,1}) = 0.36$. At the third level, calculate the stock prices according to the corresponding nodes at the second level, For example, $s_{3,1} = s_{2,1} \cdot e^{-\sigma\triangle t} = 122.15$, $s_{3,2} = s_{1,1} = 100$.

Option prices in the Black-Scholes framework are given by:

$$C(K, \tau) \quad = \quad e^{-r\tau} \int_0^{+\infty} \max(S_T - K, 0) \, p(S_t, S_T, r, \tau) dS_T, \qquad (7.7)$$

$$P(K, \tau) \quad = \quad e^{-r\tau} \int_0^{+\infty} \max(K - S_T, 0) \, p(S_t, S_T, r, \tau) dS_T, \qquad (7.8)$$

where $C(K, \tau)$ and $P(K, \tau)$ are call option price and put option price respectively, and K is the strike price. In the IBT, option prices are calculated analogously for $\tau = n\triangle t$,

$$C(K, n\triangle t) \quad = \quad \sum_{i=1}^{n+1} \lambda_{n+1,i} \max(s_{n+1,i} - K, 0), \qquad (7.9)$$

$$P(K, n\triangle t) \quad = \quad \sum_{i=1}^{n+1} \lambda_{n+1,i} \max(K - s_{n+1,i}, 0). \qquad (7.10)$$

Using the risk-neutral condition (7.4) and the discrete option price calculation from (7.9) or (7.10), one obtains the iteration formulae for constructing the IBT.

There are $(2n + 1)$ parameters which define the transition from the nth to the $(n + 1)$th level of the tree, i.e., $(n + 1)$ stock prices of the nodes at the $(n + 1)$th level, and n transition probabilities. Suppose $(2n - 1)$ parameters corresponding to the nth level are known, the $s_{n+1,i}$ and $p_{n,i}$ corresponding to the $(n + 1)$th level can be calculated depending on the following principles:

We always start from the center nodes in one level, if n is even, define $s_{n+1,i} = s_{1,1} = S$, for $i = n/2 + 1$, and if n is odd, start from the two central nodes $s_{n+1,i}$ and $s_{n+1,i+1}$ for $i = (n + 1)/2$, and suppose $s_{n+1,i} = s_{n,i}^2/s_{n+1,i+1} = S^2/s_{n+1,i+1}$, which adjusts the logarithmic spacing between $s_{n,i}$ and $s_{n+1,i+1}$ to be the same as that between $s_{n,i}$ and $s_{n+1,i}$. This principle yields the calculation formula of $s_{n+1,i+1}$, see Derman and Kani (1994),

$$s_{n+1,i+1} = \frac{S\{e^{r\triangle t}C(S, n\triangle t) + \lambda_{n,i}S - \rho_u\}}{\lambda_{n,i}F_{n,i} - e^{r\triangle t}C(S, n\triangle t) + \rho_u} \quad \text{for} \quad i = (n + 1)/2. \qquad (7.11)$$

Here ρ_u denotes the following summation term

$$\rho_u = \sum_{j=i+1}^{n} \lambda_{n,j}(F_{n,j} - s_{n,i}), \qquad (7.12)$$

$C(K, \tau)$ is the interpolated value for a call struck today at strike price K and time to maturity τ. In the D & K construction, the interpolated option price entering (7.11) is based on a CRR binomial tree with constant parameters $\sigma = \sigma_{imp}(K, \tau)$, where the BS implied volatility $\sigma_{imp}(K, \tau)$ can be calculated from the known market option prices. Calculating interpolated option prices by the CRR method has a drawback, it is computational intensive.

Once we have the initial nodes' stock prices, according to the relationships among the different parameters, we can continue to calculate those at higher nodes $(n + 1, j)$, $j = i + 2, \ldots n + 1$ and transition probabilities one by one using the formula:

$$s_{n+1,i+1} = \frac{s_{n,i}\{e^{r\triangle t}C(s_{n,i}, n\triangle t) - \rho_u\} - \lambda_{n,i}s_{n,i}(F_{n,i} - s_{n+1,i})}{\{e^{r\triangle t}C(s_{n,i}, n\triangle t) - \rho_u\} - \lambda_{n,i}(F_{n,i} - s_{n+1,i})}, \quad (7.13)$$

where the definition of ρ_u is the same as (7.12).

Similarly, we are able to continue to calculate the parameters at lower nodes $(n + 1, j)$, $j = i - 1, \ldots, 1$ according to the following recursion:

$$s_{n+1,i} = \frac{s_{n,i+1}\{e^{r\triangle t}P(s_{n,i}, n\triangle t) - \rho_l\} - \lambda_{n,i}s_{n,i}(F_{n,i} - s_{n+1,i+1})}{\{e^{r\triangle t}P(s_{n,i}, n\triangle t) - \rho_l\} + \lambda_{n,i}(F_{n,i} - s_{n+1,i+1})}, \quad (7.14)$$

where ρ_l denotes the sum $\sum_{j=1}^{i-1} \lambda_{n,j}(s_{n,i} - F_{n,j})$, and $P(K, \tau)$ is similar to $C(K, \tau)$, again these option prices are obtained by the CRR binomial tree generated from market options prices.

7.1.2 Compensation

In order to avoid arbitrage, the transition probability $p_{n,i}$ at any node should lie between 0 and 1, it makes therefore sense to limit the estimated stock prices

$$F_{n,i} < s_{n+1,i+1} < F_{n,i+1}. \quad (7.15)$$

If the stock price at any node does not satisfy the above inequality, we redefine it by assuming that the difference of the logarithm of the stock prices between this node and its adjacent node is equal to the corresponding two nodes at the previous level, i.e.,

$$\log(s_{n+1,i+1}/s_{n+1,i}) = \log(s_{n,i}/s_{n,i-1}).$$

Sometimes, the obtained price still does not satisfy inequality (7.15), then we choose the average of $F_{n,i}$ and $F_{n,i+1}$ as a proxy for $s_{n+1,i+1}$.

In fact, the product of the Arrow-Debreu prices $\lambda_{n,i}$ at the nth level with the influence of interest rate $e^{r(n-1)\triangle t}$ can be considered as a discrete estimation of the implied distribution, the SPD, $p(S_T, S_t, r, \tau)$ at $\tau = (n-1)\triangle t$. In the case of the GBM model with constant volatility, this density is corresponding to (7.1).

After the construction of an IBT, we know all stock prices, transition probabilities, and Arrow-Debreu prices at any node in the tree. We are thus able to calculate the implied local volatility $\sigma_{loc}(s_{n,i}, m\triangle t)$ (which describes the structure of the second moment of the underlying process) at any level m as a discrete estimation of the following conditional variance at $s = s_{n,i}$, $\tau = m\triangle t$. Under the risk-neutral assumption

$$
\begin{aligned}
\sigma_{loc}^2(s, \tau) &= \text{Var}(\log S_{t+\tau}|S_t = s) \\
&= \int (\log S_{t+\tau} - \text{E} \log S_{t+\tau})^2 p(S_{t+\tau}|S_t = s)\, dS_{t+\tau} \\
&= \int (\log S_{t+\tau} - \text{E} \log S_{t+\tau})^2 p(S_t, S_{t+\tau} r, \tau)\, dS_{t+\tau}. \quad (7.16)
\end{aligned}
$$

In the IBT construction, the discrete estimation can be calculated as:

$$
\sigma_{loc}(s_{n,i}, \triangle t) = \sqrt{p_{n,i}(1 - p_{n,i})} \left| \log \frac{s_{n+1,i+1}}{s_{n+1,i}} \right|.
$$

Analogously, we can calculate the implied local volatility at different times. In general, if we have calculated the transition probabilities p_j, $j = 1, \ldots, m$ from the node (n, i) to the nodes $(n + m, i + j)$, $j = i, \ldots, m$, then with

$$
mean = \text{E}(log(S_{(n+m-1)\triangle t})|S_{(n-1)\triangle t} = s_{n,i}) = \sum_{j=1}^m p_j \log(s_{n+m,i+j}),
$$

$$
\sigma_{loc}(s_{n,i}, m\triangle t) = \sqrt{\sum_{j=1}^m p_j\, (\log(s_{n+m,i+j}) - mean))^2}. \quad (7.17)
$$

Notice that the instantaneous volatility function used in (7.3) is different from the BS implied volatility function defined in (7.16), but in the GBM they are identical.

If we choose $\triangle t$ small enough, we obtain the estimated SPD at fixed time to maturity, and the distribution of implied local volatility $\sigma_{loc}(s, \tau)$. Notice that the BS implied volatility $\sigma_{imp}(K, \tau)$ (which assumes Black-Scholes model is established (at least locally)) and implied local volatility $\sigma_{loc}(s, \tau)$ is different, they have different parameters, and describe different characteristics of the second moment.

7.1.3 Barle and Cakici (B & C) algorithm

Barle and Cakici (1998) proposed an improvement of the Derman and Kani construction. The major modification is the choice of the stock price of the central nodes in the tree: their algorithm takes the riskless interest rate into account. If $(n + 1)$ is odd, then $s_{n+1,i} = s_{1,1}e^{r\,n\triangle t} = Se^{r\,n\triangle t}$ for $i = n/2 + 1$, if $(n + 1)$ is even, then start from the two central nodes $s_{n+1,i}$ and $s_{n+1,i+1}$ for $i = (n + 1)/2$, and suppose $s_{n+1,i} = F_{n,i}^2/s_{n+1,i+1}$. Thus $s_{n+1,i}$ can be calculated as:

$$s_{n+1,i} = F_{n,i}\frac{\lambda_{n,i}F_{n,i} - \{e^{r\triangle t}C(F_{n,i}, n\triangle t) - \rho_u\}}{\lambda_{n,i}F_{n,i} + \{e^{r\triangle t}C(F_{n,i}, n\triangle t) - \rho_u\}} \quad \text{for} \quad i = (n + 1)/2, \quad (7.18)$$

where $C(K, \tau)$ is defined as in the Derman and Kani algorithm, and the ρ_u is

$$\rho_u = \sum_{j=i+1}^{n} \lambda_{n,j}(F_{n,j} - F_{n,i}). \tag{7.19}$$

After stock prices of the initial nodes are obtained, then continue to calculate those at higher nodes $(n + 1, j)$, $j = i + 2, \ldots n + 1$ and transition probabilities one by one using the following recursion:

$$s_{n+1,i+1} = \frac{s_{n+1,i}\{e^{r\triangle t}C(F_{n,i}, n\triangle t) - \rho_u\} - \lambda_{n,i}F_{n,i}(F_{n,i} - s_{n+1,i})}{\{e^{r\triangle t}C(F_{n,i}, n\triangle t) - \rho_u\} - \lambda_{n,i}(F_{n,i} - s_{n+1,i})}, \tag{7.20}$$

where ρ_u is as in (7.19), $p_{n,i}$ is defined as in (7.5).

Similarly, continue to calculate the parameters iteratively at lower nodes $(n +$

$1, j)$, $j = i - 1, \ldots 1$.

$$s_{n+1,i} = \frac{\lambda_{n,i} F_{n,i}(s_{n+1,i+1} - F_{n,i}) - s_{n+1,i+1}\{e^{r\triangle t}P(F_{n,i}, n\triangle t) - \rho_l\}}{\lambda_{n,i}(s_{n+1,i+1} - F_{n,i}) - \{e^{r\triangle t}P(F_{n,i}, n\triangle t) - \rho_l\}}, \quad (7.21)$$

where ρ_l denotes the sum $\sum_{j=1}^{i-1} \lambda_{n,j}(F_{n,i} - F_{n,j})$. Notice that in (7.13) and (7.14), $C(K, \tau)$ and $P(K, \tau)$ denote the Black-Scholes call and put option prices, this construction makes the calculation faster than the interpolation technique based on the CRR method.

The balancing inequality (7.15) and a redefinition are still used in the Barle and Cakici algorithm for avoiding arbitrage: the algorithm uses the average of $F_{n,i}$ and $F_{n,i+1}$ as the re-estimation of $s_{n+1,i+1}$.

7.2   A Simulation and a Comparison of the SPDs

The example used here to show the procedure of generating the IBT, is taken from Derman and Kani (1994). Assume that the current value of the stock is $S = 100$, the annually compounded riskless interest rate is $r = 3\%$ per year for all time expirations, the stock has zero dividend. The annual BS implied volatility of an at-the-money call is assumed to be $\sigma = 10\%$, and the BS implied volatility increases (decreases) linearly by 0.5 percentage points with every 10 point drop (rise) in the strike. From the assumptions, we see that $\sigma_{imp}(K, \tau) = 0.15 - 0.0005\,K$.

In order to investigate the precision of the SPD estimation obtained from the IBT, we give a simulation example assuming that the stock price process is generated by the stochastic differential equation model (7.3), with an instantaneous local volatility function $\sigma(S_t, t) = 0.15 - 0.0005\,S_t$, $\mu_t = r = 0.03$. We may then easily compare the SPD estimations obtained from the two different methods.

7.2.1   Simulation using Derman and Kani algorithm

With the XploRe quantlet XFGIBT01.xpl, using the assumption on the BS implied volatility surface, we obtain the following one year stock price implied binomial tree, transition probability tree, and Arrow-Debreu price tree.

Derman and Kani one year (four step) implied binomial tree

stock price

```
                                             119.91
                                 115.06
                     110.04                  110.06
         105.13                  105.13
100.00                 100.00                100.00
         95.12                   95.12
                     89.93                   89.92
                                 85.22
                                             80.01
```

transition probability

```
                                 0.60
                     0.58
         0.59                    0.59
0.56                 0.56
         0.59                    0.59
                     0.54
                                 0.59
```

Arrow-Debreu price

```
                                         0.111
                             0.187
                 0.327                   0.312
         0.559               0.405
1.000            0.480                   0.343
         0.434               0.305
                 0.178                   0.172
                             0.080
                                         0.033
```

This IBT is corresponding to $\tau = 1$ year, and $\triangle t = 0.25$ year, which shows the
stock prices, and the elements at the jth column are corresponding to the stock

prices of the nodes at the $(j-1)$th level in the tree. The second one, its (n, j) element is corresponding to the transition probability from the node (n, j) to the nodes $(n+1, j+1)$. The third tree contains the Arrow-Debreu prices of the nodes. Using the stock prices together with Arrow-Debreu prices of the nodes at the final level, a discrete approximation of the implied distribution can be obtained. Notice that by the definition of the Arrow-Debreu price, the risk neutral probability corresponding to each node should be calculated as the product of the Arrow-Debreu price and the factor $e^{r\tau}$.

If we choose small enough time steps, we obtain the estimation of the implied price distribution and the implied local volatility surface $\sigma_{loc}(s, \tau)$. We still use the same assumption on the BS implied volatility surface as above here, which means $\sigma_{imp}(K, \tau) = 0.15 - 0.0005\,K$, and assume $S_0 = 100, r = 0.03, T = 5$ year.

Q XFGIBT02.xpl

Two figures are generated by running the quantlet XFGIBT02.xpl, Figure 7.2 shows the plot of the SPD estimation resulting from fitting an implied five-year tree with 20 levels. The implied local volatilities $\sigma_{loc}(s, \tau)$ in the implied tree at different time to maturity and stock price levels is shown in Figure 7.3, which obviously decreases with the stock price and increases with time to maturity as expected.

7.2.2   Simulation using Barle and Cakici algorithm

The Barle and Cakici algorithm can be applied in analogy to Derman and Kani's. The XploRe quantlets used here are similar to those presented in Section 7.2.1, one has to replace the quantlet IBTdk by IBTdc. The following figure displays the one-year (four step) stock price tree, transition probability tree, and Arrow-Debreu tree. Figure 7.4 presents the plot of the estimated SPD by fitting a five year implied binomial tree with 20 levels to the volatility smile using Barle and Cakici algorithm, and Figure 7.5, shows the characteristics of the implied local volatility surface of the generated IBT, decreases with the stock price, and increases with time.

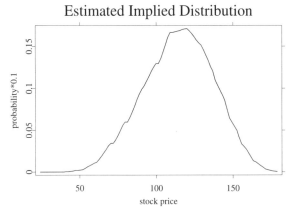

Figure 7.2.   SPD estimation by the Derman and Kani IBT.

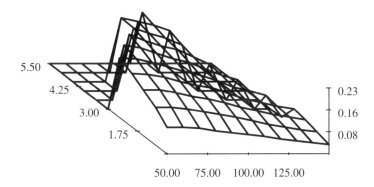

Figure 7.3.   Implied local volatility surface estimation by the Derman and Kani IBT.

```
Barle and Cakici one year implied binomial tree

stock price
```

```
                                              123.85
                                  117.02
                      112.23                  112.93
          104.84                  107.03
100.00                101.51                  103.05
          96.83                   97.73
                      90.53                   93.08
                                  87.60
                                              82.00
```

```
transition probability
                                  0.46
                      0.61
          0.38                    0.48
0.49                  0.49
          0.64                    0.54
                      0.36
                                  0.57
```

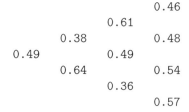

```
Arrow-Debreu price
                                          0.050
                              0.111
                  0.185                   0.240
          0.486                 0.373
1.000             0.619                   0.394
          0.506                 0.378
                  0.181                   0.237
                              0.116
                                          0.050
```

7.2.3   Comparison with Monte-Carlo Simulation

We now compare the SPD estimation at the fifth year obtained by the two IBT
methods with the estimated density function of the Monte-Carlo simulation
of $S_t, t = 5$ generated from the model (7.3), where $\sigma(S_t, t) = 0.15 - 0.0005\, S_t$,

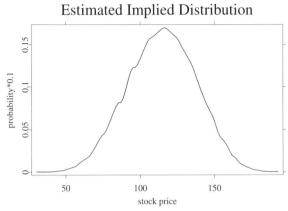

Figure 7.4.   SPD estimation by the Barle and Cakici IBT.

Implied Local Volatility Surface

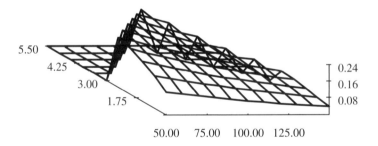

Figure 7.5.   Implied local volatility surface by the Barle and Cakici IBT.

$\mu_t = r = 0.03$. We use the Milstein scheme, Kloeden, Platen and Schurz (1994) to perform the discrete time approximation in (7.3). It has strong convergence rate δ^1. We have set the time step with $\delta = 1/1000$ here.

In order to construct the IBT, we calculate the option prices corresponding
to each node at the implied tree according to their definition by Monte-Carlo
simulation.

Q XFGIBT03.xpl **Q** XFGIBTcdk.xpl **Q** XFGIBTcbc.xpl

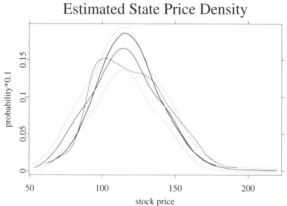

Figure 7.6.   SPD estimation by Monte-Carlo simulation, and its 95%
confidence band, the B & C IBT, from the D & K IBT (thin), level
$=20$, $T = 5$ year, $\triangle t = 0.25$ year.

Here we use the quantlets **Q** XFGIBTcdk.xpl and **Q** XFGIBTcbc.xpl. These
two are used to construct the IBT directly from the option price function,
not starting from the BS implied volatility surface as in quantlets IBTdk and
IBTbc. In the data file "IBTmcsimulation20.dat", there are 1000 Monte-Carlo
simulation samples for each S_t in the diffusion model (7.3), for $t = i/4$ year,
$i = 1, ...20$, from which we calculate the simulated values of the option prices
according to its theoretical definition and estimate the density of $S_t, T = 5$
year as the SPD estimation at the fifth year.

From the estimated distribution shown in the Figures 7.2.3, we observe their
deviation from the log-normal characteristics according to their skewness and
kurtosis. The SPD estimation obtained from the two IBT methods coincides
with the estimation obtained from the Monte-Carlo simulation well, the difference between the estimations obtained from the two IBTs is not very large.

On the other hand, we can also estimate the implied local volatility surface
from the implied binomial tree, and compare it with the one obtained by the

simulation. Compare Figure 7.7 and Figure 7.8 with Figure 7.9, and notice that in the first two figures, some edge values cannot be obtained directly from the five-year IBT. However, the three implied local volatility surface plots all actually coincide with the volatility smile characteristic, the implied local volatility of the out-the-money options decreases with the increasing stock price, and increase with time.

Implied Local Volatility Surface

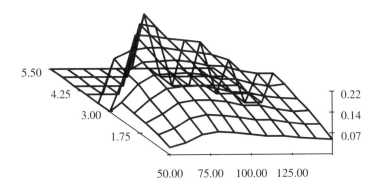

Figure 7.7.   Implied local volatility surface of the simulated model, calculated from D& K IBT.

We use the data file "IBTmcsimulation50.dat" to obtain an estimated BS implied volatility surface. There are 1000 Monte-Carlo simulation samples for each S_t in the diffusion model (7.3), for $t = i/10$ year in it, $i = 1, ...50$, because we can calculate the BS implied volatility corresponding to different strike prices and time to maturities after we have the estimated option prices corresponding to these strike price and time to maturity levels. Figure 7.10 shows that the BS implied volatility surface of our example reflects the characteristics that the BS implied volatility decrease with the strike price. But this BS implied volatility surface does not change with time a lot, which is probably due to our assumption about the local instantaneous volatility function, which only changes with the stock price.

Q XFGIBT04.xpl

Implied Local Volatility Surface

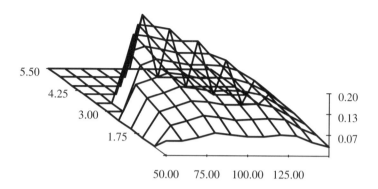

Figure 7.8.   Implied local volatility surface of the simulated model, calculated from B& C IBT.

7.3   Example – Analysis of DAX data

We now use the IBT to forecast the future price distribution of the real stock market data. We use DAX index option prices data at January 4, 1999, which are included in MD*BASE, a database located at CASE (Center for Applied Statistics and Economics) at Humboldt-Universität zu Berlin, and provide some dataset for demonstration purposes. In the following program, we estimate the BS implied volatility surface first, while the quantlet volsurf, Fengler, Härdle and Villa (2001), is used to obtain this estimation from the market option prices, then construct the IBT using Derman and Kani method and calculate the interpolated option prices using CRR binomial tree method. Fitting the function of option prices directly from the market option prices is hardly ever attempted since the function approaches a value of zero for very high strike prices and option prices are bounded by non-arbitrage conditions.

Implied Local Volatility Surface

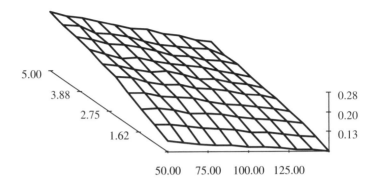

Figure 7.9.   Implied local volatility surface of the simulated model, calculated from Monte-Carlo simulation.

Q XFGIBT05.xpl

Figure 7.11 shows the price distribution estimation obtained by the Barle and Cakici IBT, for $\tau = 0.5$ year. Obviously, the estimated SPD by the Derman and Kani IBT can be obtained similarly. In order to check the precision of the estimated price distribution obtained by the IBT method, we compare it to use DAX daily prices between January 1, 1997, and January 4. 1999. The historical time series density estimation method described in Aït-Sahalia, Wang and Yared (2000) is used here. Notice that Risk-neutrality implies two kinds of SPD should be equal, historical time series SPD is in fact the conditional density function of the diffusion process. We obtain the historical time series SPD estimation by the following procedure:

1. Collect stock prices time series

Implied Volatility Surface

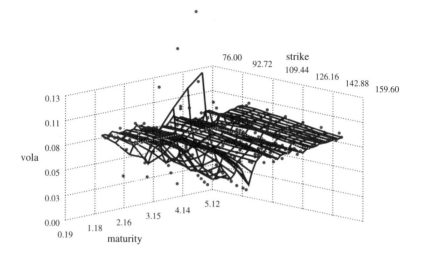

Figure 7.10.   BS implied volatility surface estimation by Monte-Carlo simulation.

2. Assume this time series is a sample path of the diffusion process

$$\frac{dS_t}{S_t} = \mu_t dt + \sigma(S_t, t)dZ_t,$$

where dZ_t is a Wiener process with mean zero and variance equal to dt.

3. Estimate diffusion function $\sigma(\cdot, \cdot)$ in the diffusion process model using nonparametric method from stock prices time series

4. Make Monte-Carlo simulation for the diffusion process with drift function is interest rate and estimated diffusion function

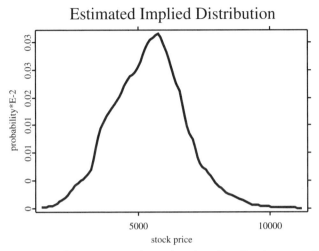

Figure 7.11.   The estimated stock price distribution, $\tau = 0.5$ year.

5. Estimate conditional density function $g = p(S_T | S_t, \hat{\mu}, \hat{\sigma})$ from Monte-Carlo simulated process

From Figure 7.12 we conclude that the SPD estimated by the Derman and Kani IBT and the one obtained by Barle and Cakici IBT can be used to forecast future SPD. The SPD estimated by different methods sometimes have deviations on skewness and kurtosis. In fact the detection of the difference between the historical time series SPD estimation and the SPD recovered from daily option prices may be used as trading rules, see Table 7.1 and Chapter 9. In Table 7.1, SPD estimated from daily option prices data set is expressed by f and the time series SPD is g. A far *out of the money* (OTM) call/put is defined as one whose exercise price is 10% higher (lower) than the future price. While a near OTM call/put is defined as one whose exercise price is 5% higher (lower) but 10% lower(higher)than the future price. When skew(f) < skew(g), agents apparently assign a lower probability to high outcomes of the underlying than would be justified by the time series SPD (see Figure 7.13). Since for call options only the right 'tail' of the support determines the theoretical price the latter is smaller than the price implied by diffusion process using the time series SPD. That is we buy calls. The same reason applies to put options.

State Price Density Estimation

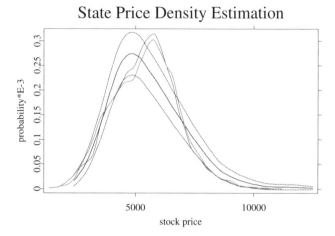

Figure 7.12.   SPD estimation by three methods, by historical estimation, and its 95% confidence band (dashed), by B & C IBT, and by D & K IBT (thin), $\tau = 0.5$ year.

Trading Rules to exploit SPD differences			
Skewness	$(S1)$	skew$(f) <$ skew(g)	sell OTM put,
			buy OTM call
Trade	$(S2)$	skew$(f) >$ skew(g)	buy OTM put
			sell OTM call
Kurtosis	$(K1)$	kurt$(f) >$ kurt(g)	sell far OTM and ATM
			buy near OTM options
Trade	$(K2)$	kurt$(f) <$ kurt(g)	buy far OTM and ATM,
			sell near OTM options

Table 7.1.   Trading Rules to exploit SPD differences.

From the simulations and real data example, we find that the implied binomial tree is an easy way to assess the future stock prices, capture the term structure of the underlying asset, and replicate the volatility smile. But the algorithms still have some deficiencies. When the time step is chosen too small, negative transition probabilities are encountered more and more often. The modification of these values loses the information about the smile at the corresponding nodes. The Barle and Cakici algorithm is a better choice when the interest rate is high.Figure 7.15 shows the deviation of the two methods under the

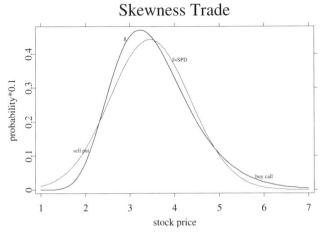

Figure 7.13.   Skewness Trade, skew(f)< skew(g).

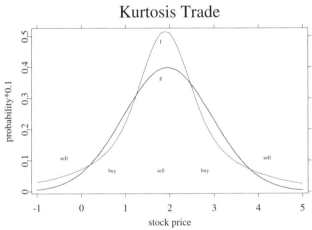

Figure 7.14.   Kurtosis Trade, kurt(f)> kurt(g).

situation that $r = 0.2$. When the interest rate is a little higher, Barle and Cakici algorithm still can be used to construct the IBT while Derman and Kani's cannot work any more. The times of the negative probabilities appear are fewer than Derman and Kani construction (see Jackwerth (1999)).

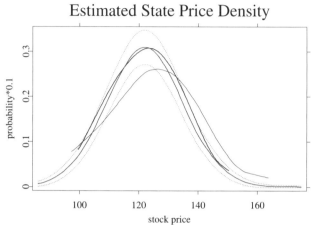

Figure 7.15. SPD estimation by Monte-Carlo simulation, and its 95%
confidence band (dashed), the B & C IBT, from the D & K IBT (thin),
level =20, $\tau = 1$ year, $r = 0.20$.

Besides its basic purpose of pricing derivatives in consistency with the market
prices, IBT is useful for other kinds of analysis, such as hedging and calculating
of implied probability distributions and volatility surfaces. It estimate the
future price distribution according to the historical data. On the practical
application aspect, the reliability of the approach depends critically on the
quality of the estimation of the dynamics of the underlying price process, such
as BS implied volatility surface obtained from the market option prices.

The IBT can be used to produce recombining and arbitrage-free binomial trees
to describe stochastic processes with variable volatility. However, some serious
limitations such as negative probabilities, even though most of them appeared
at the edge of the trees. Overriding them causes loss of the information about
the smile at the corresponding nodes. These defects are a consequence of the
requirement that a continuous diffusion is approximated by a binomial process.
Relaxation of this requirement, using multinomial trees or varinomial trees is
possible.

Bibliography

Aït-Sahalia, Y. and Lo, A. (1998). Nonparametric Estimation of State-Price Densities Implicit in Financial Asset Prices, *Journal of Finance*, **53**: 499–547.

Aït-Sahalia, Y. , Wang, Y. and Yared, F.(2001). Do Option Markets Correctly Price the Probabilities of Movement of the Underlying Asset? *Journal of Econometrics*, **102**: 67–110.

Barle, S. and Cakici, N. (1998). How to Grow a Smiling Tree *The Journal of Financial Engineering*, **7**: 127–146.

Bingham, N.H. and Kiesel, R. (1998). *Risk-neutral Valuation: Pricing and Hedging of Financial Derivatives*, Springer Verlag, London.

Cox, J., Ross, S. and Rubinstein, M. (1979). Option Pricing: A simplified Approach, *Jouranl of Financial Economics* **7**: 229–263.

Derman, E. and Kani, I. (1994). The Volatility Smile and Its Implied Tree *http://www.gs.com/qs/*

Derman, E. and Kani, I. (1998). Stochastic Implied Trees: Arbitrage Pricing with Stochastic Term and Strike Structure of Volatility, *International Journal of Theroetical and Applied Finance* **1**: 7–22.

Dupire, B. (1994). Pricing with a Smile, *Risk* **7**: 18–20.

Fengler, M. R., Härdle, W. and Villa, Chr. (2001). The Dynamics of Implied Volatilities: A Common Principal Components Approach, Discussion paper 38, Sonderforschungsbereich 373, Humboldt-Universität zu Berlin.

Härdle, W., Hlávka, Z. and Klinke, S. (2000). *XploRe Application Guide*, Springer Verlag, Heidelberg.

Härdle,W. and Yatchew, A. (2001). Dynamic Nonparametric State price Density Estimation using Constrained least Squares and the Bootstrap, Discussion paper 1, Sonderforschungsbereich 373, Humboldt-Universität zu Berlin.

Hull, J. and White, A. (1987). The Pricing of Options on Assets with Stochastic Volatility, *Journal of Finance* **42**: 281–300.

Jackwerth, J. (1999). Optional-Implied Risk-Neutral Distributions and Implied Binomial Trees: A Literature Review, *Journal of Finance* **51**: 1611–1631.

Jackwerth, J. and Rubinstein, M. (1996). Recovering Probability Distributions from Option Prices, *Journal of Finance* **51**: 1611–1631.

Kloeden, P., Platen, E. and Schurz, H. (1994). *Numerical Solution of SDE Through Computer Experiments*, Springer Verlag, Heidelberg.

Merton, R. (1976). Option Pricing When Underlying Stock Returns are Discontinuous, *Journal of Financial Economics* **January-March**: 125–144.

Rubinstein, M. (1994). Implied Binomial Trees. *Journal of Finance* **49**: 771–818.

8 Estimating State-Price Densities with Nonparametric Regression

Kim Huynh, Pierre Kervella and Jun Zheng

8.1 Introduction

Derivative markets offer a rich source of information to extract the market's expectations of the future price of an asset. Using option prices, one may derive the whole risk-neutral probability distribution of the underlying asset price at the maturity date of the options. Once this distribution also called State-Price Density (SPD) is estimated, it may serve for pricing new, complex or illiquid derivative securities.

There exist numerous methods to recover the SPD empirically. They can be separated in two classes:

- methods using option prices as identifying conditions
- methods using the second derivative of the call pricing function with respect to K

The first class includes methods which consist in estimating the parameters of a mixture of log-normal densities to match the observed option prices, Melick and Thomas (1997). Another popular approach in this class is the implied binomial trees method, see Rubinstein (1994), Derman and Kani (1994) and Chapter 7. Another technique is based on learning networks suggested by Hutchinson, Lo and Poggio (1994), a nonparametric approach using artificial neural networks, radial basis functions, and projection pursuits.

The second class of methods is based on the result of Breeden and Litzenberger (1978). This methodology is based on European options with identical time to maturity, it may therefore be applied to fewer cases than some of the techniques in the first class. Moreover, it also assumes a continuum of strike prices on $\mathbb{R}^+$ which can not be found on any stock exchange. Indeed, the strike prices are always discretely spaced on a finite range around the actual underlying price. Hence, to handle this problem an interpolation of the call pricing function inside the range and extrapolation outside may be performed. In the following, a semiparametric technique using nonparametric regression of the implied volatility surface will be introduced to provide this interpolation task. A new approach using constrained least squares has been suggested by Yatchew and Härdle (2002) but will not be explored here.

The concept of Arrow-Debreu securities is the building block for the analysis of economic equilibrium under uncertainty. Rubinstein (1976) and Lucas (1978) used this concept as a basis to construct dynamic general equilibrium models in order to determine the price of assets in an economy. The central idea of this methodology is that the price of a financial security is equal to the expected net present value of its future payoffs under the risk-neutral probability density function (PDF). The net present value is calculated using the risk-free interest rate, while the expectation is taken with respect to the weighted-marginal-rate-of-substitution PDF of the payoffs. The latter term is known as the state-price density (SPD), risk-neutral PDF, or equivalent martingale measure. The price of a security at time t (P_t) with a single liquidation date T and payoff $Z(S_T)$ is then:

$$P_t = e^{-r_{t,\tau}\tau}\mathrm{E}_t^*[Z(S_T)] = e^{-r_{t,\tau}\tau}\int_{-\infty}^{\infty} Z(S_T)f_t^*(S_T)dS_T \qquad (8.1)$$

where E_t^* is the conditional expectation given the information set in t under the equivalent martingale probability, S_T is the state variable, $r_{t,\tau}$ is the risk-free rate at time t with time to maturity τ, and $f_t^*(S_T)$ is the SPD at time t for date T payoffs.

Rubinstein (1985) shows that if one has two of the three following pieces of information:

- representative agent's preferences

- asset price dynamics or its data-generating process

- SPD

then one can recover the third. Since the agent's preferences and the true data-generating process are unknown, a no-arbitrage approach is used to recover the SPD.

8.2 Extracting the SPD using Call-Options

Breeden and Litzenberger (1978) show that one can replicate Arrow-Debreu prices using the concept of *butterfly spread* on European call options. This spread entails selling two call options at exercise price K, buying one call option at $K^- = K - \Delta K$ and another at $K^+ = K + \Delta K$, where ΔK is the stepsize between the adjacent call strikes. These four options constitute a butterfly spread centered on K. If the terminal underlying asset value S_T is equal to K then the payoff $Z(\cdot)$ of $\frac{1}{\Delta K}$ of such butterfly spreads is defined as:

$$Z(S_T, K; \Delta K) = P(S_{T-\tau}, \tau, K; \Delta K)|_{\tau=0} = \left.\frac{u_1 - u_2}{\Delta K}\right|_{S_T=K,\tau=0} = 1 \qquad (8.2)$$

where

$$u_1 = C(S_{T-\tau}, \tau, K + \Delta K) - C(S_{T-\tau}, \tau, K),$$
$$u_2 = C(S_{T-\tau}, \tau, K) - C(S_{T-\tau}, \tau, K - \Delta K).$$

$C(S, \tau, K)$ denotes the price of a European call with an actual underlying price S, a time to maturity τ and a strike price K. Here, $P(S_{T-\tau}, \tau, K; \Delta K)$ is the corresponding price of this security ($\frac{1}{\Delta K} * butterfly\ spread(K; \Delta K)$) at time $T - \tau$.

As ΔK tends to zero, this security becomes an Arrow-Debreu security paying 1 if $S_T = K$ and zero in other states. As it is assumed that S_T has a continuous distribution function on $\mathbb{R}^+$, the probability of any given level of S_T is zero and thus, in this case, the price of an Arrow-Debreu security is zero. However, dividing one more time by ΔK, one obtains the price of ($\frac{1}{(\Delta K)^2} * butterfly\ spread(K; \Delta K)$) and as ΔK tends to 0 this price tends to $f^*(S_T)e^{-r_{t,\tau}}$ for $S_T = K$. Indeed,

$$\lim_{\Delta K \to 0} \left.\left(\frac{P(S_t, \tau, K; \Delta K)}{\Delta K}\right)\right|_{K=S_T} = f^*(S_T)e^{-r_{t,\tau}}. \qquad (8.3)$$

This can be proved by setting the payoff Z_1 of this new security

$$Z_1\left(S_T\right) = \left(\frac{1}{(\Delta K)^2}(\Delta K - |S_T - K|)\mathbf{1}(S_T \in [K - \Delta K, K + \Delta K])\right)$$

in (8.1) and letting ΔK tend to 0. Indeed, one should remark that:

$$\forall(\Delta K) : \int_{K-\Delta K}^{K+\Delta K}(\Delta K - |S_T - K|)dS_T = (\Delta K)^2.$$

If one can construct these financial instruments on a continuum of states (strike prices) then at infinitely small ΔK a complete state pricing function can be defined.

Moreover, as ΔK tends to zero, this price will tend to the second derivative of the call pricing function with respect to the strike price evaluated at K:

$$\begin{aligned}
\lim_{\Delta K \to 0}\left(\frac{P(S_t, \tau, K; \Delta K)}{\Delta K}\right) &= \lim_{\Delta K \to 0}\frac{u_1 - u_2}{(\Delta K)^2} \\
&= \frac{\partial^2 C_t(\cdot)}{\partial K^2}.
\end{aligned} \tag{8.4}$$

Equating (8.3) and (8.4) across all states yields:

$$\frac{\partial^2 C_t(\cdot)}{\partial K^2}\bigg|_{K=S_T} = e^{-r_{t,\tau}\tau}f_t^*(S_T)$$

where $r_{t,\tau}$ denotes the risk-free interest rate at time t with time to maturity τ and $f_t^*(\cdot)$ denotes the risk-neutral PDF or the SPD in t. Therefore, the SPD is defined as:

$$f_t^*(S_T) = e^{r_{t,\tau}\tau}\frac{\partial^2 C_t(\cdot)}{\partial K^2}\bigg|_{K=S_T}. \tag{8.5}$$

This method constitutes a no-arbitrage approach to recover the SPD. No assumption on the underlying asset dynamics are required. Preferences are not restricted since the no-arbitrage method only assumes risk-neutrality with respect to the underlying asset. The only requirements for this method are that markets are perfect (i.e. no sales restrictions, transactions costs or taxes and that agents are able to borrow at the risk-free interest rate) and that $C(\cdot)$ is twice differentiable. The same result can be obtained by differentiating (8.1) twice with respect to K after setting for Z the call payoff function $Z(S_T) = (S_T - K)^+$.

8.2.1   Black-Scholes SPD

The Black-Scholes call option pricing formula is due to Black and Scholes (1973) and Merton (1973). In this model there are no assumptions regarding preferences, rather it relies on no-arbitrage conditions and assumes that the evolution of the underlying asset price S_t follows a geometric Brownian motion defined through

$$\frac{dS_t}{S_t} = \mu dt + \sigma dW_t. \tag{8.6}$$

Here μ denotes the drift and σ the volatility assumed to be constant.

The analytical formula for the price in t of a call option with a terminal date $T = t + \tau$, a strike price K, an underlying price S_t, a risk-free rate $r_{t,\tau}$, a continuous dividend yield $\delta_{t,\tau}$, and a volatility σ, is:

$$
\begin{aligned}
C_{BS}(S_t, K, \tau, r_{t,\tau}, \delta_{t,\tau}; \sigma) &= e^{-r_{t,\tau}} \int_0^\infty \max(S_T - K, 0) f_{BS,t}^*(S_T) dS_T \\
&= S_t e^{-\delta_{t,\tau}\tau} \Phi(d_1) - K e^{-r_{t,\tau}\tau} \Phi(d_2)
\end{aligned}
$$

where $\Phi(\cdot)$ is the standard normal cumulative distribution function and

$$
\begin{aligned}
d_1 &= \frac{\log(S_t/K) + (r_{t,\tau} - \delta_{t,\tau} + \frac{1}{2}\sigma^2)\tau}{\sigma\sqrt{\tau}}, \\
d_2 &= d_1 - \sigma\sqrt{\tau}.
\end{aligned}
$$

As a consequence of the assumptions on the underlying asset price process the Black-Scholes SPD is a log-normal density with mean $(r_{t,\tau} - \delta_{t,\tau} - \frac{1}{2}\sigma^2)\tau$ and variance $\sigma^2\tau$ for $\log(S_T/S_t)$:

$$
\begin{aligned}
f_{BS,t}^*(S_T) &= e^{r_{t,\tau}\tau} \frac{\partial^2 C_t}{\partial K^2}\Bigg|_{K=S_T} \\
&= \frac{1}{S_T\sqrt{2\pi\sigma^2\tau}} \exp\left[-\frac{[\log(S_T/S_t) - (r_{t,\tau} - \delta_{t,\tau} - \frac{1}{2}\sigma^2)\tau]^2}{2\sigma^2\tau} \right].
\end{aligned}
$$

The risk measures Delta (Δ) and Gamma (Γ) are defined as:

$$\Delta_{BS} \stackrel{\text{def}}{=} \frac{\partial C_{BS}}{\partial S_t} = \Phi(d_1)$$

$$\Gamma_{BS} \stackrel{\text{def}}{=} \frac{\partial^2 C_{BS}}{\partial S_t^2} = \frac{\Phi(d_1)}{S_t\sigma\sqrt{\tau}}$$

The Black-Scholes SPD can be calculated in XploRe using the following quant-let:

```
bsspd = spdbs(K,s,r,div,sigma,tau)
       estimates the Black-Scholes SPD
```

The arguments are the strike prices (K), underlying price (s), risk-free interest rate (r), dividend yields (div), implied volatility of the option (sigma), and the time to maturity (tau). The output consist of the Black-Scholes SPD (bsspd.fbs), Δ (bsspd.delta), and the Γ (bsspd.gamma) of the call options. Please note that spdbs can be applied to put options by using the Put-Call parity.

However, it is widely known that the Black-Scholes call option formula is not valid empirically. For more details, please refer to Chapter 6. Since the Black-Scholes model contains empirical irregularities, its SPD will not be consistent with the data. Consequently, some other techniques for estimating the SPD without any assumptions on the underlying diffusion process have been developed in the last years.

8.3   Semiparametric estimation of the SPD

8.3.1   Estimating the call pricing function

The use of nonparametric regression to recover the SPD was first investigated by Aït-Sahalia and Lo (1998). They propose to use the Nadaraya-Watson estimator to estimate the historical call prices $C_t(\cdot)$ as a function of the following state variables $(S_t, K, \tau, r_{t,\tau}, \delta_{t,\tau})^\top$. Kernel regressions are advocated because there is no need to specify a functional form and the only required assumption is that the function is smooth and differentiable, Härdle (1990). When the regressor dimension is 5, the estimator is inaccurate in practice. Hence, there is a need to reduce the dimension or equivalently the number of regressors. One method is to appeal to no-arbitrage arguments and collapse S_t, $r_{t,\tau}$ and $\delta_{t,\tau}$ into the forward price $F_t = S_t e^{(r_{t,\tau} - \delta_{t,\tau})\tau}$ in order to express the call pricing function as:

$$C(S_t, K, \tau, r_{t,\tau}, \delta_{t,\tau}) = C(F_{t,\tau}, K, \tau, r_{t,\tau}). \tag{8.7}$$

An alternative specification assumes that the call option function is homogeneous of degree one in S_t and K (as in the Black-Scholes formula) so that:

$$C(S_t, K, \tau, r_{t,\tau}, \delta_{t,\tau}) = KC(S_t/K, \tau, r_{t,\tau}, \delta_{t,\tau}). \tag{8.8}$$

Combining the assumptions of (8.7) and (8.8) the call pricing function can be further reduced to a function of three variables $(\frac{K}{F_{t,\tau}}, \tau, r_{t,\tau})$.

Another approach is to use a semiparametric specification based on the Black-Scholes implied volatility. Here, the implied volatility σ is modelled as a nonparametric function, $\sigma(F_{t,\tau}, K, \tau)$:

$$C(S_t, K, \tau, r_{t,\tau}, \delta_{t,\tau}) = C_{BS}(F_{t,\tau}, K, \tau, r_{t,\tau}; \sigma(F_{t,\tau}, K, \tau)). \tag{8.9}$$

Empirically the implied volatility function mostly depends on two parameters: the time to maturity τ and the moneyness $M = K/F_{t,\tau}$. Almost equivalently, one can set $M = \tilde{S}_t/K$ where $\tilde{S}_t = S_t - D$ and D is the present value of the dividends to be paid before the expiration. Actually, in the case of a dividend yield δ_t, we have $D = S_t(1 - e^{-\delta_t})$. If the dividends are discrete, then $D = \sum_{t_i \leq t+\tau} D_{t_i} e^{-r_{t,\tau_i}}$ where t_i is the dividend payment date of the ith dividend and τ_i is its maturity.

Therefore, the dimension of the implied volatility function can be reduced to $\sigma(K/F_{t,\tau}, \tau)$. In this case the call option function is:

$$C(S_t, K, \tau, r_{t,\tau}, \delta_{t,\tau}) = C_{BS}(F_{t,\tau}, K, \tau, r_{t,\tau}; \sigma(K/F_{t,\tau}, \tau)). \tag{8.10}$$

Once a smooth estimate of $\hat{\sigma}(\cdot)$ is obtained, estimates of $\hat{C}_t(\cdot)$, $\hat{\Delta}_t = \frac{\partial \hat{C}_t(\cdot)}{\partial S_t}$, $\hat{\Gamma}_t = \frac{\partial^2 \hat{C}_t(\cdot)}{\partial S_t^2}$, and $\hat{f}^* = e^{r_{t,\tau}\tau} \left[\frac{\partial^2 \hat{C}_t(\cdot)}{\partial K^2} \right]$ can be calculated.

8.3.2 Further dimension reduction

The previous section proposed a semiparametric estimator of the call pricing function and the necessary steps to recover the SPD. In this section the dimension is reduced further using the suggestion of Rookley (1997). Rookley uses intraday data for one maturity and estimates an implied volatility surface where the dimension are the intraday time and the moneyness of the options.

Here, a slightly different method is used which relies on all settlement prices of options of one trading day for different maturities to estimate the implied volatility surface $\sigma(K/F_{t,\tau}, \tau)$. In the second step, these estimates are used for a given time to maturity which may not necessarily correspond to the maturity of a series of options. This method allows one to compare the SPD at different dates because of the fixed maturity provided by the first step. This is interesting if one wants to study the dynamics and the stability of these densities.

Fixing the maturity also allows us to eliminate τ from the specification of the implied volatility function. In the following part, for convenience, the definition of the moneyness is $M = \tilde{S}_t/K$ and we denote by σ the implied volatility. The notation $\frac{\partial f(x_1,\ldots,x_n)}{\partial x_i}$ denotes the partial derivative of f with respect to x_i and $\frac{df(x)}{dx}$ the total derivative of f with respect to x.

Moreover, we use the following rescaled call option function:

$$c_{it} = \frac{C_{it}}{\tilde{S}_t},$$

$$M_{it} = \frac{\tilde{S}_t}{K_i}.$$

where C_{it} is the price of the ith option at time t and K_i is its strike price.

The rescaled call option function can be expressed as:

$$c_{it} = c(M_{it}; \sigma(M_{it})) = \Phi(d_1) - \frac{e^{-r\tau}\Phi(d_2)}{M_{it}},$$

$$d_1 = \frac{\log(M_{it}) + \left\{r_t + \frac{1}{2}\sigma(M_{it})^2\right\}\tau}{\sigma(M_{it})\sqrt{\tau}},$$

$$d_2 = d_1 - \sigma(M_{it})\sqrt{\tau}.$$

The standard risk measures are then the following partial derivatives (for notational convenience subscripts are dropped):

$$\Delta = \frac{\partial C}{\partial S} = \frac{\partial C}{\partial \tilde{S}} = c(M, \sigma(M)) + \tilde{S}\frac{\partial c}{\partial \tilde{S}},$$

$$\Gamma = \frac{\partial \Delta}{\partial S} = \frac{\partial^2 C}{\partial S^2} = \frac{\partial^2 C}{\partial \tilde{S}^2} = 2\frac{\partial c}{\partial \tilde{S}} + \tilde{S}\frac{\partial^2 c}{\partial \tilde{S}^2}.$$

where

$$
\frac{\partial c}{\partial \tilde{S}} = \frac{\mathrm{d}c}{\mathrm{d}M} \frac{\partial M}{\partial \tilde{S}} = \frac{\mathrm{d}c}{\mathrm{d}M} \frac{1}{K},
$$

$$
\frac{\partial^2 c}{\partial \tilde{S}^2} = \frac{\mathrm{d}^2 c}{\mathrm{d}M^2} \left(\frac{1}{K} \right)^2.
$$

The SPD is then the second derivative of the call option function with respect to the strike price:

$$
f^*(\cdot) = e^{r\tau} \frac{\partial^2 C}{\partial K^2} = e^{r\tau} \tilde{S} \frac{\partial^2 c}{\partial K^2}. \tag{8.13}
$$

The conversion is needed because $c(\cdot)$ is being estimated not $C(\cdot)$. The analytical expression of (8.13) depends on:

$$
\frac{\partial^2 c}{\partial K^2} = \frac{\mathrm{d}^2 c}{\mathrm{d}M^2} \left(\frac{M}{K} \right)^2 + 2 \frac{\mathrm{d}c}{\mathrm{d}M} \frac{M}{K^2}
$$

The functional form of $\frac{\mathrm{d}c}{\mathrm{d}M}$ is:

$$
\frac{\mathrm{d}c}{\mathrm{d}M} = \Phi'(d_1) \frac{\mathrm{d}d_1}{\mathrm{d}M} - e^{-r\tau} \frac{\Phi'(d_2)}{M} \frac{\mathrm{d}d_2}{\mathrm{d}M} + e^{-r\tau} \frac{\Phi(d_2)}{M^2}, \tag{8.14}
$$

while $\frac{\mathrm{d}^2 c}{\mathrm{d}M^2}$ is:

$$
\begin{aligned}
\frac{\mathrm{d}^2 c}{\mathrm{d}M^2} = {} & \Phi'(d_1) \left[\frac{\mathrm{d}^2 d_1}{\mathrm{d}M^2} - d_1 \left(\frac{\mathrm{d}d_1}{\mathrm{d}M} \right)^2 \right] \\
& - \frac{e^{-r\tau} \Phi'(d_2)}{M} \left[\frac{\mathrm{d}^2 d_2}{\mathrm{d}M^2} - \frac{2}{M} \frac{\mathrm{d}d_2}{\mathrm{d}M} - d_2 \left(\frac{\mathrm{d}d_2}{\mathrm{d}M} \right)^2 \right] \\
& - \frac{2 e^{-r\tau} \Phi(d_2)}{M^3} \tag{8.15}
\end{aligned}
$$

The quantities in (8.14) and (8.15) are a function of the following first derivatives:

$$\begin{aligned}
\frac{\mathrm{d}d_1}{\mathrm{d}M} &= \frac{\partial d_1}{\partial M} + \frac{\partial d_1}{\partial \sigma}\frac{\partial \sigma}{\partial M}, \\
\frac{\mathrm{d}d_2}{\mathrm{d}M} &= \frac{\partial d_2}{\partial M} + \frac{\partial d_2}{\partial \sigma}\frac{\partial \sigma}{\partial M}, \\
\frac{\partial d_1}{\partial M} &= \frac{\partial d_2}{\partial M} = \frac{1}{M\sigma\sqrt{\tau}}, \\
\frac{\partial d_1}{\partial \sigma} &= -\frac{\log(M)+r\tau}{\sigma^2\sqrt{\tau}} + \frac{\sqrt{\tau}}{2}, \\
\frac{\partial d_2}{\partial \sigma} &= -\frac{\log(M)+r\tau}{\sigma^2\sqrt{\tau}} - \frac{\sqrt{\tau}}{2}.
\end{aligned}$$

For the remainder of this chapter, we define:

$$\begin{aligned}
V &= \sigma(M), \\
V' &= \frac{\partial \sigma(M)}{\partial M}, \\
V'' &= \frac{\partial^2 \sigma(M)}{\partial M^2}.
\end{aligned} \tag{8.16}$$

The quantities in (8.14) and (8.15) also depend on the following second derivative functions:

$$\begin{aligned}
\frac{\mathrm{d}^2 d_1}{\mathrm{d}M^2} &= -\frac{1}{M\sigma\sqrt{\tau}}\left[\frac{1}{M} + \frac{V'}{\sigma}\right] + V''\left(\frac{\sqrt{\tau}}{2} - \frac{\log(M)+r\tau}{\sigma^2\sqrt{\tau}}\right) \\
&+ V'\left[2V'\frac{\log(M)+r\tau}{\sigma^3\sqrt{\tau}} - \frac{1}{M\sigma^2\sqrt{\tau}}\right],
\end{aligned} \tag{8.17}$$

$$\begin{aligned}
\frac{\mathrm{d}^2 d_2}{\mathrm{d}M^2} &= -\frac{1}{M\sigma\sqrt{\tau}}\left[\frac{1}{M} + \frac{V'}{\sigma}\right] - V''\left(\frac{\sqrt{\tau}}{2} + \frac{\log(M)+r\tau}{\sigma^2\sqrt{\tau}}\right) \\
&+ V'\left[2V'\frac{\log(M)+r\tau}{\sigma^3\sqrt{\tau}} - \frac{1}{M\sigma^2\sqrt{\tau}}\right].
\end{aligned} \tag{8.18}$$

Local polynomial estimation is used to estimate the implied volatility smile and its first two derivatives in (8.16). A brief explanation will be described now.

8.3.3   Local Polynomial Estimation

Consider the following data generating process for the implied volatilities:

$$\sigma = g(M, \tau) + \sigma^*(M, \tau)\varepsilon,$$

where $E(\varepsilon) = 0$, $Var(\varepsilon) = 1$. M, τ and ε are independent and $\sigma^*(m_0, \tau_0)$ is the conditional variance of σ given $M = m_0, \tau = \tau_0$. Assuming that all third derivatives of g exist, one may perform a Taylor expansion for the function g in a neighborhood of (m_0, τ_0):

$$
\begin{aligned}
g(m, \tau) \approx g(m_0, \tau_0) \quad &+ \quad \left.\frac{\partial g}{\partial M}\right|_{m_0,\tau_0} (m - m_0) + \frac{1}{2}\left.\frac{\partial^2 g}{\partial M^2}\right|_{m_0,\tau_0} (m - m_0)^2 \\
&+ \quad \left.\frac{\partial g}{\partial \tau}\right|_{m_0,\tau_0} (\tau - \tau_0) + \frac{1}{2}\left.\frac{\partial^2 g}{\partial \tau^2}\right|_{m_0,\tau_0} (\tau - \tau_0)^2 \\
&+ \quad \frac{1}{2}\left.\frac{\partial^2 g}{\partial M \partial \tau}\right|_{m_0,\tau_0} (m - m_0)(\tau - \tau_0). \qquad (8.19)
\end{aligned}
$$

This expansion suggests an approximation by local polynomial fitting, Fan and Gijbels (1996). Hence, to estimate the implied volatility at the target point (m_0, τ_0) from observations σ_j $(j = 1, \ldots, n)$, we minimize the following expression:

$$
\begin{aligned}
\sum_{j=1}^{n} \Big\{ \sigma_j &- \Big[\beta_0 + \beta_1(M_j - m_0) + \beta_2(M_j - m_0)^2 + \beta_3(\tau_j - \tau_0) \\
&+ \beta_4(\tau_j - \tau_0)^2 + \beta_5(M_j - m_0)(\tau_j - \tau_0) \Big] \Big\}^2 K_{h_M, h_\tau}(M_j - m_0, \tau_j - \tau_0)
\end{aligned}
\qquad (8.20)
$$

where n is the number of observations (options), h_M and h_τ are the bandwidth controlling the neighborhood in each directions and K_{h_M, h_τ} is the resulting kernel function weighting all observation points. This kernel function may be a product of two univariate kernel functions.

For convenience use the following matrix definitions:

$$
X = \begin{pmatrix}
1 & M_1 - m_0 & (M_1 - m_0)^2 & \tau_1 - \tau_0 & (\tau_1 - \tau_0)^2 & (M_1 - m_0)(\tau_1 - \tau_0) \\
1 & M_2 - m_0 & (M_2 - m_0)^2 & \tau_2 - \tau_0 & (\tau_2 - \tau_0)^2 & (M_2 - m_0)(\tau_2 - \tau_0) \\
\vdots & \vdots & \vdots & \vdots & \vdots & \vdots \\
1 & M_n - m_0 & (M_n - m_0)^2 & \tau_n - \tau_0 & (\tau_n - \tau_0)^2 & (M_n - m_0)(\tau_n - \tau_0)
\end{pmatrix},
$$

$$\sigma = \begin{pmatrix} \sigma_1 \\ \vdots \\ \sigma_n \end{pmatrix}, \quad W = diag\{K_{h_M,h_\tau}(M_j - m_0, \tau_j - \tau_0)\} \quad \text{and} \quad \beta = \begin{pmatrix} \beta_0 \\ \vdots \\ \beta_5 \end{pmatrix}.$$

Hence, the weighted least squares problem (8.20) can be written as

$$\min_\beta (\sigma - X\beta)^\top W (\sigma - X\beta). \tag{8.21}$$

and the solution is given by

$$\hat{\beta} = \left(X^\top W X\right)^{-1} X^\top W \sigma. \tag{8.22}$$

A nice feature of the local polynomial method is that it provides the estimated implied volatility and its first two derivatives in one step. Indeed, one has from (8.19) and (8.20):

$$\left. \widehat{\frac{\partial g}{\partial M}} \right|_{m_0,\tau_0} = \hat{\beta}_1,$$

$$\left. \widehat{\frac{\partial^2 g}{\partial M^2}} \right|_{m_0,\tau_0} = 2\hat{\beta}_2.$$

One of the concerns regarding this estimation method is the dependence on the bandwidth which governs how much weight the kernel function should place on an observed point for the estimation at a target point. Moreover, as the call options are not always symmetrically and equally distributed around the ATM point, the choice of the bandwidth is a key issue, especially for estimation at the border of the implied volatility surface. The bandwidth can be chosen global or locally dependent on (M, τ). There are methods providing "optimal" bandwidths which rely on plug-in rules or on data-based selectors.

In the case of the volatility surface, it is vital to determine one bandwidth for the maturity and one for the moneyness directions. An algorithm called Empirical-Bias Bandwidth Selector (EBBS) for finding local bandwidths is suggested by Ruppert (1997) and Ruppert, Wand, Holst and Hössler (1997). The basic idea of this method is to minimize the estimate of the local mean square error at each target point, without relying on asymptotic result. The variance and the bias term are in this algorithm estimated empirically.

Using the local polynomial estimations, the empirical SPD can be calculated with the following quantlet:

```
lpspd = spdbl(m,sigma,sigma1,sigma2,s,r,tau)
      estimates the semi-parametric SPD.
```

The arguments for this quantlet are the moneyness (m), V (sigma), V' (sigma1), V'' (sigma2), underlying price (s) corrected for future dividends, risk-free interest rate (r), and the time to maturity (tau). The output consist of the local polynomial SPD (lpspd.fstar), Δ (lpspd.delta), and the Γ (lpspd.gamma) of the call-options.

8.4   An Example: Application to DAX data

This section describes how to estimate the Black-Scholes and local polynomial SPD using options data on the German DAX index.

8.4.1   Data

The dataset was taken from the financial database MD*BASE located at CASE (Center for Applied Statistics and Economics) at Humboldt-Universität zu Berlin. Since MD*BASE is a proprietary database, only a limited dataset is provided for demonstration purposes.

This database is filled with options and futures data provided by Eurex. Daily series of 1, 3, 6 and 12 months DM-LIBOR rates taken from the *Thomson Financial Datastream* serve as riskless interest rates. The DAX 30 futures and options settlement data of January 1997 (21 trading days) were used in this study. Daily settlement prices for each option contract are extracted along with contract type, maturity and strike. For the futures, the daily settlement prices, maturities and volumes are the relevant information. To compute the interest rates corresponding to the option maturities a linear interpolation between the available rates was used.

The DAX is a performance index which means that dividends are reinvested. However, assuming no dividend yields when inverting the Black-Scholes formula results in different volatilities for pairs of puts and calls contrary to the no-arbitrage assumption contained in the Put-Call parity. This remark can be explained by the fact that until January 2002 domestic investors have an advantage as they may receive a portion or all of the dividend taxes back depending on their tax status. Dividend tax means here the corporate income tax for distributed gains from the gross dividend.

Since the dividends are rebated to domestic investors the DAX should fall by an amount contained between 0 and these dividend taxes. Indeed, the value of this fall depends on the level of these taxes which may be equal to zero and on the weights of domestic and foreign investors trading the DAX. These dividend taxes have the same effects as ordinary dividends and should therefore be used for computing the implied volatilities and the future price implicit in the Black Scholes formula.

Hafner and Wallmeier (2001) suggest a method in order to get around this problem which consists in computing dividends implied by the Put-Call parity. Indeed, combining the futures pricing formula

$$F_{t,\tau_F} = S_t e^{r_{t,\tau_F} \tau_F} - D_{t,\tau_f}$$

and the Put-Call parity

$$C_t - P_t = S_t - D_{t,\tau_O} - K e^{-r_{t,\tau_O} \tau_O}$$

we obtain:

$$C_t - P_t = F_{t,\tau_F} e^{-r_{t,\tau_F}} + D_{t,\tau_F,\tau_O} - K e^{-r_{t,\tau_O} \tau_O} \tag{8.23}$$

where τ_O is the maturity of the options, τ_F is the maturity of the nearest forward whose volume is positive and $D_{t,\tau_F,\tau_O} = D_{t,\tau_F} - D_{t,\tau_O}$ is the difference between the present values of the dividends.

Using (8.23), implied dividends were computed for each pair of put and call with the same strike. Theoretically, for a given time to maturity there must be only one value for these implied dividends. For each maturity the average of these implied dividends was used to compute the corrected price. Using this method implied volatilities are more reliable as the systematic "gap" between put and call volatilities disappears. The only uncertainty at this stage is due to the interpolated rates for the maturity τ_O.

The dataset consists of one file XFGData9701 with 11 columns.

1	Day
2	Month
3	Year
4	Type of option (1 for calls, 0 for puts)
5	Time to maturity (in calendar days)
6	Strike prices
7	Option prices
8	Corrected spot price (implied dividends taken into account)
9	Risk-free interest rate
10	Implied volatility
11	Non-corrected spot price

The data can be read into XploRe by loading the quantlib `finance` and then issuing the following command:

```
data=read("XFGData9701.dat")
```

Next extract all call options on January 3, 1997 with the `paf` command:

```
data=paf(data,(data[,1]==3)&&(data[,4]==1))
```

8.4.2 SPD, delta and gamma

This section provides an example using XploRe to calculate the semiparametric SPD using DAX index options data. It is assumed that the quantlib `finance` has been loaded.

Q `XFGSPDonematurity.xpl` plots the SPD of the series of options closest to maturity. This first example only uses smoothing method in one dimension.

Q `XFGSPDoneday.xpl` calculates and plots the local polynomial SPD for January 10, 1997 for different times to maturity ($\tau = 0.125, 0.25, 0.375$). After loading the data, the implied volatility is estimated using the `volsurf` quantlet, while the first and second derivatives are estimated using `lpderxest` quantlet.

In this example the grid size is 0.01. The bandwidth is chosen arbitrarily at 0.15 and 0.125 for the moneyness and maturity directions respectively. The criteria used is a visual inspection of the first and second derivatives to ensure that they are continuous and smooth. Next the quantlet `spdbl` is used to calculate the SPD which is finally displayed in Figure 8.1.

This figure shows the expected effect of time to maturity on the SPD, which is a loss of kurtosis. The x-axis represents the terminal prices S_T. The local polynomial SPD displays a negative skew compared to a theoretical Black-Scholes SPD. The major reason for the difference is the measure of implied volatility. Using the local polynomial estimators one captures the effect of the "volatility smile" and its effects on the higher moments such as skewness and kurtosis. This result is similar to what Aït-Sahalia and Lo (1998) and Rookley (1997) found in their study.

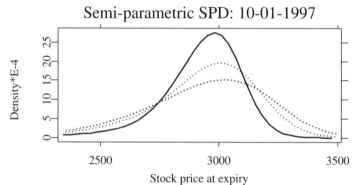

Figure 8.1. Local Polynomial SPD for $\tau = 0.125$ (blue,filled), $\tau = 0.25$ (black,dashed) and $\tau = 0.375$ (red,dotted).

Q XFGSPDoneday.xpl

Figure 8.2 and Figure 8.3 show Delta and Gamma for the full range of strikes and for three different maturities. This method allows the user to get in one step both greeks in one estimation for all strikes and maturities.

A natural question that may arise is how do the SPDs evolve over time. In this section an illustrative example is used to show the dynamics of the SPD over the month of January 1997. **Q** XFGSPDonemonth.xpl estimates and plots the SPD for each trading day in January 1997. The x-axis is the moneyness, y-axis is the trading day, and the z-axis is the SPD. Figure 8.4 shows the local polynomial SPD for the three first weeks of January, 1997.

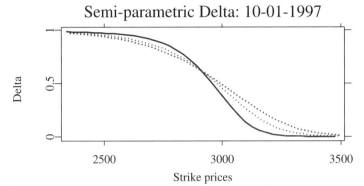

Figure 8.2. Local Polynomial Delta for $\tau = 0.125$ (blue,filled), $\tau = 0.25$ (black,dashed) and $\tau = 0.375$ (red,dotted).

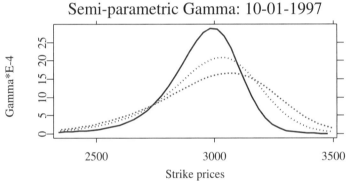

Figure 8.3. Local Polynomial Gamma for $\tau = 0.125$ (blue,filled), $\tau = 0.25$ (black,dashed) and $\tau = 0.375$ (red,dotted).

Q XFGSPDoneday.xpl

8.4.3 Bootstrap confidence bands

Rookley's method serves to estimate the SPD, where V, V' and V'' from (8.16) are computed via local polynomials. The method is now applied to estimate a SPD whose maturity is equal to the maturity of a series of options. In this case, the nonparametric regression is a univariate one.

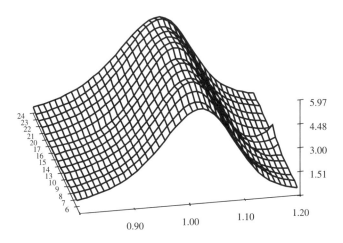

Local-Polynomial SPD: 01-1997, tau=0.250

Figure 8.4. Three weeks State-Price Densities on a moneyness scale.

XFGSPDonemonth.xpl

With a polynomial of order $p = 2$ and a bandwidth $h = \left(n^{-1/9}\right)$, it can be shown that

$$E|\hat{f}_n^* - f^*|^2 = \mathcal{O}\left(n^{-4/9}\right),$$

because

$$
\begin{aligned}
E|\hat{V}_n - V|^2 &= \mathcal{O}\left(n^{-8/9}\right), \\
E|\hat{V}_n' - V'|^2 &= \mathcal{O}\left(n^{-4/9}\right), \\
E|\hat{V}_n'' - V''|^2 &= \mathcal{O}\left(n^{-4/9}\right).
\end{aligned}
$$

This result can be obtained using some theorems related to local polynomial estimation, for example in Fan and Gijbels (1996), if some boundary conditions are satisfied.

An asymptotic approximation of $\hat{f}_n^*$ is complicated by the fact that $\hat{f}_n^*$ is a non linear function of V, V' and V''. Analytical confidence intervals can be obtained using delta methods proposed by Aït-Sahalia (1996). However, an alternative method is to use the bootstrap to construct confidence bands. The idea for estimating the bootstrap bands is to approximate the distribution of

$$\sup_k |\hat{f}^*(k) - f^*(k)|.$$

The following procedure illustrates how to construct bootstrap confidence bands for local polynomial SPD estimation.

1. Collect daily option prices from MD*BASE, only choose those options with the same expiration date, for example, those with time to maturity 49 days on Jan 3, 1997.

2. Use the local polynomial estimation method to obtain the empirical SPD. Notice that when τ is fixed the forward price F is also fixed. So that the implied volatility function $\sigma(K/F)$ can be considered as a fixed design situation, where K is the strike price.

3. Obtain the confidence band using the wild bootstrap method. The wild bootstrap method entails:

   - Suppose that the regression model for the implied volatility function $\sigma(K/F)$ is:
   $$Y_i = \sigma\left(\frac{K_i}{F}\right) + \varepsilon_i, \quad i = 1, \cdots, n.$$

   - Choose a bandwidth g which is larger than the optimal h in order to have oversmoothing. Estimate the implied volatility function $\sigma(K/F)$ nonparametrically and then calculate the residual errors:
   $$\tilde{\varepsilon}_i = Y_i - \hat{\sigma}_h\left(\frac{K_i}{F}\right).$$

   - Replicate B times the series of the $\{\tilde{\varepsilon}_i\}$ with wild bootstrap obtaining $\{\varepsilon_i^{*,j}\}$ for $j = 1, \cdots, B$, Härdle (1990), and build B new bootstrapped samples:

$$Y_i^{*,j} = \hat{\sigma}_g \left(\frac{K_i}{F} \right) + \varepsilon_i^{*,j}.$$

- Estimate the SPD $f^{*,j}$ using bootstrap samples, Rookley's method and the bandwidth h, and build the statistics

$$T_f^* = \sup_z |f^{*,j}(z) - \hat{f}^*(z)|.$$

- Form the $(1 - \alpha)$ bands $[\hat{f}^*(z) - t_{f^*,1-\alpha}, \hat{f}^*(z) + t_{f^*,1-\alpha}]$, where $t_{f^*,1-\alpha}$ denotes the empirical $(1 - \alpha)$-quantile of T_f^*.

Two SPDs (Jan 3 and Jan 31, 1997) whose times to maturity are 49 days were estimated and are plotted in Figure (8.5). The bootstrap confidence band corresponding to the first SPD (Jan 3) is also visible on the chart. In Figure (8.6), the SPDs are displayed on a moneyness metric. It seems that the differences between the SPDs can be eliminated by switching to the moneyness metric. Indeed, as can be extracted from Figure 8.6, both SPDs lie within the 95 percent confidence bands. The number of bootstrap samples is set to $B = 100$. The local polynomial estimation was done on standardized data, h is then set to 0.75 for both plots and g is equal to 1.1 times h. Notice that greater values of g are tried and the conclusion is that the confidence bands are stable to an increase of g.

8.4.4   Comparison to Implied Binomial Trees

In Chapter 7, the Implied Binomial Trees (IBT) are discussed. This method is a close approach to estimate the SPD. It also recovers the SPD nonparametrically from market option prices and uses the Black Scholes formula to establish the relationship between the option prices and implied volatilities as in Rookley's method. In Chapter 7, the Black Scholes formula is only used for Barle and Cakici IBT procedure, but the CRR binomial tree method used by Derman and Kani (1994) has no large difference with it in nature. However, IBT and nonparametric regression methods have some differences caused by different modelling strategies.

The IBT method might be less data-intensive than the nonparametric regression method. By construction, it only requires one cross section of prices. In the

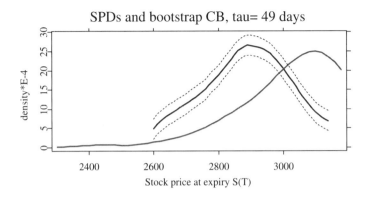

Figure 8.5. SPD estimation and bootstrap confidence band.

Q XFGSPDcb.xpl

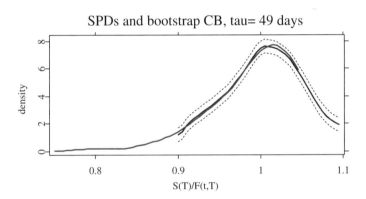

Figure 8.6. SPD estimation and bootstrap confidence band (moneyness metric).

Q XFGSPDcb2.xpl

earlier application with DAX data, option prices are used with different times to maturity for one day to estimate the implied volatility surface first in order

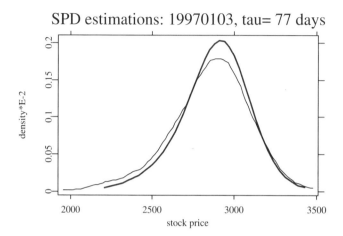

SPD estimations: 19970103, tau= 77 days

Figure 8.7. Comparison of different SPD estimations, by Rookley's method (blue) and IBT (black, thin).

Q XFGSPDcom.xpl

to construct the tree using the relation formula between option prices and risk-neutral probabilities. The precision of the SPD estimation using IBT is heavily affected by the quality of the implied volatility surface and the choice of the levels of the implied tree. Furthermore, from the IBT method only risk-neutral probabilities are obtained. They can be considered as a discrete estimation of the SPD. However, the IBT method is not only useful for estimating SPD, but also for giving a discrete approximation of the underlying process.

The greatest difference between IBTs and nonparametric regression is the requirement of smoothness. The precision of Rookley's SPD estimation is highly dependent on the selected bandwidth. Even if very limited option prices are given, a part of the SPD estimation still can be obtained using nonparametric regression, while the IBT construction has to be given up if no further structure is invoked on the volatility surface. Rookley's method has on first sight no obvious difference with Aït-Sahalia's method theoretically, Aït-Sahalia and Lo (1998). But investigating the convergence rate of the SPD estimation using Aït-Sahalia's method allows one to conduct statistical inference such as test of the stability of the SPD and tests of risk neutrality.

The quantlet ⊙ XFGSPDcom.xpl shows a comparison of the SPD estimates by IBT and Rookley's methods. The differences between these two SPD estimates may be due to the selection of the bandwidths in Rookley's method, the choice of steps in the construction of the IBT and the use of DAX implied dividends in Rookley's method. Figure 8.7 shows the implied binomial trees and the local polynomial SPDs for January, 3 1997.

Both densities seems to be quiet different. Indeed, the IBTs SPD shows a fatter left tail than the Rookley's one and the Rookley's SPD shows a larger kurtosis. To test which of both densities is more reliable, a cross-validation procedure is performed. The idea of this test is to compare the theoretical prices based on (8.1) with those observed on the market. However, as the whole tails are not available for the Rookley's SPD, the test is done on butterfly spreads defined in Section 8.2 since their prices should not be influenced by the tails of the SPDs. For cross-validation, we remove the three calls used to calculate the observed butterfly prices from the sample before estimating the SPD. Moreover, since the largest difference between both SPDs is observed at the ATM point (see Figure 8.7), the test is applied only to the two butterfly spreads whose centers surround the ATM point. The width $2\Delta K$ of the butterfly spread is set to 200.

This procedure is done for the 21 days of January 1997. Figure 8.8 displays the results in term of relative pricing error E:

$$E = \frac{P_{observed} - P_{SPD}}{P_{observed}}$$

where $P_{observed}$ is the observed price of the butterfly spread and P_{SPD} is the price computed using the SPD estimate and (8.1). It seems that both SPDs have a too small kurtosis since the observed prices of butterfly spreads are larger than those of both SPDs in most of the cases. However, Rookley's SPD is in mean nearer to the observed price than the IBT's one.

Bibliography

Aït-Sahalia, Y. (1996). The Delta method for Nonparametric Kernel Functionals, mimeo.

Aït-Sahalia, Y. and Lo, A. W. (1998). Nonparametric estimation of state-price densities implicit in financial asset prices, *Journal of Finance* **53**: 499–547.

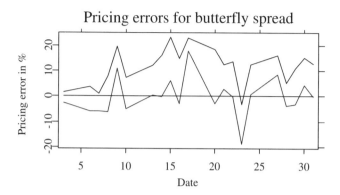

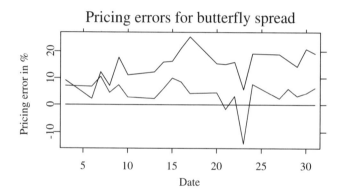

Figure 8.8. The upper graph display the relative pricing errors for the butterfly spread centered on the nearest strike on the left side of the ATM point. The second graph corresponds to the butterfly spread centered on the nearest strike on the right side of the ATM point. The black lines represent the IBT's pricing errors and the blue the Rookley's errors.

Arrow, K. (1964). The role of securities in the optimal allocation of risk bearing, *Review of Economic Studies* **31**: 91–96.

Bahra, B. (1997). Implied risk-neutral probability density functions from option prices: theory and application. Bank of England Working Paper 66.

Black, F. and Scholes, M. (1973). The pricing of options and corporate liabilities, *Journal of Political Economy* **81**: 637–654.

Breeden, D. and Litzenberger, R. H. (1978). Prices of state-contingent claims implicit in option prices, *Journal of Business* **51**: 621–651.

Debreu, G. (1959). *Theory of Value*, John Wiley and Sons, New York.

Derman, E. and Kani, I. (1994). Riding on the smile, *Risk* **7**: 32–39.

Fan, J. and Gijbels, I. (1996). *Local Polynomial Modelling and Its Apllications*, Chapman and Hall, New York. Vol. 66 of Monographs on Statistics and Applied Probability.

Hafner, R. and Wallmeier, M. (2001). The dynamics of DAX implied volatilities, *Quarterly International Journal of Finance* **1**: 1–27.

Härdle, W. (1990). *Applied Nonparametric Regression*, Cambridge University Press, New York.

Härdle, W., Hlávka, Z. and Klinke, S. (2000). *XploRe Application Guide*, Springer-Verlag, Berlin.

Hutchinson, J., Lo, A. and Poggio, A. (1994). A nonparametric approach to the pricing and hedging of derivative securities via learning networks, *Journal of Finance* **49**: 851–889.

Lucas, R. E. (1978). Asset prices in an exchange economy, *Econometrica* **46**(1429-1446).

Melick, W. and Thomas, C. (1997). Recovering an Asset's Implied PDF from Option Prices: An application to Crude Oil During the Gulf Crisis, *Journal of Financial and Quantitative Analysis* **32**: 91–115.

Merton, R. B. (1973). Rational theory of option pricing, *Bell Journal of Economics and Management Science* **4**: 141–183.

Rookley, C. (1997). Fully exploiting the information content of intra-day option quotes: Applications in option pricing and risk management. mimeo.

Rubinstein, M. (1976). The valuation of uncertain income streams and the pricing of options, *Bell Journal of Economics* **7**(407-425).

Rubinstein, M. (1985). Nonparametric tests of alternative option pricing models using all reported trades and quotes on the 30 most active cboe option classes from august 23, 1976 to august 31, 1978, *Journal of Finance* **40**: 455–480.

Rubinstein, M. (1994). Implied binomial trees, *Journal of Finance* **49**: 771–818.

Ruppert, D. (1997). Empirical-bias bandwidths for local polynomial nonparametric regression and density estimation, *Journal of the American Statistical Association* **92**: 1049–1062.

Ruppert, D., Wand, M. P., Holst, U. and Hössler, O. (1997). Local polynomial variance-function estimation, *Technometrics* **39**: 262–273.

Yatchew, A. and Härdle, W. (2002). Dynamic nonparametric state price density estimation using constrained least squares and the bootstrap. *Journal of Econometrics, forthcoming.*

9 Trading on Deviations of Implied and Historical Densities

Oliver Jim Blaskowitz and Peter Schmidt

9.1 Introduction

In recent years a number of methods have been developed to infer implied state price densities (SPD) from cross sectional option prices, Chapter 7 and 8. Instead of comparing this density to a historical density extracted from the observed time series of the underlying asset prices, i.e. a risk neutral density to an actual density, Ait–Sahalia, Wang and Yared (2000) propose to compare two risk neutral densities, one obtained from cross sectional S&P 500 option data and the other from the S&P 500 index time series. Furthermore, they propose trading strategies designed to exploit differences in skewness and kurtosis of both densities. The goal of this article is to apply the procedure to the german DAX index. While the option implied SPD is estimated by means of the Barle and Cakici, Barle and Cakici (1998), implied binomial tree version, the time series density is inferred from the time series of the DAX index by applying a method used by Ait–Sahalia, Wang and Yared (2000). Based on the comparison of both SPDs the performance of skewness and kurtosis trades is investigated.

We use options data included in MD*BASE. This is a database located at CASE (Center for Applied Statistics and Economics) of Humboldt–Universität zu Berlin. The time period is limited to data of the period between 01/01/97 and 12/31/99 for which MD*BASE contains daily closing prices of the DAX index, EUREX DAX option settlement prices and annual interest rates which are adjusted to the time to maturity of the above mentioned EUREX DAX options.

While Section 9.2 applies the Barle and Cakici implied binomial tree algorithm which estimates the option implied SPD using a two week cross section of DAX index options, Section 9.3 explains and applies the method to estimate DAX time series SPD from 3 months of historical index prices. Following, in Section 9.4 we compare the conditional skewness and kurtosis of both densities. Section 9.5 and 9.6 complete the chapter with the investigation of 4 trading strategies and Section 9.7 completes with some critical remarks.

9.2   Estimation of the Option Implied SPD

Barle–Cakici's modification of Derman–Kani's Implied Binomial Tree (IBT) yields a proxy for the option implied SPD, f^*, see Chapter 7. XploRe provides quantlets computing Derman–Kani's and Barle–Cakici's IBT's. Since the latter proved to be slightly more robust than the former, Jackwerth (1999), we decide to use Barle–Cakici's IBT to compute the option implied SPD. In the following subsection, we follow closely the notation used in Chapter 7. That is, N denotes the number of evenly spaced time steps of length Δt in which the tree is divided into (so we have $N+1$ levels). $F_{n,i} = e^{r\Delta t}s_{n,i}$ is the forward price of the underlying, $s_{n,i}$, at node i at, level n. Each level n corresponds to time $t_n = n\Delta t$.

9.2.1   Application to DAX Data

Using the DAX index data from MD*BASE, we estimate the 3 month option implied IBT SPD f^* by means of the XploRe quantlets IBTbc and volsurf and a two week cross section of DAX index option prices for 30 periods beginning in April 1997 and ending in September 1999. We measure time to maturity (TTM) in days and annualize it using the factor 360, giving the annualized time to maturity $\tau = \text{TTM}/360$. For each period, we assume a flat yield curve. We extract from MD*BASE the maturity consistent interest rate.

We describe the procedure in more detail for the first period. First of all, we estimate the implied volatility surface given the two week cross section of DAX option data and utilizing the XploRe quantlet volsurf which computes the 3 dimensional implied volatility surface (implied volatility over time to maturity and moneyness) using a kernel smoothing procedure. Friday, April 18, 1997 is the 3rd Friday of April 1997. On Monday, April 21, 1997, we estimate the volatility surface, using two weeks of option data from Monday, April 7, 1997, to Friday, April 18, 1997. Following, we start the IBT computation using the

DAX price of this Monday, April 21, 1997. The volatility surface is estimated
for the moneyness interval $[0.8, 1.2]$ and the time to maturity interval $[0.0, 1.0]$.
Following, the XploRe quantlet IBTbc takes the volatility surface as input and
computes the IBT using Barle and Cakici's method. Note that the observed
smile enters the IBT via the analytical Black–Scholes pricing formula for a call
$C(F_{n,i}, t_{n+1})$ and for a put $P(F_{n,i}, t_{n+1})$ which are functions of $S_{t_1} = s_{1,1}$,
$K = F_{n,i}$, r, t_{n+1} and $\sigma_{impl}(F_{n,i}, t_{n+1})$. We note, it may happen that at the
edge of the tree option prices, with associated strike prices $F_{n,i}$ and node prices
$s_{n+1,i+1}$, have to be computed for which the moneyness ratio $s_{n+1,i+1}/F_{n,i}$ is
outside the intverall $[0.8, 1.2]$ on which the volatility surface has been estimated.
In these cases, we use the volatility at the edge of the surface. Note, as well,
that the mean of the IBT SPD is equal to the futures price by construction of
the IBT.

Finally, we transform the SPD over $s_{N+1,i}$ into a SPD over log–returns $u_{N+1,i} = \ln(s_{N+1,i}/s_{1,1})$ as follows:

$$P(s_{N+1,i} = x) \quad = \quad P\left(\ln\left(\tfrac{s_{N+1,i}}{s_{1,1}} \right) = \ln\left(\tfrac{x}{s_{1,1}} \right) \right) \quad = \quad P\left(u_{N+1,i} = u \right)$$

where $u = \ln(x/s_{1,1})$. That is, $s_{N+1,i}$ has the same probability as $u_{N+1,i}$. See
Figure 9.1 for the SPD computed with parameters $N = 10$ time steps and
interest rate $r = 3.23$.

A crucial aspect using binomial trees is the choice of the number of time steps
N in which the time interval $[t, T]$ is divided. In general one can state, the more
time steps are used the better is the discrete approximation of the continuous
diffusion process and of the SPD. Unfortunately, the bigger N, the more node
prices $s_{n,i}$ possibly have to be overridden in the IBT framework. Thereby we are
effectively losing the information about the smile at the corresponding nodes.
Therefore, we computed IBT's for different numbers of time steps. We found
no hint for convergence of the variables of interest, skewness and kurtosis. Since
both variables seemed to fluctuate around a mean, we compute IBT's with time
steps $10, 20, \ldots, 100$ and consider the average of these ten values for skewness
and kurtosis as the option implied SPD skewness and kurtosis.

Applying this procedure for all 30 periods, beginning in April 1997 and ending
in September 1999, we calculate the time series of skewness and kurtosis of the
3 month implied SPD f^* shown in Figures 9.3 and 9.4. We see that the implied
SPD is clearly negatively skewed for all periods but one. In September 1999 it
is slightly positively skewed. The pattern is similar for the kurtosis of f^* which
is leptokurtic in all but one period. In October 1998 the density is platykurtic.

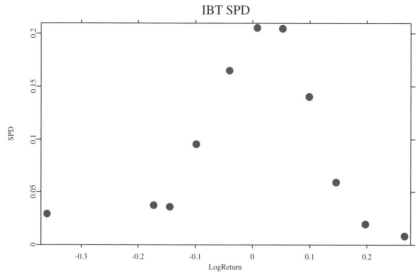

Figure 9.1. Option implied SPD estimated on April 21, 1997, by an IBT with $N = 10$ time steps, $S_0 = 3328.41$, $r = 3.23$ and $\tau = 88/360$.

9.3   Estimation of the Historical SPD

While the previous section was dedicated to finding a proxy for f^* used by investors to price options, this section approximates the historical underlyings' density g^* for date $t = T$ using all the information available at date $t = 0$. Of course, if the process governing the underlying asset dynamics were common knowledge and if agents had perfect foresight, then by no arbitrage arguments both SPDs should be equal. Following Ait–Sahalia, Wang and Yared (2000), the density extracted from the observed underlyings' data is not comparable to the density implied by observed option data without assumptions on investor's preferences. As in Härdle and Tsybakov (1995), they apply an estimation method which uses the observed asset prices to infer indirectly the time series SPD. First, we will explain the estimation method for the underlyings' SPD. Second, we apply it to DAX data.

9.3.1   The Estimation Method

Assuming the underlying S to follow an Îto diffusion process driven by a Brownian motion W:

$$dS_t = \mu(S_t)dt + \sigma(S_t)dW_t. \tag{9.1}$$

Ait–Sahalia, Wang and Yared (2000) rely on Girsanov's characterization of the change of measure from the actual density to the SPD. It says the diffusion function of the asset's dynamics is identical under both the risk neutral and the actual measure and only the drift function needs to be adjusted, leading to the risk neutral asset dynamics:

$$dS_t^* = (r_{t,\tau} - \delta_{t,\tau})S_t^* dt + \sigma(S_t^*)dW_t^*. \tag{9.2}$$

Let $g_t(S_t, S_T, \tau, r_{t,\tau}, \delta_{t,\tau})$ denote the conditional density of S_T given S_t generated by the dynamics defined in equation (9.1) and $g_t^*(S_t, S_T, \tau, r_{t,\tau}, \delta_{t,\tau})$ denote the conditional density generated by equation (9.2) then f^* can only be compared to the risk neutral density g^* and not to g.

A crucial feature of this method is that the diffusion functions are identical under both the actual and the risk neutral dynamics (which follows from Girsanov's theorem). Therefore, it is not necessary to observe the risk neutral path of the DAX index $\{S_t^*\}$. The function $\sigma(\bullet)$ is estimated using N^* observed index values $\{S_t\}$ and applying Florens–Zmirou's (1993) (FZ) nonparametric version of the minimum contrast estimators:

$$\hat{\sigma}_{FZ}(S) = \frac{\sum_{i=1}^{N^*-1} K_{FZ}(\frac{S_i-S}{h_{FZ}})N^*\{S_{(i+1)/N^*} - S_{i/N^*}\}^2}{\sum_{i=1}^{N^*} K_{FZ}(\frac{S_i-S}{h_{FZ}})}, \tag{9.3}$$

where $K_{FZ}(\bullet)$ is a kernel function and h_{FZ} is a bandwidth parameter such that:

$$(N^* h_{FZ})^{-1} ln(N^*) \quad \to \quad 0 \quad \text{and} \quad N^* h_{FZ}^4 \quad \to \quad 0$$

as $N^* \to \infty$. Without imposing restrictions on the drift function $\hat{\sigma}_{FZ}$ is an unbiased estimator of σ in the model specified in equation (9.2). Since the DAX index is a performance index ($\delta_{t,\tau} = 0$), the risk neutral drift rate of equation (9.2) is equal to $r_{t,\tau}$.

Once $\sigma(\bullet)$ is estimated, the time series SPD g^* can be computed by Monte Carlo integration. Applying the Milstein scheme (Kloeden, Platen and Schurz

(1994)), we simulate $M = 10,000$ paths of the diffusion process:

$$dS_t^* \;=\; r_{t,\tau}S_t^* dt + \hat{\sigma}_{FZ}(S_t^*)dW_t^* \tag{9.4}$$

for a time period of 3 months, starting value $S_{t=0}$ equal to the DAX index value at the beginning of the period, collect the endpoints at T of these simulated paths $\{S_{T,m} : m = 1,\ldots,M\}$ and annualize the index log–returns. Then g^* is obtained by means of a nonparametric kernel density estimation of the continuously compounded log–returns u:

$$\hat{p}_t^*(u) \;=\; \frac{1}{Mh_{MC}}\sum_{m=1}^{M} K_{MC}\left(\frac{u_m - u}{h_{MC}}\right) \tag{9.5}$$

where u_m is the log–return at the end of the mth path and $K_{MC}(\bullet)$ is a kernel function and h_{MC} is a bandwidth parameter. The equation:

$$\mathrm{P}(S_T \leq S) \;=\; \mathrm{P}(u \leq \log(S/S_t)) \;=\; \int_{-\infty}^{\log(S/S_t)} p_t^*(u)du$$

with $u = \ln(S_T/S_t)$ relates this density estimator to the SPD g^*:

$$g_t^*(S) \;=\; \tfrac{\partial}{\partial S}\mathrm{P}(S_T \leq S) \;=\; \frac{p_t^*(\log(S/S_t))}{S}.$$

This method results in a nonparametric estimator $\hat{g}^*$ which is $\sqrt{N^*}$–consistent as $M \to \infty$ even though $\hat{\sigma}_{FZ}$ converges at a slower rate (Ait–Sahalia, Wang and Yared (2000)).

In the absence of arbitrage, the futures price is the expected future value of the spot price under the risk neutral measure. Therefore the time series distribution is translated such that its mean matches the implied future price. Then the bandwidth h_{MC} is chosen to best match the variance of the IBT implied distribution. In order to avoid over– or undersmoothing of g^*, h_{MC} is constrained to be within 0.5 to 5 times the optimal bandwidth implied by Silverman's rule of thumb. This procedure allows us to focus the density comparison on the skewness and kurtosis of the two densities.

9.3.2   Application to DAX Data

Using the DAX index data from MD*BASE we estimate the diffusion function $\sigma^2(\bullet)$ from equation (9.2) by means of past index prices and simulate (forward) $M = 10,000$ paths to obtain the time series density, g^*.

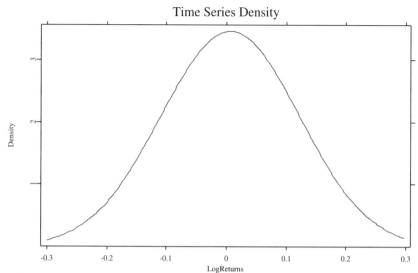

Figure 9.2. Mean and variance adjusted estimated time series density on Friday, April 18, 1997. Simulated with $M = 10,000$ paths, $S_0 = 3328.41$, $r = 3.23$ and $\tau = 88/360$.

To be more precise, we explain the methodology for the first period in more detail. First, note that Friday, April 18, 1997, is the 3rd Friday of April 1997. Thus, on Monday, April 21, 1997, we use 3 months of DAX index prices from Monday, January 20, 1997, to Friday, April 18, 1997, to estimate σ^2. Following, on the same Monday, we start the 3 months 'forward' Monte Carlo simulation. The bandwidth h_{FZ} is determined by Cross Validation applying the XploRe quantlet `regxbwcrit` which determines the optimal bandwidth from a range of bandwidths by using the resubstitution estimator with the penalty function 'Generalized Cross Validation'.

Knowing the diffusion function it is now possible to Monte Carlo simulate the index evolution. The Milstein scheme applied to equation (9.2) is given by:

$$S_{i/N^{**}} = S_{(i-1)/N^{**}} + rS_{(i-1)/N^{**}}\Delta t + \sigma(S_{(i-1)/N^{**}})\Delta W_{i/N^{**}} +$$
$$\frac{1}{2}\sigma(S_{(i-1)/N^{**}})\frac{\partial \sigma}{\partial S}(S_{(i-1)/N^{**}})\Big((\Delta W_{(i-1)/N^{**}})^2 - \Delta t\Big),$$

where we set the drift equal to r which is extracted from MD*BASE and corresponds to the time to maturity used in the simulation and N^{**} is the number of days to maturity. The first derivative of $\sigma(\cdot)$ is approximated by:

$$\frac{\partial \sigma}{\partial S}(S_{(i-1)/N^{**}}) \;=\; \frac{\sigma(S_{(i-1)/N^{**}}) - \sigma(S_{(i-1)/N^{**}} - \Delta S)}{\Delta S},$$

where ΔS is 1/2 of the width of the bingrid on which the diffusion function is estimated. Finally the estimated diffusion function is linearly extrapolated at both ends of the bingrid to accommodate potential outliers.

With these ingredients we start the simulation with index value $S_0 = 3328.41$ (Monday, April 21, 1997) and time to maturity $\tau = 88/360$ and $r = 3.23$. The expiration date is Friday, July 18, 1997. From these simulated index values we calculate annualized log–returns which we take as input of the nonparametric density estimation (see equation (9.5)). The XploRe quantlet denxest accomplishes the estimation of the time series density by means of the Gaussian kernel function:

$$K(u) \;=\; \frac{1}{\sqrt{2\pi}} \exp\left(-\frac{1}{2}u^2 \right).$$

The bandwidth h_{MC} is computed by the XploRe quantlet denrot which applies Silverman's rule of thumb.

First of all, we calculate the optimum bandwidth h_{MC} given the vector of $10,000$ simulated index values. Then we search the bandwidth h'_{MC} which implies a variance of g^* to be closest to the variance of f^* (but to be still within 0.5 to 5 times h_{MC}). We stop the search if $\mathrm{var}(g^*)$ is within a range of 5% of $\mathrm{var}(f^*)$. Following, we translate g^* such that its mean matches the futures price F. Finally, we transform this density over DAX index values S_T into a density $g^{*'}$ over log–returns u_T. Since

$$P(S_T < x) \;=\; P\left(\ln\left(\tfrac{S_T}{S_t}\right) < \ln\left(\tfrac{x}{S_t}\right) \right) \;=\; P(u_T < u)$$

where $x = S_t e^u$, we have

$$P(S_T \in [x, x + \Delta x]) \;=\; P(u_T \in [u, u + \Delta u])$$

and

$$P(S_T \in [x, x + \Delta x]) \;\approx\; g^*(x)\Delta x$$
$$P(u_T \in [u, u + \Delta u]) \;\approx\; g^{*'}(u)\Delta u.$$

Therefore, we have as well (see Härdle and Simar (2002) for density transformation techniques)

$$g^{*\prime}(u) \quad \approx \quad \frac{g^*(S_t e^u)\Delta(S_t e^u)}{\Delta u} \quad \approx \quad g^*(S_t e^u) S_t e^u.$$

To simplify notations, we will denote both densities g^*. Figure 9.2 displays the resulting time series density over log–returns on Friday, April 18, 1997. Proceeding in the same way for all 30 periods beginning in April 1997 and ending in September 1999, we obtain the time series of the 3 month 'forward' skewness and kurtosis values of g^* shown in Figures 9.3 and 9.4. The figures reveal that the time series distribution is systematically slightly negatively skewed. Skewness is very close to zero. As far as kurtosis is concerned we can extract from Figure 9.4 that it is systematically smaller than but nevertheless very close to 3. Additionally, all time series density plots looked like the one shown in Figure 9.2.

9.4   Comparison of Implied and Historical SPD

At this point it is time to compare implied and historical SPDs. Since by construction, expectation and variance are adjusted, we focus the comparison on skewness and kurtosis. Starting with skewness, we can extract from Figure 9.3 that except for one period the IBT implied SPD is systematically more negatively skewed than the time series SPD, a fact that is quite similar to what Ait–Sahalia, Wang and Yared (2000) already found for the S&P 500. The 3 month IBT implied SPD for Friday, September 17, 1999 is slightly positively skewed. It may be due to the fact that in the months preceeding June 1999, the month in which the 3 month implied SPD was estimated, the DAX index stayed within a quite narrow horizontal range of index values after a substantial downturn in the 3rd quarter of 1998 (see Figure 9.11) and agents therefore possibly believed index prices lower than the average would be more realistic to appear. However, this is the only case where $\text{skew}(f^*) > \text{skew}(g^*)$.

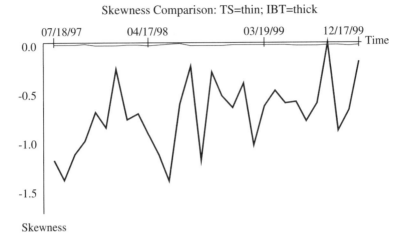

Figure 9.3. Comparison of Skewness time series for 30 periods.

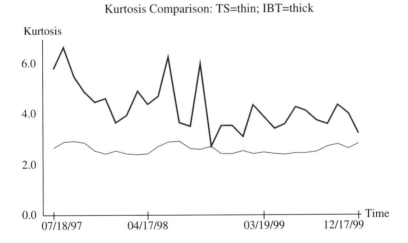

Figure 9.4. Comparison of Kurtosis time series for 30 periods.

The kurtosis time series reveals a similar pattern as the skewness time series. The IBT SPD has except for one period systematically more kurtosis than the time series SPD. Again this feature is in line with what Ait–Sahalia, Wang and Yared (2000) found for the S&P 500. The 3 month IBT implied SPD for Friday, October 16, 1998 has a slightly smaller kurtosis than the time series SPD. That is, investors assigned less probability mass to high and low index prices. Note that the implied SPD was estimated in July 1998 after a period of 8 months of booming asset prices (see Figure 9.11). It is comprehensible in such an environment that high index prices seemed less realistic to appear. Since the appearance of low index prices seemed to be unrealistic as well, agents obviously expected the DAX move rather sideways.

9.5 Skewness Trades

In the previous section we learned that the implied and the time series SPD's reveal differences in skewness and kurtosis. In the following two sections, we investigate how to profit from this knowledge. In general, we are interested in what option to buy or to sell at the day at which both densities were estimated. We consider exclusively European call or put options.

According to Ait–Sahalia, Wang and Yared (2000), all strategies are designed such that we do not change the resulting portfolio until maturity, i.e. we keep all options until they expire. We use the following terms for moneyness which we define as $K/(S_t e^{(T-t)r})$:

	Moneyness(FOTM Put)	$<$	0.90
0.90	$\leq$	Moneyness(NOTM Put)	$<$	0.95
0.95	$\leq$	Moneyness(ATM Put)	$<$	1.00
1.00	$\leq$	Moneyness(ATM Call)	$<$	1.05
1.05	$\leq$	Moneyness(NOTM Call)	$<$	1.10
1.10	$\leq$	Moneyness(FOTM Call)		

Table 9.1. Definitions of moneyness regions.

where FOTM, NOTM, ATM stand for far out–of–the–money, near out–of–the–money and at–the–money respectively.

A skewness trading strategy is supposed to exploit differences in skewness of two distributions by buying options in the range of strike prices where they are underpriced and selling options in the range of strike prices where they are overpriced. More specifically, if the implied SPD f^* is less skewed (for example more negatively skewed) than the time series SPD g^*, i.e. skew(f^*) < skew(g^*), we sell the whole range of strikes of OTM puts and buy the whole range of strikes of OTM calls (S1 trade). Conversely, if the implied SPD is more skewed, i.e. skew(f^*) > skew(g^*), we initiate the S2 trade by buying the whole range of strikes of OTM puts and selling the whole range of strikes of OTM calls. In both cases we keep the options until expiration.

Skewness s is a measure of asymmetry of a probability distribution. While for a distribution symmetric around its mean $s = 0$, for an asymmetric distribution $s > 0$ indicates more weight to the left of the mean. Recalling from option pricing theory the pricing equation for a European call option, Franke, Härdle and Hafner (2001):

$$C(S_t, K, r, T - t) \quad = \quad e^{-r(T-t)} \int_0^\infty \max(S_T - K, 0) f^*(S_T) dS_T, \quad (9.6)$$

where f^* is the implied SPD, we see that when the two SPD's are such that skew(f^*) < skew(g^*), agents apparently assign a lower probability to high outcomes of the underlying than would be justified by the time series density, see Figure 7.13. Since for call options only the right 'tail' of the support determines the theoretical price, the latter is smaller than the price implied by equation (9.6) using the time series density. That is, we buy underpriced calls. The same reasoning applies to European put options. Looking at the pricing equation for such an option:

$$P(S_t, K, r, T - t) \quad = \quad e^{-r(T-t)} \int_0^\infty \max(K - S_T, 0) f^*(S_T) dS_T, \quad (9.7)$$

we conclude that prices implied by this pricing equation using f^* are higher than the prices using the time series density. That is, we sell puts.

Since we hold all options until expiration and due to the fact that options for all strikes are not always available in markets we are going to investigate the payoff profile at expiration of this strategy for two compositions of the portfolio. To get an idea about the exposure at maturity let us begin with a simplified portfolio consisting of one short position in a put option with moneyness of 0.95 and one long position in a call option with moneyness of 1.05. To further simplify, we assume that the future price F is equal to 100 EUR. Thus, the portfolio has a payoff which is increasing in S_T, the price of the underlying at maturity. For $S_T < 95$ EUR the payoff is negative and for $S_T > 105$ EUR it is positive.

However, in the application we encounter portfolios containing several long/short calls/puts with increasing/decreasing strikes as indicated in Table 9.2.

Figure 9.5. S1 trade payoff at maturity of portfolio detailed in Table 9.2.

Figure 9.5 shows the payoff of a portfolio of 10 short puts with strikes ranging from 86 EUR to 95 EUR and of 10 long calls striking at 105 EUR to 114 EUR, the future price is still assumed to be 100 EUR. The payoff is still increasing in S_T but it is concave in the left tail and convex in the right tail. This is due to the fact that our portfolio contains, for example, at $S_T = 106$ EUR two call options which are in the money instead of only one compared to the portfolio considered above. These options generate a payoff which is twice as much. At $S_T = 107$ EUR the payoff is influenced by three ITM calls procuring a payoff which is three times higher as in the situation before etc. In a similar way we can explain the slower increase in the left tail. Just to sum up, we can state that this trading rule has a favorable payoff profile in a bull market where the underlying is increasing. But in bear markets it possibly generates negative cash flows. Buying (selling) two or more calls (puts) at the same strike would change the payoff profile in a similar way leading to a faster increase (slower decrease) with every call (put) bought (sold).

The S2 strategy payoff behaves in the opposite way. The same reasoning can be applied to explain its payoff profile. In contradiction to the S1 trade the S2 trade is favorable in a falling market.

	S1 Moneyness	OTM–S1 Moneyness
short put	0.95	$0.86 - 0.95$
long call	1.05	$1.05 - 1.14$

Table 9.2. Portfolios of skewness trades.

9.5.1 Performance

Given the skewness values for the implied SPD and the time series SPD we now have a look on the performance of the skewness trades. Performance is measured in net EUR cash flows which is the sum of the cash flows generated at initiation in $t = 0$ and at expiration in $t = T$. We ignore any interest rate between these two dates. Using EUREX settlement prices of 3 month DAX put and calls we initiated the S1 strategy at the Monday immediately following the 3rd Friday of each month, beginning in April 1997 and ending in September 1999. January, February, March 1997 drop out due to the time series density estimation for the 3rd Friday of April 1997. October, November and December 1999 drop out since we look 3 months forward. The cash flow at initiation stems from the inflow generated by the written options and the outflow generated by the bought options and hypothetical 5% transaction costs on prices of bought and sold options. Since all options are kept in the portfolio until maturity (time to expiration is approximately 3 months, more precisely $\tau = \text{TTM}/360$) the cash flow in $t = T$ is composed of the sum of the inner values of the options in the portfolio.

Figure 9.6 shows the EUR cash flows at initiation, at expiration and the resulting net cash flow for each portfolio. The sum of all cash flows, the total net cash flow, is strongly positive (9855.50 EUR). Note that the net cash flow (blue bar) is always positive except for the portfolios initiated in June 1998 and in September 1998 where we incur heavy losses compared to the gains in the other periods. In other words, this strategy would have procured 28 times moderate gains and two times large negative cash flows. As Figure 9.5 suggests this strategy is exposed to a directional risk, a feature that appears in December 1997 and June 1998 where large payoffs at expiration (positive and negative) occur. Indeed, the period of November and December 1997 was a turning point of the DAX and the beginning of an 8 month bull market, explaining the large payoff in March 1998 of the portfolio initiated in December 1997. The same

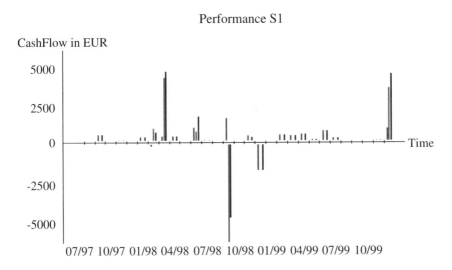

Figure 9.6. Performance of S1 trade with 5% transaction costs. The first (red), second (magenta) and the third bar (blue) show for each period the cash flow in $t = 0$, in $t = T$ and the net cash flow respectively. Cash flows are measured in EUR. ◨ XFGSpdTradeSkew.xpl

arguing explains the large negative payoff of the portfolio set up in June 1998 expiring in September 1998 (refer to Figure 9.11). Another point to note is that there is a zero cash flow at expiration in 24 periods. Periods with a zero cash flow at initiation and at expiration are due to the fact that there was not set up any portfolio (there was no OTM option in the database).

Since there is only one period (June 1999), when the implied SPD is more skewed than the time series SPD a comparison of the S1 trade with knowledge of the latter SPD's and without this knowledge is not useful. A comparison of the skewness measures would have filtered out exactly one positive net cash flow, more precisely the cash flow generated by a portfolio set up in June 1999. But to what extend this may be significant is uncertain. For the same reason the S2 trade has no great informational content. Applied to real data it would have procured a negative total net cash flow. Actually, only in June 1999 a portfolio would have been set up. While the S1 trade performance was independent of the knowledge of the implied and the time series SPD's the S2 trade performance changed significantly as it was applied in each period (without knowing both SPD's). The cash flow profile seemed to be the inverse of Figure 9.6 indicating that should there be an options mispricing it would probably be in the sense that the implied SPD is more negatively skewed than the time series SPD.

9.6   Kurtosis Trades

A kurtosis trading strategy is supposed to exploit differences in kurtosis of two distributions by buying options in the range of strike prices where they are underpriced and selling options in the range of strike prices where they are overpriced. More specifically, if the implied SPD f^* has more kurtosis than the time series SPD g^*, i.e. kurt(f^*) > kurt(g^*), we sell the whole range of strikes of FOTM puts, buy the whole range of strikes of NOTM puts, sell the whole range of strikes of ATM puts and calls, buy the whole range of strikes of NOTM calls and sell the whole range of strikes of FOTM calls (K1 trade). Conversely, if the implied SPD has less kurtosis than the time series density g^*, i.e. kurt(f^*) < kurt(g^*), we initiate the K2 trade by buying the whole range of strikes of FOTM puts, selling the whole range of strikes of NOTM puts, buying the whole range of strikes of ATM puts and calls, selling the whole range of strikes of NOTM calls and buying the whole range of strikes of FOTM calls. In both cases we keep the options until expiration.

Kurtosis κ measures the fatness of the tails of a distribution. For a normal distribution we have $\kappa = 3$. A distribution with $\kappa > 3$ is said to be leptokurtic and has fatter tails than the normal distribution. In general, the bigger κ is, the fatter the tails are. Again we consider the option pricing formulae (9.6) and (9.7) and reason as above using the probability mass to determine the moneyness regions where we buy or sell options. Look at Figure 7.14 for a situation in which the implied density has more kurtosis than the time series density triggering a K1 trade.

To form an idea of the K1 strategy's exposure at maturity we start once again with a simplified portfolio containing two short puts with moneyness 0.90 and 1.00, one long put with moneyness 1.00, two short calls with moneyness 1.00 and 1.10 and one long call with moneyness 1.05. Figure 9.7 reveals that this portfolio inevitably leads to a negative payoff at maturity regardless the movement of the underlying.

Should we be able to buy the whole range of strikes as the K1 trading rule suggests, the portfolio is given in Table 9.3, FOTM–NOTM–ATM–K1, we get

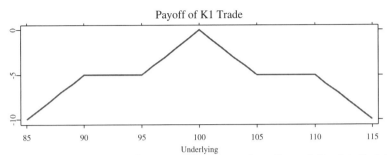

Figure 9.7. Kurtosis trade 1 payoff at maturity of portfolio detailed in Table 9.3.

a payoff profile (Figure 9.8) which is quite similar to the one from Figure 9.7. In fact, the payoff function looks like the 'smooth' version of Figure 9.7.

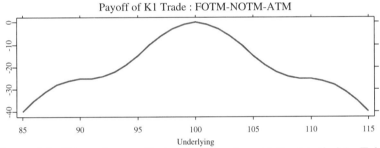

Figure 9.8. K1 trade payoff at maturity of portfolio detailed in Table 9.3.

Changing the number of long puts and calls in the NOTM regions can produce a positive payoff. Setting up the portfolio given in Table 9.3, NOTM–K1, results in a payoff function shown in Figure 9.9. It is quite intuitive that the more long positions the portfolio contains the more positive the payoff will be. Conversely, if we added to that portfolio FOTM short puts and calls the payoff would decrease in the FOTM regions.

As a conclusion we can state that the payoff function can have quite different shapes depending heavily on the specific options in the portfolio. If it is possible to implement the K1 trading rule as proposed the payoff is negative. But it may

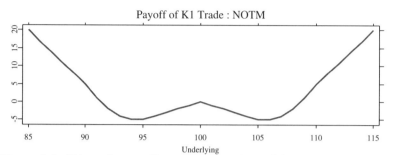

Figure 9.9. K1 trade payoff at maturity of portfolio detailed in Table 9.3.

happen that the payoff function is positive in case that more NOTM options (long positions) are available than FOTM or ATM (short positions) options.

	K1 Moneyness	FOTM–NOTM–ATM–K1 Moneyness	NOTM–K1 Moneyness
short put	0.90	0.86 − 0.90	0.90
long put	0.95	0.91 − 0.95	0.91 − 0.95
short put	1.00	0.96 − 1.00	1.00
short call	1.00	1.00 − 1.04	1.00
long call	1.05	1.05 − 1.09	1.05 − 1.09
short call	1.10	1.10 − 1.14	1.10

Table 9.3. Portfolios of kurtosis trades.

9.6.1   Performance

To investigate the performance of the kurtosis trades, K1 and K2, we proceed in the same way as for the skewness trade. The total net EUR cash flow of the K1 trade, applied when $\text{kurt}(f^*) > \text{kurt}(g^*)$, is strongly positive ($10,915.77$ EUR). As the payoff profiles from figures 9.7 and 9.8 already suggested, all portfolios generate negative cash flows at expiration (see magenta bar in Figure 9.10). In contrast to that, the cash flow at initiation in $t = 0$ is always positive. Given the positive total net cash flow, we can state that the K1 trade earns its profit in $t = 0$. Looking at the DAX evolution shown in Figure 9.11, we understand why

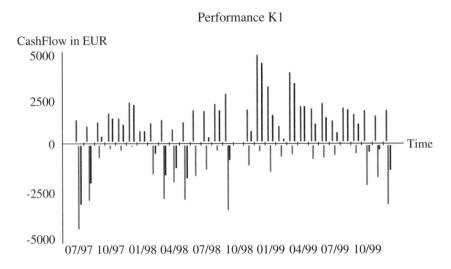

Figure 9.10. Performance of K1 trade with 5% transaction costs. The first (red), second (magenta) and the third bar (blue) show for each period the cash flow in $t = 0$, in $t = T$ and the net cash flow respectively. Cash flows are measured in EUR. ⊡ XFGSpdTradeKurt.xpl

the payoff of the portfolios set up in the months of April 1997, May 1997 and in the months from November 1997 to June 1998 is relatively more negative than for the portfolios of June 1997 to October 1997 and November 1998 to June 1999. The reason is that the DAX is moving up or down for the former months and stays within an almost horizontal range of quotes for the latter months (see the payoff profile depicted in Figure 9.8). In July 1998 no portfolio was set up since $\text{kurt}(f^*) < \text{kurt}(g^*)$.

What would have happened if we had implemented the K1 trade without knowing both SPD's? Again, the answer to this question can only be indicated due to the rare occurences of periods in which $\text{kurt}(f^*) < \text{kurt}(g^*)$. Contrarily to the S1 trade, the density comparison would have filtered out a strongly negative net cash flow that would have been generated by a portfolio set up in July 1998. But the significance of this feature is again uncertain.

About the K2 trade can only be said that without a SPD comparison it would have procured heavy losses. The K2 trade applied as proposed can not be evaluated completely since there was only one period in which $\text{kurt}(f^*) <$ $\text{kurt}(g^*)$.

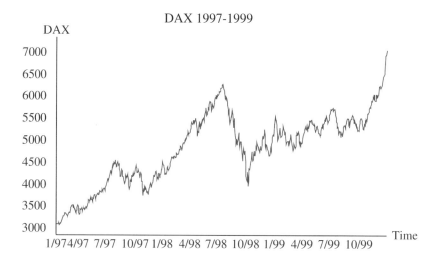

Figure 9.11. Evolution of DAX from January 1997 to December 1999

9.7   A Word of Caution

Interpreting the implied SPD as the SPD used by investors to price options, the historical density as the 'real' underlyings' SPD and assuming that no agent but one know the underlyings' SPD one should expect this agent to make higher profits than all others due to its superior knowledge. That is why, exploiting deviations of implied and historical density appears to be very promising at a first glance. Of course, if all market agents knew the underlyings' SPD, both f^* would be equal to g^* . In view of the high net cash flows generated by both skewness and kurtosis trades of type 1, it seems that not all agents are aware of discrepancies in the third and fourth moment of both densities. However, the strategies seem to be exposed to a substantial directional risk. Even if the dataset contained bearish and bullish market phases, both trades have to be tested on more extensive data. Considering the current political and economic developments, it is not clear how these trades will perform being exposed to 'peso risks'. Given that profits stem from highly positive cash flows at portfolio initiation, i.e. profits result from possibly mispriced options, who knows how the pricing behavior of agents changes, how do agents assign probabilities to future values of the underlying?

We measured performance in net EUR cash flows. This approach does not take risk into account as, for example the Sharpe ratio which is a measure of the risk adjusted return of an investment. But to compute a return an initial investment has to be done. However, in the simulation above, some portfolios generated positive payoffs both at initiation and at maturity. It is a challenge for future research to find a way how to adjust for risk in such situations.

The SPD comparison yielded the same result for each period but one. The implied SPD f^* was in all but one period more negatively skewed than the time series SPD g^*. While g^* was in all periods platykurtic, f^* was in all but one period leptokurtic. In this period the kurtosis of g^* was slightly greater than that of f^*. Therefore, there was no alternating use of type 1 and type 2 trades. But in more turbulent market environments such an approach might prove useful. The procedure could be extended and fine tuned by applying a density distance measure as in Ait–Sahalia, Wang and Yared (2000) to give a signal when to set up a portfolio either of type 1 of type 2. Furthermore, it is tempting to modify the time series density estimation method such that the monte carlo paths be simulated drawing random numbers not from a normal distribution but from the distribution of the residuals resulting from the nonparametric estimation of $\sigma_{FZ}(\bullet)$, Härdle and Yatchew (2001).

Bibliography

Ait–Sahalia, Y., Wang, Y. and Yared, F. (2001). Do Option Markets correctly Price the Probabilities of Movement of the Underlying Asset?, *Journal of Econometrics* **102**: 67–110.

Barle, S. and Cakici, N., (1998). How to Grow a Smiling Tree, *The Journal of Financial Engineering* **7**: 127–146.

Black, F. and Scholes, M., (1998). The Pricing of Options and Corporate Liabilities, *Journal of Political Economy* **81**: 637–659.

Blaskowitz, O. (2001). *Trading on Deviations of Implied and Historical Density*, Diploma Thesis, Humboldt–Universität zu Berlin.

Breeden, D. and Litzenberger, R., (1978). Prices of State Contingent Claims Implicit in Option Prices, *Journal of Business*, **9**, 4: 621–651.

Cox, J., Ross, S. and Rubinstein, M. (1979). Option Pricing: A simplified Approach, *Journal of Financial Economics* **7**: 229–263.

Derman, E. and Kani, I. (1994). The Volatility Smile and Its Implied Tree, *http://www.gs.com/qs/*

Dupire, B. (1994). Pricing with a Smile, *Risk* **7**: 18–20.

Florens–Zmirou, D. (1993). On Estimating the Diffusion Coefficient from Discrete Observations, *Journal of Applied Probability* **30**: 790–804.

Franke, J., Härdle, W. and Hafner, C. (2001). *Einführung in die Statistik der Finanzmärkte*, Springer Verlag, Heidelberg.

Härdle, W. and Simar, L. (2002). *Applied Multivariate Statistical Analysis*, Springer Verlag, Heidelberg.

Härdle, W. and Tsybakov, A., (1995). *Local Polynomial Estimators of the Volatility Function in Nonparametric Autoregression*, Sonderforschungsbereich 373 Discussion Paper, Humboldt–Universität zu Berlin.

Härdle, W. and Yatchew, A. (2001). *Dynamic Nonparametric State Price Density Estimation using Constrained Least Squares and the Bootstrap*, Sonderforschungsbereich 373 Discussion Paper, Humboldt–Universität zu Berlin.

Härdle, W. and Zheng, J. (2001). *How Precise Are Price Distributions Predicted by Implied Binomial Trees?*, Sonderforschungsbereich 373 Discussion Paper, Humboldt–Universität zu Berlin.

Jackwerth, J.C. (1999). Option Implied Risk Neutral Distributions and Implied Binomial Trees: A Literatur Review, *The Journal of Derivatives* **Winter**: 66–82.

Kloeden, P., Platen, E. and Schurz, H. (1994). *Numerical Solution of SDE Through Computer Experiments*, Springer Verlag, Heidelberg.

Rubinstein, M. (1994). Implied Binomial Trees, *Journal of Finance* **49**: 771–818.

Part IV

Econometrics

10 Multivariate Volatility Models

Matthias R. Fengler and Helmut Herwartz

Multivariate volatility models are widely used in Finance to capture both volatility clustering and contemporaneous correlation of asset return vectors. Here we focus on multivariate GARCH models. In this common model class it is assumed that the covariance of the error distribution follows a time dependent process conditional on information which is generated by the history of the process. To provide a particular example, we consider a system of exchange rates of two currencies measured against the US Dollar (USD), namely the Deutsche Mark (DEM) and the British Pound Sterling (GBP). For this process we compare the dynamic properties of the bivariate model with univariate GARCH specifications where cross sectional dependencies are ignored. Moreover, we illustrate the scope of the bivariate model by ex-ante forecasts of bivariate exchange rate densities.

10.1 Introduction

Volatility clustering, i.e. positive correlation of price variations observed on speculative markets, motivated the introduction of autoregressive conditionally heteroskedastic (ARCH) processes by Engle (1982) and its popular generalizations by Bollerslev (1986) (Generalized ARCH, GARCH) and Nelson (1991) (exponential GARCH, EGARCH). Being univariate in nature, however, such models neglect a further stylized fact of empirical price variations, namely contemporaneous cross correlation e.g. over a set of assets, stock market indices, or exchange rates.

Cross section relationships are often implied by economic theory. Interest rate parities, for instance, provide a close relation between domestic and foreign bond rates. Assuming absence of arbitrage, the so-called triangular equation formalizes the equality of an exchange rate between two currencies on the one hand and an implied rate constructed via exchange rates measured towards a third currency. Furthermore, stock prices of firms acting on the same market often show similar patterns in the sequel of news that are important for the entire market (Hafner and Herwartz, 1998). Similarly, analyzing global volatility transmission Engle, Ito and Lin (1990) and Hamao, Masulis and Ng (1990) found evidence in favor of volatility spillovers between the world's major trading areas occurring in the sequel of floor trading hours. From this point of view, when modeling time varying volatilities, a multivariate model appears to be a natural framework to take cross sectional information into account. Moreover, the covariance between financial assets is of essential importance in finance. Effectively, many problems in financial practice like portfolio optimization, hedging strategies, or Value-at-Risk evaluation require multivariate volatility measures (Bollerslev et al., 1988; Cecchetti, Cumby and Figlewski, 1988).

10.1.1   Model specifications

Let $\varepsilon_t = (\varepsilon_{1t}, \varepsilon_{2t}, \dots, \varepsilon_{Nt})^\top$ denote an N-dimensional error process, which is either directly observed or estimated from a multivariate regression model. The process ε_t follows a multivariate GARCH process if it has the representation

$$\varepsilon_t = \Sigma_t^{1/2} \xi_t, \tag{10.1}$$

where Σ_t is measurable with respect to information generated up to time $t-1$, denoted by the filtration $\mathcal{F}_{t-1}$. By assumption the N components of ξ_t follow a multivariate Gaussian distribution with mean zero and covariance matrix equal to the identity matrix.

The conditional covariance matrix, $\Sigma_t = \mathrm{E}[\varepsilon_t \varepsilon_t^\top | \mathcal{F}_{t-1}]$, has typical elements σ_{ij} with $\sigma_{ii}, i = 1, \dots, N$, denoting conditional variances and off-diagonal elements $\sigma_{ij}, i, j = 1, \dots, N, i \neq j$, denoting conditional covariances. To make the specification in (10.1) feasible a parametric description relating Σ_t to $\mathcal{F}_{t-1}$ is necessary. In a multivariate setting, however, dependencies of the second order moments in Σ_t on $\mathcal{F}_{t-1}$ become easily computationally intractable for practical purposes.

Let vech(A) denote the half-vectorization operator stacking the elements of a quadratic $(N \times N)$-matrix A from the main diagonal downwards in a $\frac{1}{2}N(N+1)$ dimensional column vector. Within the so-called vec-representation of the

GARCH(p,q) model Σ_t is specified as follows:

$$\text{vech}(\Sigma_t) = c + \sum_{i=1}^{q} \tilde{A}_i \text{vech}(\varepsilon_{t-i}\varepsilon_{t-i}^{\top}) + \sum_{i=1}^{p} \tilde{G}_i \text{vech}(\Sigma_{t-i}). \qquad (10.2)$$

In (10.2) the matrices $\tilde{A}_i$ and $\tilde{G}_i$ each contain $\{N(N+1)/2\}^2$ elements. Deterministic covariance components are collected in c, a column vector of dimension $N(N+1)/2$. We consider in the following the case $p = q = 1$ since in applied work the GARCH(1,1) model has turned out to be particularly useful to describe a wide variety of financial market data (Bollerslev, Engle and Nelson, 1994).

On the one hand the vec–model in (10.2) allows for a very general dynamic structure of the multivariate volatility process. On the other hand this specification suffers from high dimensionality of the relevant parameter space, which makes it almost intractable for empirical work. In addition, it might be cumbersome in applied work to restrict the admissible parameter space such that the implied matrices Σ_t, $t = 1, \ldots, T$, are positive definite. These issues motivated a considerable variety of competing multivariate GARCH specifications.

Prominent proposals reducing the dimensionality of (10.2) are the constant correlation model (Bollerslev, 1990) and the diagonal model (Bollerslev et al., 1988). Specifying diagonal elements of Σ_t both of these approaches assume the absence of cross equation dynamics, i.e. the only dynamics are

$$\sigma_{ii,t} = c_{ii} + a_i \varepsilon_{i,t-1}^2 + g_i \sigma_{ii,t-1}, \; i = 1, \ldots, N. \qquad (10.3)$$

To determine off-diagonal elements of Σ_t Bollerslev (1990) proposes a constant contemporaneous correlation,

$$\sigma_{ij,t} = \rho_{ij}\sqrt{\sigma_{ii}\sigma_{jj}}, \; i, j = 1, \ldots, N, \qquad (10.4)$$

whereas Bollerslev et al. (1988) introduce an ARMA-type dynamic structure as in (10.3) for $\sigma_{ij,t}$ as well, i.e.

$$\sigma_{ij,t} = c_{ij} + a_{ij}\varepsilon_{i,t-1}\varepsilon_{j,t-1} + g_{ij}\sigma_{ij,t-1}, \; i, j = 1, \ldots, N. \qquad (10.5)$$

For the bivariate case ($N = 2$) with $p = q = 1$ the constant correlation model contains only 7 parameters compared to 21 parameters encountered in the full model (10.2). The diagonal model is specified with 9 parameters. The price that both models pay for parsimony is in ruling out cross equation dynamics as allowed in the general vec-model. Positive definiteness of Σ_t is easily guaranteed for the constant correlation model ($|\rho_{ij}| < 1$), whereas the diagonal model requires more complicated restrictions to provide positive definite covariance matrices.

The so-called BEKK-model (named after Baba, Engle, Kraft and Kroner, 1990) provides a richer dynamic structure compared to both restricted processes mentioned before. Defining $N \times N$ matrices A_{ik} and G_{ik} and an upper triangular matrix C_0 the BEKK–model reads in a general version as follows:

$$\Sigma_t = C_0^\top C_0 + \sum_{k=1}^{K}\sum_{i=1}^{q} A_{ik}^\top \varepsilon_{t-i}\varepsilon_{t-i}^\top A_{ik} + \sum_{k=1}^{K}\sum_{i=1}^{p} G_{ik}^\top \Sigma_{t-i} G_{ik}. \tag{10.6}$$

If $K = q = p = 1$ and $N = 2$, the model in (10.6) contains 11 parameters and implies the following dynamic model for typical elements of Σ_t:

$$
\begin{aligned}
\sigma_{11,t} &= c_{11} + a_{11}^2\varepsilon_{1,t-1}^2 + 2a_{11}a_{21}\varepsilon_{1,t-1}\varepsilon_{2,t-1} + a_{21}^2\varepsilon_{2,t-1}^2 \\
&+ g_{11}^2\sigma_{11,t-1} + 2g_{11}g_{21}\sigma_{21,t-1} + g_{21}^2\sigma_{22,t-1}, \\
\sigma_{21,t} &= c_{21} + a_{11}a_{22}\varepsilon_{1,t-1}^2 + (a_{21}a_{12} + a_{11}a_{22})\varepsilon_{1,t-1}\varepsilon_{2,t-1} + a_{21}a_{22}\varepsilon_{2,t-1}^2 \\
&+ g_{11}g_{22}\sigma_{11,t-1} + (g_{21}g_{12} + g_{11}g_{22})\sigma_{12,t-1} + g_{21}g_{22}\sigma_{22,t-1}, \\
\sigma_{22,t} &= c_{22} + a_{12}^2\varepsilon_{1,t-1}^2 + 2a_{12}a_{22}\varepsilon_{1,t-1}\varepsilon_{2,t-1} + a_{22}^2\varepsilon_{2,t-1}^2 \\
&+ g_{12}^2\sigma_{11,t-1} + 2g_{12}g_{22}\sigma_{21,t-1} + g_{22}^2\sigma_{22,t-1}.
\end{aligned}
$$

Compared to the diagonal model the BEKK–specification economizes on the number of parameters by restricting the vec–model within and across equations. Since A_{ik} and G_{ik} are not required to be diagonal, the BEKK-model is convenient to allow for cross dynamics of conditional covariances. The parameter K governs to which extent the general representation in (10.2) can be approximated by a BEKK-type model. In the following we assume $K = 1$. Note that in the bivariate case with $K = p = q = 1$ the BEKK-model contains 11 parameters. If $K = 1$ the matrices A_{11} and $-A_{11}$, imply the same conditional covariances. Thus, for uniqueness of the BEKK-representation $a_{11} > 0$ and $g_{11} > 0$ is assumed. Note that the right hand side of (10.6) involves only quadratic terms and, hence, given convenient initial conditions, Σ_t is positive definite under the weak (sufficient) condition that at least one of the matrices C_0 or G_{ik} has full rank (Engle and Kroner, 1995).

10.1.2   Estimation of the BEKK-model

As in the univariate case the parameters of a multivariate GARCH model are estimated by maximum likelihood (ML) optimizing numerically the Gaussian log-likelihood function.

With f denoting the multivariate normal density, the contribution of a single observation, l_t, to the log-likelihood of a sample is given as:

$$
\begin{aligned}
l_t &= \ln\{f(\varepsilon_t|\mathcal{F}_{t-1})\} \\
&= -\frac{N}{2}\ln(2\pi) - \frac{1}{2}\ln(|\Sigma_t|) - \frac{1}{2}\varepsilon_t^\top \Sigma_t^{-1}\varepsilon_t.
\end{aligned}
$$

Maximizing the log-likelihood, $l = \sum_{t=1}^{T} l_t$, requires nonlinear maximization methods. Involving only first order derivatives the algorithm introduced by Berndt, Hall, Hall, and Hausman (1974) is easily implemented and particularly useful for the estimation of multivariate GARCH processes.

If the actual error distribution differs from the multivariate normal, maximizing the Gaussian log-likelihood has become popular as Quasi ML (QML) estimation. In the multivariate framework, results for the asymptotic properties of the (Q)ML-estimator have been derived recently. Jeantheau (1998) proves the QML-estimator to be consistent under the main assumption that the considered multivariate process is strictly stationary and ergodic. Further assuming finiteness of moments of ε_t up to order eight, Comte and Lieberman (2000) derive asymptotic normality of the QML-estimator. The asymptotic distribution of the rescaled QML-estimator is analogous to the univariate case and discussed in Bollerslev and Wooldridge (1992).

10.2 An empirical illustration

10.2.1 Data description

We analyze daily quotes of two European currencies measured against the USD, namely the DEM and the GBP. The sample period is December 31, 1979 to April 1, 1994, covering $T = 3720$ observations. Note that a subperiod of our sample has already been investigated by Bollerslev and Engle (1993) discussing common features of volatility processes.

The data is provided in `fx`. The first column contains DEM/USD and the second GBP/USD. In XploRe a preliminary statistical analysis is easily done by the `summarize` command. Before inspecting the summary statistics, we load the data, R_t, and take log differences, $\varepsilon_t = \ln(R_t) - \ln(R_{t-1})$. Q `XFGmvol01.xpl` produces the following table:

```
[2,]  "          Minimum    Maximum     Mean    Median Std.Error"
[3,]  "-----------------------------------------------------------"
[4,]  "DEM/USD  -0.040125   0.031874 -4.7184e-06      0   0.0070936"
[5,]  "GBP/USD  -0.046682   0.038665  0.00011003      0   0.0069721"
```

Q XFGmvol01.xpl

Evidently, the empirical means of both processes are very close to zero (-4.72e-06 and 1.10e-04, respectively). Also minimum, maximum and standard errors are of similar size. First differences of the respective log exchange rates are shown in Figure 10.1. As is apparent from Figure 10.1, variations of exchange rate returns exhibit an autoregressive pattern: Large returns in foreign exchange markets are followed by large returns of either sign. This is most obvious in periods of excessive returns. Note that these volatility clusters tend to coincide in both series. It is precisely this observation that justifies a multivariate GARCH specification.

10.2.2 Estimating bivariate GARCH

{coeff, likest} = bigarch(theta,et)
        estimates a bivariate GARCH model

The quantlet `bigarch` provides a fast algorithm to estimate the BEKK representation of a bivariate GARCH(1,1) model. QML-estimation is implemented by means of the BHHH-algorithm which minimizes the negative Gaussian log-likelihood function. The algorithm employs analytical first order derivatives of the log-likelihood function (Lütkepohl, 1996) with respect to the 11-dimensional vector of parameters containing the elements of C_0, A_{11} and G_{11} as given in (10.6).

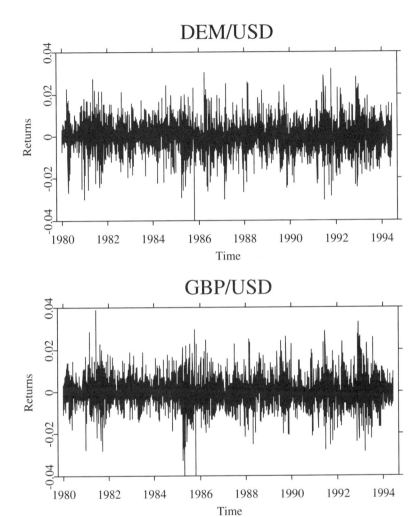

Figure 10.1. Foreign exchange rate data: returns.

XFGmvol01.xpl

The standard call is

```
{coeff, likest}=bigarch(theta, et),
```

where as input parameters we have initial values `theta` for the iteration algorithm and the data set, e.g. financial returns, stored in `et`. The estimation
output is the vector `coeff` containing the stacked elements of the parameter
matrices C_0, A_{11} and G_{11} in (10.6) after numerical optimization of the Gaussian
log-likelihood function. Being an iterative procedure the algorithm requires to
determine suitable initial parameters `theta`. For the diagonal elements of the
matrices A_{11} and G_{11} values around 0.3 and 0.9 appear reasonable, since in univariate GARCH(1,1) models parameter estimates for a_1 and g_1 in (10.3) often
take values around $0.3^2 = 0.09$ and $0.81 = 0.9^2$. There is no clear guidance how
to determine initial values for off diagonal elements of A_{11} or G_{11}. Therefore
it might be reasonable to try alternative initializations of these parameters.
Given an initialization of A_{11} and G_{11} the starting values for the elements in
C_0 are immediately determined by the algorithm assuming the unconditional
covariance of ε_t to exist, Engle and Kroner (1995).

Given our example under investigation the bivariate GARCH estimation yields
as output:

```
Contents of coeff

[ 1,]   0.0011516
[ 2,]   0.00031009
[ 3,]   0.00075685
[ 4,]   0.28185
[ 5,] -0.057194
[ 6,] -0.050449
[ 7,]   0.29344
[ 8,]   0.93878
[ 9,]   0.025117
[10,]   0.027503
[11,]   0.9391

Contents of likest

[1,]    -28599
```

Q XFGmvol02.xpl

The last number is the obtained minimum of the negative log-likelihood function. The vector `coeff` given first contains as first three elements the parameters of the upper triangular matrix C_0, the following four belong to the ARCH (A_{11}) and the last four to the GARCH parameters (G_{11}), i.e. for our model

$$\Sigma_t = C_0^\top C_0 + A_{11}^\top \varepsilon_{t-1}\varepsilon_{t-1}^\top A_{11} + G_{11}^\top \Sigma_{t-1} G_{11} \tag{10.7}$$

stated again for convenience, we find the matrices C_0, A, G to be:

$$C_0 = 10^{-3} \begin{pmatrix} 1.15 & .31 \\ 0 & .76 \end{pmatrix},$$

$$A_{11} = \begin{pmatrix} .282 & -.050 \\ -.057 & .293 \end{pmatrix}, \; G_{11} = \begin{pmatrix} .939 & .028 \\ .025 & .939 \end{pmatrix}. \tag{10.8}$$

10.2.3   Estimating the (co)variance processes

The (co)variance is obtained by sequentially calculating the difference equation (10.7) where we use the estimator for the unconditional covariance matrix as initial value ($\Sigma_0 = \frac{E^\top E}{T}$). Here, the $T \times 2$ vector E contains log-differences of our foreign exchange rate data. Estimating the covariance process is also accomplished in the quantlet **Q** `XFGmvol02.xpl` and additionally provided in `sigmaprocess`.

We display the estimated variance and covariance processes in Figure 10.2. The upper and the lower panel of Figure 10.2 show the variances of the DEM/USD and GBP/USD returns respectively, whereas in the middle panel we see the covariance process. Except for a very short period in the beginning of our sample the covariance is positive and of non-negligible size throughout. This is evidence for cross sectional dependencies in currency markets which we mentioned earlier to motivate multivariate GARCH models.

Instead of estimating the realized path of variances as shown above, we could also use the estimated parameters to *simulate* volatility paths (**Q** `XFGmvol03.xpl`).

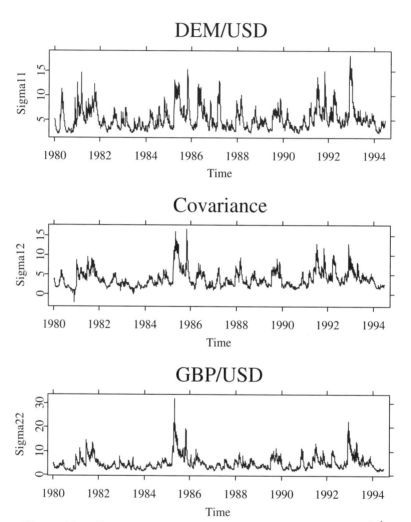

Figure 10.2. Estimated variance and covariance processes, $10^5 \hat{\Sigma}_t$.

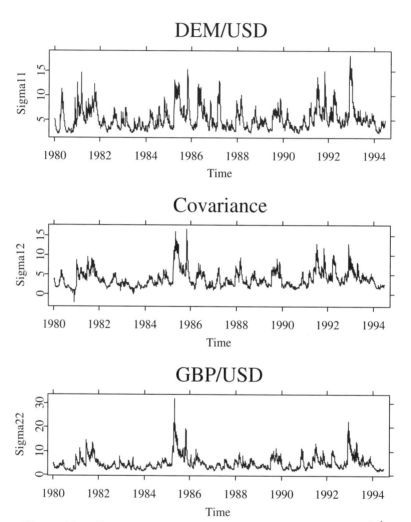 XFGmvol02.xpl

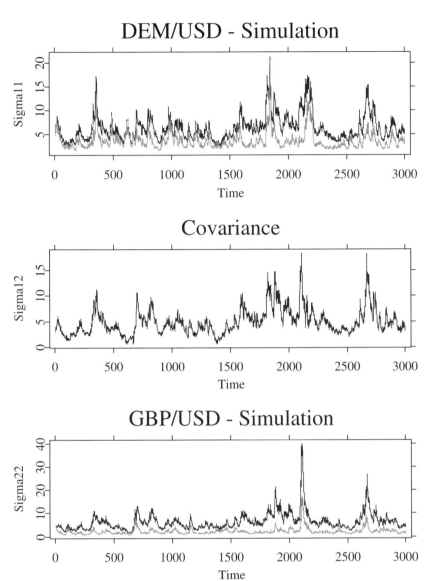

Figure 10.3. Simulated variance and covariance processes, both bivariate (blue) and univariate case (green), $10^5\hat{\Sigma}_t$.

Q XFGmvol03.xpl

For this at each point in time an observation ε_t is drawn from a multivariate normal distribution with variance Σ_t. Given these observations, Σ_t is updated according to (10.7). Then, a new residual is drawn with covariance Σ_{t+1}. We apply this procedure for $T = 3000$. The results, displayed in the upper three panels of Figure 10.3, show a similar pattern as the original process given in Figure 10.2. For the lower two panels we generate two variance processes from the *same* residuals ξ_t. In this case, however, we set off-diagonal parameters in A_{11} and G_{11} to zero to illustrate how the unrestricted BEKK model incorporates cross equation dynamics. As can be seen, both approaches are convenient to capture volatility clustering. Depending on the particular state of the system, spillover effects operating through conditional covariances, however, have a considerable impact on the magnitude of conditional volatility.

10.3   Forecasting exchange rate densities

The preceding section illustrated how the GARCH model may be employed effectively to describe empirical price variations of foreign exchange rates. For practical purposes, as for instance scenario analysis, VaR estimation (Chapter 1), option pricing (Chapter 16), one is often interested in the future joint density of a set of asset prices. Continuing the comparison of the univariate and bivariate approach to model volatility dynamics of exchange rates it is thus natural to investigate the properties of these specifications in terms of forecasting performance.

We implement an iterative forecasting scheme along the following lines: Given the estimated univariate and bivariate volatility models and the corresponding information sets $\mathcal{F}_{t-1}, t = 1, \ldots, T - 5$ (Figure 10.2), we employ the identified data generating processes to simulate one-week-ahead forecasts of both exchange rates. To get a reliable estimate of the future density we set the number of simulations to 50000 for each initial scenario. This procedure yields two bivariate samples of future exchange rates, one simulated under bivariate, the other one simulated under univariate GARCH assumptions.

A review on the current state of evaluating competing density forecasts is offered by Tay and Wallis (1990). Adopting a Bayesian perspective the common approach is to compare the expected loss of actions evaluated under alternative density forecasts. In our pure time series framework, however, a particular action is hardly available for forecast density comparisons. Alternatively one could concentrate on statistics directly derived from the simulated densities,

Time window J		Success ratio SR_J
1980	1981	0.744
1982	1983	0.757
1984	1985	0.793
1986	1987	0.788
1988	1989	0.806
1990	1991	0.807
1992	1994/4	0.856

Table 10.1. Time varying frequencies of the bivariate GARCH model outperforming the univariate one in terms of one-week-ahead forecasts (success ratio)

such as first and second order moments or even quantiles. Due to the multivariate nature of the time series under consideration it is a nontrivial issue to rank alternative density forecasts in terms of these statistics. Therefore, we regard a particular volatility model to be superior to another if it provides a higher simulated density estimate of the actual bivariate future exchange rate. This is accomplished by evaluating both densities at the actually realized exchange rate obtained from a bivariate kernel estimation. Since the latter comparison might suffer from different unconditional variances under univariate and multivariate volatility, the two simulated densities were rescaled to have identical variance. Performing the latter forecasting exercises iteratively over 3714 time points we can test if the bivariate volatility model outperforms the univariate one.

To formalize the latter ideas we define a success ratio SR_J as

$$SR_J = \frac{1}{|J|} \sum_{t \in J} \mathbf{1}\{\hat{f}_{biv}(R_{t+5}) > \hat{f}_{uni}(R_{t+5})\}, \qquad (10.9)$$

where J denotes a time window containing $|J|$ observations and $\mathbf{1}$ an indicator function. $\hat{f}_{biv}(R_{t+5})$ and $\hat{f}_{uni}(R_{t+5})$ are the estimated densities of future exchange rates, which are simulated by the bivariate and univariate GARCH processes, respectively, and which are evaluated at the actual exchange rate levels R_{t+5}. The simulations are performed in **Q** XFGmvol04.xpl.

Our results show that the bivariate model indeed outperforms the univariate one when both likelihoods are compared under the actual realizations of the exchange rate process. In 81.6% of all cases across the sample period, $SR_J = 0.816$, $J = \{t : t = 1, ..., T-5\}$, the bivariate model provides a better forecast.

Covariance and success ratio

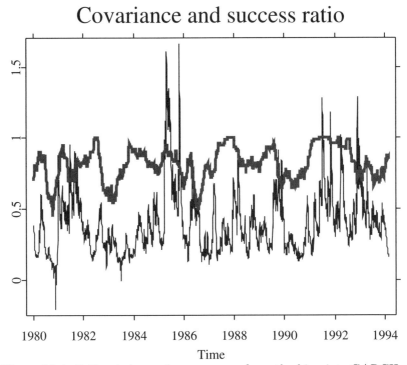

Figure 10.4. Estimated covariance process from the bivariate GARCH model ($10^4\hat{\sigma}_{12}$, blue) and success ratio over overlapping time intervals with window length 80 days (red).

This is highly significant. In Table 10.1 we show that the overall superiority of the bivariate volatility approach is confirmed when considering subsamples of two-years length. A-priori one may expect the bivariate model to outperform the univariate one the larger (in absolute value) the covariance between both return processes is. To verify this argument we display in Figure 10.4 the empirical covariance estimates from Figure 10.2 jointly with the success ratio evaluated over overlapping time intervals of length $|J| = 80$.

As is apparent from Figure 10.4 there is a close co-movement between the success ratio and the general trend of the covariance process, which confirms our expectations: the forecasting power of the bivariate GARCH model is particularly strong in periods where the DEM/USD and GBP/USD exchange rate returns exhibit a high covariance. For completeness it is worthwhile to mention that similar results are obtained if the window width is varied over reasonable choices of $|J|$ ranging from 40 to 150.

With respect to financial practice and research we take our results as strong support for a multivariate approach towards asset price modeling. Whenever contemporaneous correlation across markets matters, the system approach offers essential advantages. To name a few areas of interest multivariate volatility models are supposed to yield useful insights for risk management, scenario analysis and option pricing.

Bibliography

Baba, Y., Engle, R.F., Kraft, D.F., and Kroner, K.F. (1990). Multivariate Simultaneous Generalized ARCH, *mimeo*, Department of Economics, University of California, San Diego.

Berndt, E.K., Hall B.H., Hall, R.E., and Hausman, J.A. (1974). Estimation and Inference in Nonlinear Structural Models, *Annals of Economic and Social Measurement* **3/4**: 653–665.

Bollerslev, T. (1986). Generalized Autoregressive Conditional Heteroscedasticity, *Journal of Econometrics* **31**: 307-327.

Bollerslev, T. (1990). Modeling the Coherence in Short-Run Nominal Exchange Rates: A Multivariate Generalized ARCH Approach, *Review of Economics and Statistics* **72**: 498–505.

Bollerslev, T. and Engle, R.F. (1993). Common Persistence in Conditional Variances, *Econometrica* **61**: 167–186.

Bollerslev, T., Engle, R.F. and Nelson, D.B. (1994). GARCH Models, in: Engle, R.F., and McFadden, D.L. (eds.) Handbook of Econometrics, Vol. 4, Elsevier, Amsterdam, 2961–3038.

Bollerslev, T., Engle, R.F. and Wooldridge, J.M. (1988). A Capital Asset Pricing Model with Time-Varying Covariances, *Journal of Political Economy* **96**: 116–131.

Bollerslev, T. and Wooldridge, J.M. (1992). Quasi–Maximum Likelihood Estimation and Inference in Dynamic Models with Time–Varying Covariances, *Econometric Reviews*, **11**: 143–172.

Cecchetti, S.G., Cumby, R.E. and Figlewski, S. (1988). Estimation of the Optimal Futures Hedge, *Review of Economics and Statistics* **70**: 623-630.

Comte, F. and Lieberman, O. (2000). Asymptotic Theory for Multivariate GARCH Processes, *Manuscript, Universities Paris 6 and Paris 7*.

Engle, R.F. (1982). Autoregressive Conditional Heteroscedasticity with Estimates of the Variance of UK Inflation. *Econometrica* **50**: 987-1008.

Engle, R.F., Ito, T. and Lin, W.L. (1990). Meteor Showers or Heat Waves? Heteroskedastic Intra-Daily Volatility in the Foreign Exchange Market, *Econometrica* **58**: 525–542.

Engle, R.F. and Kroner, K.F. (1995). Multivariate Simultaneous Generalized ARCH, *Econometric Theory* **11**: 122–150.

Hafner, C.M. and Herwartz, H. (1998). Structural Analysis of Portfolio Risk using Beta Impulse Response Functions, *Statistica Neerlandica* **52**: 336-355.

Hamao, Y., Masulis, R.W. and Ng, V.K. (1990). Correlations in Price Changes and Volatility across International Stock Markets, *Review of Financial Studies* **3**: 281–307.

Jeantheau, T. (1998). Strong Consistency of Estimators for Multivariate ARCH Models, *Econometric Theory* **14**: 70-86.

Lütkepohl, H. (1996). *Handbook of Matrices*, Wiley, Chichester.

Nelson, D.B. (1991). Conditional Heteroskedasticity in Asset Returns: A New Approach, *Econometrica* **59**: 347–370.

Tay, A. and Wallis, K. (2000). Density forecasting: A Survey, *Journal of Forecasting* **19**: 235–254.

11 Statistical Process Control

Sven Knoth

Statistical Process Control (SPC) is the misleading title of the area of statistics which is concerned with the statistical monitoring of sequentially observed data. Together with the theory of sampling plans, capability analysis and similar topics it forms the field of Statistical Quality Control. SPC started in the 1930s with the pioneering work of Shewhart (1931). Then, SPC became very popular with the introduction of new quality policies in the industries of Japan and of the USA. Nowadays, SPC methods are considered not only in industrial statistics. In finance, medicine, environmental statistics, and in other fields of applications practitioners and statisticians use and investigate SPC methods.

A SPC scheme – in industry mostly called control chart – is a sequential scheme for detecting the so called change point in the sequence of observed data. Here, we consider the most simple case. All observations $X_1, X_2, \ldots$ are independent, normally distributed with known variance σ^2. Up to an unknown time point $m - 1$ the expectation of the X_i is equal to μ_0, starting with the change point m the expectation is switched to $\mu_1 \neq \mu_0$. While both expectation values are known, the change point m is unknown. Now, based on the sequentially observed data the SPC scheme has to detect whether a change occurred.

SPC schemes can be described by a stopping time L – known as run length – which is adapted to the sequence of sigma algebras $\mathcal{F}_n = \mathcal{F}(X_1, X_2, \ldots, X_n)$. The performance or power of these schemes is usually measured by the Average Run Length (ARL), the expectation of L. The ARL denotes the average number of observations until the SPC scheme signals. We distinguish false alarms – the scheme signals before m, i.e. before the change actually took place – and right ones. A suitable scheme provides large ARLs for $m = \infty$ and small ARLs for $m = 1$. In case of $1 < m < \infty$ one has to consider further performance measures. In the case of the oldest schemes – the Shewhart charts – the typical inference characteristics like the error probabilities were firstly used.

The chapter is organized as follows. In Section 11.1 the charts in consideration are introduced and their graphical representation is demonstrated. In the Section 11.2 the most popular chart characteristics are described. First, the characteristics as the ARL and the Average Delay (AD) are defined. These performance measures are used for the setup of the applied SPC scheme. Then, the three subsections of Section 11.2 are concerned with the usage of the SPC routines for determination of the ARL, the AD, and the probability mass function (PMF) of the run length. In Section 11.3 some results of two papers are reproduced with the corresponding XploRe quantlets.

11.1   Control Charts

Recall that the data $X_1, X_2, \ldots$ follow the change point model

$$
\begin{cases}
X_t \sim N(\mu_0, \sigma^2) & , t = 1, 2, \ldots, m-1 \\
X_t \sim N(\mu_1 \neq \mu_0, \sigma^2) & , t = m, m+1, \ldots
\end{cases}
\tag{11.1}
$$

The observations are independent and the time point m is unknown. The control chart (the SPC scheme) corresponds to a stopping time L. Here we consider three different schemes – the Shewhart chart, EWMA and CUSUM schemes. There are one- and two-sided versions. The related stopping times in the one-sided upper versions are:

1. The Shewhart chart introduced by Shewhart (1931)

$$
L^{\text{Shewhart}} = \inf \left\{ t \in I\!\!N : Z_t = \frac{X_t - \mu_0}{\sigma} > c_1 \right\}
\tag{11.2}
$$

   with the design parameter c_1 called critical value.

2. The EWMA scheme (exponentially weighted moving average) initially presented by Roberts (1959)

$$
L^{\text{EWMA}} = \inf \left\{ t \in I\!\!N : Z_t^{\text{EWMA}} > c_2 \sqrt{\lambda/(2-\lambda)} \right\},
\tag{11.3}
$$

$$
Z_0^{\text{EWMA}} = z_0 = 0,
$$

$$
Z_t^{\text{EWMA}} = (1-\lambda) Z_{t-1}^{\text{EWMA}} + \lambda \frac{X_t - \mu_0}{\sigma} , \, t = 1, 2, \ldots
\tag{11.4}
$$

   with the smoothing value λ and the critical value c_2. The smaller λ the faster EWMA detects small $\mu_1 - \mu_0 > 0$.

3. The CUSUM scheme (cumulative sum) introduced by Page (1954)

$$L^{\text{CUSUM}} = \inf \left\{ t \in I\!N : Z_t^{\text{CUSUM}} > c_3 \right\}, \tag{11.5}$$

$$Z_0^{\text{CUSUM}} = z_0 = 0,$$

$$Z_t^{\text{CUSUM}} = \max \left\{ 0, Z_{t-1}^{\text{CUSUM}} + \frac{X_t - \mu_0}{\sigma} - k \right\}, \quad t = 1, 2, \ldots \tag{11.6}$$

with the reference value k and the critical value c_3 (known as decision interval). For fastest detection of $\mu_1 - \mu_0$ CUSUM has to be set up with $k = (\mu_1 + \mu_0)/(2\,\sigma)$.

The above notation uses normalized data. Thus, it is not important whether X_t is a single observation or a sample statistic as the empirical mean.

Remark, that for using one-sided lower schemes one has to apply the upper schemes to the data multiplied with -1. A slight modification of one-sided Shewhart and EWMA charts leads to their two-sided versions. One has to replace in the comparison of chart statistic and threshold the original statistic Z_t and Z_t^{EWMA} by their absolute value. The two-sided versions of these schemes are more popular than the one-sided ones. For two-sided CUSUM schemes we consider a combination of two one-sided schemes, Lucas (1976) or Lucas and Crosier (1982), and a scheme based on Crosier (1986). Note, that in some recent papers the same concept of combination of two one-sided schemes is used for EWMA charts.

Recall, that Shewhart charts are a special case of EWMA schemes ($\lambda = 1$). Therefore, we distinguish 5 SPC schemes – ewma1, ewma2, cusum1, cusum2 (two one-sided schemes), and cusumC (Crosier's scheme). For the two-sided EWMA charts the following quantlets are provided in the XploRe quantlib spc.

SPC quantlets for two-sided EWMA scheme	
spcewma2	– produces chart figure
spcewma2arl	– returns ARL
spcewma2c	– returns critical value c_2
spcewma2ad	– returns AD (steady-state ARL)
spcewma2pmf	– returns probability mass and distribution function of the run-length for single time points
spcewma2pmfm	– the same up to a given time point

By replacing `ewma2` by one of the remaining four scheme titles the related characteristics can be computed.

The quantlets `spcewma1`,...,`spccusumC` generate the chart figure. Here, we apply the 5 charts to artificial data. 100 pseudo random values from a normal distribution are generated. The first 80 values have expectation 0, the next 20 values have expectation 1, i.e. model (11.1) with $\mu_0 = 0$, $\mu_1 = 1$, and $m = 81$. We start with the two-sided EWMA scheme and set $\lambda = 0.1$, i.e. the chart is

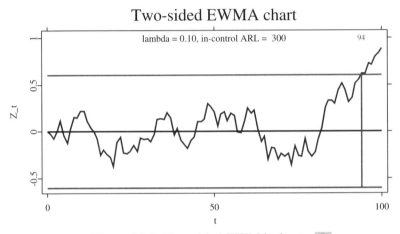

Figure 11.1. Two-sided EWMA chart **Q** XFGewma2fig.xpl

very sensitive to small changes. The critical value c_2 (see (11.3)) is computed to provide an in-control ARL of 300 (see Section 11.2). Thus, the scheme leads in average after 300 observations to a false alarm.

In Figure 11.1 the graph of Z_t^{EWMA} is plotted against time $t = 1, 2, \ldots, 100$. Further, the design parameter λ, the in-control ARL, and the time of alarm (if there is one) are printed. One can see, that the above EWMA scheme detects the change point $m = 81$ at time point 94, i.e. the delay is equal to 14. The related average values, i.e. ARL and Average Delay (AD), for $\mu_1 = 1$ are 9.33 and 9.13, respectively. Thus, the scheme needs here about 5 observations more than average.

In the same way the remaining four SPC schemes can be plotted. Remark, that in case of `ewma1` one further parameter has to be set. In order to obtain a suitable figure and an appropriate scheme the EWMA statistic Z_t^{EWMA} (see (11.4)) is reflected at a pre-specified border $\mathtt{zreflect} \leq 0 \,(= \mu_0)$, i.e.

$$Z_t^{\mathrm{EWMA}} = \max\{\mathtt{zreflect}, Z_t^{\mathrm{EWMA}}\} \quad , t = 1, 2, \ldots$$

for an upper EWMA scheme. Otherwise, the statistic is unbounded, which leads to schemes with poor worst case performance. Further, the methods

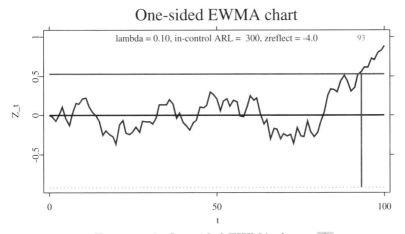

Figure 11.2. One-sided EWMA chart Q `XFGewma1fig.xpl`

used in Section 11.2 for computing the chart characteristics use bounded continuation regions of the chart. If `zreflect` is small enough, then the ARL and the AD (which are not worst case criterions) of the reflected scheme are the same as of the unbounded scheme. Applying the quantlet Q `XFGewma1fig.xpl` with `zreflect`$= -4$ leads to Figure 11.2. Thereby, `zreflect` has the same normalization factor $\sqrt{\lambda/(2 - \lambda)}$ like the critical value c_2 (see 2.). The corresponding normalized border is printed as dotted line (see Figure 11.2). The chart signals one observation earlier than the two-sided version in Figure 11.1. The related ARL and AD values for $\mu_1 = 1$ are now 7.88 and 7.87, respectively.

In Figure 11.3 the three different CUSUM charts with $k = 0.5$ are presented. They signal at the time points 87, 88, and 88 for `cusum1`, `cusum2`, and `cusumC`, respectively.   For the considered dataset the CUSUM charts are faster be-

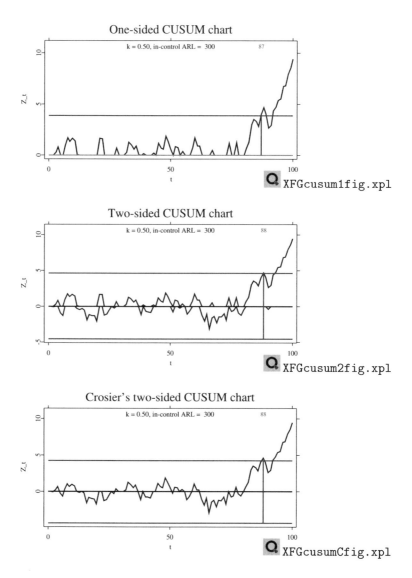

Figure 11.3. CUSUM charts: one-sided, two-sided, Crosier's two-sided

cause of their better worst case performance. The observations right before
the change point at $m = 81$ are smaller than average. Therefore, the EWMA
charts need more time to react to the increased average. The related average
values of the run length, i.e. ARL and AD, are 8.17 and 7.52, 9.52 and 8.82,
9.03 and 8.79 for `cusum1`, `cusum2`, and `cusumC`, respectively.

11.2   Chart characteristics

Consider the change point model (11.1). For fixed m denote $P_m(\cdot)$ and $E_m(\cdot)$
the corresponding probability measure and expectation, respectively. Hereby,
$m = \infty$ stands for the case of no change, i.e. the so called in-control case. Then
the Average Run Length (ARL) (expectation of the run length L) is defined
as

$$\mathcal{L}_\mu = \begin{cases} E_\infty(L) & , \ \mu = \mu_0 \\ E_1(L) & , \ \mu \neq \mu_0 \end{cases}. \tag{11.7}$$

Thus, the ARL denotes the average number of observations until signal for a
sequence with constant expectation. $\mu = \mu_0$ or $m = \infty$ stands for no change,
$\mu \neq \mu_0$ and $m = 1$ mark, that just at the first time point (or earlier) a change
takes place from μ_0 to μ. Therefore, the ARL evaluates only the special scenario of $m = 1$ of the SPC scheme. Other measures, which take into account
that usually $1 < m < \infty$, were introduced by Lorden (1971) and Pollak and
Siegmund (1975), Pollak and Siegmund (1975). Here, we use a performance
measure which was firstly proposed by Roberts (1959). The so called (conditional) Average Delay (AD, also known as steady-state ARL) is defined as

$$\mathcal{D}_\mu = \lim_{m \to \infty} \mathcal{D}_\mu^{(m)}, \tag{11.8}$$

$$\mathcal{D}_\mu^{(m)} = E_m\left(L - m + 1 | L \geq m\right),$$

where μ is the value of μ_1 in (11.1), i.e. the expectation after the change.
While $\mathcal{L}_\mu$ measures the delay for the case $m = 1$, $\mathcal{D}_\mu$ determines the delay for
a SPC scheme which ran a long time without signal. Usually, the convergence
in (11.8) is very fast. For quite small m the difference between $\mathcal{D}_\mu^{(m)}$ and $\mathcal{D}_\mu$ is
very small already. $\mathcal{L}_\mu$ and $\mathcal{D}_\mu$ are average values for the random variable L.
Unfortunately, L is characterized by a large standard deviation. Therefore, one
might be interested in the whole distribution of L. Again, we restrict on the
special cases $m = 1$ and $m = \infty$. We consider the probability mass function
$P_\mu(L = n)$ (PMF) and the cumulative distribution function $P_\mu(L \leq n)$ (CDF).
Based on the CDF, one is able to compute quantiles of the run length L.

For normally distributed random variables it is not possible to derive exact solutions for the above characteristics. There are a couple of approximation techniques. Besides very rough approximations based on the Wald approximation known from sequential analysis, Wiener process approximations and similar methods, three main methods can be distinguished:

1. Markov chain approach due to Brook and Evans (1972): Replacement of the continuous statistic Z_t by a discrete one

2. Quadrature of integral equations which are derived for the ARL, Vance (1986) and Crowder (1986) and for some eigenfunctions which lead to the AD

3. Waldmann (1986) approach: Iterative computation of $P(L = n)$ by using quadrature and exploiting of monotone bounds for the considered characteristics

Here we use the first approach, which has the advantage, that all considered characteristics can be presented in a straightforward way. Next, the Markov chain approach is briefly described. Roughly speaking, the continuous statistic Z_t is approximated by a discrete Markov chain M_t. The transition $Z_{t-1} = x \rightarrow Z_t = y$ is approximated by the transition $M_{t-1} = i\,w \rightarrow M_t = j\,w$ with $x \in [i\,w - w/2, i\,w + w/2]$ and $y \in [j\,w - w/2, j\,w + w/2]$. That is, given an integer r the continuation region of the scheme $[-c, c]$, $[\texttt{zreflect}, c]$, or $[0, c]$ is separated into $2\,r + 1$ or $r + 1$ intervals of the kind $[i\,w - w/2, i\,w + w/2]$ (one exception is $[0, w/2]$ as the first subinterval of $[0, c]$). Then, the transition kernel f of Z_t is approximated by the discrete kernel of M_t, i. e.

$$f(x, y) \approx P(i\,w \rightarrow [j\,w - w/2, j\,w + w/2])/w$$

for all $x \in [i\,w - w/2, i\,w + w/2]$ and $y \in [j\,w - w/2, j\,w + w/2]$. Eventually, we obtain a Markov chain $\{M_t\}$ with $2\,r + 1$ or $r + 1$ transient states and one absorbing state. The last one corresponds to the alarm (signal) of the scheme.

Denote by $Q = (q_{ij})$ the matrix of transition probabilities of the Markov chain $\{M_t\}$ on the transient states, $\underline{1}$ a vector of ones, and $\underline{L} = (L_i)$ the ARL vector. L_i stands for the ARL of a SPC scheme which starts in point $i\,w$ (corresponds to z_0). In the case of a one-sided CUSUM scheme with $z_0 = 0 \ni [0, w/2]$ the value L_0 approximates the original ARL. By using $\underline{L}$ we generalize the original schemes to schemes with possibly different starting values z_0. Now, the following linear equation system is valid, Brook and Evans (1972):

$$(I - Q)\,\underline{L} = \underline{1}, \tag{11.9}$$

where I denotes the identity matrix. By solving this equation system we get the ARL vector $\underline{L}$ and an approximation of the ARL of the considered SPC scheme. Remark that the larger r the better is the approximation. In the days of Brook and Evans (1972) the maximal matrix dimension $r+1$ (they considered `cusum1`) was 15 because of the restrictions of the available computing facilities. Nowadays, one can use dimensions larger than some hundreds. By looking at different r one can find a suitable value. The quantlet **Q** `XFGrarl.xpl` demonstrates this effect for the Brook and Evans (1972) example. 9 different values of r from 5 to 500 are used to approximate the in-control ARL of a one-sided CUSUM chart with $k = 0.5$ and $c_3 = 3$ (variance $\sigma^2 = 1$). We get

r	5	10	20	30	40	50	100	200	500
$\mathcal{L}_0$	113.47	116.63	117.36	117.49	117.54	117.56	117.59	117.59	117.60

Q `XFGrarl.xpl`

The true value is 117.59570 (obtainable via a very large r or by using the quadrature methods with a suitable large number of abscissas). The computation of the average delay (AD) requires more extensive calculations. For details see, e. g., Knoth (1998) on CUSUM for Erlang distributed data. Here we apply the Markov chain approach again, Crosier (1986). Given one of the considered schemes and normally distributed data, the matrix Q is primitive, i. e. there exists a power of Q which is positive. Then Q has one single eigenvalue which is larger in magnitude than the remaining eigenvalues. Denote this eigenvalue by ϱ. The corresponding left eigenvector $\underline{\psi}$ is strictly positive, i. e.

$$\underline{\psi} Q = \varrho \underline{\psi} \, , \, \underline{\psi} > 0 \, . \tag{11.10}$$

It can be shown, Knoth (1998), that the conditional density $f(\cdot | L \geq m)$ of both the continuous statistic Z_t and the Markov chain M_t tends for $m \to \infty$ to the normalized left eigenfunction and eigenvector, respectively, which correspond to the dominant eigenvalue ϱ. Therefore, the approximation of $\mathcal{D} = \lim_{m \to \infty} E_m(L - m + 1 | L \geq m)$ can be constructed by

$$\mathcal{D} = (\underline{\psi}^T \underline{L})/(\underline{\psi}^T \underline{1}) \, .$$

Note, that the left eigenvector $\underline{\psi}$ is computed for the in-control mean μ_0, while the ARL vector $\underline{L}$ is computed for a specific out-of-control mean or μ_0 again.

If we replace in the above quantlet (**Q** `XFGrarl.xpl`) the phrase `arl` by `ad`, then we obtain the following output which demonstrates the effect of the parameter r again.

r	5	10	20	30	40	50	100	200	500
$\mathcal{D}_0$	110.87	114.00	114.72	114.85	114.90	114.92	114.94	114.95	114.95

Q XFGrad.xpl

Fortunately, for smaller values of r than in the ARL case we get good accuracy already. Note, that in case of cusum2 the value r has to be smaller (less than 30) than for the other charts, since it is based on the computation of the dominant eigenvalue of a very large matrix. The approximation in case of combination of two one-sided schemes needs a twodimensional approximating Markov chain. For the ARL only exists a more suitable approach. As, e. g., Lucas and Crosier (1982) shown it is possible to use the following relation between the ARLs of the one- and the two-sided schemes. Here, the two-sided scheme is a combination of two symmetric one-sided schemes which both start at $z_0 = 0$. Therefore, we get a very simple formula for the ARL $\mathcal{L}$ of the two-sided scheme and the ARLs $\mathcal{L}_{upper}$ and $\mathcal{L}_{lower}$ of the upper and lower one-sided CUSUM scheme

$$\mathcal{L} = \frac{\mathcal{L}_{upper} \cdot \mathcal{L}_{lower}}{\mathcal{L}_{upper} + \mathcal{L}_{lower}} . \tag{11.11}$$

Eventually, we consider the distribution function of the run length L itself. By using the Markov chain approach and denoting with p_i^n the approximated probability of $(L > n)$ for a SPC scheme started in $i\,w$, such that $\underline{p}^n = (p_i^n)$, we obtain

$$\underline{p}^n = \underline{p}^{n-1} Q = \underline{p}^0 Q^n . \tag{11.12}$$

The vector $\underline{p}^0$ is initialized with $p_i^0 = 1$ for the starting point $z_0 \in [i\,w - w/2, i\,w + w/2]$ and $p_j^0 = 0$ otherwise. For large n we can replace the above equation by

$$p_i^n \approx g_i \, \varrho^n . \tag{11.13}$$

The constant g_i is defined as

$$g_i = \phi_i / (\underline{\phi}^T \underline{\psi}) ,$$

where ϕ denotes the right eigenvector of Q, i. e. $Q\,\underline{\phi} = \varrho\,\underline{\phi}$. Based on (11.12) and (11.13) the probability mass and the cumulative distribution function of the run length L can be approximated. (11.12) is used up to a certain n. If the difference between (11.12) and (11.13) is smaller than 10^{-9}, then exclusively (11.13) is exploited. Remark, that the same is valid as for the AD. For the two-sided CUSUM scheme (cusum2) the parameter r has to be small (≤ 30).

11.2.1   Average Run Length and Critical Values

The spc quantlib provides the quantlets spcewma1arl,...,spccusumCarl for computing the ARL of the corresponding SPC scheme. All routines need the actual value of μ as a scalar or as a vector of several μ, two scheme parameters, and the integer r (see the beginning of the section). The XploRe example **Q** XFGarl.xpl demonstrates all ...arl routines for $k = 0.5$, $\lambda = 0.1$, zreflect$= -4$, $r = 50$, $c = 3$, in-control and out-of-control means $\mu_0 = 0$ and $\mu_1 = 1$, respectively. The next table summarizes the ARL results

chart	ewma1	ewma2	cusum1	cusum2	cusumC
$\mathcal{L}_0$	1694.0	838.30	117.56	58.780	76.748
$\mathcal{L}_1$	11.386	11.386	6.4044	6.4036	6.4716

Q XFGarl.xpl

Remember that the ARL of the two-sided CUSUM (cusum2) scheme is based on the one-sided one, i. e. $58.78 = 117.56/2$ and $6.4036 = (6.4044 \cdot 49716)/(6.4044 + 49716)$ with $49716 = \mathcal{L}_{-1}$.

For the setup of the SPC scheme it is usual to give the design parameter λ and k for EWMA and CUSUM, respectively, and a value ξ for the in-control ARL. Then, the critical value c (c_2 or c_3) is the solution of the equation $\mathcal{L}_{\mu_0}(c) = \xi$. Here, the regula falsi is used with an accuracy of $|\mathcal{L}_{\mu_0}(c) - \xi| < 0.001$. The quantlet **Q** XFGc.xpl demonstrates the computation of the critical values for SPC schemes with in-control ARLs of $\xi = 300$, reference value $k = 0.5$ (CUSUM), smoothing parameter $\lambda = 0.1$ (EWMA), zreflect$= -4$, and the Markov chain parameter $r = 50$.

chart	ewma1	ewma2	cusum1	cusum2	cusumC
c	2.3081	2.6203	3.8929	4.5695	4.288

Q XFGc.xpl

The parameter $r = 50$ guarantees fast computation and suitable accuracy. Depending on the power of the computer one can try values of r up to 1000 or larger (see **Q** XFGrarl.xpl in the beginning of the section).

11.2.2   Average Delay

The usage of the routines for computing the Average Delay (AD) is similar to the ARL routines. Replace only the code `arl` by `ad`. Be aware that the computing time is larger than in case of the ARL, because of the computation of the dominant eigenvalue. It would be better to choose smaller r, especially in the case of the two-sided CUSUM. Unfortunately, there is no relation between the one- and two-sided schemes as for the ARL in (11.11). Therefore, the library computes the AD for the two-sided CUSUM based on a twodimensional Markov chain with dimension $(r + 1)^2 \times (r + 1)^2$. Thus with values of r larger than 30, the computing time becomes quite large. Here the results follow for the above quantlet **Q** XFGrarl.xpl with `ad` instead of `arl` and $r = 30$ for `spccusum2ad`:

chart	ewma1	ewma2	cusum1	cusum2	cusumC
$\mathcal{D}_0$	1685.8	829.83	114.92	56.047	74.495
$\mathcal{D}_1$	11.204	11.168	5.8533	5.8346	6.2858

Q XFGad.xpl

11.2.3   Probability Mass and Cumulative Distribution Function

The computation of the probability mass function (PMF) and of the cumulative distribution function (CDF) is implemented in two different types of routines. The first one with the syntax `spcchartpmf` returns the values of the PMF $P(L = n)$ and CDF $P(L \leq n)$ at given single points of n, where *chart* has to be replaced by `ewma1`, ..., `cusumC`. The second one written as `spcchartpmfm` computes the whole vectors of the PMF and of the CDF up to a given point n, i. e. $\big(P(L = 1), P(L = 2), \ldots, P(L = n)\big)$ and the similar one of the CDF.

Note, that the same is valid as for the Average Delay (AD). In case of the two-sided CUSUM scheme the computations are based on a twodimensional

Markov chain. A value of parameter r less than 30 would be computing time friendly.

With the quantlet **Q** XFGpmf1.xpl the 5 different schemes ($r = 50$, for cusum2 $r = 25$) are compared according their in-control PMF and CDF ($\mu = \mu_0 = 0$) at the positions n in $\{1, 10, 20, 30, 50, 100, 200, 300\}$. Remark, that the in-control ARL of all schemes is chosen as 300.

chart	ewma1	ewma2	cusum1	cusum2	cusumC
$P(L = 1)$	$6 \cdot 10^{-8}$	$2 \cdot 10^{-9}$	$6 \cdot 10^{-6}$	$4 \cdot 10^{-7}$	$2 \cdot 10^{-6}$
$P(L = 10)$	0.00318	0.00272	0.00321	0.00307	0.00320
$P(L = 20)$	0.00332	0.00324	0.00321	0.00325	0.00322
$P(L = 30)$	0.00315	0.00316	0.00310	0.00314	0.00311
$P(L = 50)$	0.00292	0.00296	0.00290	0.00294	0.00290
$P(L = 100)$	0.00246	0.00249	0.00245	0.00248	0.00245
$P(L = 200)$	0.00175	0.00177	0.00175	0.00176	0.00175
$P(L = 300)$	0.00125	0.00126	0.00124	0.00125	0.00125
$P(L = 1)$	$6 \cdot 10^{-8}$	$2 \cdot 10^{-9}$	$6 \cdot 10^{-6}$	$4 \cdot 10^{-7}$	$2 \cdot 10^{-6}$
$P(L \leq 10)$	0.01663	0.01233	0.02012	0.01675	0.01958
$P(L \leq 20)$	0.05005	0.04372	0.05254	0.04916	0.05202
$P(L \leq 30)$	0.08228	0.07576	0.08407	0.08109	0.08358
$P(L \leq 50)$	0.14269	0.13683	0.14402	0.14179	0.14360
$P(L \leq 100)$	0.27642	0.27242	0.27728	0.27658	0.27700
$P(L \leq 200)$	0.48452	0.48306	0.48480	0.48597	0.48470
$P(L \leq 300)$	0.63277	0.63272	0.63272	0.63476	0.63273

Q XFGpmf1.xpl

A more appropriate, graphical representation provides the quantlet **Q** XFGpmf2.xpl. Figure 11.4 shows the corresponding graphs.

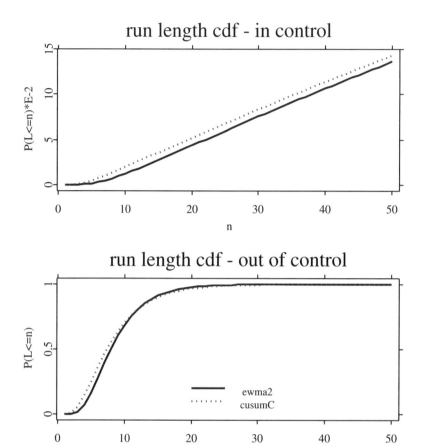

Figure 11.4. CDF for two-sided EWMA and Crosier's CUSUM for $\mu = 0$ (in control) and $\mu = 1$ (out of control)

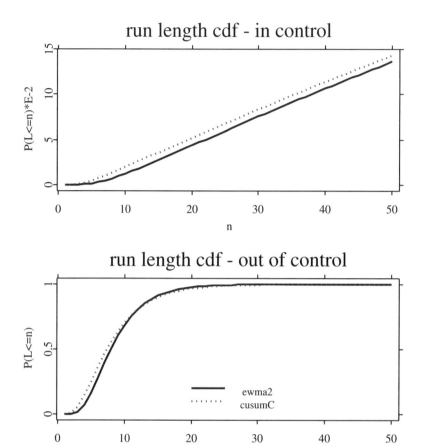 XFGpmf2.xpl

11.3 Comparison with existing methods

11.3.1 Two-sided EWMA and Lucas/Saccucci

Here, we compare the ARL and AD computations of Lucas and Saccucci (1990) with XploRe results. In their paper they use as in-control ARL $\xi = 500$. Then for, e.g., $\lambda = 0.5$ and $\lambda = 0.1$ the critical values are 3.071 and 2.814, respectively. By using XploRe the related values are 3.0712 and 2.8144, respectively. It is known, that the smaller λ the worse the accuracy of the Markov chain approach. Therefore, r is set greater for $\lambda = 0.1$ ($r = 200$) than for $\lambda = 0.5$ ($r = 50$). Table 11.1 shows some results of Lucas and Saccucci (1990) on ARLs and ADs. Their results are based on the Markov chain approach as well. However, they used some smaller matrix dimension and fitted a regression model on r (see Subsection 11.3.2). The corresponding XploRe results

μ	0	0.25	0.5	0.75	1	1.5	2	3	4	5
					$\lambda = 0.5$					
$\mathcal{L}_\mu$	500	255	88.8	35.9	17.5	6.53	3.63	1.93	1.34	1.07
$\mathcal{D}_\mu$	499	254	88.4	35.7	17.3	6.44	3.58	1.91	1.36	1.10
					$\lambda = 0.1$					
$\mathcal{L}_\mu$	500	106	31.3	15.9	10.3	6.09	4.36	2.87	2.19	1.94
$\mathcal{D}_\mu$	492	104	30.6	15.5	10.1	5.99	4.31	2.85	2.20	1.83

Table 11.1. ARL and AD values from Table 3 of Lucas and Saccucci (1990)

by using the quantlet **Q** XFGlucsac.xpl coincide with the values of Lucas and Saccucci (1990).

Q XFGlucsac.xpl

11.3.2 Two-sided CUSUM and Crosier

Crosier (1986) derived a new two-sided CUSUM scheme and compared it with the established combination of two one-sided schemes. Recall Table 3 of Crosier (1986), where the ARLs of the new and the old scheme were presented. The reference value k is equal to 0.5. First, we compare the critical values. By

μ	0	0.25	0.5	0.75	1	1.5	2	2.5	3	4	5
				old scheme, $h = 4$							
$\mathcal{L}_\mu$	168	74.2	26.6	13.3	8.38	4.74	3.34	2.62	2.19	1.71	1.31
				new scheme, $h = 3.73$							
$\mathcal{L}_\mu$	168	70.7	25.1	12.5	7.92	4.49	3.17	2.49	2.09	1.60	1.22
				old scheme, $h = 5$							
$\mathcal{L}_\mu$	465	139	38.0	17.0	10.4	5.75	4.01	3.11	2.57	2.01	1.69
				new scheme, $h = 4.713$							
$\mathcal{L}_\mu$	465	132	35.9	16.2	9.87	5.47	3.82	2.97	2.46	1.94	1.59

Table 11.2. ARLs from Table 3 of Crosier (1986)

using XploRe (**Q** XFGcrosc.xpl) with $r = 100$ one gets $c = 4.0021$ (4), 3.7304 (3.73), 4.9997 (5), 4.7133 (4.713), respectively – the original values of Crosier are written in parentheses. By comparing the results of Table 11.2 with the results obtainable by the quantlet **Q** XFGcrosarl.xpl ($r = 100$) it turns out, that again the ARL values coincide with one exception only, namely $\mathcal{L}_{1.5} = 4.75$ for the old scheme with $h = 4$.

Q XFGcrosarl.xpl

Further, we want to compare the results for the Average Delay (AD), which is called Steady-State ARL in Crosier (1986). In Table 5 of Crosier we find the related results. A slight modification of the above quantlet **Q** XFGcrosarl.xpl

μ	0	0.25	0.5	0.75	1	1.5	2	2.5	3	4	5
				old scheme, $h = 4$							
$\mathcal{L}_\mu$	163	71.6	25.2	12.3	7.68	4.31	3.03	2.38	2.00	1.55	1.22
				new scheme, $h = 3.73$							
$\mathcal{L}_\mu$	164	69.0	24.3	12.1	7.69	4.39	3.12	2.46	2.07	1.60	1.29
				old scheme, $h = 5$							
$\mathcal{L}_\mu$	459	136	36.4	16.0	9.62	5.28	3.68	2.86	2.38	1.86	1.53
				new scheme, $h = 4.713$							
$\mathcal{L}_\mu$	460	130	35.1	15.8	9.62	5.36	3.77	2.95	2.45	1.91	1.57

Table 11.3. ADs (steady-state ARLs) from Table 5 of Crosier (1986)

allows to compute the ADs. Remember, that the computation of the AD for the two-sided CUSUM scheme is based on a twodimensional Markov chain. Therefore the parameter r is set to 25 for the scheme called old scheme by Crosier. The results are summarized in Table 11.4.

μ	0	0.25	0.5	0.75	1	1.5	2	2.5	3	4	5
				old scheme, $h = 4$							
$\mathcal{L}_\mu$	163	71.6	25.2	*12.4*	*7.72*	*4.33*	*3.05*	*2.39*	*2.01*	1.55	1.22
				new scheme, $h = 3.73$							
$\mathcal{L}_\mu$	*165*	69.1	*24.4*	12.2	7.70	*4.40*	3.12	*2.47*	2.07	1.60	1.29
				old scheme, $h = 5$							
$\mathcal{L}_\mu$	*455*	136	36.4	16.0	*9.65*	*5.30*	*3.69*	2.87	2.38	1.86	*1.54*
				new scheme, $h = 4.713$							
$\mathcal{L}_\mu$	460	130	35.1	15.8	*9.63*	*5.37*	3.77	2.95	2.45	1.91	1.57

Table 11.4. ADs (steady-state ARLs) computed by XploRe, different values to Table 11.3 are printed as italics **Q** XFGcrosad.xpl

While the ARL values in the paper and computed by XploRe coincide, those for the AD differ slightly. The most prominent deviation (459 vs. 455) one observes for the old scheme with $h = 5$. One further in-control ARL difference one notices for the new scheme with $h = 3.73$. All other differences are small.

There are different sources for the deviations:

1. Crosier computed $D^{(32)} = (\underline{p}^{32^T}\underline{L})/(\underline{p}^{32^T}\underline{1})$ and not the actual limit D (see 11.8, 11.10, and 11.12).

2. Crosier used $ARL(r) = ARL_\infty + B/r^2 + C/r^4$ and fitted this model for $r = 8, 9, 10, 12, 15$. Then, ARL_∞ is used as final approximation. In order to get the above $D^{(32)}$ one needs the whole vector $\underline{L}$, such that this approach might be more sensitive to approximation errors than in the single ARL case.

11.4   Real data example – monitoring CAPM

There are different ways of applying SPC to financial data. Here, we use a twosided EWMA chart for monitoring the Deutsche Bank (DBK) share. More precisely, a capital asset pricing model (CAPM) is fitted for DBK and the DAX which is used as proxy of the efficient market portfolio. That is, denoting with $r_{\mathrm{DAX},t}$ and $r_{\mathrm{DBK},t}$ the log returns of the DAX and the DBK, respectively, one assumes that the following regression model is valid:

$$r_{\mathrm{DBK},t} = \alpha + \beta\, r_{\mathrm{DAX},t} + \varepsilon_t \qquad (11.14)$$

Usually, the parameters of the model are estimated by the ordinary least squares method. The parameter β is a very popular measure in applied finance, Elton and Gruber (1991). In order to construct a real portfolio, the β coefficient is frequently taken into account. Research has therefore concentrated on the appropriate estimation of constant and time changing β. In the context of SPC it is therefore useful to construct monitoring rules which signal changes in β. Contrary to standard SPC application in industry there is no obvious state of the process which one can call "in-control", i.e. there is no target process. Therefore, pre-run time series of both quotes (DBK, DAX) are exploited for building the in-control state. The daily quotes and log returns, respectively, from january, 6th, 1995 to march, 18th, 1997 (about 450 observations) are used for fitting (11.14):

```
A  N  0  V  A                    SS       df     MSS      F-test   P-value
----------------------------------------------------------------------------
Regression                      0.025     1     0.025    445.686   0.0000
Residuals                       0.025    448    0.000
Total Variation                 0.050    449    0.000

Multiple R     = 0.70619
R^2            = 0.49871
Adjusted R^2   = 0.49759
Standard Error = 0.00746

PARAMETERS          Beta         SE         StandB     t-test   P-value
----------------------------------------------------------------------------
b[ 0,]=           -0.0003      0.0004      -0.0000    -0.789    0.4307
b[ 1,]=            0.8838      0.0419       0.7062    21.111    0.0000
```

With $\mathtt{b[1,]} = \beta = 0.8838$ a typical value has been obtained. The $R^2 = 0.49871$ is not very large. However, the simple linear regression is considered in the sequel. The (empirical) residuals of the above model are correlated (see Figure 11.5). The SPC application should therefore be performed with the (standardized) residuals of an AR(1) fit to the regression residuals. For an application of the XploRe quantlet $\mathtt{armacls}$ (quantlib $\mathtt{times}$) the regression residuals were standardized. By using the conditional least squares method an

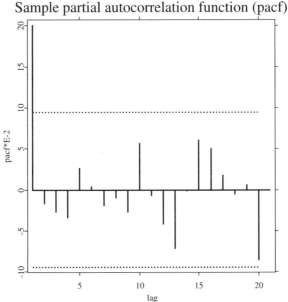

Figure 11.5. Partial autocorrelation function of CAPM regression residuals

estimate of $\hat{\varrho} = 0.20103$ for the AR(1) model

$$\varepsilon_t = \varrho\,\varepsilon_{t-1} + \eta_t \tag{11.15}$$

has been obtained. Eventually, by plugging in the estimates of α, β and ϱ,
and standardizing with the sample standard deviation of the pre-run residuals
series (see (11.15)) one gets a series of uncorrelated data with expectation 0 and
variance 1, i.e. our in-control state. If the fitted model (CAPM with AR(1)
noise) remains valid after the pre-run, the related standardized residuals behave
like in the in-control state. Now, the application of SPC, more precisely of a
twosided EWMA chart, allows to monitor the series in order to get signals, if
the original model was changed. Changes in α or β in (11.14) or in ϱ in (11.15)
or in the residual variance of both models lead to shifts or scale changes in the
empirical residuals series. Hence, the probability of an alarm signaled by the
EWMA chart increases (with one exception only – decreased variances). In
this way a possible user of SPC in finance is able to monitor an estimated and
presumed CAPM.

In our example we use the parameter $\lambda = 0.2$ and an in-control ARL of 500, such that the critical value is equal to $c = 2.9623$ (the Markov chain parameter r was set to 100). Remark, that the computation of c is based on the normality assumption, which is seldom fulfilled for financial data. In our example the hypothesis of normality is rejected as well with a very small p value (Jarque-Bera test with quantlet `jarber`). The estimates of skewness 0.136805 and kurtosis 6.64844 contradict normality too. The fat tails of the distribution are a typical pattern of financial data. Usually, the fat tails lead to a higher false alarm rate. However, it would be much more complicated to fit an appropriate distribution to the residuals and use these results for the "correct" critical value.

The Figures 11.6 and 11.7 present the EWMA graphs of the pre-run and the monitoring period (from march, 19th, 1997 to april, 16th, 1999). In the pre-run

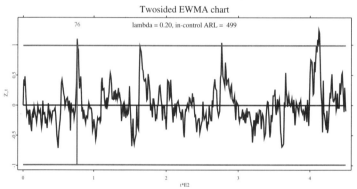

Figure 11.6. Twosided EWMA chart of the standardized CAPM-AR(1) residuals for the pre-run period (06/01/95 - 03/18/97)

period the EWMA chart signals 4 times. The first 3 alarms seem to be outliers, while the last points on a longer change. Nevertheless, the chart performs quite typical for the pre-run period. The first signal in the monitoring period was obtained at the 64th observation (i.e. 06/24/97). Then, we observe more frequently signals than in the pre-run period, the changes are more persistent and so one has to assume, that the pre-run model is no longer valid. A new CAPM has therefore to be fitted and, if necessary, the considered portfolio has to be reweighted. Naturally, a new pre-run can be used for the new monitoring

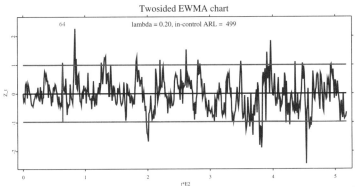

Figure 11.7. Twosided EWMA chart of the standardized CAPM-AR(1) residuals for the monitoring period (03/19/97 - 04/16/99)

period.

Q XFGcapmar1.xpl

Bibliography

Brook, D. and Evans, D. A. (1972). An approach to the probability distribution of cusum run length, *Biometrika* **59**: 539–548.

Crosier, R. B. (1986). A new two-sided cumulative quality control scheme, *Technometrics* **28**: 187–194.

Crowder, S. V. (1986). A simple method for studying run-length distributions of exponentially weighted moving average charts, *Technometrics* **29**: 401–407.

Elton, EJ. and Gruber, MJ. (1991). *Modern portfolio theory and investment analysis*, Wiley, 4. edition.

Knoth, S. (1998). Quasi-stationarity of CUSUM schemes for Erlang distributions, *Metrika* **48**: 31–48.

Lorden, G. (1971). Procedures for reacting to a change in distribution, *Annals of Mathematical Statistics* **42**: 1897–1908.

Lucas, J. M. (1976). The design and use of V-mask control schemes, *Journal of Quality Technology* **8**: 1–12.

Lucas, J. M. and Crosier, R. B. (1982). Fast initial response for cusum quality-control schemes: Give your cusum a headstart, *Technometrics* **24**: 199–205.

Lucas, J. M. and Saccucci, M. S. (1990). Exponentially weighted moving average control schemes: properties and enhancements, *Technometrics* **32**: 1–12.

Page, E. S. (1954). Continuous inspection schemes, *Biometrika* **41**: 100–115.

Pollak, M. and Siegmund, D. (1975). Approximations to the expected sample size of certain sequential tests, *Annals of Statistics* **3**: 1267–1282.

Pollak, M. and Siegmund, D. (1985). A diffusion process and its applications to detection a change in the drift of brownian motion, *Biometrika* **72**: 267–280.

Roberts, S. W. (1959). Control-charts-tests based on geometric moving averages, *Technometrics* **1**: 239–250.

Shewhart, W. A. (1931). *Economic Control of Quality of Manufactured Product*, D. van Nostrand Company, Inc., Toronto, Canada.

Vance, L. (1986). ARL of cumulative sum control chart for controlling normal mean, *Journal of Quality Technology* **18**: 189–193.

Waldmann, K.-H. (1986). Bounds to the distribution of the run length in general quality–control schemes, *Statistische Hefte* **27**: 37–56.

12 An Empirical Likelihood Goodness-of-Fit Test for Diffusions

Song Xi Chen, Wolfgang Härdle and Torsten Kleinow

The analysis and prediction of diffusion processes plays a fundamental role in the statistical analysis of financial markets. The techniques applied rely on the actual model assumed for the drift and diffusion coefficient functions. Mismodelling these coefficients might result in biased prediction and incorrect parameter specification. We show in this chapter how the empirical likelihood technique, Owen (1988) and Owen (1990), may be used to construct test procedures for the Goodness-of-Fit of a diffusion model. The technique is based on comparison with kernel smoothing estimators. The Goodness-of-Fit test proposed is based on the asymptotics of the empirical likelihood, which has two attractive features. One is its automatic consideration of the variation associated with the nonparametric fit due to the empirical likelihood's ability to studentize internally. The other one is that the asymptotic distributions of the test statistic are free of unknown parameters which avoids secondary plug-in estimation.

12.1 Introduction

Let us assume a strictly stationary one-dimensional diffusion Z solving the stochastic differential equation (SDE)

$$dZ(t) = m\{Z(t)\}dt + v\{Z(t)\}dW(t) \qquad (12.1)$$

where the driving process $W = \{W(t),\ t \in [0, \infty)\}$ in (12.1) is a standard Wiener process. In a mathematical finance setting, Z might be the price process of a stock, a stock market index or any other observable process. For the rest of the chapter the drift $m : \mathbb{R} \mapsto \mathbb{R}$, and the diffusion coefficient $v : \mathbb{R} \mapsto [0, \infty)$ in (12.1) are assumed to be sufficiently smooth, so that a unique solution of (12.1) exists.

In applications we are mostly interested in the stationary solutions of (12.1). For the existence of a stationary solution, the drift and the diffusion coefficient must satisfy some conditions, Bibby and Sørensen (1995). The most important condition is that the stationary forward Kolmogorov equation

$$(1/2) \left\{ v^2(z)p(z) \right\}' - m(z)p(z) = 0$$

has a solution $p(z)$ which is a probability density. If the initial value $Z(0)$ is distributed in accordance with p_0, and if it is independent of the Wiener process $W(t)$ in (12.1), then (12.1) defines a stationary process. The above condition holds for the Ornstein-Uhlenbeck process with a normal stationary distribution, and for the Cox-Ingersoll-Ross process with a Γ-distribution. For the statistical analysis we assume that Z is observed at discrete times $t_i = i\Delta$, $i = 1, 2, \ldots, n$, with a time step size $\Delta > 0$. From these observations we get a time series Z^Δ with certain dynamics specified in Section 12.2.

The aim of this chapter is to test a parametric model for the drift function m against a nonparametric alternative, i.e.

$$H_0(m) : m(z) = m_\theta(z) \qquad (12.2)$$

where θ is an unknown parameter. The test statistic we apply is based on the empirical likelihood. This concept was introduced by Chen, Härdle and Kleinow (2001) for time series. To apply it in our situation we start with the discretization of the diffusion process Z.

12.2   Discrete Time Approximation of a Diffusion

Let us assume that the diffusion process Z is observed at discrete times $t_i = i\Delta$, $i = 1, 2, \ldots, n$, with a time step size $\Delta > 0$. Here we suppose that Δ is small or, more precisely, will tend to zero asymptotically. Under rather weak assumptions, see Kloeden and Platen (1999), on the functions m and v^2, it can be shown that the Euler approximation

$$Z^\Delta(t) = Z^\Delta(0) + \int_0^t m\{Z^\Delta(t_{i_s})\}ds + \int_0^t v\{Z^\Delta(t_{i_s})\}dW(s) \qquad (12.3)$$

with $t_{i_s} = \max\{t_i, t_i \leq s\}$, converges in a mean square sense to Z as $\Delta \to 0$, i.e.,

$$\lim_{\Delta \to 0} \mathrm{E}(\sup_{0 \leq t \leq T} |Z^{\Delta}(t) - Z(t)|^2) = 0, \ T > 0. \tag{12.4}$$

From now on, we assume that a discrete time approximation Z^{Δ} exists in the form of (12.3), and that the property (12.4) holds. For the purposes of this chapter, Δ will always be considered small enough that one can substitute Z by Z^{Δ} in our interpretation of the observed data. The increments of the Euler approximation and so the observed data will have the form

$$Z^{\Delta}(t_{i+1}) - Z^{\Delta}(t_i) = m\{Z^{\Delta}(t_i)\}\Delta + v\{Z^{\Delta}(t_i)\}\{W(t_{i+1}) - W(t_i)\} \tag{12.5}$$

for $i = 0, 1, \ldots$. The observations $\{Z^{\Delta}(t_i)\}$, $i = 0, 1, \ldots n$ form a time series. As long as the step size Δ is small enough the concrete choice of Δ does not matter since all the relevant information about the model is contained in the drift m and diffusion coefficient v.

For the following we introduce the notation

$$\begin{aligned}
X_i &\stackrel{\text{def}}{=} Z^{\Delta}(t_i), &\quad X &\stackrel{\text{def}}{=} (X_1, \ldots, X_n)\\
\varepsilon_i &\stackrel{\text{def}}{=} W(t_{i+1}) - W(t_i), &\quad \varepsilon &\stackrel{\text{def}}{=} (\varepsilon_1, \ldots, \varepsilon_n)\\
Y_i &\stackrel{\text{def}}{=} X_{i+1} - X_i = m(X_i)\Delta + v(X_i)\varepsilon_i, &\quad Y &\stackrel{\text{def}}{=} (Y_1, \ldots, Y_n) \tag{12.6}
\end{aligned}$$

We can now apply the empirical likelihood Goodness-of-Fit test for stationary time series developed by Chen et al. (2001).

12.3 Hypothesis Testing

Suppose (X, Y) is defined as in (12.6) and let $m(x) = \mathrm{E}(Y|X = x)$ be the conditional mean function, f be the density of the design points X, and $\sigma^2(x) = \mathrm{Var}(Y|X = x)$ be the conditional variance function of Y given $X = x \in S$, a closed interval $S \subset \mathbb{R}$. Suppose that $\{m_\theta | \theta \in \Theta\}$ is a parametric model for the mean function m and that $\hat{\theta}$ is an estimator of θ under this parametric model. The interest is to test the null hypothesis:

$$H_0 : m(x) = m_\theta(x) \quad \text{for all } x \in S$$

against a series of local smooth nonparametric alternatives:

$$H_1 : m(x) = m_\theta(x) + c_n \Delta_n(x),$$

where c_n is a non-random sequence tending to zero as $n \to \infty$ and $\Delta_n(x)$ is a sequence of bounded functions.

The problem of testing against a nonparametric alternative is not new for an independent and identically distributed setting, Härdle and Mammen (1993) and Hart (1997). In a time series context the testing procedure has only been considered by Kreiß, Neumann and Yao (1998) as far as we are aware. Also theoretical results on kernel estimators for time series appeared only very recently, Bosq (1998). This is surprising given the interests in time series for financial engineering.

We require a few assumptions to establish the results in this chapter. These assumptions are the following:

(i)   The kernel K is Lipschitz continuous in $[-1, 1]$, that is $|K(t_1) - K(t_2)| \le C||t_1 - t_2||$ where $|| \cdot ||$ is the Euclidean norm, and $h = \mathcal{O}\{n^{-1/5}\}$;

(ii) f, m and σ^2 have continuous derivatives up to the second order in S.

(iii) $\hat{\theta}$ is a parametric estimator of θ within the family of the parametric model, and
$$\sup_{x \in S} |m_{\hat{\theta}}(x) - m_\theta(x)| = \mathcal{O}_p(n^{-1/2}).$$

(iv) $\Delta_n(x)$, the local shift in the alternative H_1, is uniformly bounded with respect to x and n, and $c_n = n^{-1/2}h^{-1/4}$ which is the order of the difference between H_0 and H_1.

(v)   The process $\{(X_i, Y_i)\}$ is strictly stationary and α-mixing, i.e.
$$\alpha(k) \stackrel{\text{def}}{=} \sup_{A \in \mathcal{F}_1^i, B \in \mathcal{F}_{i+k}^\infty} |P(AB) - P(A)P(B)| \le a\rho^k$$

for some $a > 0$ and $\rho \in [0, 1)$. Here $\mathcal{F}_k^l$ denotes the σ-algebra of events generated by $\{(X_i, Y_i), k \le i \le l\}$ for $l \ge k$. For an introduction into α-mixing processes, see Bosq (1998) or Billingsley (1999). As shown by Genon-Catalot, Jeantheau and Larédo (2000) this assumption is fulfilled if Z_t is an α-mixing process.

(vi) $E\{\exp(a_0|Y_1 - m(X_1)|)\} < \infty$ for some $a_0 > 0$; The conditional density of X given Y and the joint conditional density of (X_1, X_l) given (Y_1, Y_l) are bounded for all $l > 1$.

Assumptions (i) and (ii) are standard in nonparametric curve estimation and are satisfied for example for bandwidths selected by cross validation, whereas (iii) and (iv) are common in nonparametric Goodness-of-Fit tests. Assumption (v) means the data are weakly dependent. It is satisfied for a wide class of diffusion processes.

12.4 Kernel Estimator

To develop a test about H_0 we first introduce a nonparametric kernel estimator for m. For an introduction into kernel estimation see Härdle (1990), Wand and Jones (1995) and (Härdle, Müller, Sperlich and Werwatz, 2000). Without loss of generality we assume that we are only interested in $m(x)$ for $x \in [0,1]$ and that $f(x) \geq C_1 \ \forall x \in [0,1]$ with a positive constant C_1. If in a particular problem the data are supported by another closed interval, this problem can be transformed by rescaling into an equivalent problem with data support $[0,1]$.

Let K be a bounded probability density function with a compact support on $[-1,1]$ that satisfies the moment conditions:

$$\int uK(u)du = 0, \ \int u^2 K(u)du = \sigma_K^2$$

where σ_K^2 is a positive constant. Let h be a positive smoothing bandwidth which will be used to smooth (X,Y).

The nonparametric estimator considered is the Nadaraya-Watson (NW) estimator

$$\hat{m}(x) = \frac{\sum_{i=1}^n Y_i K_h(x - X_i)}{\sum_{i=1}^n K_h(x - X_i)} \tag{12.7}$$

with $K_h(u) = h^{-1}K(h^{-1}u)$. This estimator is calculated in XploRe by the quantlets `regest` or `regxest`.

The parameter estimation of θ depends on the null hypothesis. We assume here, that the parameter θ is estimated by a $\sqrt{n}$-consistent estimator. Let

$$\tilde{m}_{\hat{\theta}}(x) = \frac{\sum K_h(x - X_i)m_{\hat{\theta}}(X_i)}{\sum_{i=1}^n K_h(x - X_i)}$$

be the smoothed parametric model. The test statistic we are going to consider is based on the difference between $\tilde{m}_{\hat{\theta}}$ and $\hat{m}$, rather than directly between $\hat{m}$

and $m_{\hat{\theta}}$, in order to avoid the issue of bias associated with the nonparametric fit.

The local linear estimator can be used to replace the NW estimator in estimating m. However, as we compare $\hat{m}$ with $\tilde{m}_{\hat{\theta}}$ in formulating the Goodness-of-Fit test, the possible bias associated with the NW estimator is not an issue here. In addition, the NW estimator has a simpler analytic form.

12.5   The Empirical Likelihood concept

12.5.1   Introduction into Empirical Likelihood

Let us now as in Owen (1988) and Owen (1990) introduce the empirical likelihood (EL) concept. Suppose a sample $(U_1, \ldots, U_n)$ of independent identically distributed random variables in $\mathbb{R}^1$ according to a probability law with unknown distribution function F and unknown density f. For an observation $(u_1, \ldots, u_n)$ of $(U_1, \ldots, U_n)$ the likelihood function is given by

$$\bar{L}(f) = \prod_{i=1}^{n} f(u_i) \qquad (12.8)$$

The empirical density calculated from the observations $(u_1, \ldots, u_n)$ is

$$f_n(u) \stackrel{\text{def}}{=} \frac{1}{n} \sum_{i=1}^{n} \mathbf{1}\{u_i = u\} \qquad (12.9)$$

where $\mathbf{1}$ denotes the indicator function. It is easy to see that f_n maximizes $\bar{L}(f)$ in the class of all probability density functions.

The objective of the empirical likelihood concept is the construction of tests and confidence intervals for a parameter $\theta = \theta(F)$ of the distribution of U_i. To keep things simple we illustrate the empirical likelihood method for the expectation $E[U_i]$. The null hypothesis is $E[U_i] = \theta$. We can test this assumption based on the empirical likelihood ratio

$$R(F) \stackrel{\text{def}}{=} \frac{\bar{L}\{f(\theta)\}}{\bar{L}(f_n)} \qquad (12.10)$$

where $f(\theta)$ maximizes $\bar{L}(f)$ subject to

$$\int U_i dF = \theta. \qquad (12.11)$$

On a heuristic level we can reject the null hypothesis "under the true distribution F, U has expectation θ" if the ratio $R(F)$ is small relative to 1, i.e. the test rejects if $R(F) < r$ for a certain level $r \in (0, 1)$. More precisely, Owen (1990) proves the following

THEOREM 12.1 *Let* $(U_1, \ldots, U_n)$ *be iid one-dimensional random variables with expectation* θ *and variance* σ^2. *For a positive* $r < 1$ *let*

$$C_{r,n} = \left\{ \int U_i dF \ \middle| \ F \ll F_n, R(F) \geq r \right\}$$

be the set of all possible expectations of U *with respect to distributions* F *dominated by* F_n *($F \ll F_n$). Then it follows*

$$\lim_{n \to \infty} P[\theta \in C_{r,n}] = P[\chi^2 \leq -2 \log r] \qquad (12.12)$$

where χ^2 *is a* χ^2-*distributed random variable with one degree of freedom.*

From Theorem 12.1 it follows directly

$$\lim_{n \to \infty} P\left[-2 \log \left\{ \max_{\{F | F \ll F_n, \int U_i dF = \theta\}} R(F) \right\} \leq r \ \middle| \ EU_i = \theta \right] = P[\chi^2 \leq r]$$

This result suggests therefore to use the log-EL ratio

$$-2 \log \left\{ \max_{\{F | F \ll F_n, \int U_i dF = \theta\}} R(F) \right\} = -2 \log \left\{ \max_{\{F | F \ll F_n, \int U_i dF = \theta\}} \frac{\bar{L}\{f(\theta)\}}{\bar{L}(f_n)} \right\}$$

as the basic element of a test about a parametric hypothesis for the drift function of a diffusion process.

12.5.2   Empirical Likelihood for Time Series Data

We will now expand the results in Section 12.5.1 to the case of time series data. For an arbitrary $x \in [0, 1]$ and any function μ we have

$$E\left[K\left(\frac{x - X_i}{h} \right) \{Y_i - \mu(x)\} \ \middle| \ E[Y_i | X_i = x] = \mu(x) \right] = 0. \qquad (12.13)$$

Let $p_i(x)$ be nonnegative numbers representing a density for

$$K\left(\frac{x - X_i}{h} \right) \{Y_i - \mu(x)\} \qquad i = 1, \ldots, n$$

The empirical likelihood for $\mu(x)$ is

$$L\{\mu(x)\} \stackrel{\text{def}}{=} \max \prod_{i=1}^{n} p_i(x) \tag{12.14}$$

subject to $\sum_{i=1}^{n} p_i(x) = 1$ and $\sum_{i=1}^{n} p_i(x)K\left(\frac{x-X_i}{h}\right)\{Y_i - \mu(x)\} = 0$. The second condition reflects (12.13).

We find the maximum by introducing Lagrange multipliers and maximizing the Lagrangian function

$$\mathcal{L}(p, \lambda_1, \lambda_2) \;=\; \sum_{i=1}^{n} \log p_i(x)$$

$$-\lambda_1 \sum_{i=1}^{n} p_i(x)K\left(\frac{x-X_i}{h}\right)\{Y_i - \mu(x)\} - \lambda_2\left\{\sum_{i=1}^{n} p_i(x) - 1\right\}$$

The partial derivatives are

$$\frac{\partial \mathcal{L}(p, \lambda_1, \lambda_2)}{\partial p_i(x)} = \frac{1}{p_i(x)} - \lambda_1 K\left(\frac{x-X_i}{h}\right)\{Y_i - \mu(x)\} - \lambda_2 \qquad \forall i = 1, \dots, n.$$

With $\lambda = \lambda_1/\lambda_2$ we obtain as a solution to (12.14) the optimal weights

$$p_i(x) = n^{-1}\left[1 + \lambda(x)K\left(\frac{x-X_i}{h}\right)\{Y_i - \mu(x)\}\right]^{-1} \tag{12.15}$$

where $\lambda(x)$ is the root of

$$\sum_{i=1}^{n} \frac{K\left(\frac{x-X_i}{h}\right)\{Y_i - \mu(x)\}}{1 + \lambda(x)K\left(\frac{x-X_i}{h}\right)\{Y_i - \mu(x)\}} = 0. \tag{12.16}$$

Note, that $\lambda_2 = n$ follows from

$$\sum_{i=1}^{n} p_i(x) + \lambda \sum_{i=1}^{n} p_i(x)K\left(\frac{x-X_i}{h}\right)\{Y_i - \mu(x)\} = 1.$$

The maximum empirical likelihood is achieved at $p_i(x) = n^{-1}$ corresponding to the nonparametric curve estimate $\mu(x) = \hat{m}(x)$. For a parameter estimate $\hat{\theta}$ we get the maximum empirical likelihood for the smoothed parametric model $L\{\tilde{m}_{\hat{\theta}}(x)\}$. The log-EL ratio is

$$\ell\{\tilde{m}_{\hat{\theta}}(x)\} \stackrel{\text{def}}{=} -2\log\frac{L\{\tilde{m}_{\hat{\theta}}(x)\}}{L\{\hat{m}(x)\}} = -2\log[L\{\tilde{m}_{\hat{\theta}}(x)\}n^n].$$

To study properties of the empirical likelihood based test statistic we need to evaluate $\ell\{\tilde{m}_{\hat{\theta}}(x)\}$ at an arbitrary x first, which requires the following lemma on $\lambda(x)$ that is proved in Chen et al. (2001).

LEMMA 12.1 *Under the assumptions (i)-(vi),*

$$\sup_{x \in [0,1]} |\lambda(x)| = \mathcal{O}_p\{(nh)^{-1/2} \log(n)\}.$$

Let $\gamma(x)$ be a random process with $x \in [0,1]$. Throughout this chapter we use the notation $\gamma(x) = \tilde{\mathcal{O}}_p(\delta_n)$ ($\tilde{o}_p(\delta_n)$) to denote the facts that $\sup_{x \in [0,1]} |\gamma(x)| = \mathcal{O}_p(\delta_n)$ ($o_p(\delta_n)$) for a sequence δ_n.

Let $\bar{U}_j(x) = (nh)^{-1} \sum_{i=1}^{n} \left[K\left(\frac{x-X_i}{h}\right) \{Y_i - \tilde{m}_{\hat{\theta}}(x)\} \right]^j$ for $j = 1, 2, \ldots$. An application of the power series expansion of $1/(1 - \bullet)$ applied to (12.16) and Lemma 12.1 yields

$$\sum_{i=1}^{n} K\left(\frac{x-X_i}{h}\right) \{Y_i - \tilde{m}_{\hat{\theta}}(x)\} \left[\sum_{j=0}^{\infty} (-\lambda(x))^j K^j \left(\frac{x-X_i}{h}\right) \{Y_i - \tilde{m}_{\hat{\theta}}(x)\}^j \right] = 0.$$

Inverting the above expansion, we have

$$\lambda(x) = \bar{U}_2^{-1}(x)\bar{U}_1(x) + \tilde{o}_p\{(nh)^{-1} \log^2(n)\}. \tag{12.17}$$

From (12.15), Lemma 12.1 and the Taylor expansion of $\log(1 + \bullet)$ we get

$$\begin{aligned}
\ell\{\tilde{m}_{\hat{\theta}}(x)\} &= -2 \log[L\{\tilde{m}_{\hat{\theta}}(x)\}n^n] \\
&= 2 \sum_{i=1}^{n} \log[1 + \lambda(x)K\left(\frac{x-X_i}{h}\right) \{Y_j - \tilde{m}_{\hat{\theta}}(x)\}] \\
&= 2nh\lambda(x)\bar{U}_1 - nh\lambda^2(x)\bar{U}_2 + \tilde{o}_p\{(nh)^{-1/2} \log^3(n)\}
\end{aligned}$$
$$\tag{12.18}$$

Inserting (12.17) in (12.18) yields

$$\ell\{\tilde{m}_{\hat{\theta}}(x)\} = nh\bar{U}_2^{-1}(x)\bar{U}_1^2(x) + \tilde{o}_p\{(nh)^{-1/2} \log^3(n)\}. \tag{12.19}$$

For any $x \in [0,1]$, let

$$v(x;h) = h \int_0^1 K_h^2(x-y)dy \text{ and } b(x;h) = h \int_0^1 K_h(x-y)dy$$

be the variance and the bias coefficient functions associated with the NW estimator, respectively, see Wand and Jones (1995). Let

$$S_{I,h} = \{x \in [0,1] | \min(|x-1|, |x|) > h\}.$$

For $h \to 0$, $S_{I,h}$ converges to the set of interior points in $[0,1]$. If $x \in S_{I,h}$, we have $v(x;h) \stackrel{\text{def}}{=} \int K^2(x)dx$ and $b(x;h) = 1$. Define

$$V(x;h) = \frac{v(x;h)\sigma^2(x)}{f(x)b^2(x;h)}.$$

Clearly, $V(x;h)/(nh)$ is the asymptotic variance of $\hat{m}(x)$ when $nh \to \infty$ which is one of the conditions we assumed.

It was shown by Chen et al. (2001), that

$$
\begin{aligned}
\bar{U}_1(x) &= n^{-1}\sum_{i=1}^{n} K_h(x - X_i)\{Y_i - \tilde{m}_{\hat{\theta}}(x)\} \\
&= n^{-1}\sum_{i=1}^{n} K_h(x - X_i)\{Y_i - m_{\theta}(X_i)\} + \tilde{\mathcal{O}}_p(n^{-1/2}) \\
&= \hat{f}(x)\{\hat{m}(x) - \tilde{m}_{\theta}(x)\} + \tilde{\mathcal{O}}_p(n^{-1/2}) \\
&= f(x)b(x;h)\{\hat{m}(x) - \tilde{m}_{\theta}(x)\} + \tilde{\mathcal{O}}_p\{n^{-1/2} + (nh)^{-1}\log^2(n)\}.
\end{aligned}
$$

In the same paper it is shown, that condition (iii) entails $\sup_{x \in [0,1]} |\bar{U}_2(x) - f(x)v(x;h)\sigma^2(x)| = \mathcal{O}_p(h)$. These and (12.19) mean that

$$
\begin{aligned}
\ell\{\tilde{m}_{\hat{\theta}}(x)\} &= (nh)\bar{U}_2^{-1}\bar{U}_1^2 + \tilde{o}_p\{(nh)^{-1/2}\log^3(n)\} \\
&= V^{-1}(x;h)\{\hat{m}(x) - \tilde{m}_{\theta}(x)\}^2 + \tilde{\mathcal{O}}\{(nh)^{-1}h\log^2(n)\} \quad (12.20)
\end{aligned}
$$

Therefore, $\ell\{\tilde{m}_{\hat{\theta}}(x)\}$ is asymptotically equivalent to a studentized L_2 distance between $\tilde{m}_{\hat{\theta}}(x)$ and $\hat{m}(x)$. It is this property that leads us to use $\ell\{\tilde{m}_{\hat{\theta}}(x)\}$ as the basic building block in the construction of a global test statistic for distinction between $\tilde{m}_{\hat{\theta}}$ and $\hat{m}$ in the next section. The use of the empirical likelihood as a distance measure and its comparison with other distance measures have been discussed in Owen (1991) and Baggerly (1998).

12.6   Goodness-of-Fit Statistic

To extend the empirical likelihood ratio statistic to a global measure of Goodness-of-Fit, we choose k_n-equally spaced lattice points $t_1, t_2, \cdots, t_{k_n}$ in

$[0, 1]$ where $t_1 = 0$, $t_{k_n} = 1$ and $t_i \leq t_j$ for $1 \leq i < j \leq k_n$. We let $k_n \to \infty$ and $k_n/n \to 0$ as $n \to \infty$. This essentially divides $[0, 1]$ into k_n small bins of size $(k_n)^{-1}$. A simple choice is to let $k_n = [1/(2h)]$ where $[a]$ is the largest integer less than a. This choice as justified later ensures asymptotic independence among $\ell\{\tilde{m}_{\hat{\theta}}(t_j)\}$ at different t_js. Bins of different size can be adopted to suit situations where there are areas of low design density. This corresponds to the use of different bandwidth values in adaptive kernel smoothing. The main results of this chapter is not affected by un-equal bins. For the purpose of easy presentation, we will treat bins of equal size.

As $\ell\{\tilde{m}_{\hat{\theta}}(t_j)\}$ measures the Goodness-of-Fit at a fixed t_j, an empirical likelihood based statistic that measures the global Goodness-of-Fit is defined as

$$\ell_n(\tilde{m}_{\hat{\theta}}) \overset{\text{def}}{=} \sum_{j=1}^{k_n} \ell\{\tilde{m}_{\hat{\theta}}(t_j)\}.$$

The following theorem was proven by Chen et al. (2001).

THEOREM 12.2 *Under the assumptions (i) - (vi),*

$$k_n^{-1}\ell_n(\tilde{m}_{\hat{\theta}}) = (nh) \int \frac{\{\hat{m}(x) - \tilde{m}_{\theta}(x)\}^2}{V(x)} dx + \mathcal{O}_p\{k_n^{-1}\log^2(n) + h\log^2(n)\}$$

$$(12.21)$$

where $V(x) \overset{\text{def}}{=} \lim_{h \to 0} V(x, h)$.

Härdle and Mammen (1993) proposed the L_2 distance

$$T_n = nh^{1/2} \int \{\hat{m}(x) - \tilde{m}_{\hat{\theta}}(x)\}^2 \pi(x) dx$$

as a measure of Goodness-of-Fit where $\pi(x)$ is a given weight function. Theorem 12.2 indicates that the leading term of $k_n^{-1}\ell_n(\tilde{m}_{\hat{\theta}})$ is $h^{1/2}T_n$ with $\pi(x) = V^{-1}(x)$. The differences between the two test statistics are (a) the empirical likelihood test statistic automatically studentizes via its internal algorithm conducted at the background, so that there is no need to explicitly estimate $V(x)$; (b) the empirical likelihood statistic is able to capture other features such as skewness and kurtosis exhibited in the data without using the bootstrap resampling which involves more technical details when data are dependent. If we choose $k_n = [1/(2h)]$ as prescribed, then the remainder term in (12.21) becomes $\mathcal{O}_p\{h\log^2(n)\}$.

We will now discuss the asymptotic distribution of the test statistic $\ell_n(\tilde{m}_{\hat{\theta}})$. Theorem 12.3 was proven by Chen et al. (2001).

THEOREM 12.3 *Suppose assumptions (i) - (vi), then*

$$k_n^{-1}\ell_n(\tilde{m}_{\hat{\theta}}) \xrightarrow{\mathcal{L}} \int_0^1 \mathcal{N}^2(s)ds$$

where $\mathcal{N}$ is a Gaussian process on $[0,1]$ with mean

$$E\{\mathcal{N}(s)\} = h^{1/4}\Delta_n(s)/\sqrt{V(s)}$$

and covariance

$$\Omega(s,t) = Cov\{\mathcal{N}(s),\mathcal{N}(t)\} = \sqrt{\frac{f(s)\sigma^2(s)}{f(t)\sigma^2(t)}} \frac{W_0^{(2)}(s,t)}{\sqrt{W_0^{(2)}(s,s)W_0^{(2)}(t,t)}}$$

where

$$W_0^{(2)}(s,t) = \int_0^1 h^{-1}K\{(s-y)/h\}K\{(t-y)/h\}dy. \qquad (12.22)$$

As K is a compact kernel on $[-1,1]$, when both s and t are in S_I (the interior part of $[0,1]$), we get from (12.22) with $u = (s-y)/h$

$$
\begin{aligned}
W_0^{(2)}(s,t) &= \int_{\frac{s-1}{h}}^{\frac{s}{h}} K(u)K\{u-(s-t)/h\}du \\
&= \int_{-\infty}^{\infty} K(u)K\{u-(s-t)/h\}du \\
&= K^{(2)}\left(\frac{s-t}{h}\right) \qquad (12.23)
\end{aligned}
$$

where $K^{(2)}$ is the convolution of K. The compactness of K also means that $W_0^{(2)}(s,t) = 0$ if $|s-t| > 2h$ which implies $\Omega(s,t) = 0$ if $|s-t| > 2h$. Hence $\mathcal{N}(s)$ and $\mathcal{N}(t)$ are independent if $|s-t| > 2h$. As

$$f(s)\sigma^2(s) = f(s)\sigma^2(t) + \mathcal{O}(h)$$

when $|s-t| \le 2h$, we get

$$\Omega(s,t) = \frac{W_0^{(2)}(s,t)}{\sqrt{W_0^{(2)}(s,s)W_0^{(2)}(t,t)}} + \mathcal{O}(h), \qquad (12.24)$$

So, the leading order of the covariance function is free of σ^2 and f, i.e. $\Omega(s,t)$ is completely known.

Let

$$\mathcal{N}_0(s) = \mathcal{N}(s) - \frac{h^{1/4}\Delta_n(s)}{\sqrt{V(s)}}. \tag{12.25}$$

Then $\mathcal{N}_0(s)$ is a normal process with zero mean and covariance Ω. The boundedness of K implies $W_0^{(2)}$ being bounded, and hence $\int_0^1 \Omega(t,t)dt < \infty$. We will now study the expectation and variance of $\int_0^1 \mathcal{N}^2(s)ds$. Let $T = T_1 + T_2 + T_3 \overset{\text{def}}{=} \int_0^1 \mathcal{N}^2(s)ds$ where

$$
\begin{aligned}
T_1 &= \int_0^1 \mathcal{N}_0^2(s)ds, \\
T_2 &= 2h^{1/4}\int_0^1 V^{-1/2}(s)\Delta_n(s)\mathcal{N}_0(s)ds \quad \text{and} \\
T_3 &= h^{1/2}\int_0^1 V^{-1}(s)\Delta_n^2(s)ds.
\end{aligned}
$$

From some basic results on stochastic integrals, Lemma 12.2 and (12.24) follows,

$$
\begin{aligned}
\mathrm{E}(T_1) &= \int_0^1 \Omega(s,s)ds = 1 \quad \text{and} \\
\mathrm{Var}(T_1) &= \mathrm{E}[T_1^2] - 1 \tag{12.26} \\
&= \int_0^1\int_0^1 \mathrm{E}\left[\mathcal{N}_0^2(s)\mathcal{N}_0^2(t)\right]dsdt - 1 \tag{12.27} \\
&= 2\int_0^1\int_0^1 \Omega^2(s,t)dsdt \\
&= 2\int_0^1\int_0^1 \{W_0^{(2)}(s,t)\}^2\{W_0^{(2)}(s,s)W_0^{(2)}(t,t)\}^{-1}dsdt\,\{1 + \mathcal{O}(h^2)\}
\end{aligned}
$$

From (12.23) and the fact that the size of the region $[0,1] \setminus S_{I,h}$ is $\mathcal{O}(h)$, we have

$$
\begin{aligned}
&\int_0^1\int_0^1 \{W_0^{(2)}(s,t)\}^2\{W_0^{(2)}(s,s)W_0^{(2)}(t,t)\}^{-1}dsdt \\
&= \{K^{(2)}(0)\}^{-2}\int_0^1\int_0^1 [K^{(2)}\{(s-t)/h\}]^2 dsdt\,\{1 + o(1)\} \\
&= hK^{(4)}(0)\{K^{(2)}(0)\}^{-2} + o(h).
\end{aligned}
$$

Therefore,
$$\mathrm{Var}(T_1) = 2hK^{(4)}(0)\{K^{(2)}(0)\}^{-2} + o(h^2).$$

It is obvious that $\mathrm{E}(T_2) = 0$ and

$$\mathrm{Var}(T_2) \quad = \quad 4h^{1/2} \int \int V^{-1/2}(s)\Delta_n(s)\Omega(s,t)V^{-1/2}(t)\Delta_n(t)dsdt.$$

As Δ_n and V^{-1} are bounded in $[0,1]$, there exists a constant C_1 such that

$$\mathrm{Var}(T_2) \leq C_1 h^{1/2} \int \int \Omega(s,t)dsdt.$$

Furthermore we know from the discussion above,

$$
\begin{aligned}
\int \int \Omega(s,t)dsdt \quad &= \quad \int \int \frac{W_0^{(2)}(s,t)}{\sqrt{W_0^{(2)}(s,s)W_0^{(2)}(t,t)}}dsdt + \mathcal{O}(h) \\
&= \quad \int \int_{t-2h}^{t+2h} \frac{W_0^{(2)}(s,t)}{K^{(2)}(0)}dsdt + \mathcal{O}(h) \\
&\leq \quad 4\frac{1}{K^{(2)}(0)}C_1'h + C_1''h
\end{aligned}
$$

with other constants C'_1 and C''_1, and thus, there exists a constant C_2, such that

$$\mathrm{Var}(T_2) \leq C_2 h^{\frac{3}{2}}.$$

As T_3 is non-random, we have

$$\mathrm{E}(T) \quad = \quad 1 + h^{1/2} \int_0^1 V^{-1}(s)\Delta_n^2(s)ds \quad \text{and} \tag{12.28}$$

$$\mathrm{Var}\{T\} \quad = \quad 2hK^{(4)}(0)\{K^{(2)}(0)\}^{-2} + o(h) \tag{12.29}$$

(12.28) and (12.29) together with Theorem 13.3 give the asymptotic expectation and variance of the test statistic $k_n^{-1}\ell_n(\tilde{m}_{\hat{\theta}})$.

12.7   Goodness-of-Fit test

We now turn our interest to the derivation of the asymptotic distribution of $k_n^{-1}\ell_n(\tilde{m}_{\hat{\theta}})$. We do this by discretizing $\int_0^1 \mathcal{N}^2(s)ds$ as $(k_n)^{-1}\sum_{j=1}^{k_n} \mathcal{N}^2(t_j)$

where $\{t_j\}_{j=1}^{k_n}$ are the mid-points of the original bins in formulating $\ell_n(\tilde{m}_{\hat{\theta}})$. If we choose $k_n = [(2h)^{-1}]$ such that $|t_{j+1} - t_j| \geq 2h$ for all j, then $\{\mathcal{N}(t_j)\}$ are independent and each $\mathcal{N}(t_j) \sim \mathrm{N}(h^{1/4}\Delta_n(t_j)/\sqrt{V(t_j)}, 1)$. This means that under the alternative H_1

$$\sum_{j=1}^{k_n} \mathcal{N}^2(t_j) \sim \chi_{k_n}^2(\gamma_{k_n}),$$

a non-central χ^2 random variable with k_n degree of freedom and the non-central component $\gamma_{k_n} = h^{1/4}\{\sum_{j=1}^{k_n} \Delta_n^2(t_j)/V(t_j)\}^{1/2}$. Under H_0,

$$\sum_{j=1}^{k_n} \mathcal{N}^2(t_j) \sim \chi_{k_n}^2$$

is χ^2-distributed with k_n degrees of freedom. This leads to a χ^2 test with significance level α which rejects H_0 if $\ell_n(\tilde{m}_{\hat{\theta}}) > \chi_{k_n,\alpha}^2$ where $\chi_{k_n,\alpha}^2$ is the $(1 - \alpha)$-quantile of $\chi_{k_n}^2$. The asymptotic power of the χ^2 test is $\mathrm{P}\{\chi_{k_n}^2(\gamma_{k_n}) > \chi_{k_n,\alpha}^2\}$, which is sensitive to alternative hypotheses differing from H_0 in all directions.

We may also establish the asymptotic normality of $(k_n)^{-1}\sum_{i=1}^{k_n} \mathcal{N}^2(t_j)$ by applying the central limit theorem for a triangular array, which together with (12.28) and (12.29) means that

$$k_n^{-1}\ell_n(\tilde{m}_{\hat{\theta}}) \overset{\mathcal{L}}{\to} N\left(1 + h^{1/2}\int \Delta_n^2(s)V^{-1}(s)ds, 2hK^{(4)}(0)\{K^{(2)}(0)\}^{-2}\right).$$

A test for H_0 with an asymptotic significance level α is to reject H_0 if

$$k_n^{-1}\ell_n(\tilde{m}_{\hat{\theta}}) > 1 + z_\alpha\{K^{(2)}(0)\}^{-1}\sqrt{2hK^{(4)}(0)} \qquad (12.30)$$

where $\mathrm{P}(Z > z_\alpha) = \alpha$ and $Z \sim \mathrm{N}(0,1)$. The asymptotic power of this test is

$$1 - \Phi\left\{z_\alpha - \frac{K^{(2)}(0)\int \Delta_n^2(s)V^{-1}(s)ds}{\sqrt{2K^{(4)}(0)}}\right\}. \qquad (12.31)$$

We see from the above that the binning based on the bandwidth value h provides a key role in the derivation of the asymptotic distributions. However, the binning discretizes the null hypothesis and unavoidably leads to some loss of power as shown in the simulation reported in the next section. From the point of view of retaining power, we would like to have the size of the bins smaller than that prescribed by the smoothing bandwidth in order to increase the resolution of the discretized null hypothesis to the original H_0. However, this will create dependence between the empirical likelihood evaluated at neighbouring bins and make the above asymptotic distributions invalid. One possibility is to evaluate the distribution of $\int_0^1 \mathcal{N}_0^2(s)ds$ by using the approach of Wood and Chan (1994) by simulating the normal process $\mathcal{N}^2(s)$ under H_0. However, this is not our focus here and hence is not considered in this chapter.

12.8   Application

Figure 12.1 shows the daily closing value of the S&P 500 share index from the 31st December 1976 to the 31st December 1997, which covers 5479 trading days. In the upper panel, the index series shows a trend of exponential form which is estimated using the method given in Härdle, Kleinow, Korostelev, Logeay and Platen (2001). The lower panel is the residual series after removing the exponential trend. In mathematical finance one assumes often a specific dynamic form of this residual series, Platen (2000). More precisely, Härdle et al. (2001) assume the following model for an index process $S(t)$

$$S(t) = S(0)X(t)\exp\left(\int_0^t \eta(s)ds\right) \tag{12.32}$$

with a diffusion component $X(t)$ solving the stochastic differential equation

$$dX(t) = a\{1 - X(t)\}dt + \sigma X^{1/2}(t)dW(t) \tag{12.33}$$

where $W(t)$ is a Brownian motion and α and σ are parameters. Discretizing this series with a sampling interval Δ leads to the observations (X_i, Y_i) with $Y_i = X_{(i+1)\Delta} - X_{i\Delta}$ and $X_i = X_{i\Delta}$, which will be α-mixing and fulfill all the other conditions assumed in Section 12.3.

We now apply the empirical likelihood test procedure on the S&P 500 data presented in Figure 12.1 to test the parametric mean function $m(x) = a(1 - x)$ given in the Cox-Ingersoll-Ross diffusion model (12.33). The process X is restored from the observed residuals by the approach introduced in Härdle et al. (2001). The parametric estimate for a is $\hat{a} = 0.00968$ by using methods based on the marginal distribution and the autocorrelation structure of X. For details about the procedure see Härdle et al. (2001). The cross validation

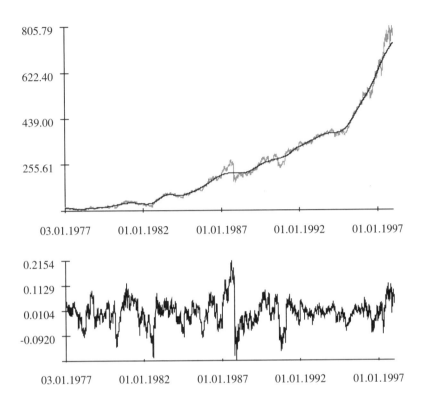

Figure 12.1. The S&P 500 Data. The upper plot shows the S&P 500 together with the exponential trend. The lower plot shows the residual process X.

is used to find the bandwidth h. However, the score function is monotonic decreasing for $h < 0.15$ and then become a flat line for $h \in [0.15, 0.8]$. This may be caused by the different intensity level of the design points. Further investigation shows that a h-value larger (smaller) than 0.06 (0.02) produces an oversmoothed (undersmoothed) curve estimate. Therefore, the test is carried out for a set of h values ranging from 0.02 to 0.06. The P-values of the test as a function of h are plotted in Figure 12.2.

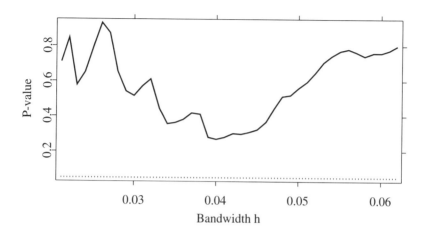

Figure 12.2. The p-values of the S&P 500 Data

The P-values indicate that there is insufficient evidence to reject the diffusion model.

12.9   Simulation Study and Illustration

We investigate our testing procedure in two simulation studies. In our first simulation we consider the time series model

$$Y_i = 2Y_{i-1}/(1 + Y_{i-1}^2) + c_n \sin(Y_{i-1}) + \sigma(Y_{i-1})\eta_i$$

where $\{\eta_i\}$ are independent and identically distributed uniform random variables in $[-1, 1]$, η_i is independent of $X_i = Y_{i-1}$ for each i, and $\sigma(x) = exp(-x^2/4)$. Note that the mean and the variance functions are both bounded which ensures the series is asymptotically stationary. To realize the stationarity, we pre-run the series 100 times with an initial value $Y_{-100} = 0$. The empirical likelihood test statistic is calculated via the `elmtest` quantlet.

{el,p,kn,h2} = elmtest(x,y,model{,kernel{,h{,theta}}})
calculates the empirical likelihood test statistic

The first and the second parameter are the vectors of observations of X and Y. The third parameter model is the name of a quantlet that implements the parametric model for the null hypothesis. The optimal parameter kernel is the name of the kernel K that is used to calculate the test statistic and h is the bandwidth used to calculate $\bar{U}_1$ and $\bar{U}_2$ in (12.18). theta is directly forwarded to the parametric model.

Q XFGelsim1.xpl

For the simulation study the sample sizes considered for each trajectory are $n = 500$ and 1000 and c_n, the degree of difference between H_0 and H_1, takes value of 0, 0.03 and 0.06. As the simulation shows that the two empirical likelihood tests have very similar power performance, we will report the results for the test based on the χ^2 distribution only. To gauge the effect of the smoothing bandwidth h on the power, ten levels of h are used for each simulated sample to formulate the test statistic.

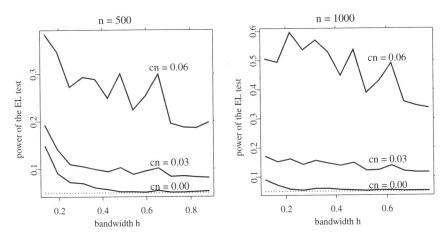

Figure 12.3. Power of the empirical likelihood test. The dotted lines indicate the 5% level

Figure 12.3 presents the power of the empirical likelihood test based on 5000 simulation with a nominal 5% level of significance. We notice that when $c_n = 0$ the simulated significance level of the test is very close to the nominal level for large range of h values which is especially the case for the larger sample size $n = 1000$. When c_n increases, for each fixed h the power increases as the distance between the null and the alternative hypotheses becomes larger. For each fixed c_n, there is a general trend of decreasing power when h increases. This is due to the discretization of H_0 by binning as discussed at the end of the previous section. We also notice that the power curves for $c_n = 0.06$ are a little erratic although they maintain the same trend as in the case of $c_n = 0.03$. This may be due to the fact that when the difference between H_0 and H_1 is large, the difference between the nonparametric and the parametric fits becomes larger and the test procedure becomes more sensitive to the bandwidths.

In our second simulation study we consider an Ornstein-Uhlenbeck process Z fluctuating about 0 that satisfies the stochastic differential equation

$$dZ(t) = aZ(t)dt + \sigma dW(t)$$

where W is a standard Brownian Motion. The speed of adjustment parameter a has to be negative to ensure stationarity. To apply the empirical likelihood test we construct the time series X and Y as in Section 12.2, i.e.

$$
\begin{aligned}
X_i &= Z^\Delta(t_i), & X &= (X_1, \ldots, X_n) \\
\varepsilon_i &= W(t_{i+1}) - W(t_i), & \varepsilon &= (\varepsilon_1, \ldots, \varepsilon_n) \\
Y_i &= X_{i+1} - X_i = aX_i\Delta + \sigma\varepsilon_i, & Y &= (Y_1, \ldots, Y_n) \quad (12.34)
\end{aligned}
$$

It is well known that the transition probability of an Ornstein-Uhlenbeck process is normal with conditional mean

$$E[Z_{t+\Delta}|Z_t = x] = E[X_{i+1}|X_i = x] = xe^{a\Delta}$$

and conditional variance

$$\text{Var}(Z_{t+\Delta}|Z_t = x) = \text{Var}(X_{i+1}|X_i = x) = \frac{\gamma^2}{-2\beta}\left(e^{-2\beta\Delta} - 1\right).$$

To simulate the process we use the simou quantlet.

```
x = simou(n,a,s,delta)
    simulates a discretely observed path of an Ornstein-Uhlenbeck
    process via its transition probability law.
```

The number of observations is given by n+1/, a is the speed of adjustment parameter a, s is the diffusion coefficient σ and delta is the time difference Δ between two observations.

The proposed simulation procedure and the Goodness-of-Fit test are illustrated in ⌕ XFGelsim2.xpl.

⌕ XFGelsim2.xpl

.

12.10 Appendix

LEMMA 12.2 *Let X, Y be standard normal random variables with covariance $Cov(X, Y) = \rho$, i.e.*

$$\begin{pmatrix} X \\ Y \end{pmatrix} \sim N\left(\begin{pmatrix} 0 \\ 0 \end{pmatrix}, \begin{pmatrix} 1 & \rho \\ \rho & 1 \end{pmatrix}\right). \tag{12.37}$$

Then we have:

$$Cov(X^2, Y^2) = 2\rho^2$$

PROOF:
Define $Z \sim N(0, 1)$ independent of X and $X' \stackrel{\text{def}}{=} \rho X + \sqrt{1 - \rho^2} Z$. Then we get:

$$\begin{pmatrix} X \\ X' \end{pmatrix} \sim N\left(\begin{pmatrix} 0 \\ 0 \end{pmatrix}, \begin{pmatrix} 1 & \rho \\ \rho & 1 \end{pmatrix}\right).$$

$$Cov(X^2, Y^2) = Cov(X^2, X'^2) = 2\rho^2$$

$\square$

Bibliography

Baggerly, K. A. (1998). Empirical likelihood as a goodness-of-fit measure, *Biometrika* **85**: 535–547.

Bibby, B. M. and Sørensen, M. (1995). Martingale estimation functions for discretely observed diffusion processes, *Bernoulli* **1**(1/2): 17 – 40.

Billingsley, P. (1999). *Convergence of Probability Measures*, Wiley, New York.

Bosq, D. (1998). *Nonparametric Statistics for Stochastic Processes*, Vol. 110 of *Lecture Notes in Statistics*, Springer-Verlag, Heidelberg.

Chen, S. X., Härdle, W. and Kleinow, T. (2001). An empirical likelihood goodness-of-fit test for time series, Discussion paper 1, Sonderforschungsbereich 373, Humboldt-Universität zu Berlin.

Genon-Catalot, V., Jeantheau, T. and Larédo, C. (2000). Stochastic volatility models as hidden markov models and statistical applications, *Bernoulli* **6**(6).

Härdle, W. (1990). *Applied Nonparametric Regression*, number 19 in *Econometric Society Monographs*, Cambridge University Press.

Härdle, W., Kleinow, T., Korostelev, A., Logeay, C. and Platen, E. (2001). Semiparametric diffusion estimation and application to a stock market index, Discussion Paper 24, Sonderforschungsbereich 373, Humboldt-Universität zu Berlin.

Härdle, W. and Mammen, E. (1993). Comparing nonparametric versus parametric regression fits, *Ann. Statist.* **21**: 1926–1947.

Härdle, W., Müller, M., Sperlich, S. and Werwatz, A. (2000). Non- and semi-parametric modelling, XploRe e-book, www.xplore-stat.de.

Hart, J. D. (1997). *Nonparametric smoothing and lack-of-fit tests.*, Springer, New York.

Kloeden, P. E. and Platen, E. (1999). *Numerical Solution of Stochastic Differential Equations*, Vol. 23 of *Applications of Mathematics*, Springer Verlag Berlin Heidelberg.

Kreiß, J.-P., Neumann, M. and Yao, Q. (1998). Bootstrap tests for simple structures in nonparametric time series regression. Discussion paper, Sonderforschungsbereich 373.

Owen, A. (1988). Empirical likelihood ratio confidence intervals for a single functional, *Biometrika* **75**: 237–249.

Owen, A. (1990). Empirical likelihood ratio confidence regions, *Ann. Statist.* **18**: 90–120.

Owen, A. (1991). Empirical likelihood for linear model, *Ann. Statist.* **19**: 1725–1747.

Platen, E. (2000). Risk premia and financial modelling without measure transformation. University of Technology Sydney, School of Finance & and Economics and Department of Mathematical Sciences.

Wand, M. and Jones, M. (1995). *Kernel Smoothing*, number 60 in *Monographs in Statistics and Applied Probability*, Chapman & Hall.

Wood, A. T. A. and Chan, G. (1994). Simulation of stationary gaussian process in $[0, 1]^d$, *J. Comp. Graph. Stat.* **3**: 409–432.

13 A simple state space model of house prices

Rainer Schulz and Axel Werwatz

13.1   Introduction

For most people, purchasing a house is a major decision. Once purchased, the house will by far be the most important asset in the buyer's portfolio. The development of its price will have a major impact on the buyer's wealth over the life cycle. It will, for instance, affect her ability to obtain credit from commercial banks and therefore influence her consumption and savings decisions and opportunities. The behavior of house prices is therefore of central interest for (potential) house buyers, sellers, developers of new houses, banks, policy makers or, in short, the general public.

An important property of houses is that they are different from each other. Hence, while houses in the same market (i.e., the same city, district or neighborhood) will share some common movements in their price there will at all times be idiosyncratic differences due to differences in maintenance, design or furnishing. Thus, the average or median price will depend not only on the general tendency of the market, but also on the composition of the sample. To calculate a price index for real estate, one has to control explicitly for idiosyncratic differences. The hedonic approach is a popular method for estimating the impact of the characteristics of heterogenous goods on their prices.

The statistical model used in this chapter tries to infer the common component in the movement of prices of 1502 single-family homes sold in a district of Berlin, Germany, between January 1980 and December 1999. It combines hedonic regression with Kalman filtering. The Kalman filter is the standard statistical tool for filtering out an unobservable, common component from idiosyncratic, noisy observations. We will interpret the common price component as an index of house prices in the respective district of Berlin. We assume that the index follows an autoregressive process. Given this assumption, the model is writable in state space form.

The remainder of this chapter is organized as follows. In the next section we propose a statistical model of house prices and discuss its interpretation and estimation. Section 13.4 introduces the data, while Section 13.5 describes the quantlets used to estimate the statistical model. In this section we present also the estimation results for our data. The final section gives a summary.

13.2   A Statistical Model of House Prices

13.2.1   The Price Function

The standard approach for constructing a model of the prices of heterogeneous assets is hedonic regression (Bailey, Muth and Nourse, 1963; Hill, Knight and Sirmans, 1997; Shiller, 1993). A hedonic model starts with the assumption that on the average the observed price is given by some function $f(I_t, X_{n,t}, \beta)$. Here, I_t is a common price component that "drives" the prices of all houses, the vector $X_{n,t}$ comprises the characteristics of house n and the vector β contains all coefficients of the functional form.

Most studies assume a log-log functional form and that I_t is just the constant of the regression for every period (Clapp and Giaccotto, 1998; Cho, 1996). In that case

$$p_{n,t} = I_t + x_{n,t}^\top \beta + \varepsilon_{n,t} . \tag{13.1}$$

Here, $p_{n,t}$ denotes the log of the transaction price. The vector $x_{n,t}$ contains the transformed characteristics of house n that is sold in period t. The idiosyncratic influences $\varepsilon_{n,t}$ are white noise with variance σ_ε^2.

Following Schwann (1998), we put some structure on the behavior of the common price component over time by assuming that the common price component follows an autoregressive moving average (ARMA) process. For our data it turns out that the following AR(2) process

$$I_t = \phi_1 I_{t-1} + \phi_2 I_{t-2} + \nu_t \tag{13.2}$$

with $I_0 = 0$ suffices. This autoregressive specification reflects that the market for owner-occupied houses reacts sluggish to changing conditions and that any price index will thus exhibit some autocorrelation. This time-series-based way of modelling the behavior of I_t is more parsimonious than the conventional hedonic regressions (which need to include a seperate dummy variable for each time period) and makes forecasting straightforward.

13.2.2 State Space Form

We can rewrite our model (13.1) and (13.2) in *State Space Form* (SSF) (Gourieroux and Monfort, 1997). In general, the SSF is given as:

$$\alpha_t = c_t + T_t\alpha_{t-1} + \varepsilon_t^s \tag{13.3a}$$

$$y_t = d_t + Z_t\alpha_t + \varepsilon_t^m \tag{13.3b}$$

$$\varepsilon_t^s \sim (0, R_t) \ , \ \varepsilon_t^m \sim (0, H_t) \ . \tag{13.3c}$$

The notation partially follows Harvey (1989; 1993). The first equation is the *state equation* and the second is the *measurement equation*. The characteristic structure of state space models relates a series of unobserved values α_t to a set of observations y_t. The unobserved values α_t represent the behavior of the system over time (Durbin and Koopman, 2001).

The unobservable state vector α_t has the dimension $K \geqslant 1$, T_t is a square matrix with dimension $K \times K$, the vector of the observable variables y_t has the dimension $N_t \times 1$. Here, N_t denotes the number of observations $y_{t,n}$ in period $t \leqslant T$. If the number of observations varies through periods, we denote

$$N \stackrel{\text{def}}{=} \max_{t=1,\cdots,T} N_t \ .$$

The matrix Z_t contains constant parameters and other exogenous observable variables. Finally, the vectors c_t and d_t contain some constants. The system matrices c_t, T_t, R_t, d_t, Z_t, and H_t may contain unknown parameters that have to be estimated from the data.

In our model—that is (13.1) and (13.2)—, the common price component I_t and the quality coefficients β are unobservable. However, whereas these coefficients are constant through time, the price component evolves according to (13.2). The parameters ϕ_1, ϕ_2, and σ_ν^2 of this process are unknown.

The observed log prices are the entries in y_t of the measurement equation and the characteristics are entries in Z_t. In our data base we observe three characteristics per object. Furthermore, we include the constant β_0. We can put (13.1) and (13.2) into SSF by setting

$$
\alpha_t = \begin{bmatrix} I_t \\ \phi_2 I_{t-1} \\ \beta_0 \\ \beta_1 \\ \beta_2 \\ \beta_3 \end{bmatrix}, \; T_t = \begin{bmatrix} \phi_1 & 1 & 0 & 0 & 0 & 0 \\ \phi_2 & 0 & 0 & 0 & 0 & 0 \\ 0 & 0 & 1 & 0 & 0 & 0 \\ 0 & 0 & 0 & 1 & 0 & 0 \\ 0 & 0 & 0 & 0 & 1 & 0 \\ 0 & 0 & 0 & 0 & 0 & 1 \end{bmatrix}, \; \varepsilon_t^s = \begin{bmatrix} \nu_t \\ 0 \\ 0 \\ 0 \\ 0 \\ 0 \end{bmatrix} \tag{13.4a}
$$

$$
y_t = \begin{bmatrix} p_{1,t} \\ \dots \\ p_{N_t,t} \end{bmatrix}, \; Z_t = \begin{bmatrix} 1 & 0 & x_{1,t}^\top \\ \vdots & \vdots & \vdots \\ 1 & 0 & x_{N_t,t}^\top \end{bmatrix}, \; \varepsilon_t^m = \begin{bmatrix} \varepsilon_{1,t} \\ \vdots \\ \varepsilon_{N_t,t} \end{bmatrix} \tag{13.4b}
$$

For our model, both c_t and d_t are zero vectors. The transition matrices T_t are non time-varying. The variance matrices of the state equation R_t are identical for all t and equal to a 6×6 matrix, where the first element is σ_ν^2 and all other elements are zeros. H_t is a $N_t \times N_t$ diagonal matrix with σ_ε^2 on the diagonal. The variance σ_ε^2 is also an unknown parameter.

The first two elements of the state equation just resemble the process of the common price component given in (13.2). However, we should mention that there are other ways to put an AR(2) process into a SSF (see Harvey, 1993, p. 84). The remaining elements of the state equation are the implicit prices β of the hedonic price equation (13.1). Multiplying the state vector α_t with row n of the matrix Z_t gives $I_t + x_{t,n}^\top \beta$. This is just the functional relation (13.1) for the log price without noise. The noise terms of (13.1) are collected in the SSF in the vector ε_t^m. We assume that ε_t^m and ε_t^s are uncorrelated. This is required for identification (Schwann, 1998, p. 274).

13.3   Estimation with Kalman Filter Techniques

13.3.1   Kalman Filtering given all parameters

Given the above SSF and all unknown parameters $\psi \overset{\text{def}}{=} (\phi_1, \phi_2, \sigma_\nu^2, \sigma_\varepsilon^2)$, we can use Kalman filter techniques to estimate the unknown coefficients β and the process of I_t. The Kalman filter technique is an algorithm for estimating the unobservable state vectors by calculating its expectation conditional on information up to $s \leqslant T$. In the ongoing, we use the following general notation:

$$a_{t|s} \stackrel{\text{def}}{=} \mathrm{E}[\alpha_t|\mathcal{F}_s] \tag{13.5a}$$

denotes the filtered state vector and

$$P_{t|s} \stackrel{\text{def}}{=} \mathrm{E}[(\alpha_t - a_{t|s})(\alpha_t - a_{t|s})^\top|\mathcal{F}_s] \tag{13.5b}$$

denotes the covariance matrix of the estimation error and $\mathcal{F}_s$ is a shorthand for the information available at time s.

Generally, the estimators delivered by Kalman filtering techniques have minimum mean-squared error among all linear estimators (Shumway and Stoffer, 2000, Chapter 4.2). If the initial state vector, the noise ε^m and ε^s are multivariate Gaussian, then the Kalman filter delivers the optimal estimator among all estimators, linear and nonlinear (Hamilton, 1994, Chapter 13).

The Kalman filter techniques can handle missing observations in the measurement equation (13.3b). For periods with less than N observations, one has to adjust the measurement equations. One can do this by just deleting all elements of the measurement matrices d_t, Z_t, H_t for which the corresponding entry in y_t is a missing value. The quantlets in XploRe use this procedure. Another way to take missing values into account is proposed by Shumway and Stoffer (1982; 2000): replace all missing values with zeros and adjust the other measurement matrices accordingly. We show in Appendix 13.6.1 that both methods deliver the same results. For periods with no observations the Kalman filter techniques recursively calculate an estimate given recent information (Durbin and Koopman, 2001).

13.3.2 Filtering and state smoothing

The Kalman *filter* is an algorithm for sequently updating our knowledge of the system given a new observation y_t. It calculates one step predictions conditional on $s = t$. Using our general expressions, we have

$$a_t = \mathrm{E}[\alpha_t|\mathcal{F}_t]$$

and

$$P_t = \mathrm{E}[(\alpha_t - a_t)(\alpha_t - a_t)^\top|\mathcal{F}_t] \, .$$

Here we use the standard simplified notation a_t and P_t for $a_{t|t}$ and $P_{t|t}$. As a by-product of the filter, the recursions calculate also

$$a_{t|t-1} = \mathrm{E}[\alpha_t|\mathcal{F}_{t-1}]$$

and

$$P_{t|t-1} = \mathrm{E}[(\alpha_t - a_{t|t-1})(\alpha_t - a_{t|t-1})^\top | \mathcal{F}_{t-1}] \,.$$

We give the filter recursions in detail in Subsection 13.5.3.

The Kalman *smoother* is an algorithm to predict the state vector α_t given the whole information up to T. Thus we have with our general notation $s = T$ and

$$a_{t|T} = \mathrm{E}[\alpha_t | \mathcal{F}_T]$$

the corresponding covariance matrix

$$P_{t|T} = \mathrm{E}[(\alpha_t - a_{t|T})(\alpha_t - a_{t|T})^\top | \mathcal{F}_T] \,.$$

We see that the filter makes one step predictions given the information up to $t \in \{1, \ldots, T\}$ whereas the smoother is backward looking. We give the smoother recursions in detail in Subsection 13.5.5.

13.3.3   Maximum likelihood estimation of the parameters

Given the system matrices c_t, T_t, R_t, d_t, Z_t, and H_t, Kalman filtering techniques are the right tool to estimate the elements of the state vector. However, in our model some of these system matrices contain unknown parameters ψ. These parameters have to be estimated by maximum likelihood.

Given a multivariate Gaussian error distribution, the value of the log likelihood function $l(\psi)$ for a general SSF is up to an additive constant equal to:

$$-\frac{1}{2} \sum_{t=1}^{T} \ln |F_t| - \frac{1}{2} \sum_{t=1}^{T} v_t^\top F_t^{-1} v_t \,. \tag{13.9}$$

Here,

$$v_t \overset{\mathrm{def}}{=} y_t - d_t - Z_t a_{t|t-1} \tag{13.10}$$

are the *innovations* of the filtering procedure and $a_{t|t-1}$ is the conditional expectation of α_t given information up to $t-1$. As we have already mentioned, these expressions are a by-product of the filter recursions. The matrix F_t is the covariance matrix of the innovations at time t and also a by-product of the Kalman filter. The above log likelihood is known as the *prediction error decomposition form* (Harvey, 1989). Periods with no observations do not contribute to the log likelihood function.

Starting with some initial value, one can use numerical maximization methods to obtain an estimate of the parameter vector ψ. Under certain regularity conditions, the maximum likelihood estimator $\tilde{\psi}$ is consistent and asymptotically normal. One can use the information matrix to calculate standard errors of $\tilde{\psi}$ (Hamilton, 1994).

13.3.4 Diagnostic checking

After fitting a SSF, one should check the appropriateness of the results by looking at the *standardized residuals*

$$v_t^{st} = F_t^{-1/2} v_t \ . \tag{13.11}$$

If all parameters of the SSF were known, v_t^{st} would follow a multivariate standardized normal distribution (Harvey, 1989, see also (13.9)). We know that F_t is a symmetric matrix and that it should be positive definite (recall that it is just the covariance matrix of the innovations v_t). So

$$F_t^{-1/2} = C_t \Lambda_t^{-1/2} C_t^{\top} \ , \tag{13.12}$$

where the diagonal matrix Λ_t contains all eigenvalues of F_t and C_t is the matrix of corresponding normalized eigenvectors (Greene, 2000, p.43). The standardized residuals should be distributed normally with constant variance, and should show no serial correlation. It is a signal for a misspecified model when the residuals do not possess these properties. To check the properties, one can use standard test procedures. For example, a Q-Q plot indicates if the quantiles of the residuals deviate from the corresponding theoretical quantiles of a normal distribution. This plot can be used to detect non-normality. The Jarque-Bera test for normality can also be used for testing non-normality of the residuals (Bera and Jarque, 1982). This test is implemented in XploRe as `jarber`.

In the empirical part, we combine Kalman filter techniques and maximum likelihood to estimate the unknown parameters and coefficients of the SSF for the house prices in a district of Berlin.

13.4 The Data

The data set is provided by the *Gutachterausschuß für Grundstückswerte in Berlin*, an expert commission for Berlin's real estate market. The commission

collects information on all real estate transactions in Berlin in a data base called
Automatisierte Kaufpreissammlung.

Here, we use data for 1502 sales of detached single-family houses in a district
of Berlin for the years 1980 to 1999, stored in MD*BASE. Besides the price,
we observe the size of the lot, the floor space, and the age of the house. The
data set XFGhouseprice contains the log price observations for all 80 quarters.
There are at most $N = 43$ observations in any quarter. The following lines of
XploRe code

```
Y = read("XFGhouseprice.dat")
Y[1:20,41:44]
```

can be used to take a look at the entries of XFGhouseprice. Every column
gives the observations for one quarter. Thus, in columns 41 to 44 we find the
observations for all quarters of 1990. If less than 43 transactions are observed
in a quarter the remaining entries are filled with the missing value code NaN.
Only in the first quarter of the year 1983 we observe 43 transactions.

The corresponding data set XFGhousequality contains the observed characteristics of all houses sold. They are ordered in the following way: each column
contains all observations for a given quarter. Remember that for every house
we observe log size of the lot, log size of the floor space and age. The first
three rows of a column refer to the first house in t, the next three to the second
house and so on.

Let us look at the characteristics of the first two observations in 1990:1. Just
type the following lines in the XploRe input window

```
X = read("XFGhousequality.dat")
X[1:6,41]'
```

After compiling, you get the output

```
[1,]   6.1048   4.7707   53   6.5596   5.1475   13
```

The size of the lot for the second house is about 706 square meters (just take
the antilog). The size of the floor space is 172 square meters and the age is 13
years.

The following table shows summary statistics of our Berlin house price data.

```
"==========================================================="
" Summary statistics for the Berlin house price data      "
"==========================================================="
" Sample for 80 quarters with 1502 observations           "
"                                                          "
"      Observations per period                            "
"      ----------------------------------------------------"
"        Minimum =   4     Average = 18.77     Maximum = 43 "
"                                                          "
"      Transaction prices (in thousand DM)                "
"      ----------------------------------------------------"
"          Minimum =   100.00       Average   = 508.46     "
"          Maximum = 1750.01        Std. Dev. = 197.92     "
"                                                          "
"      Size of the lot (in square meters)                 "
"      ----------------------------------------------------"
"          Minimum =   168.00       Average   = 626.18     "
"          Maximum = 2940.00        Std. Dev. = 241.64     "
"                                                          "
"      Size of the floor space (in square meters)         "
"      ----------------------------------------------------"
"          Minimum =   46.00        Average   = 144.76     "
"          Maximum = 635.00         Std. Dev. = 48.72      "
"                                                          "
"      Age of the building (in years)                     "
"      ----------------------------------------------------"
"          Minimum =    0           Average   = 28.59      "
"          Maximum = 193            Std. Dev. = 21.58      "
"==========================================================="
```

Q XFGsssm1.xpl

Not surprisingly for detached houses there are large differences in the size of the lot. Some houses were new in the period of the sale while one was 193 years old. That is a good example for the potential bias of the average price per quarter as a price index. If we do not control explicitly for depreciation we might obtain a low price level simply because the houses sold in a quarter were old.

Nevertheless, the average price per quarter can give an indication of the price
level. Figure 13.1 shows the average price per quarter along with confidence
intervals at the 90% level. Instead of the average price, we could also calculate
an average adjusted price, where the most important characteristic is used for
the adjustment. Such adjustment is attained by dividing the price of every
house by—for example—the respective size of the lot. However, even in that
case we would control only for one of the observed characteristics. In our model
we will control for all of the observed characteristics.

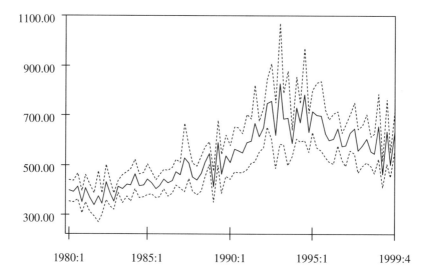

Figure 13.1. Average price per quarter, units are Deutsche Mark (1
DM ≈ 0.511 EURO). Confidence intervals are calculated for the 90%
level.

Q XFGsssm2.xpl

13.5   Estimating and filtering in XploRe

13.5.1   Overview

The procedure for Kalman filtering in XploRe is as follows: first, one has to set up the system matrices using gkalarray. The quantlet adjusts the measurement matrices for missing observations.

After the set up of the system matrices, we calculate the Kalman filter with gkalfilter. This quantlet also calculates the value of the log likelihood function given in equation (13.9). That value will be used to estimate the unknown parameters of the system matrices with numerical maximization (Hamilton, 1994, Chapter 5). The first and second derivatives of the log likelihood function will also be calculated numerically. To estimate the unknown state vectors—given the estimated parameters—we use the Kalman smoother gkalsmoother. For diagnostic checking, we use the standardized residuals (13.11). The quantlet gkalresiduals calculates these residuals.

13.5.2   Setting the system matrices

---

gkalarrayOut = gkalarray(Y,M,IM,XM)
    sets the system matrices for a time varying SSF

The Kalman filter quantlets need as arguments arrays consisting of the system matrices. The quantlet **gkalarray** sets these arrays in a user-friendly way. The routine is especially convenient if one works with time varying system matrices. In our SSF (13.4), only the system matrix Z_t is time varying. As one can see immediately from the general SSF (13.3), possibly every system matrix can be time varying.

The quantlet uses a three step procedure to set up the system matrices.

1. To define a system matrix all constant entries must be set to their respective values and all time varying entries must be set to an arbitrary number (for example to 0).

2. One must define an index matrix for every system matrix. An entry is set to 0 when its corresponding element in the system matrix is constant and to some positive integer when it is not constant.

3. In addition, for every time varying system matrix, one also has to specify a data matrix that contains the time varying entries.

gkalarray uses the following notation: Y denotes the matrix of all observations $[y_1, \ldots, y_T]$, M denotes the system matrix, IM denotes the corresponding index matrix and XM the data matrix.

If all entries of a system matrix are constant over time, then the parameters have already been put directly into the system matrix. In this case, one should set the index and the data matrix to 0.

For every time varying system matrix, only constant parameters—if there are any—have already been specified with the system matrix. The time-varying coefficients have to be specified in the index and the data matrix.

In our example, only the matrices Z_t are time varying. We have

$$
Z \stackrel{\text{def}}{=} \begin{bmatrix} 1 & 0 & 1 & 0 & 0 & 0 \\ \vdots & \vdots & \vdots & \vdots & \vdots & \vdots \\ 1 & 0 & 1 & 0 & 0 & 0 \end{bmatrix}
$$

$$
IZ \stackrel{\text{def}}{=} \begin{bmatrix} 0 & 0 & 0 & 1 & 2 & 3 \\ 0 & 0 & 0 & 4 & 5 & 6 \\ \vdots & \vdots & \vdots & \vdots & \vdots & \vdots \\ 0 & 0 & 0 & (3N+1) & (3N+2) & (3N+3) \end{bmatrix}
$$

$$
XZ \stackrel{\text{def}}{=} \quad \text{XFGhousequality}
$$

The system matrix Z_t has the dimension $(N \times 6)$. The non-zero entries in the index matrix IZ prescribe the rows of XFGhousequality, which contain the time varying elements.

The output of the quantlet is an array that stacks the system matrices one after the other. For example, the first two rows of the system matrix Z_{41} are

[1,]	1	0	1	6.1048	4.7707	53
[2,]	1	0	1	6.5596	5.1475	13

Q XFGsssm3.xpl

It is easy to check that the entries in the last three columns are just the characteristics of the first two houses that were sold in 1990:1 (see p. 290).

13.5.3 Kalman filter and maximized log likelihood

```
{gkalfilOut,loglike} = gkalfilter(Y,mu,Sig,ca,Ta,Ra,
                                      da,Za,Ha,l)
    Kalman filters a time-varying SSF
```

We assume that the initial state vector at $t = 0$ has mean μ and covariance matrix Σ. Recall, that R_t and H_t denote the covariance matrix of the state noise and—respectively—of the measurement noise. The general filter recursions are as follows:

Start at $t = 1$: use the initial guess for μ and Σ to calculate

$$
\begin{aligned}
a_{1|0} &= c_1 + T_1\mu \\
P_{1|0} &= T_1\Sigma T_1^\top + R_1 \\
F_1 &= Z_1 P_{1|0} Z_1^\top + H_1
\end{aligned}
$$

and

$$
\begin{aligned}
a_1 &= a_{1|0} + P_{1|0} Z_1^\top F_1^{-1}(y_1 - Z_1 a_{1|0} - d_1) \\
P_1 &= P_{1|0} - P_{1|0} Z_1^\top F_1^{-1} Z_1 P_{1|0}
\end{aligned}
$$

Step at $t \leqslant T$: using a_{t-1} and P_{t-1} from the previous step, calculate

$$
\begin{aligned}
a_{t|t-1} &= c_t + T_t a_{t-1} \\
P_{t|t-1} &= T_t P_{t-1} T_t^\top + R_t \\
F_t &= Z_t P_{t|t-1} Z_t^\top + H_t
\end{aligned}
$$

and

$$
\begin{aligned}
a_t &= a_{t|t-1} + P_{t|t-1} Z_t^\top F_t^{-1}(y_t - Z_t a_{t|t-1} - d_t) \\
P_t &= P_{t|t-1} - P_{t|t-1} Z_t^\top F_t^{-1} Z_t P_{t|t-1}
\end{aligned}
$$

The implementation for our model is as follows: The arguments of `gkalfilter` are the data matrix Y, the starting values mu (μ), Sig (Σ) and the array for every system matrix (see section 13.5.2). The output is a $T + 1$ dimensional array of $[a_t \quad P_t]$ matrices. If one chooses $l = 1$ the value of the log likelihood function (13.9) is calculated.

Once again, the $T + 1$ matrices are stacked "behind each other", with the $t = 0$ matrix at the front and the $t = T$ matrix at the end of the array. The first entry is $[\mu \quad \Sigma]$.

How can we provide initial values for the filtering procedure? If the state matrices are non time-varying and the transition matrix T satisfies some stability condition, we should set the initial values to the unconditional mean and variance of the state vector. Σ is given implicitly by

$$\text{vec}(\Sigma) = (I - T \otimes T)^{-1} \text{vec}(R) \ .$$

Here, vec denotes the vec-operator that places the columns of a matrix below each other and $\otimes$ denotes the Kronecker product. Our model is time-invariant. But does our transition matrix fulfill the stability condition? The necessary and sufficient condition for stability is that the characteristic roots of the transition matrix T should have modulus less than one (Harvey, 1989, p. 114). It is easy to check that the characteristic roots λ_j of our transition matrix (13.4a) are given as

$$\lambda_{1,2} = \frac{\phi_1 \pm \sqrt{\phi_1^2 + 4\phi_2}}{2} \ .$$

For example, if ϕ_1 and ϕ_2 are both positive, then $\phi_1 + \phi_2 < 1$ guarantees real characteristic roots that are smaller than one (Baumol, 1959, p. 221). However, when the AR(2) process of the common price component I_t has a unit root, the stability conditions are not fulfilled. If we inspect Figure 13.1, a unit root seems quite plausible. Thus we can not use this method to derive the initial values.

If we have some preliminary estimates of μ, along with preliminary measures of uncertainty—that is a estimate of Σ—we can use these preliminary estimates as initial values. A standard way to derive such preliminary estimates is to use OLS. If we have no information at all, we must take diffuse priors about the initial conditions. A method adopted by Koopman, Shephard and Doornik (1999) is setting $\mu = 0$ and $\Sigma = \kappa I$ where κ is an large number. The large variances on the diagonal of Σ reflect our uncertainty about the true μ.

We will use the second approach for providing some preliminary estimates as initial values. Given the hedonic equation (13.1), we use OLS to estimate I_t, β, and σ_m^2 by regressing log prices on lot size, floor space, age and quarterly time dummies. The estimated coefficients of lot size, floor space and age are

	coefficient		t-statistic	p-value
log lot size	0.2675		15.10	0.0000
log floor space	0.4671		23.94	0.0000
age	-0.0061		-20.84	0.0000
	Regression diagnostics			
R^2	0.9997	Number of observations		1502
$\overline{R}^2$	0.9997	F-statistic		64021.67
$\hat{\sigma}^2_\varepsilon$	0.4688	Prob(F-statistic)		0.0000

Table 13.1. Results for hedonic regression

reported in Table 13.1. They are highly significant and reasonable in sign and magnitude. Whereas lot size and floor space increase the price on average, age has the opposite effect. According to (13.1), the common price component I_t is a time-varying constant term and is therefore estimated by the coefficients of the quarterly time dummies, denoted by $\{\hat{I}_t\}_{t=1}^{80}$. As suggested by (13.2), these estimates are regressed on their lagged values to obtain estimates of the unknown parameters ϕ_1, ϕ_2, and σ_s^2. Table 13.2 presents the results for an AR(2) for the $\hat{I}_t$ series. The residuals of this regression behave like white noise.

	coefficient		t-statistic	p-value
constant	0.5056		1.3350	0.1859
$\hat{I}_{t-1}$	0.4643		4.4548	0.0000
$\hat{I}_{t-2}$	0.4823		4.6813	0.0000
	Regression diagnostics			
R^2	0.8780	Number of observations		78
$\overline{R}^2$	0.8747	F-statistic		269.81
$\hat{\sigma}^2_\nu$	0.0063	Prob(F-statistic)		0.0000

Table 13.2. Time series regression for the quarterly dummies

We should remark that

$$\hat{\phi}_1 + \hat{\phi}_2 \approx 1$$

and thus the process of the common price component seems to have a unit root.

Given our initial values we maximize the log likelihood (13.9) numerically with respect to the elements of $\psi^* \stackrel{\text{def}}{=} (\phi_1, \phi_2, \log(\sigma_\nu^2), \log(\sigma_\varepsilon^2))$. Note that ψ^* differs from ψ by using the logarithm of the variances σ_ν^2 and σ_ε^2. This transformation is known to improve the numerical stability of the maximization algorithm, which employs nmBFGS of XploRe's nummath library. Standard errors are computed from inverting the Hessian matrix provided by nmhessian. The output of the maximum likelihood estimation procedure is summarized in Table 13.3, where we report the estimates of σ_ν^2 and σ_ε^2 obtained by retransforming the estimates of $\log(\sigma_\nu^2)$ and $\log(\sigma_\varepsilon^2)$.

	estimate	std error	t-value	p-value
$\hat{\psi}_1 = \hat{\phi}_1$	0.783	0.501	1.56	0.12
$\hat{\psi}_2 = \hat{\phi}_2$	0.223	0.504	0.44	0.66
$\hat{\psi}_1 = \hat{\sigma}_\nu^2$	0.0016	0.012	1.36	0.17
$\hat{\psi}_2 = \hat{\sigma}_\varepsilon^2$	0.048	0.002	26.7	0
average log likelihood	0.9965			

Table 13.3.   Maximum likelihood estimates of the elements of ψ
⊙ XFGsssm4.xpl

Note that the maximum likelihood estimates of the AR coefficients ϕ_1 and ϕ_2 approximately sum to 1, again pointing towards a unit root process for the common price component.

13.5.4   Diagnostic checking with standardized residuals

```
{V,Vs} = gkalresiduals(Y,Ta,Ra,da,Za,Ha,gkalfilOut)
    calculates innovations and standardized residuals
```

The quantlet gkalresiduals checks internally for the positive definiteness of F_t. An error message will be displayed when F_t is not positive definite. In such a case, the standardized residuals are not calculated.

The output of the quantlet are two $N \times T$ matrices V and Vs. V contains the innovations (13.10) and Vs contains the standardized residuals (13.11).

The Q-Q plot of the standardized residuals in Figure 13.2 shows deviations from normality at both tails of the distribution.

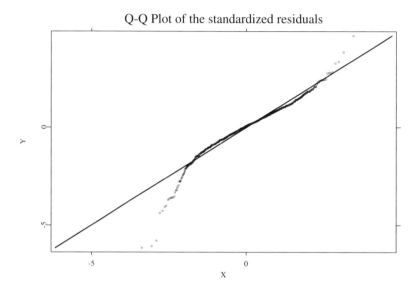

Figure 13.2. Deviations of the dotted line from the straight line are evidence for a nonnormal error distribution

ⓠ XFGsssm5.xpl

This is evidence, that the true error distribution might be a unimodal distribution with heavier tails than the normal, such as the *t*-distribution. In this case the projections calculated by the Kalman filter no longer provide the conditional expectations of the state vector but rather its best linear prediction. Moreover the estimates of ψ calculated from the likelihood (13.9) can be interpreted as pseudo-likelihood estimates.

13.5.5   Calculating the Kalman smoother

```
gkalsmoothOut = gkalsmoother(Y,Ta,Ra,gkalfilOut)
      provides Kalman smoothing of a time-varying SSF
```

The Kalman filter is a convenient tool for calculating the conditional expectations and covariances of our SSF (13.4). We have used the innovations of this filtering technique and its covariance matrix for calculating the log likelihood. However, for estimating the unknown state vectors, we should use in every step the whole sample information up to period T. For this task, we use the Kalman smoother.

The quantlet `gkalsmoother` needs as argument the output of `gkalfilter`. The output of the smoother is an array with $[a_{t|T} \quad P_{t|T}]$ matrices. This array of dimension $T + 1$ starts with the $t = 0$ matrix and ends with the matrix for $t = T$. For the smoother recursions, one needs a_t, P_t and $P_{t|t-1}$ for $t = 1 \ldots T$. Then the calculation procedure is as follows:

Start at $t = T$:

$$
\begin{aligned}
a_{T|T} &= a_T \\
P_{T|T} &= P_T
\end{aligned}
$$

Step at $t < T$:

$$
\begin{aligned}
P_t^* &= P_t T_{t+1}^\top P_{t+1|t}^{-1} \\
a_{t|T} &= a_t + P_t^* (a_{t+1|T} - T_{t+1} a_t) \\
P_{t|T} &= P_t + P_t^* (P_{t+1|T} - P_{t+1|t}) P_t^{*\top}
\end{aligned}
$$

The next program calculates the smoothed state vectors for our SSF form, given the estimated parameters $\tilde{\psi}$. The smoothed series of the common price component is given in Figure 13.3. The confidence intervals are calculated using the variance of the first element of the state vector.

Comparison with the average prices given in Figure 13.1 reveals that the common price component is less volatile than the simple average. Furthermore, a table for the estimated hedonic coefficients—that is β—is generated, Table 13.4.

Recall that these coefficients are just the last three entries in the state vector α_t. According to our state space model, the variances for these state variables are

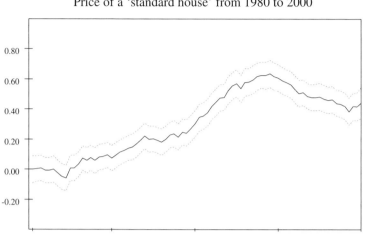

Figure 13.3. Smoothed common price component. Confidence intervals
are calculated for the 90% level.

Q XFGsssm6.xpl

```
[1,] "==========================================="
[2,] " Estimated hedonic coefficients            "
[3,] "==========================================="
[4,] " Variable          coeff.   t-Stat.  p-value "
[5,] " ----------------------------------------- "
[6,] " log lot size      0.2664   21.59    0.0000  "
[7,] " log floor area    0.4690   34.33    0.0000  "
[8,] " age              -0.0061  -29.43    0.0000  "
[9,] "==========================================="
```

Table 13.4. Estimated hedonic coefficients β. Q XFGsssm6.xpl

zero. Thus, it is not surprising that the Kalman smoother produces constant
estimates through time for these coefficients. In the Appendix 13.6.2 we give
a formal proof of this intuitive result.

The estimated coefficient of log lot size implies that, as expected, the size of the lot has an positive influence on the price. The estimated relative price increase for an one percent increase in the lot size is about 0.27%. The estimated effect of an increase in the floor space is even larger. Here, a one percent increase in the floor space lets the price soar by about 0.48%. Finally, note that the price of a houses is estimated to decrease with age.

13.6   Appendix

13.6.1   Procedure equivalence

We show that our treatment of missing values delivers the same results as the procedure proposed by Shumway and Stoffer (1982; 2000). For this task, let us assume that the $(N \times 1)$ vector of observations t

$$y_t^\top = \begin{bmatrix} y_{1,t} & \cdot & y_{3,t} & \cdot & y_{5,t} & \cdots & y_{N,t} \end{bmatrix}$$

has missing values. Here, observations 2 and 4 are missing. Thus, we have only $N_t < N$ observations. For Kalman filtering in XploRe, all missing values in y_t and the corresponding rows and columns in the measurement matrices d_t, Z_t, and H_t, are deleted. Thus, the adjusted vector of observations is

$$y_{t,1} = \begin{bmatrix} y_{1,t} & y_{3,t} & y_{5,t} & \cdots & y_{N,t} \end{bmatrix}$$

where the subscript 1 indicates that this is the vector of observations used in the XploRe routines. The procedure of Shumway and Stoffer instead rearranges the vectors in such a way that the first N_t entries are the observations—and thus given by $y_{t,1}$—and the last $(N - N_t)$ entries are the missing values. However, all missing values must be replaced with zeros.

For our proof, we use the following generalized formulation of the measurement equation

$$\begin{bmatrix} y_{t,1} \\ y_{t,2} \end{bmatrix} = \begin{bmatrix} d_{t,1} \\ d_{t,2} \end{bmatrix} + \begin{bmatrix} Z_{t,1} \\ Z_{t,2} \end{bmatrix} \alpha_t + \begin{bmatrix} \varepsilon_{t,1}^m \\ \varepsilon_{t,2}^m \end{bmatrix}$$

and

$$\mathrm{cov} \begin{pmatrix} \varepsilon_{t,1}^m \\ \varepsilon_{t,2}^m \end{pmatrix} = \begin{bmatrix} H_{t,11} & H_{t,12} \\ H_{t,12} & H_{t,22} \end{bmatrix}.$$

$y_{t,1}$ contains the observations and $y_{t,2}$ the missing values. The procedure of Shumway and Stoffer employs the generalized formulation given above and sets

$y_{t,2} = 0$, $d_{t,2} = 0$, $Z_{t,2} = 0$, and $H_{t,12} = 0$ (Shumway and Stoffer, 2000, p. 330). We should remark that the dimensions of these matrices also depend on t via $(N - N_t)$. However, keep notation simple we do not make this time dependency explicit. It is important to mention that matrices with subscript 1 and 11 are equivalent to the adjusted matrices of XploRe's filtering routines.

First, we show by induction that both procedures deliver the same results for the Kalman filter. Once this equivalence is established, we can conclude that the smoother also delivers identical results.

PROOF:

Given μ and Σ, the terms $a_{1|0}$ and $P_{1|0}$ are the same for both procedures. This follows from the simple fact that the first two steps of the Kalman filter do not depend on the vector of observations (see Subsection 13.5.3).

Now, given $a_{t|t-1}$ and $P_{t|t-1}$, we have to show that also the filter recursions

$$a_t = a_{t|t-1} + P_{t|t-1} Z_t^\top F_t^{-1} v_t , \quad P_t = P_{t|t-1} - P_{t|t-1} Z_t^\top F_t^{-1} Z_t P_{t|t-1} \quad (13.13)$$

deliver the same results. Using ss to label the results of the Shumway and Stoffer procedure, we obtain by using

$$Z_{t,ss} \stackrel{\text{def}}{=} \begin{bmatrix} Z_{t,1} \\ 0 \end{bmatrix}$$

that

$$F_{t,ss} = \begin{bmatrix} Z_{t,1} P_{t|t-1} Z_{t,1}^\top & 0 \\ 0 & 0 \end{bmatrix} + \begin{bmatrix} H_{t,11} & 0 \\ 0 & H_{t,22} \end{bmatrix} .$$

The inverse is given by (Sydsæter, Strøm and Berck, 2000, 19.49)

$$F_{t,ss}^{-1} = \begin{bmatrix} F_{t,1}^{-1} & 0 \\ 0 & H_{t,22}^{-1} \end{bmatrix} \quad (13.14)$$

where $F_{t,1}$ is just the covariance matrix of the innovations of XploRe's procedure. With (13.14) we obtain that

$$Z_{t,ss}^\top F_{t,ss}^{-1} = \begin{bmatrix} Z_{t,1}^\top F_{t,1}^{-1} & 0 \end{bmatrix}$$

and accordingly for the innovations

$$v_{t,ss} = \begin{bmatrix} v_{t,1} \\ 0 \end{bmatrix} .$$

We obtain immediately

$$Z_{t,ss}^\top F_{t,ss}^{-1} v_{t,ss} = Z_{t,1}^\top F_{t,1}^{-1} v_{t,1} \ .$$

Plugging this expression into (13.13)—taking into account that $a_{t|t-1}$ and $P_{t|t-1}$ are identical—delivers

$$a_{t,ss} = a_{t,1} \quad \text{and} \quad P_{t,ss} = P_{t,1} \ .$$

This completes the first part of our proof.

The Kalman smoother recursions use only system matrices that are the same for both procedures. In addition to the system matrices, the output of the filter is used as an input, see Subsection 13.5.5. But we have already shown that the filter output is identical. Thus the results of the smoother are the same for both procedures as well.   □

13.6.2   Smoothed constant state variables

We want to show that the Kalman smoother produces constant estimates through time for all state variables that are constant by definition. To proof this result, we use some of the smoother recursions given in Subsection 13.5.5. First of all, we rearrange the state vector such that the last $k \leqslant K$ variables are constant. This allows the following partition of the transition matrix

$$T_{t+1} = \begin{bmatrix} T_{11,t+1} & T_{12,t+1} \\ 0 & I \end{bmatrix} \tag{13.15}$$

with the $k \times k$ identity matrix I. Furthermore, we define with the same partition

$$\tilde{P}_t \overset{\text{def}}{=} T_{t+1} P_t T_{t+1}^\top = \begin{bmatrix} \tilde{P}_{11,t} & \tilde{P}_{12,t} \\ \tilde{P}_{12,t} & \tilde{P}_{22,t} \end{bmatrix}$$

The filter recursion for the covariance matrix are given as

$$P_{t+1|t} = T_{t+1} P_t T_{t+1}^\top + R_{t+1}$$

where the upper left part of R_{t+1} contains the covariance matrix of the disturbances for the stochastic state variables. We see immediately that only the upper left part of $P_{t+1|T}$ is different from $\tilde{P}_t$.

Our goal is to show that for the recursions of the smoother holds

$$P_t^* = \begin{bmatrix} M_{11,t} & M_{12,t} \\ 0 & I \end{bmatrix} , \tag{13.16}$$

where both Ms stand for some complicated matrices. With this result at hand, we obtain immediately

$$a_{t|T}^k = a_{t+1|T}^k = a_T^k \tag{13.17}$$

for all t, where $a_{t|T}^k$ contains the last k elements of the smoothed state $a_{t|T}$.

Furthermore, it is possible to show with the same result that the lower right partition of $P_{t|T}$ is equal to the lower right partition of P_T for all t. This lower right partition is just the covariance matrix of $a_{t|T}^k$. Just write the smoother recursion

$$P_{t|T} = P_t(I - T_{t+1}^\top P_t^{*\top}) + P_t^* P_{t+1|T} P_t^{*\top} .$$

Then check with (13.15) and (13.16) that the lower-right partition of the first matrix on the right hand side is a $k \times k$ matrix of zeros. The lower-right partition of the second matrix is given by the the lower-right partition of $P_{t+1|T}$.

PROOF:
Now we derive (13.16): We assume that the inverse of T_{t+1} and $T_{11,t+1}$ exist. The inverses for our model exist because we assume that $\phi_2 \neq 0$. For the partitioned transition matrix (Sydsæter, Strøm and Berck, 2000, 19.48) we derive

$$T_{t+1}^{-1} = \begin{bmatrix} T_{11,t+1}^{-1} & -T_{11,t+1}^{-1} T_{12,t+1} \\ 0 & I \end{bmatrix} . \tag{13.18}$$

Now, it is easy to see that

$$P_t^* = T_{t+1}^{-1} \tilde{P}_t P_{t+1|t}^{-1} . \tag{13.19}$$

We have (Sydsæter, Strøm and Berck, 2000, 19.49)

$$P_{t+1|t}^{-1} = \begin{bmatrix} \Delta_t & -\Delta_t \tilde{P}_{12,t} \tilde{P}_{22,t}^{-1} \\ -\tilde{P}_{22,t}^{-1} \tilde{P}_{12,t} \Delta_t & \tilde{P}_{22,t}^{-1} + \tilde{P}_{22,t}^{-1} \tilde{P}_{12,t} \Delta_t \tilde{P}_{12,t} \tilde{P}_{22,t}^{-1} \end{bmatrix} \tag{13.20}$$

with Δ_t as a known function of the partial matrices. If we multiply this matrix with the lower partition of $\tilde{P}_t$ we obtain immediately $[0\ I]$. With this result and (13.18) we derive (13.16). $\square$

Bibliography

Bailey, M. J., Muth, R. F. and Nourse, H.O. (1963). A regression method for real estate price index construction, *Journal of the American Statistical Association* **58**: 933–942.

Baumol, W. (1959). *Economic Dynamics*, 2nd ed., Macmillan, New York.

Bera, A. K. and Jarque, C. M. (1982). Model Specification Tests: a Simultaneous Approach, *Journal of Econometrics* **20**: 59–82.

Cho, M. (1996). House price dynamics: a survey of theoretical and empirical issues, *Journal of Housing Research* **7:2**: 145–172.

Clapp, J. M. and Giaccotto, C. (1998). Price indices based on the hedonic repeat-sales method: application to the housing market, *Journal of Real Estate Finance and Economics* **16:1**: 5–26.

Durbin, J. and Koopman, J. S. (2001). *Time Series Analysis by State Space Methods*, Oxford University Press, Oxford.

Engle, R. F. and M. W. Watson (1981). A One-Factor Multivariate Time Series Model of Metropolitan Wage Rates, *Journal of the American Statistical Association* **76**: 774–781.

Gourieroux, C. and Monfort, A. (1997). *Time Series and Dynamic Models*, Cambridge University Press, Cambridge.

Greene, W. H. (2000). *Econometric Analysis. Fourth Edition*, Prentice Hall, Upper Saddle River, New Jersey.

Hamilton, J. D. (1994). *Time Series Analysis*, Princeton University Press, Princeton, New Jersey.

Harvey, A. C. (1989). *Forecasting, Structural Time Series Models and the Kalman Filter*, Cambridge University Press, Cambridge.

Harvey, A. C. (1993). *Time Series Models*, 2. edn, Harvester Wheatsheaf, New York.

Hill, R. C., Knight, J. R. and Sirmans, C. F. (1997). Estimating Capital Asset Price Indexes, *Review of Economics and Statistics* **79**: 226–233.

Koopman, S. J., Shepard, N. and Doornik, J. A. (1999). Statistical Algorithms for Models in State Space Using SsfPack 2.2, *Econometrics Journal* **2**: 107–160.

Peña, D., Tiao, G. C. and Tsay, R. S. (2001). *A Course in Time Series Analysis*, Wiley, New York.

Schwann, G. M. (1998). A real estate price index for thin markets, *Journal of Real Estate Finance and Economics* **16:3**: 269–287.

Shiller, R. J. (1993). *Macro Markets. Creating Institutions for Managing Society's Largest Economic Risks*, Clarendon Press, Oxford.

Shumway, R. H. and Stoffer, D. S. (1982). An approach to time series smoothing and forecasting using the EM algorithm, *Journal of Time Series Analysis* **3**: 253–264.

Shumway, R. H. and Stoffer, D. S. (2000). *Time Series Analysis and Its Applications*, Springer, New York, Berlin.

Sydsæter, K., Strøm, A. and Berck, P. (2000). *Economists' Mathematical Manual*, 3. edn, Springer, New York, Berlin.

14 Long Memory Effects Trading Strategy

Oliver Jim Blaskowitz and Peter Schmidt

14.1 Introduction

Long range dependence is widespread in nature and has been extensively documented in economics and finance, as well as in hydrology, meteorology, and geophysics by authors such as Heyman, Tabatabai and Lakshman (1991), Hurst (1951), Jones and Briffa (1992), Leland, Taqqu, Willinger and Wilson (1993) and Peters (1994). It has a long history in economics and finance, and has remained a topic of active research in the study of financial time series, Beran (1994).

Historical records of financial data typically exhibit distinct nonperiodical cyclical patterns that are indicative of the presence of significant power at low frequencies (i.e. long range dependencies). However, the statistical investigations that have been performed to test for the presence of long range dependence in economic time series representing returns of common stocks have often become sources of major controversies. Asset returns exhibiting long range dependencies are inconsistent with the efficient market hypothesis, and cause havoc on stochastic analysis techniques that have formed the basis of a broad part of modern finance theory and its applications, Lo (1991). In this chapter, we examine the methods used in Hurst analysis, present a process exhibiting long memory features, and give market evidence by applying Hurst's R/S analysis and finally sketch a trading strategy for German voting and non–voting stocks.

14.2   Hurst and Rescaled Range Analysis

Hurst (1900–1978) was an English hydrologist, who worked in the early 20th century on the Nile River Dam project. When designing a dam, the yearly changes in water level are of particular concern in order to adapt the dam's storage capacity according to the natural environment. Studying an Egyptian 847–year record of the Nile River's overflows, Hurst observed that flood occurrences could be characterized as persistent, i.e. heavier floods were accompanied by above average flood occurrences, while below average occurrences were followed by minor floods. In the process of this findings he developed the Rescaled Range (R/S) Analysis.

We observe a stochastic process Y_t at time points $t \in \mathcal{I} = \{0, \ldots, N\}$. Let n be an integer that is small relative to N, and let A denote the integer part of N/n. Divide the 'interval' $\mathcal{I}$ into A consecutive 'subintervals', each of length n and with overlapping endpoints. In every subinterval correct the original datum Y_t for location, using the mean slope of the process in the subinterval, obtaining $Y_t - (t/n)\,(Y_{an} - Y_{(a-1)n})$ for all t with $(a-1)n \leq t \leq an$ and for all $a = 1, \ldots, A$. Over the a'th subinterval $\mathcal{I}_a = \{(a-1)n, (a-1)n + 1, \ldots, an\}$, for $1 \leq a \leq A$, construct the smallest box (with sides parallel to the coordinate axes) such that the box contains all the fluctuations of $Y_t - (t/n)\,(Y_{an} - Y_{(a-1)n})$ that occur within $\mathcal{I}_a$. Then, the height of the box equals

$$R_a = \max_{(a-1)n \leq t \leq an} \left\{ Y_t - \frac{t}{n}(Y_{an} - Y_{(a-1)n}) \right\}$$
$$- \min_{(a-1)n \leq t \leq an} \left\{ Y_t - \frac{t}{n}(Y_{an} - Y_{(a-1)n}) \right\}$$

Figure 14.1 illustrates the procedure. Let S_a denote the empirical standard error of the n variables $Y_t - Y_{t-1}$, for $(a-1)n + 1 \leq t \leq an$. If the process Y is stationary then S_a varies little with a; in other cases, dividing R_a by S_a corrects for the main effects of scale inhomogeneity in both spatial and temporal domains.

The total area of the boxes, corrected for scale, is proportional in n to

$$\left(\frac{R}{S}\right)_n := A^{-1} \sum_{a=1}^{A} \frac{R_a}{S_a}. \tag{2.1}$$

The slope $\hat{H}$ of the regression of $\log(R/S)_n$ on $\log n$, for k values of n, may be taken as an estimator of the Hurst constant H describing long-range dependence of the process Y, Beran (1994) and Peters (1994).

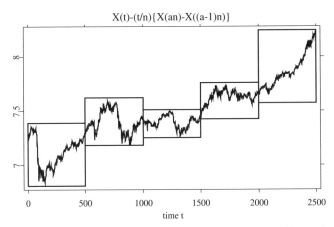

Figure 14.1. The construction of the boxes in the R/S analysis.

If the process Y is stationary then correction for scale is not strictly necessary, and we may take each S_a to be the constant 1. In that case the R–S statistic $\hat{H}$ is a version of the box-counting estimator that is widely used in physical science applications, Carter, Cawley and Mauldin (1988), Sullivan and Hunt (1988) and Hunt (1990). The box-counting estimator is related to the capacity definition of fractal dimension, Barnsley (1988) p. 172ff, and the R–S estimator may be interpreted in the same way. Statistical properties of the box-counting estimator have been discussed by Hall and Wood (1993).

A more detailed analysis, exploiting dependence among the errors in the regression of $\log(R/S)_n$ on $\log n$, may be undertaken in place of R–S analysis. See Kent and Wood (1997) for a version of this approach in the case where scale correction is unnecessary. However, as Kent and Wood show, the advantages of the approach tend to be asymptotic in character, and sample sizes may need to be extremely large before real improvements are obtained.

Hurst used the coefficient H as an index for the persistence of the time series considered. For $0.5 < H < 1$, it is positively persistent and characterized by 'long memory' effects, as described in the next section. A rather informal interpretation of H used by practitioners is this: H may be interpreted as the chance of movements with the same sign, Peters (1994). For $H > 0.5$, it is more likely that an upward movement is followed by a movement of the same (positive) sign, and a downward movement is more likely to be followed by another downward movement. For $H < 0.5$, a downward movement is more likely to be reversed by an upward movement thus implying the reverting behavior.

14.3 Stationary Long Memory Processes

A stationary process X has the long memory property, if for its autocorrelation function $\rho(k) = \mathrm{Cov}(X_i, X_{i+k})/\mathrm{Var}(X_1)$ holds:

$$\sum_{k=-\infty}^{\infty} \rho(k) \;=\; \infty .\tag{14.1}$$

That is, the autocorrelations decay to zero so slowly that their sum does not converge, Beran (1994).

With respect to (14.1), note that the classical expression for the variance of the sample mean, $\bar{X} \stackrel{\text{def}}{=} n^{-1} \sum_{i=1}^{n} X_i$, for independent and identically distributed $X_1, \ldots, X_n$,

$$\mathrm{Var}(\bar{X}) = \frac{\sigma^2}{n} \text{ with } \sigma^2 = \mathrm{Var}(X_i)\tag{14.2}$$

is not valid anymore. If correlations are neither zero and nor so small to be negligible, the variance of $\bar{X}$ is equal to

$$\mathrm{Var}(\bar{X}) \;=\; \frac{\sigma^2}{n}\left(1 + 2\sum_{k=1}^{n-1}\left(1 - \frac{k}{n}\right)\rho(k)\right).\tag{14.3}$$

Thus, for long memory processes the variance of the sample mean converges to zero at a slower rate than n^{-1}, Beran (1994). Note that long memory implies positive long range correlations. It is essential to understand that long range dependence is characterized by slowly decaying correlations, although nothing is said about the size of a particular correlation at lag k. Due to the slow decay it is sometimes difficult to detect non zero but very small correlations by looking at the $\pm 2/\sqrt{n}$–confidence band. Beran (1994) gives an example where the correct correlations are slowly decaying but within the $\pm 2/\sqrt{n}$–band. So even if estimated correctly we would consider them as non significant.

Note that (14.1) holds in particular if the autocorrelation $\rho(k)$ is approximately $c|k|^{-\alpha}$ with a constant c and a parameter $\alpha \in (0,1)$. If we know the autocorrelations we also know the spectral density $f(\lambda)$, defined as

$$f(\lambda) \quad = \quad \frac{\sigma^2}{2\pi} \sum_{k=-\infty}^{\infty} \rho(k)e^{ik\lambda}. \tag{14.4}$$

The structure of the autocorrelation then implies, that the spectral density is approximately of the form $c_f|k|^{\alpha-1}$ with a constant c_f as $\lambda \to 0$. Thus the spectral density has a pole at 0.

To connect the long memory property with the Hurst coefficient, we introduce self similar processes. A stochastic process Y_t is called self similar with self similarity parameter H, if for any positive stretching factor c, the rescaled process $c^{-H}Y_{ct}$ has the same distribution as the original process Y_t. If the increments $X_t = Y_t - Y_{t-1}$ are stationary, there autocorrelation function is given by

$$\rho(k) = \frac{1}{2} \left(|k+1|^{2H} - 2|k|^{2H} + |k-1|^{2H} \right) ,$$

Beran (1994). From a Taylor expansion of ρ it follows

$$\frac{\rho(k)}{H(2H-1)k^{2H-2}} \to 1 \text{ for } k \to \infty .$$

This means, that for $H > 0.5$, the autocorrelation function $\rho(k)$ is approximately $H(2H-1)k^{-\alpha}$ with $\alpha = 2 - 2H \in (0,1)$ and thus X_t has the long memory property.

14.3.1   Fractional Brownian Motion and Noise

In this section, we introduce a particular self similar process with stationary increments, namely the fractional Brownian motion (FBM) and fractional Gaussian noise (FGN), Mandelbrot and van Ness (1968), Beran (1994).

DEFINITION 14.1 *Let $B_H(t)$ be a stochastic process with continuous sample paths and such that*

- $B_H(t)$ *is Gaussian*

- $B_H(0) = 0$

- $E\{B_H(t) - B_H(s)\} = 0$

- $Cov\{B_H(t), B_H(s)\} = \frac{\sigma^2}{2}\left(|t|^{2H} - |t-s|^{2H} + |s|^{2H}\right)$

for any $H \in (0,1)$ and σ^2 a variance scaling parameter. Then $B_H(t)$ is called fractional Brownian motion.

Essentially, this definition is the same as for standard Brownian motion besides that the covariance structure is different. For $H = 0.5$, definition 14.1 contains standard Brownian motion as a special case but in general ($H \neq 0.5$), increments $B_H(t) - B_H(s)$ are not independent anymore. The stochastic process resulting by computing first differences of FBM is called FGN with parameter H. The covariance at lag k of FGN follows from definition 14.1:

$$\begin{aligned}
\gamma(k) &= Cov\{B_H(t) - B_H(t-1), B_H(t+k) - B_H(t+k-1)\} \\
&= \frac{\sigma^2}{2}\left(|k+1|^{2H} - 2|k|^{2H} + |k-1|^{2H}\right)
\end{aligned} \tag{14.5}$$

For $0.5 < H < 1$ the process has long range dependence, and for $0 < H < 0.5$ the process has short range dependence.

Figures 14.2 and 14.3 show two simulated paths of $N = 1000$ observations of FGN with parameter $H = 0.8$ and $H = 0.2$ using an algorithm proposed by Davies and Harte (1987). For $H = 0.2$, the FBM path is much more jagged and the range of the y–axis is about ten times smaller than for $H = 0.8$ which is due to the reverting behavior of the time series.

The estimated autocorrelation function (ACF) for the path simulated with $H = 0.8$ along with the $\pm 2/\sqrt{N}$–confidence band is shown in Figure 14.4. For comparison the ACF used to simulate the process given by (14.5) is superimposed (dashed line). The slow decay of correlations can be seen clearly.

Applying R/S analysis we can retrieve the Hurst coefficient used to simulate the process. Figure 14.5 displays the estimated regression line and the data points used in the regression. We simulate the process with $H = 0.8$ and the R/S statistic yields $\hat{H} = 0.83$.

Finally, we mention that fractional Brownian motion is not the only stationary process revealing properties of systems with long memory. Fractional ARIMA processes are an alternative to FBM, Beran (1994). As well, there are non stationary processes with infinite second moments that can be used to model long range dependence, Samrodnitsky and Taqqu (1994).

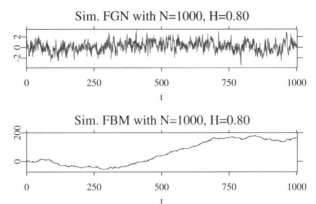

Figure 14.2. Simulated FGN with $H = 0.8$, $N = 1000$ and path of corresponding FBM.

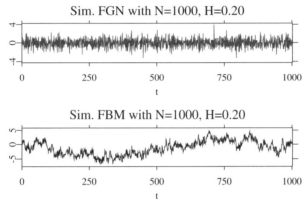

Figure 14.3. Simulated FGN with $H = 0.2$, $N = 1000$ and path of corresponding FBM. **Q** XFGSimFBM.xpl

14.4   Data Analysis

A set of four pairs of voting and non–voting German stocks will be subject to our empirical analysis. More precisely, our data sample retrieved from the data information service Thompson Financial Datastream, consists of 7290 daily

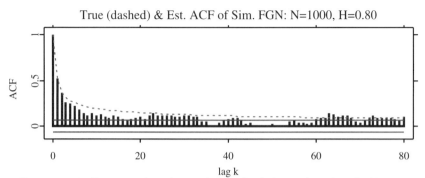

Figure 14.4. Estimated and true ACF of FGN simulated with $H = 0.8$, $N = 1000$. **Q** XFGSimFBM.xpl

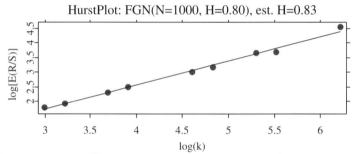

Figure 14.5. Hurst regression and estimated Hurst coefficient ($\hat{H} = 0.83$) of FBM simulated with $H = 0.8$, $N = 1000$. **Q** XFGSimFBMHurst.xpl

closing prices of stocks of WMF, Dyckerhoff, KSB and RWE from January 01, 1973, to December 12, 2000.

Figure 14.6 shows the performance of WMF stocks in our data period. The plot indicates an intimate relationship of both assets. Since the performance of both kinds of stocks are influenced by the same economic underlyings, their relative value should be stable over time. If this holds, the log–difference X_t of the pairs of voting (S_t^v) and non–voting stocks (S_t^{nv}),

$$X_t \stackrel{\text{def}}{=} \log S_t^v - \log S_t^{nv} \tag{14.6}$$

should exhibit a reverting behavior and therefore an R/S analysis should yield estimates of the Hurst coefficient smaller than 0.5. In order to reduce the number of plots we show only the plot of WMF stocks. One may start the quantlet Q XFGStocksPlots.xpl to see the time series for the other companies as well. First, we perform R/S analysis on both individual stocks and the voting/non–voting log–differences. In a second step, a trading strategy is applied to all four voting/non–voting log–differences.

Time Series of Voting(dashed) and Non Voting WMF Stocks

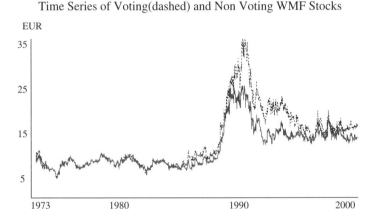

Figure 14.6. Time series of voting and non–voting WMF stocks.
Q XFGStocksPlots.xpl

Table 14.1 gives the R/S statistic of each individual stock and of the log–difference process of voting and non–voting stocks. While $\hat{H}$ is close to 0.5 for each time series taken separately, we find for the log differences a Hurst coefficient indicating negative persistence, i.e. $H < 0.5$.

	WMF		Dyck.		KSB		RWE	
	nv	v	nv	v	nv	v	nv	v
Stock	0.51	0.53	0.57	0.52	0.53	0.51	0.50	0.51
Differences	0.33		0.37		0.33		0.41	

Table 14.1. Estimated Hurst coefficients of each stock and of log–differences.

To test for the significance of the estimated Hurst coefficients we need to know the finite sample distribution of the R/S statistic. Usually, if the probabilistic behavior of a test statistic is unknown, it is approximated by its asymptotic distribution when the number of observations is large. Unfortunately, as, for example, Lo (1991) shows, such an asymptotic approximation is inaccurate in the case of the R/S statistic. This problem may be solved by means of bootstrap and simulation methods. A semiparametric bootstrap approach to hypothesis testing for the Hurst coefficient has been introduced by Hall, Härdle, Kleinow and Schmidt (2000), In the spirit of this chapter we use Brownian motion ($H = 0.5$) to simulate under the null hypothesis. Under the null hypothesis the log–difference process follows a standard Brownian motion and by Monte Carlo simulation we compute 99%, 95% and 90% confidence intervals of the R/S statistic. The results are given in Table 14.2. While the estimated Hurst coefficients for each individual stock are at least contained in the 99% confidence interval, we consider the R/S statistic for voting/non–voting log differences as significant.

N	Mean	90%	95%	99%
7289	0.543	$[0.510, 0.576]$	$[0.504, 0.582]$	$[0.491, 0.595]$

Table 14.2. Simulated confidence intervals for R/S statistic for Brownian motion.

14.5   Trading the Negative Persistence

The data analysis conducted so far indicates a negative persistence ($H < 0.5$) of the log differences of pairs of voting and non–voting stocks of a company. It should be possible to take advantage of this knowledge. If we found a profitable trading strategy, we would interpret this result as a further indication for the reverting behavior of voting/non–voting log–differences.

The average relationship between voting and non–voting stocks in the sample period may be expressed in the following way,

$$\log(\text{voting}) = \beta \log(\text{non-voting}) + \varepsilon$$

where β may be estimated by linear regression. If the log–differences of voting and non–voting stocks are reverting as the R/S analysis indicates, negative differences, $X_t < 0$, are often followed by positive differences and vice versa. In terms of the Hurst coefficient interpretation, given a negative difference, a positive difference has a higher chance to appear in the future than a negative one and vice versa, implying voting stocks probably to become relatively more expensive than their non–voting counterparts. Thus, we go long the voting and short the non–voting stock. In case of the inverse situation, we carry out the inverse trade (short voting and long non–voting). When initiating a trade we take a cash neutral position. That is, we go long one share of the voting and sell short m shares of the non–voting stock to obtain a zero cash flow from this action.

But how to know that a 'turning point' is reached? What is a signal for the reverse? Naturally, one could think, the longer a negative difference persisted, the more likely the difference is going to be positive. In our simulation, we calculate the maximum and minimum difference of the preceding M trading days (for example $M = 50, 100, 150$). If the current difference is more negative than the minimum over the last M trading days, we proceed from the assumption that a reverse is to come and that the difference is going to be positive, thereby triggering a long voting and short non–voting position. A difference greater than the M day maximum releases the opposite position.

When we take a new position, we compute the cash flow from closing the old one. Finally, we calculate the total cash flow, i.e. we sum up all cash flows without taking interests into account. To account for transaction costs, we compute the total net cash flow. For each share bought or sold, we calculate a hypothetical percentage, say 0.5%, of the share price and subtract the sum of all costs incurred from the total cash flow. In order to compare the total net cash flows of our four pairs of stocks which have different levels of stock prices, we normalize them by taking WMF stocks as a numeraire.

In Table 14.3 we show the total net cash flows and in Table 14.4 the number of trade reverses are given. It is clear that for increasing transaction costs the performance deteriorates, a feature common for all 4 pairs of stocks. Moreover, it is quite obvious that the number of trade reverses decreases with the number of days used to compute the signal. An interesting point to note is that for RWE, which is in the German DAX30, the total net cash flow is worse in all situations. A possible explanation would be that since the Hurst coefficient is the highest, the log–differences contain less 'reversion'. Thus, the strategy designed to exploit the reverting behavior should perform rather poorly. WMF and KSB have a smaller Hurst coefficient than RWE and the strategy performs better than for RWE. Furthermore, the payoff pattern is very similar in all situations. Dyckerhoff with a Hurst coefficient of $H = 0.37$ exhibits a payoff structure that rather resembles the one of WMF/KSB.

Transaction Costs	M	WMF $H = 0.33$	Dyckerhoff $H = 0.37$	KSB $H = 0.33$	RWE $H = 0.41$
0.00	50	133.16	197.54	138.68	39.93
	100	104.44	122.91	118.85	20.67
	150	71.09	62.73	56.78	8.80
0.005	50	116.92	176.49	122.32	21.50
	100	94.87	111.82	109.26	12.16
	150	64.78	57.25	51.86	2.90
0.01	50	100.69	155.43	105.96	3.07
	100	85.30	100.73	99.68	3.65
	150	58.48	51.77	49.97	−3.01

Table 14.3. Performance of Long Memory Strategies (TotalNetCash-Flow in EUR). Q XFGLongMemTrade.xpl

M	WMF	Dyckerhoff	KSB	RWE
50	120	141	132	145
100	68	69	69	59
150	47	35	41	42

Table 14.4. Number of Reverses of Long Memory Trades

Regarding the interpretation of the trading strategy, one has to be aware that neither the cash flows are adjusted for risk nor did we account for interest rate effects although the analysis spread over a period of time of about 26 years.

Bibliography

Barnsley, M. (1988). *Fractals everywhere.*, Boston, MA etc.: Academic Press, Inc.

Beran, J. (1994). *Statistics for Long Memory Processes*, Chapman and Hall, New York.

Carter, P., Cawley, R. and Mauldin, R. (1988). Mathematics of dimension measurements of graphs of functions, *in* D. Weitz, L. Sander and B. Mandelbrot (eds), *Proc. Symb. Fractal Aspects of Materials, Disordered Systems*, pp. 183–186.

Davies, R. B. and Harte, D. S. (1987). Test for Hurst Effect, *Biometrica* **74**: 95–102.

Hall, P., Härdle, W., Kleinow, T. and Schmidt, P. (2000). Semiparametric bootstrap approach to hypothesis tests and confidence intervals for the hurst coefficient, *Statistical Inference for stochastic Processes* **3**.

Hall, P. and Wood, A. (1993). On the performance of box-counting estimators of fractal dimension., *Biometrika* **80**(1): 246–252.

Heyman, D., Tabatabai, A. and Lakshman, T.V. (1993). Statistical analysis and simulation of video teleconferencing in ATM networks, *IEEE Trans. Circuits. Syst. Video Technol.*, **2**, 49–59.

Hunt, F. (1990). Error analysis and convergence of capacity dimension algorithms., *SIAM J. Appl. Math.* **50**(1): 307–321.

Hurst, H. E. (1951). Long Term Storage Capacity of Reservoirs, *Trans. Am. Soc. Civil Engineers* **116**, 770–799.

Jones, P.D. and Briffa, K.R. (1992). Global surface air temperature variations during the twentieth century: Part 1, spatial, temporal and seasonals details, *The Holocene* **2**, 165–179.

Kent, J. T. and Wood, A. T. (1997). Estimating the fractal dimension of a locally self-similar Gaussian process by using increments., *J. R. Stat. Soc., Ser. B* **59**(3): 679–699.

Leland, W.E., Taqqu, M.S., Willinger, W. and Wilson, D.V. (1993). Ethernet traffic is self–similar: Stochastic modelling of packet traffic data, *preprint*, Bellcore, Morristown.

Lo, A.W. (1991). Long-term memory in stock market prices, *Econometrica*, **59**, 1279–1313.

Mandelbrot, B.B. and van Ness, J.W. (1968). Fractional Brownian Motion, fractional Noises and Applications, *SIAM* Rev.10, **4**, 422–437.

Peters, E.E. (1994). *Fractal Market Analysis: Applying Chaos Theory to Investment and Economics*, John Wiley & Sons, New York.

Samrodnitsky, G. and Taqqu, M.S. (1994). *Stable non-Gaussian Random Processes: Stochastic Models with infinite variance,* Chapman and Hall, New York.

Sullivan, F. and Hunt, F. (1988). How to estimate capacity dimension, *Nuclear Physics B (Proc. Suppl.)* pp. 125–128.

15 Locally time homogeneous time series modeling

Danilo Mercurio

15.1 Intervals of homogeneity

An adaptive estimation algorithm for time series is presented in this chapter. The basic idea is the following: given a time series and a linear model, we select on-line the largest sample of the most recent observations, such that the model is not rejected. Assume for example that the data can be well fitted by a regression, an autoregression or even by a constant in an unknown interval. The main problem is then to detect the time interval where the model approximately holds. We call such an interval: *interval of time homogeneity*.

This approach appears to be suitable in financial econometrics, where an on-line analysis of large data sets, like e.g. in backtesting, has to be performed. In this case, as soon as a new observation becomes available, the model is checked, the sample size is optimally adapted and a revised forecast is produced.

In the remainder of the chapter we briefly present the theoretical foundations of the proposed algorithm which are due to Liptser and Spokoiny (1999) and we describe its implementation. Then, we provide two applications to financial data. In the first one we estimate the possibly time varying coefficients of an exchange rate basket, while in the second one the volatility of an exchange rate time series is fitted to a locally constant model. The main references can be found in Härdle, Herwartz and Spokoiny (2001), Mercurio and Spokoiny (2000), Härdle, Spokoiny and Teyssière (2000) and Mercurio and Torricelli (2001).

Let us consider the following linear regression equation:

$$Y_t = X_t^\top \theta + \sigma \varepsilon_t, \quad t = 1, \dots, T \tag{15.1}$$

where Y_t is real valued, $X_t = (X_{1,t} \dots X_{p,t})^\top$ and $\theta = (\theta_1 \dots \theta_p)^\top$ are $\mathbb{R}^p$ valued and ε_t is a standard normally distributed random variable. If the matrix $\sum_{t=1}^{T} X_t X_t^\top$ is nonsingular with inverse W, then the least squares estimator of θ is:

$$\widehat{\theta} = W \sum_{t=1}^{T} X_t Y_t. \tag{15.2}$$

Define w_{kk} as the k-th element on the diagonal of W and let λ be a positive scalar. For nonrandom regressors,the following exponential probability bound is easy to prove:

$$\mathrm{P}(|\widehat{\theta}_k - \theta_k| > \lambda \sigma \sqrt{w_{kk}}) \leq 2e^{-\frac{\lambda^2}{2}}, \quad k = 1, \dots, p. \tag{15.3}$$

Indeed, the estimation error $\widehat{\theta}_k - \theta_k$ is $N(0, w_{kk}^2 \sigma^2)$ distributed, therefore:

$$
\begin{aligned}
1 &= \mathrm{E} \exp\left(\frac{\lambda(\widehat{\theta}_k - \theta_k)}{\sigma \sqrt{w_{kk}}} - \frac{\lambda^2}{2} \right) \\
&\geq \mathrm{E} \exp\left(\frac{\lambda(\widehat{\theta}_k - \theta_k)}{\sigma \sqrt{w_{kk}}} - \frac{\lambda^2}{2} \right) \mathbf{1}(\widehat{\theta}_k - \theta_k > \lambda \sigma \sqrt{w_{kk}}) \\
&\geq \exp\left(\frac{\lambda^2}{2} \right) \mathrm{P}(\widehat{\theta}_k - \theta_k > \lambda \sigma \sqrt{w_{kk}}).
\end{aligned}
$$

The result in (15.3) follows from the symmetry of the normal distribution. Equation (15.3) has been generalized by Liptser and Spokoiny (1999) to the case of nonrandom regressors. More precisely, they allow the X_t to be only conditionally independent of ε_t, and they include lagged values of Y_t as regressors. In this case the bound reads roughly as follows:

$$\mathrm{P}(|\widehat{\theta}_k - \theta_k| > \lambda \sigma \sqrt{w_{kk}}; W \text{ is nonsingular }) \leq \mathcal{P}(\lambda)e^{-\frac{\lambda^2}{2}}. \tag{15.4}$$

Where $\mathcal{P}(\lambda)$ is a polynomial in λ. It must be noticed that (15.4) is not as sharp as (15.3), furthermore, because of the randomness of W, (15.4) holds only on the set where W is nonsingular, nevertheless this set has in many cases a large probability. For example when Y_t follows an ergodic autoregressive process and the number of observations is at least moderately large. More technical details are given in Section 15.4.

We now describe how the bound (15.4) can be used in order to estimate the coefficients θ in the regression equation (15.1) when the regressors are (possibly) stochastic and the coefficients are not constant, but follow a jump process.

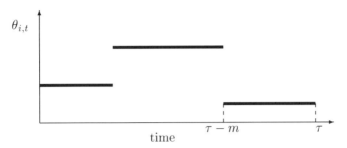

Figure 15.1. Example of a locally homogeneous process.

The procedure that we describe does not require an explicit expression of the law of the process θ_t, but it only assumes that θ_t is constant on some unknown time interval $I = [\tau - m, \tau]$, $\tau - m > 0$, $\tau, m \in \mathbb{N}$. This interval is referred as an *interval of time homogeneity* and a model which is constant only on some time interval is called *locally time homogeneous*.

Let us now define some notation. The expression $\widehat{\theta}_\tau$ will describe the (filtering) estimator of the process $(\theta_t)_{t \in \mathbb{N}}$ at time τ; that is to say, the estimator which uses only observations up to time τ. For example if θ is constant, the recursive estimator of the form:

$$\widehat{\theta}_\tau = \left(\sum_{s=1}^{\tau} X_s X_s^\top \right)^{-1} \sum_{s=1}^{\tau} X_s Y_s,$$

represents the best linear estimator for θ. But, if the coefficients are not constant and follow a jump process, like in the picture above a recursive estimator cannot provide good results. Ideally, only the observations in the interval $I = [\tau - m, \tau]$ should be used for the estimation of θ_τ. Actually, an estimator of θ_τ using the observation of a subinterval $J \subset I$ would be less efficient, while an estimator using the observation of a larger interval $K \supset I$ would be biased. The main objective is therefore to estimate the largest interval of time homogeneity. We refer to this estimator as $\widehat{I} = [\tau - \widehat{m}, \tau]$. On this interval $\widehat{I}$

we estimate θ_τ with ordinary least squares (OLS):

$$\widehat{\theta}_\tau = \widehat{\theta}_{\widehat{I}} = \left(\sum_{s \in \widehat{I}} X_s X_s^\top \right)^{-1} \sum_{s \in \widehat{I}} X_s Y_s. \tag{15.5}$$

In order to determine $\widehat{I}$ we use the idea of pointwise adaptive estimation described in Lepski (1990), Lepski and Spokoiny (1997) and Spokoiny (1998). The idea of the method can be explained as follows.

Suppose that I is an interval-candidate, that is, we expect time-homogeneity in I and hence in every subinterval $J \subset I$. This implies that the mean values of the $\widehat{\theta}_I$ and $\widehat{\theta}_J$ nearly coincide. Furthermore, we know on the basis of equation (15.4) that the events

$$|\widehat{\theta}_{i,I} - \theta_\tau| \leq \mu\sigma\sqrt{w_{ii,I}} \quad \text{and} \quad |\widehat{\theta}_{i,J} - \theta_\tau| \leq \lambda\sigma\sqrt{w_{ii,J}}$$

occur with high probability for some sufficiently large constants λ and μ. The adaptive estimation procedure therefore roughly corresponds to a family of tests to check whether $\widehat{\theta}_I$ does not differ significantly from $\widehat{\theta}_J$. The latter is done on the basis of the triangle inequality and of equation (15.4) which assigns a large probability to the event

$$|\widehat{\theta}_{i,I} - \widehat{\theta}_{i,J}| \leq \mu\sigma\sqrt{w_{ii,I}} + \lambda\sigma\sqrt{w_{ii,J}}$$

under the assumption of homogeneity within I, provided that μ and λ are sufficiently large. Therefore, if there exists an interval $J \subset I$ such that the hypothesis $\widehat{\theta}_{i,I} = \widehat{\theta}_{i,J}$ cannot be accepted, we reject the hypothesis of time homogeneity for the interval I. Finally, our adaptive estimator corresponds to the largest interval I such that the hypothesis of homogeneity is not rejected for I itself and all smaller intervals.

15.1.1   The adaptive estimator

Now we present a formal description. Suppose that a family $\mathcal{I}$ of interval candidates I is fixed. Each of them is of the form $I = [\tau - m, \tau]$, so that the set $\mathcal{I}$ is ordered due to m. With every such interval we associate an estimate $\widehat{\theta}_{i,I}$ of the parameter $\theta_{i,\tau}$ and the corresponding conditional standard deviation $\sqrt{w_{ii,I}}$. Next, for every interval I from $\mathcal{I}$, we suppose to be given a set $\mathcal{J}(I)$ of testing subintervals J. For every $J \in \mathcal{J}(I)$, we construct the corresponding estimate $\widehat{\theta}_{i,J}$ from the observations for $t \in J$ and compute $\sqrt{w_{ii,J}}$. Now, with two constants μ and λ, define the adaptive choice of the interval of homogeneity by the following iterative procedure:

- Initialization: Select the smallest interval in $\mathcal{I}$

- Iteration: Select the next interval I in $\mathcal{I}$ and calculate the corresponding estimate $\widehat{\theta}_{i,I}$ and the conditional standard deviation $\sqrt{w_{ii,I}}\sigma$

- Testing homogeneity: Reject I, if there exists one $J \in \mathcal{J}(I)$, and $i = 1,\ldots,p$ such that

$$|\widehat{\theta}_{i,I} - \widehat{\theta}_{i,J}| > \mu\sigma\sqrt{w_{ii,I}} + \lambda\sigma\sqrt{w_{ii,J}}. \qquad (15.6)$$

- Loop: If I is not rejected, then continue with the iteration step by choosing a larger interval. Otherwise, set $\widehat{I} = $ "the latest non rejected I".

The adaptive estimator $\widehat{\theta}_{\tau}$ of θ_{τ} is defined by applying the selected interval $\widehat{I}$:

$$\widehat{\theta}_{i,\tau} = \widehat{\theta}_{i,\widehat{I}} \text{ for } i = 1,\ldots,p.$$

As for the variance estimation, note that the previously described procedure requires the knowledge of the variance σ^2 of the errors. In practical applications, σ^2 is typically unknown and has to be estimated from the data. The regression representation (15.1) and local time homogeneity suggests to apply a residual-based estimator. Given an interval $I = [\tau - m, \tau]$, we construct the parameter estimate $\widehat{\theta}_I$. Next the pseudo-residuals $\widehat{\varepsilon}_t$ are defined as $\widehat{\varepsilon}_t = Y_t - X_t^\top\widehat{\theta}_I$. Finally the variance estimator is defined by averaging the squared pseudo-residuals:

$$\widehat{\sigma}^2 = \frac{1}{|I|}\sum_{t\in I}\widehat{\varepsilon}_t^2.$$

15.1.2   A small simulation study

The performance of the adaptive estimator is evaluated with data from the following process:

$$Y_t = \theta_{1,t} + \theta_{2,t}X_{2,t} + \theta_{3,t}X_{3,t} + \sigma\varepsilon_t.$$

The length of the sample is 300. The regressors X_2 and X_3 are two independent random walks. The regressor coefficients are constant in the first half of the

$1 \leq t \leq 150$	$151 \leq t \leq 300$		
	large jump	medium jump	small jump
$\theta_{1,t} = 1$	$\theta_{1,t} = .85$	$\theta_{1,t} = .99$	$\theta_{1,t} = .9995$
$\theta_{2,t} = .006$	$\theta_{2,t} = .0015$	$\theta_{2,t} = .004$	$\theta_{2,t} = .0055$
$\theta_{3,t} = .025$	$\theta_{3,t} = .04$	$\theta_{3,t} = .028$	$\theta_{3,t} = .0255$

Table 15.1. Simulated models.

sample, then they make a jump after which they continue being constant until the end of the sample. We simulate three models with jumps of different magnitude. The values of the simulated models are presented in Table 15.1.

The error term ε_t is a standard Gaussian white noise, and $\sigma = 10^{-2}$. Note that the average value of $\sigma|\varepsilon_t|$ equals $10^{-2}\sqrt{2/\pi} \approx 0.008$, therefore the small jump of magnitude 0.0005 is clearly not visible by eye. For each of the three models above 100 realizations of the white noise ε_t are generated and the adaptive estimation is performed.

In order to implement the procedure we need two parameters: μ and λ, and two sets of intervals: $\mathcal{I}$ and $\mathcal{J}(I)$. As far as the latter are concerned the simplest proposal is to use a regular grid $G = \{t_k\}$ with $t_k = m_0 k$ for some integer m_0 and with $\tau = t_{k^*}$ belonging to the grid. We next consider the intervals $I_k = [t_k, t_{k^*}[= [t_k, \tau[$ for all $t_k < t_{k^*} = \tau$. Every interval I_k contains exactly $k^* - k$ smaller intervals $J' = [t_{k'}, t_{k^*}[$. So that for every interval $I_k = [t_k, t_{k^*}[$ and $k' : k < k' < k^*$ we define the set $\mathcal{J}(I_k)$ of testing subintervals J' by taking all smaller intervals with right end point t_{k^*}: $J' = [t_{k'}, t_{k^*}[$ and all smaller intervals with left end point t_k: $J' = [t_k, t_{k'}[$:

$$\mathcal{J}(I_k) = \{J = [t_{k'}, t_{k^*}[\text{ or } J = [t_k, t_{k'}[: k < k' < k^*\}.$$

The testing interval sets $\mathcal{I}$ and $\mathcal{J}(I)$ are therefore identified by the parameter m_0: the grid step.

We are now left with the choice of three parameters: λ, μ and m_0. These parameters act as the smoothing parameters in the classical nonparametric estimation. The value of m_0 determines the number of points at which the time homogeneity is tested and it defines the minimal delay after which a jump can be discovered. Simulation results have shown that small changes of m_0 do not essentially affect the results of the estimation and, depending on the number of parameters to be estimated, it can be set between 10 and 50.

The choice of λ and μ is more critical because these parameters determine the acceptance or the rejection of the interval of time homogeneity as it can be seen from equation (15.6). Large values of λ and μ reduce the sensitivity of the algorithm and may delay the detection of the change point, while small values make the procedure more sensitive to small changes in the values of the estimated parameters and may increase the probability of a type-I error.

For the simulation, we set: $m_0 = 30$, $\lambda = 2$ and $\mu = 4$, while a rule for the selection of λ and μ for real application will be discussed in the next section. Figure 15.2 shows the results of the simulation. The true value of the coefficients is plotted ($\theta_{1,t}$: first row, $\theta_{2,t}$: second row, $\theta_{3,t}$: third row) along with the median, the maximum and the minimum of the estimates from all realizations for each model at each time point. The simulation results are very satisfactory. The change point is quickly detected, almost within the minimal delay of 30 periods for all three models, so that the adaptive estimation procedure show a good performance even for the small jump model.

15.2 Estimating the coefficients of an exchange rate basket

In this section we compare the *adaptive estimator* with standard procedures which have been designed to cope with time varying regressor coefficients. A simple solution to this problem consists in applying a window estimator, i.e. an estimator which only uses the most recent k observations:

$$\widehat{\theta}_t = \left(\sum_{s=t-k}^{t} X_s X_s^\top \right)^{-1} \sum_{s=t-k}^{t} X_s Y_s, \qquad (15.7)$$

where the value of k is specified by the practitioner. Another, more refined technique, consists in describing the coefficients θ as an unobserved stochastic process: $(\theta_t)_{t \in \mathbb{N}}$, see Elliot, Aggoun and Moore (1995). Apart from the cases when there is some knowledge about the data generating process of θ_t, the most common specification is as a multivariate random walk:

$$\theta_t = \theta_{t-1} + \zeta_t \qquad \zeta_t \sim N(0, \Sigma). \qquad (15.8)$$

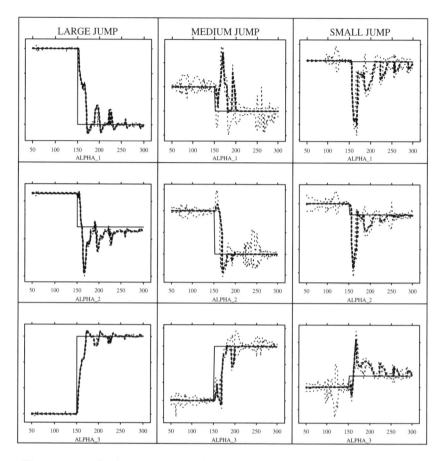

Figure 15.2. On-line estimates of the regression coefficients with jumps of different magnitude. Median (thick dotted line), maximum and minimum (thin dotted line) among all estimates.

In this context, equations (15.8) and (15.1) can be regarded as a state space model, where equation (15.8) is the state equation (the signal) and equation (15.1) is the measurement equation and it plays the role of a noisy observation of θ_t. A Kalman filter algorithm can be used for the estimation, see Cooley and Prescott (1973). The Kalman filter algorithm requires the initialization of two variables: $\widehat{\theta}_{0|0}$ and $P_{0|0} = \mathrm{Cov}(\widehat{\theta}_{0|0})$ and its recursions read as follows, see Chui and Chen (1998):

$$
\begin{cases}
P_{0|0} & = & \mathrm{Cov}(\widehat{\theta}_{0|0}) \\
P_{t|t-1} & = & P_{t-1|t-1} + \Sigma\sigma^2 \\
G_t & = & P_{t|t-1}X_t(X_t^{\top}P_{t|t-1}X_t + \sigma^2)^{-1} \\
P_{t|t} & = & (I - G_t X_t^{\top})P_{t|t-1} \\
\widehat{\theta}_{t|t-1} & = & \widehat{\theta}_{t-1|t-1} \\
\widehat{\theta}_{t|t} & = & \widehat{\theta}_{t|t-1} + G_t(Y_t - X_t^{\top}\widehat{\theta}_{t|t-1}).
\end{cases}
$$

The question of the initialization of the Kalman filter will be discussed in the next section together with the Thai Baht basket example. In the notation above, the index $t|t-1$ denotes the estimate performed using all the observation before time t (forecasting estimate), while $t|t$ refers to the estimate performed using all the observations up to time t (filtering estimate). The four estimators described above: the adaptive, the recursive, the window and the Kalman filter Estimator are now applied to the data set of the Thai Baht basket. For deeper analysis of these data see Christoffersen and Giorgianni (2000) and Mercurio and Torricelli (2001).

15.2.1   The Thai Baht basket

An exchange rate basket is a form of pegged exchange rate regime and it takes place whenever the domestic currency can be expressed as a linear combination of foreign currencies. A currency basket can be therefore expressed in the form of equation (15.1), where: $X_{1,t}$ is set constantly equal to one and is taken as numeraire, Y_t represents the home currency exchange rate with respect to the numeraire, and $X_{j,t}$ is the amount of currency 1 per unit of currency j, i.e. the cross currency exchange rate. The above relationship usually holds only on the average, because the central bank cannot control the exchange rate exactly, therefore the error term ε_t is added.

Because modern capital mobility enables the investors to exploit the interest rate differentials which may arise between the domestic and the foreign currencies, a pegged exchange rate regime can become an incentive to speculation and eventually lead to destabilization of the exchange rate, in spite of the fact that its purpose is to reduce exchange rate fluctuations, see Eichengreen, Masson, Savastano and Sharma (1999). Indeed, it appears that one of the causes which have led to the Asian crisis of 1997 can be searched in short term capital investments.

From 1985 until its suspension on July 2, 1997 (following a speculative attack) the Bath was pegged to a basket of currencies consisting of Thailand's main trading partners. In order to gain greater discretion in setting monetary policy, the Bank of Thailand neither disclosed the currencies in the basket nor the weights. Unofficially, it was known that the currencies composing the basket were: US Dollar, Japanese Yen and German Mark. The fact that the public was not aware of the values of the basket weights, also enabled the monetary authorities to secretly adjust their values in order to react to changes in economic fundamentals and/or speculative pressures. Therefore one could express the USD/THB exchange rate in the following way:

$$Y_{USD/THB,t} = \theta_{USD,t} + \theta_{DEM,t} X_{USD/DEM,t} + \theta_{JPY,t} X_{USD/JPY,t} + \sigma\varepsilon_t.$$

This exchange rate policy had provided Thailand with a good stability of the exchange rate as it can be seen in Figure 15.3. During the same period, though, the interest rates had maintained constantly higher than the ones of the countries composing the basket, as it is shown in Figure 15.4.

This facts suggest the implementation of a speculative strategy, which con sists in borrowing from the countries with a lower interest rate and lending to the ones with an higher interest rate. A formal description of the problem can be made relying on a mean-variance hedging approach, see Musiela and Rutkowski (1997). The optimal investment strategy $\xi_1^*, \ldots, \xi_p^*$ is obtained by the minimization of the quadratic cost function below:

$$E\left\{ \left(Y_{t+h} - \sum_{j=1}^{p} \xi_j X_{j,t+h} \right)^2 \bigg| \mathcal{F}_t \right\}.$$

The solution is:

$$\xi_j^* = E(\theta_{j,t+h} | \mathcal{F}_t) \quad \text{for } j = 1, \ldots, p.$$

It can be seen that, when the interest rates in Thailand (r_0) are sufficiently high with respect to the foreign interest rates $(r_j, \ j = 1, \ldots, p)$ the following inequality holds

$$(1+r_0)^{-1} Y_t < \sum_{j=1}^{p} (1+r_j)^{-1} E(\theta_{j,t+h} | \mathcal{F}_t) X_{j,t}. \tag{15.9}$$

This means that an investment in Thailand is cheaper than an investment with the same expected revenue in the countries composing the basket. In the

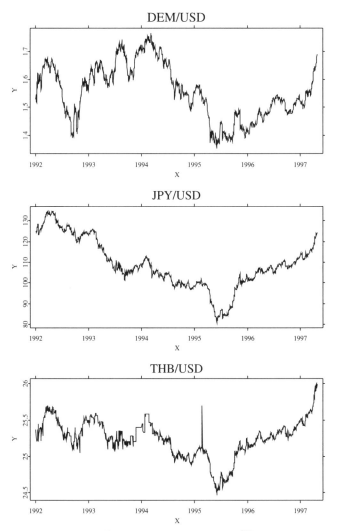

Figure 15.3. Exchange rate time series. Q XFGbasket.xpl

empirical analysis we find out that the relationship (15.9) is fulfilled during
the whole period under investigation for any of the four methods that we use
to estimate the basket weights. Therefore it is possible to construct a mean

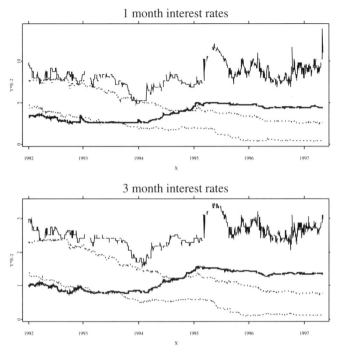

Figure 15.4. Interest rates time series: German (thick dotted line), Japanese (thin dotted line), American (thick straight line), Thai (thin straight line). **Q** XFGbasket.xpl

self-financing strategy which produces a positive expected payoff:

- at time t

  - borrow the portfolio $\sum(1+r_j)^{-1}E(\theta_{j,t+h}|\mathcal{F}_t)X_{j,t}$ from the countries composing the basket,

  - lend $(1+r_0)^{-1}Y_t$ to Thailand,

  - invest the difference $\sum(1+r_j)^{-1}E(\theta_{j,t+h}|\mathcal{F}_t)X_{j,t} - (1+r_0)^{-1}Y_t$ in the numeraire currency at the risk-free rate r_1,

- at time $t+h$

  - withdraw the amount Y_{t+h} from Thailand,

    – pay back the loan of $\sum E(\theta_{j,t+h}|\mathcal{F}_t)X_{j,t+h}$,

    – keep the difference.

The expression for the profit and for its expected value are:

$$\Pi_{t+h} \quad = \quad Y_{t+h} - \sum_{j=1}^{p} E(\theta_{j,t+h}|\mathcal{F}_t)X_{j,t+h}$$

$$+(1+r_1)\left(\sum_{j=1}^{p}(1+r_j)^{-1}E(\theta_{j,t+h}|\mathcal{F}_t)X_{j,t} - (1+r_0)^{-1}Y_t\right)$$

$$E(\Pi_{t+h}|\mathcal{F}_t) \quad = \quad (1+r_1)\left(\sum_{j=1}^{p}(1+r_j)^{-1}E(\theta_{j,t+h}|\mathcal{F}_t)X_{j,t} - (1+r_0)^{-1}Y_t\right).$$

15.2.2   Estimation results

For the implementation of the investment strategy described above one needs the estimate of the, possibly time-varying, basket weights. The precision of the estimation has a direct impact on the economic result of the investment. Therefore, we compare four different estimators of the basket weights: the adaptive, the recursive, the window and the Kalman filter estimator using economic criteria for a one month and for a three month investment horizon. In particular we compute the average expected profit and the average realized profit.

The adaptive estimation procedure requires three parameters: m, λ and μ. The choice of m_0 does not influence the results very much and it can be reasonably set to 30. This value represents the minimal amount of data which are used for the estimation, and in the case of a structural break, the minimal delay before having the chance of detecting the change point. The selection of λ and μ is more critical. These two values determine the sensitivity of the algorithm. Small values would imply a fast reaction to changes in the regressor coefficients, but but they would also lead to the selection of intervals of homogeneity which are possibly too small. Large values would imply a slower reaction and consequently the selection of intervals which can be too large. To overcome this problem we suggest the following approach.

The main idea is that small changes in the values of λ and μ should not affect the estimation results. Therefore we restrict our attention on a set $\mathcal{S}$ of possible

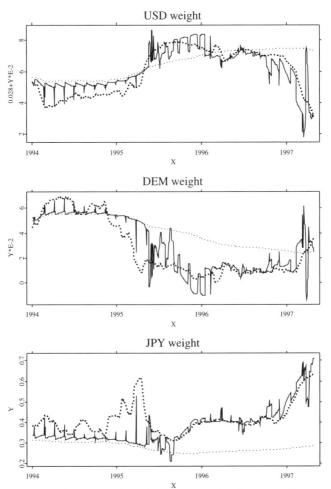

Figure 15.5.   Estimated exchange rate basket weights: adaptive
(straight line), recursive (thine dotted line), window (thick dotted line).

pairs (λ, μ). In the present context we chose all the even number between 2
and 8:

$$\mathcal{S} = \{(\lambda, \mu) | \ \lambda, \ \mu \in \{2, 4, 6, 8\}\}$$

Then we compare the 16 pairs with the following criterion at each time t:

$$(\lambda^*,\mu^*) = \arg\min_{(\lambda,\mu)\in\mathcal{S}} \sum_{s=t-200}^{t-1} \left(Y_s - \sum_{j=1}^{d} \widehat{\theta}_{j,s|s-h} X_{j,s} \right)^2.$$

Finally, we estimate the value of $\widehat{\theta}_{t+h|t}$ with the selected pair (λ^*,μ^*). The appeal of the above selection criterion consists of the fact that it leads to the choice of the pair (λ,μ) which has provided the least quadratic hedging costs over the past trading periods. Notice that in general we have different results depending on the length of the forecasting horizon: here one and three month. Figure 15.5 shows the results for the three month horizon. It is interesting to see that the adaptive estimate tends to coincide with the recursive estimate during the first half of the sample, more or less, while during the second half of the sample it tends to follow the rolling estimate.

We remark that the problem of selecting free parameters is not specific to the adaptive estimator. The window estimator requires the choice of the length of the window: k, while the Kalman filter needs the specification of the data generating process of θ_t and the determination of Σ and σ. In this application k is set equal to 250, Σ and σ are estimated recursively from the data using the OLS, while $\widehat{\theta}_{0|0}$ and $P_{0|0}$ are initialized using the first 350 observations which are then discarded. We remark that this choice is consistent with the one of Christoffersen and Giorgianni (2000).

Table 15.2 shows the result of the simulated investment. The investments are normalized such that at each trading day we take a short position of 100 USD in the optimal portfolio of the hard currencies. The result refers to the period April 9 1993 to February 12 1997 for the one month horizon investment and June 7 1993 to February 12 1997 for the three month horizon investment. Notice first that the *average realized profits* are positive and, as far as the three month investment horizon is concerned, they are significantly larger than zero among all methods. This provides a clear evidence for the fact that arbitrage profits were possible with in the framework of the Thai Bath basket for the period under study. The comparison of the estimator also show the importance of properly accounting for the time variability of the parameters. The recursive estimator shows modest result as far as the realized profits are concerned and the largest bias between expected the realized profit. On one side, the bias is reduced by the window estimator and by the Kalman filter, but on the other side these two methods provide a worse performance as far as the realized profit are concerned. Finally, the adaptive estimator appears to be the best one, its

ONE MONTH HORIZON	Recursive	Window	KF	Adaptive
Average Expected Profits	.772	.565	.505	.553
Average Realized Profit	.403	.401	.389	.420
Standard errors	(.305)	(.305)	(.330)	(.333)
THREE MONTH HORIZON	Recursive	Window	KF	Adaptive
Average Expected Profits	1.627	1.467	1.375	1.455
Average Realized Profit	1.166	1.141	1.147	1.182
Standard errors	(.464)	(.513)	(.475)	(.438)

Table 15.2. Summary statistics of the profits.

bias is much smaller than the one of the recursive estimator and it delivers the largest realized profits for both investment horizons.

15.3 Estimating the volatility of financial time series

The locally time homogeneous approach appears to be also appropriate for the estimation of the volatility of financial time series. In order to provide some motivation we first describe the stylized facts of financial time series. Let S_t define the price process of a financial asset such as stocks or exchange rates, then the returns are defined as follows:

$$R_t = \ln S_t - \ln S_{t-1}.$$

Stylized facts of financial asset returns are: a leptokurtic density, variance clustering and highly persistent autocorrelation of square and absolute returns (see Figure 15.6). Further details and examples on this topic can be found in Taylor (1986) and in Franke, Härdle and Hafner (2001).

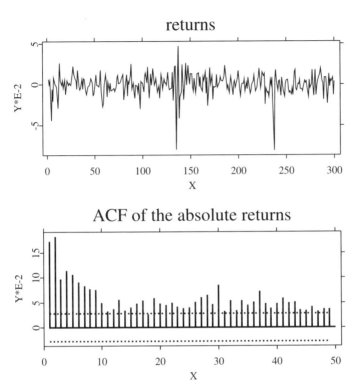

Figure 15.6. JPY/USD returns ◘XFGretacf.xpl

15.3.1   The standard approach

The returns of financial time series are usually modeled by the following equation:

$$R_t = \sigma_t \varepsilon_t$$

Where σ_t is a strictly positive process, which describes the dynamics of the variance of R_t, and ξ_t has a standard normal distribution: $\xi_t \sim N(0,1)$. Standard parametric models of the volatility are of (G)ARCH type:

$$\sigma_t^2 = \omega + \alpha R_{t-1}^2 + \beta \sigma_{t-1}^2,$$

like in Engle (1995) and Bollerslev (1995), and of stochastic volatility type:

$$\ln \sigma_t^2 = \theta_0 + \theta_1 \ln \sigma_{t-1}^2 + \nu_t,$$

as described by Harvey, Ruiz and Shephard (1995). These models have been
expanded in order to incorporate other characteristics of the financial return
time series: TARCH, EGARCH and QARCH explicitly assume an asymmetric reaction of the volatility process to the sign of the observed returns, while
IGARCH and FIGARCH model the long memory structure of the autocorrelations of the square returns.

15.3.2   The locally time homogeneous approach

A common feature to all the models which have been cited in the previous
section is that they completely describe the volatility process by a finite set of
parameters. The availability of very large samples of financial data has given
the possibility of constructing models which display quite complicated param-
eterizations in order to explain all the observed stylized facts. Obviously those
models rely on the assumption that the parametric structure of the process
remains constant through the whole sample. This is a nontrivial and possibly dangerous assumption in particular as far as forecasting is concerned as
pointed out in Clements and Hendry (1998). Furthermore checking for parameter instability becomes quite difficult if the model is nonlinear, and/or the
number of parameters is large. Whereby those characteristics of the returns
which are often explained by the long memory and (fractal) integrated nature
of the volatility process, could also depend on the parameters being time varying. We want to suggest an alternative approach which relies on a locally time
homogeneous parameterization, i.e. we assume that the volatility σ follows a
jump process and is constant over some unknown interval of time homogeneity.
The adaptive algorithm, which has been presented in the previous sections,
also applies in this case; its aim consists in the data-driven estimation of the
interval of time homogeneity, after which the estimate of the volatility can be
simply obtained by local averaging.

15.3.3   Modeling volatility via power transformation

Let S_t be an observed asset process in discrete time, $t = 1, 2, \ldots, \tau$ and R_t
are the corresponding returns: $R_t = \log(S_t/S_{t-1})$. We model this process via

the *conditional heteroscedasticity* assumption

$$R_t = \sigma_t \varepsilon_t, \tag{15.10}$$

where ε_t, $t \geq 1$, is a sequence of independent standard Gaussian random variables and σ_t is the *volatility* process which is in general a predictable random process, that is, σ_t is measurable with respect to $\mathcal{F}_{t-1}$ with $\mathcal{F}_{t-1} = \sigma(R_1, \ldots, R_{t-1})$.

The model equation (15.10) links the volatility σ_t with the observations R_t via the multiplicative errors ε_t. In order to apply the theory presented in Section 15.1 we need a regression like model with additive errors. For this reason we consider the power transformation, which leads to a regression with additive noise and so that the noise is close to a Gaussian one, see Carroll and Ruppert (1988). Due to (15.10) the random variable R_t is conditionally on $\mathcal{F}_{t-1}$ Gaussian and it holds

$$\mathrm{E}\left(R_t^2 | \mathcal{F}_{t-1}\right) = \sigma_t^2.$$

Similarly, for every $\gamma > 0$,

$$\mathrm{E}\left(|R_t|^\gamma | \mathcal{F}_{t-1}\right) = \sigma_t^\gamma \mathrm{E}\left(|\xi|^\gamma | \mathcal{F}_{t-1}\right) = C_\gamma \sigma_t^\gamma,$$

$$\mathrm{E}\left(|R_t|^\gamma - C_\gamma \sigma_t^\gamma | \mathcal{F}_{t-1}\right)^2 = \sigma_t^{2\gamma} \mathrm{E}\left(|\xi|^\gamma - C_\gamma\right)^2 = \sigma_t^{2\gamma} D_\gamma^2$$

where ξ denotes a standard Gaussian r.v., $C_\gamma = \mathrm{E}|\xi|^\gamma$ and $D_\gamma^2 = \mathrm{Var}|\xi|^\gamma$. Therefore, the process $|R_t|^\gamma$ allows for the representation

$$|R_t|^\gamma = C_\gamma \sigma_t^\gamma + D_\gamma \sigma_t^\gamma \zeta_t, \tag{15.11}$$

where ζ_t is equal $\left(|\xi|^\gamma - C_\gamma\right)/D_\gamma$. A suitable choice of the value of γ provides that the distribution of

$$\left(|\xi|^\gamma - C_\gamma\right)/D_\gamma$$

is close to the normal. In particular the value of $\gamma = 0.5$ appears to be almost optimal, see Figure 15.7.

15.3.4   Adaptive estimation under local time-homogeneity

The assumption of local time homogeneity means that the function σ_t is constant within an interval $I = [\tau - m, \tau]$, and the process R_t follows the

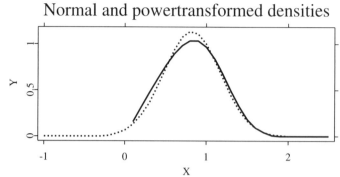

Figure 15.7.   Normal and power transformed densities for $\gamma = 0.5$.
▣ XFGpowtrans.xpl

regression-like equation (15.11) with the constant trend $\theta_I = C_\gamma \sigma_I^\gamma$ which can
be estimated by averaging over this interval I:

$$\widehat{\theta}_I = \frac{1}{|I|} \sum_{t \in I} |R_t|^\gamma. \tag{15.12}$$

By (15.11)

$$\widehat{\theta}_I = \frac{C_\gamma}{|I|} \sum_{t \in I} \sigma_t^\gamma + \frac{D_\gamma}{|I|} \sum_{t \in I} \sigma_t^\gamma \zeta_t = \frac{1}{|I|} \sum_{t \in I} \theta_t + \frac{s_\gamma}{|I|} \sum_{t \in I} \theta_t \zeta_t \tag{15.13}$$

with $s_\gamma = D_\gamma / C_\gamma$ so that

$$\mathrm{E}\widehat{\theta}_I = \mathrm{E}\frac{1}{|I|} \sum_{t \in I} \theta_t, \tag{15.14}$$

$$\frac{s_\gamma^2}{|I|^2} \mathrm{E} \left(\sum_{t \in I} \theta_t \zeta_t \right)^2 = \frac{s_\gamma^2}{|I|^2} \mathrm{E} \sum_{t \in I} \theta_t^2. \tag{15.15}$$

Define also

$$v_I^2 = \frac{s_\gamma^2}{|I|^2} \sum_{t \in I} \theta_t^2.$$

In view of (15.15) this value is called the *conditional variance* of $\widehat{\theta}_I$. Under local homogeneity it holds θ_t is constantly equal to θ_I for $t \in I$, and hence,

$$\mathrm{E}\widehat{\theta}_I = \theta_I$$

$$v_I^2 = \mathrm{Var}\,\widehat{\theta}_I = \frac{s_\gamma^2 \theta_I^2}{|I|}.$$

A probability bound analogous to the one in Section 15.1 holds also in this case. Let the volatility coefficient σ_t satisfy the condition $b \leq \sigma_t^2 \leq bB$ with some constants $b > 0$, $B > 1$. Then there exists $a_\gamma > 0$ such that it holds for every $\lambda \geq 0$

$$\mathrm{P}\left(|\widehat{\theta}_I - \theta_\tau| > \lambda v_I\right) \leq 4\sqrt{e}\lambda(1 + \log B)\exp\left(-\frac{\lambda^2}{2a_\gamma}\right). \tag{15.16}$$

The proof of the statement above and some related theoretical results can be found in Mercurio and Spokoiny (2000).

For practical application one has to substitute the unknown conditional standard deviation with its estimate: $\widehat{v}_I = s_\gamma \widehat{\theta}_I |I|^{-1/2}$. Under the assumption of time homogeneity within an interval $I = [\tau - m, \tau]$ equation (15.16) allows to bound $|\widehat{\theta}_I - \widehat{\theta}_J|$ by $\lambda \widehat{v}_I + \mu \widehat{v}_J$ for any $J \subset I$, provided that λ and μ are sufficiently large. Therefore we can apply the same algorithm described in Section 15.1 in order to estimate the largest interval of time homogeneity and the related value of $\widehat{\theta}_\tau$. Here, as in the previous section, we are faced with the choice of three tuning parameters: m_0, λ, and μ. Simulation studies and repeated trying on real data by Mercurio and Spokoiny (2000) have shown that the choice of m_0 is not particularly critical and it can be selected between 10 and 50 without affecting the overall results of the procedure.

As described in Section 15.2.2, the choice of λ and μ is more delicate. The influence of λ and μ is similar to the one of the smoothing parameters in the nonparametric regression. The likelihood of rejecting a time homogeneous interval decreases with increasing λ and/or μ. This is clear from equation (15.6). Therefore if λ and μ are too large this would make the algorithm too conservative, increasing the bias of the estimator, while too small values of λ and μ would lead to a frequent rejection and to a high variability of the estimate. Once again, a way of choosing the optimal values of λ and μ can be made through the minimization of the squared forecast error. One has to define a finite set S of the admissible pair of λ and μ. Then for each pair belonging to $\mathcal{S}$ one can compute the corresponding estimate: $\widehat{\theta}_t^{(\lambda,\mu)}$ and then select the optimal pair and the corresponding estimate by the following criterion:

$$(\widehat{\lambda}, \widehat{\mu}) = \min_{\lambda,\mu \in \mathcal{S}} \sum_{t=0}^{T} \left(|R_t|^\gamma - \widehat{\theta}_t^{(\lambda,\mu)} \right)^2.$$

Figure 15.8 shows the result of the on-line estimation of the locally time homogeneous volatility model for the JPY/USD exchange rate. The bottom plot, in particular, shows the estimated length of the interval of time homogeneity: $\widehat{m}$, at each time point.

15.4   Technical appendix

In this section we give the precise conditions under which the bound (15.4) holds. Define:

$$V_I = \sigma^{-2} \sum_{t \in I} X_t X_t^\top \qquad W_I = V_I^{-1},$$

furthermore let $w_{ij,I}$ denote the elements of W_I. For some positive constants $b > 0$, $B > 1$, $\rho < 1$, $r \geq 1$, $\lambda > \sqrt{2}$ and for $i = 1 \ldots p$ consider the random set were the following conditions are fulfilled:

$$A_{i,I} \;=\; \left\{ \begin{array}{c} b \leq w_{jj,I}^{-1} \leq bB \\[2mm] \sup\limits_{\{\mu \in \mathbb{R}^K : ||\mu|| = 1\}} ||V_I \mu||_2 w_{jj,I} \leq r \\[2mm] |w_{ji,I}/w_{jj,I}| \leq \rho \quad \forall i = 1, \ldots, p \end{array} \right\}$$

Let $(Y_1, X_1) \ldots (Y_\tau, X_\tau)$ obey (15.1), where the regressors are possibly stochastic, then it holds holds for the estimate $\widehat{\theta}_I$:

$$\mathrm{P}\left(|\widehat{\theta}_{i,I} - \theta_{i,\tau}| > \lambda \sqrt{w_{ii,I}} \,;\, A_{i,I} \right)$$
$$\leq 4e\ln(4B)(1 + 2\rho\sqrt{r(d-1)}\lambda)^{p-1}\lambda \exp(-\lambda^2/2), \qquad i = 1, \ldots, p.$$

A proof of this statement can be found in Liptser and Spokoiny (1999). For a further generalization, where the hypothesis of local time homogeneity holds only approximatively, see Härdle et al. (2000).

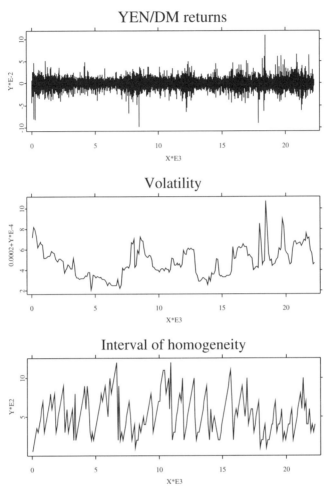

Figure 15.8. From the top: returns, estimated locally time homogeneous volatility and estimated length of the interval of time homogeneity. Q XFGlochom.xpl

Bibliography

Bollerslev, T. (1995). Generalised autoregressive conditional heteroskedasticity, *in* Engle (1995).

Carroll, R. and Ruppert, D. (1988). *Transformation and Weighting in Regression*, Chapman and Hall, New York.

Christoffersen, P. and Giorgianni, L. (2000). Interest rate in currency basket: Forecasting weights and measuring risk, *Journal of Business and Economic Statistics* **18**: 321–335.

Chui, C. and Chen, G. (1998). *Kalman Filtering*, Information Sciences, third edn, Springer-Verlag, Berlin.

Clements, M. P. and Hendry, D. F. (1998). *Forecastng Economic Time Series*, Cambridge University Press, Cambridge.

Cooley, T. F. and Prescott, E. C. (1973). An adaptive regression model, *International Economic Review* **14**: 364–371.

Eichengreen, B., Masson, P., Savastano, M. and Sharma, S. (1999). *Transition Strategies and Nominal Anchors on the Road to Greater Exchange Rate Flexibility*, number 213 in *Essays in International Finance*, Princeton University Press.

Elliot, R. J., Aggoun, L. and Moore, J. B. (1995). *Hidden Markov Models*, Springer-Verlag, Berlin.

Engle, R. F. (ed.) (1995). *ARCH, selected readings*, Oxford University Press, Oxford.

Franke, J., Härdle, W. and Hafner, C. (2001). *Einführung in die Statistik der Finanzmärkte*, Springer, Berlin.

Härdle, W., Herwartz, H. and Spokoiny, V. (2001). Time inhomogeous multiple volatility modelling. Discussion Paper 7, Sonderforschungsbereich 373, Humboldt-Universität zu Berlin. To appear in *Financial Econometrics*.

Härdle, W., Spokoiny, V. and Teyssière, G. (2000). Adaptive estimation for a time inhomogeneouse stochastic volatility model. Discussion Paper 6, Sonderforschungsbereich 373, Humboldt-Universität zu Berlin.

Harvey, A., Ruiz, E. and Shephard, N. (1995). Multivariate stochastic variance models, *in* Engle (1995).

Lepski, O. (1990). One problem of adaptive estimation in gaussian white noise, *Theory Probab. Appl.* **35**: 459–470.

Lepski, O. and Spokoiny, V. (1997). Optimal pointwise adaptive methods in nonparametric estimation, *Annals of Statistics* **25**: 2512–2546.

Liptser, R. and Spokoiny, V. (1999). Deviation probability bound for martingales with applications to statistical estimation, *Stat. & Prob. Letter* **46**: 347–357.

Mercurio, D. and Spokoiny, V. (2000). Statistical inference for time-inhomogeneous volatility models. Discussion Paper 583, Weierstrass Institute for Applied Analysis and Stochastic, Berlin.

Mercurio, D. and Torricelli, C. (2001). Estimation and arbitrage opportunities for exchange rate baskets. Discussion Paper 37, Sonderforschungsbereich 373, Humboldt-Universität zu Berlin.

Musiela, M. and Rutkowski, M. (1997). *Martingale Methods in Financial Modelling*, number 36 in *Application of Mathemathics. Stochastic Modelling and Applied Probability*, Springer, New York.

Spokoiny, V. (1998). Estimation of a function with discontinuities via local polynomial fit with an adaptive window choice, *Annals of Statistics* **26**: 1356–1378.

Taylor, S. J. (1986). *Modelling Financial Time Series*, Wiley, Chichester.

16 Simulation based Option Pricing

Jens Lüssem and Jürgen Schumacher

16.1 Simulation techniques for option pricing

We introduce Monte Carlo techniques and Quasi Monte Carlo techniques for option pricing. First, we give an idea how to use simulation techniques to determine option prices, then - using the developed basic methods - we give examples how to price more complex i.e. exotic options even on more than one underlying. Finally we present a short guideline how to price exotic options with the proposed techniques.

First, we take a look at a European put on one underlying stock, a pricing problem which can be solved analytically e.g. by using the Black-Scholes formula. We start with this problem not only because it has become a kind of "standard problem" but also to have the possibility to compare the results of our approximation with an analytical solution. At the same time we look at the time-complexity of the used simulation technique. Next, we show how to price path dependent options with Monte Carlo methods. Afterwards, we show how to price a stock option on several underlyings. This implies that we have to solve a multi-dimensional simulation problem.

16.1.1 Introduction to simulation techniques

The idea behind randomized algorithms is that a random sample from a population (of input variables) is representative for the whole population. As a consequence, a randomized algorithm can be interpreted as a probability distribution on a set of deterministic algorithms.

We will see that there are three main advantages to randomized algorithms: 1. Performance: For many problems, it can be shown that randomized algorithms run faster than the best known deterministic algorithm. 2. Simplicity: Randomized algorithms are easier to describe and implement than comparable deterministic algorithms. 3. Flexibility: Randomized algorithms can be easily adapted.

In general one distinguishes two types of randomized algorithms. Las Vegas algorithms are randomized algorithms that always give correct results with only the variation from one run to another being its running time. Monte Carlo algorithms are randomized algorithms that may produce an incorrect solution for which one can bound the probability of occurrence. The quality of the solution can be seen as a random variable.

Within this chapter, we focus on Monte Carlo algorithms calculating the value of the following integral

$$\int_{[0,1]^d} f(x)dx \tag{16.1}$$

by evaluation of $f(x)$ for independent uniform distributed random vectors $X_1, X_2, \ldots, X_n$, $X_i \in [0,1]^d$.

The arithmetic mean of the values $f(X_i)$ can be seen as a guess for the expected value of the random variable $f(X_i)$ and therefore can be interpreted as an approximation for the value of the integral. According to the strong law of large numbers the estimator for the expected value (the arithmetic mean of the random function values) is converging to the expected value (the value of the integral) with an increasing sample size. The probability that the absolute error of the approximation result exceeds a fixed positive value ϵ is limited and decreases to zero with an increasing sample size if the variance of f is finite.

16.1.2 Pricing path independent European options on one underlying

For the case of a European option on one underlying we have to approximate the following integral via Monte Carlo simulation:

$$e^{r(T-t)}\mathrm{E}\left[C_T(S_T)|S_t\right] \;=\; \int_0^\infty C_T(S_T)g(S_T|S_t,r,\sigma,T-t)dS_T \tag{16.2}$$

$$=\; \int_{[0,1)} C_T\{f(x,S_t,r,\sigma,T-t)\}dx \tag{16.3}$$

Where

$$g(S_T|S_t, r, \sigma, T - t) = \frac{\exp\left\{-\frac{(\log S_T - (\log S_t - (r - 0.5\sigma^2)(T - t)))^2}{2\sigma^2(T - t)}\right\}}{\sqrt{2\pi\sigma^2(T - t)}S_T}$$

is the risk neutral density function of the Black Scholes model with parameters:

S_T :   price of the underlying at maturity
S_t :   price of the underlying at time t
r :   risk free interest rate
σ :   volatility of log returns of the underlying
$T - t$:   time to maturity

$$S_T = f(x, S_t, r, \sigma, T - t) = S_t \exp\{(r - \frac{1}{2}\sigma^2)(T - t) + \sigma\sqrt{T - t}F^{-1}(x)\}$$

transforms the uniform distributed values x in $g(S_T|S_t, r, \sigma, T - t)$ distributed underlying values S_T. $F^{-1}(x)$ is the inverse of the cumulative normal distribution function and $C_T(y)$ is the payoff function of the option.

The Monte Carlo simulation calculates the value of the integral in the following way:

1. n independent random underlying values $S_T^1 \ldots S_T^n$ are generated by computing $f(x, S_t, r, \sigma, T - t)$ for a set of uniformly distributed pseudo random numbers $X_1, \ldots, X_n$.

2. the option payoff $C_T(S_T^i)$ is calculated for each S_T^i.

3. the value of the integral in (16.3) is then approximated by the arithmetic mean of the option payoffs:

$$\bar{C} = \frac{1}{n} \sum_{i=1}^{n} C_T(S_T^i)$$

We will now derive an estimate of the approximation error of the arithmetic mean. We assume that $S_T^1 \ldots S_T^n$ are independent random underlying samples of the $g(S_T|S_t, r, \sigma, T - t)$ density. Using this assumption we can conclude that $\bar{C}$ is a random variable with expected value

$$\mathrm{E}[\bar{C}] = e^{r(T - t)}C_t(S_t)$$

Additionally we have to assume that the variance of the option payoffs $C_T(S_T)$ is given by:

$$\text{Var}\left[C_T(S_T)\right] = \int_{[0,\infty]} C_T(S_T)^2 g(S_T|S_t, r, \sigma, T - t) dS_T - \text{E}\left[C_T(S_T)\right]^2 \quad (16.4)$$

exists. Then we get:

$$\text{Var}\left[\bar{C}\right] = \frac{1}{n^2} \sum_{i=1}^{n} \text{Var}\left[C_T(S_T^i)\right] = \frac{1}{n} \text{Var}\left[C_T(S_T)\right] \quad (16.5)$$

because of the independence of $S_T^1, \ldots, S_T^n$.

The expected value of the random variable $\bar{C}$ equals the value of the integral $e^{r(T-t)} C_t(S_t)$ and its variance converges to zero with increasing n. The probability that the approximation error is greater than a fixed positive value decreases to 0 with an increasing number n. A first estimation of the error is given by the Chebychev inequality for $\bar{C}$,

$$\text{P}\left(|\bar{C} - e^{r(T-t)} C_t(S_t)| \geq a\right) \leq \frac{\frac{1}{n} \text{Var}\left[C_T(S_T)\right]}{a^2}$$

The bound given by this equation is rather imprecise since we do not make any assumptions on the distribution of the random variable. Only the expected value and the variance are used in the previous equation. According to the central limit theorem the distribution of $\bar{C}$ converges to a normal distribution for $n \to \infty$. It follows that the difference between the approximation and the integral, $\bar{C} - e^{r(T-t)} C_t(S_t)$ is approximately normally distributed with mean 0 and standard deviation

$$\sigma_{\bar{C}} = \sqrt{\frac{\text{Var}\left[C_T(S_T)\right]}{n}} \quad (16.7)$$

for large n. According to Boyle (1977) a value of $n > 1000$ is sufficiently large in order to use the normal distribution for error estimation purposes.

We get the following equation if we assume that $\bar{C} - e^{r(T-t)} C_t(S_t)$ is normal distributed:

$$\text{P}\left(\left|\bar{C} - e^{r(T-t)} C_t(S_t)\right| \leq \epsilon\right) = \frac{1}{\sqrt{2\pi}} \int_{-\epsilon}^{\epsilon} \exp\left\{-\frac{u^2}{2\sigma_{\bar{C}}}\right\} du \quad (16.8)$$

If we choose k as a multiple of the standard deviation $\sigma_{\bar{C}}$ of $\bar{C}$, then we get:

$$
\begin{aligned}
\mathrm{P}\left(\left|\bar{C} - e^{r(T-t)}C_t(S_t)\right| \le k\sigma_{\bar{C}}\right) &= \mathrm{P}\left(\frac{\left|\bar{C} - e^{r(T-t)}C_t(S_t)\right|}{\sigma_{\bar{C}}} \le k\right) \\
&= \frac{1}{\sqrt{2\pi}}\int_{-k}^{k}\exp\left\{-\frac{u^2}{2}\right\}du \\
&= p
\end{aligned}
\tag{16.9}
$$

Given a fixed probability level p, the error converges to zero with $\mathcal{O}(1/\sqrt{n})$. The error interval holds for $k = 1, 2, 3$ with the respective probabilities $p = 0.682, 0.955, 0.997$

The confidence intervals for a given probability level depend on the standard deviation of the payoff function $C_T(S_T)$:

$$
\sigma_{C_T} = \sqrt{\operatorname{Var}\left[C_T(S_T)\right]}\,.
\tag{16.10}
$$

In general, this standard deviation cannot be calculated with analytical methods. Therefore one calculates the empirical standard deviation $\bar{\sigma}$ and uses it as a proxy for the error bounds:

$$
\bar{\sigma} = \sqrt{\frac{1}{n-1}\sum_{k=1}^{n}\left\{C_T(S_T^i) - \bar{C}\right\}^2}\,.
\tag{16.11}
$$

Figure 16.1 shows the evolution of the absolute error of the price for a European call option calculated by Monte Carlo methods compared with the analytic solution. One can observe that the error tends to zero with $\mathcal{O}\left(1/\sqrt{n}\right)$.

We would like to give some of the main properties of algorithms using Monte Carlo techniques. First from (16.9) it follows that the error bound tends to zero with $\mathcal{O}\left(1/\sqrt{n}\right)$ for a fixed probability level p. Second, the probability that a fixed error bound holds converges to 1 with $\mathcal{O}\left(1/\sqrt{n}\right)$, Mavin H. Kalos (1986). Since these results hold independent of the dimension of the problem, which affects only the variance of the payoff function with respect to the Black-Scholes risk neutral density, the Monte Carlo method is especially well suited for the evaluation of option prices in multidimensional settings. Competing pricing methods e.g finite differences have exponential growing computational costs in

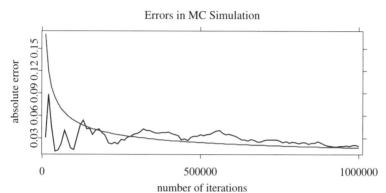

Figure 16.1.   Absolute error of a European Call option price calculated by Monte Carlo simulations vs. $n^{-1/2}$

the dimension of the problem. Another advantage of the Monte Carlo pricing method is the error estimate given by the empirical standard deviation which can be computed with a small additional effort.

The two most important drawbacks of the Monte Carlo simulation, mentioned in literature are its small convergence speed compared to other techniques for options on few underlyings and the difficulties occurring for options with early exercise possibilities. For example, American options giving the investor the possibility to exercise the option at any time before and at maturity, are difficult to price. To evaluate an American option means to find an optimal exercise strategy which leads - using only basic Monte Carlo techniques - to a recursive algorithm with exponential time-complexity. But more advanced techniques using importance sampling methods show that Monte Carlo simulations can be applied to evaluate American contracts, Broadie (2000).

16.1.3   Pricing path dependent European options on one underlying

There are two categories of options. Path-independent options are options whose payoff depends only on the underlying prices at maturity. Path-dependent options are options whose payoff depends on underlying price outcomes $S_{t_1}, \ldots, S_{t_m}$ at several time points $t_1 \leq \ldots \leq t_m$ within the lifetime of the respective option.

Within the group of path-dependent options one can distinguish options with a payoff function depending on a continuously defined path variable and options with a payoff function depending on a fixed number of underlying values. The price of an option with many - usually equally spaced - exercise dates is often approximated by the price of an option with a continuously defined path variable and vice versa.

Examples for path-dependent options are barrier options, lookback options, and Asian options. The latter have a payoff function which is linked to the average value of the underlying on a specific set of dates during the life of the option. One distinguishes two basic forms of Asian options: options on the geometric mean (for which the price can be calculated with standard techniques) and options on the arithmetic mean (for which the price can not be determined using standard approaches). Asian options are frequently used in commodity markets. The volatility of the underlying prices of the commodities is usually very high so that prices for vanilla options are more expensive than for comparable Asian-style options.

16.1.4 Pricing options on multiple underlyings

In this section we show how to extend the Monte Carlo simulation technique to higher dimensions. The problem is not only that one has to deal with higher dimensional integrals, but also that one has to incorporate the underlying correlation structure between the considered securities. In our framework we need the covariance matrix of the log returns on an annual basis.

In general, a basket option is an option on several underlyings (a basket of underlyings). Basket options can be European-, American or even Asian-style options. Normally, the average of the underlying prices is taken to calculate the price of the basket option, but sometimes other functions are used.

The advantage of the usage of basket options instead of a series of one dimensional options is that the correlation between securities is taken into account. This may lead to better portfolio hedges. We will look at a basket option on five underlyings where the underlying price of the best security in the basket is taken to calculate the option price.

16.2   Quasi Monte Carlo (QMC) techniques for option pricing

16.2.1   Introduction to Quasi Monte Carlo techniques

QMC methods can be considered as an alternative to Monte Carlo simulation. Instead of (pseudo) random numbers, Quasi Monte Carlo algorithms use the elements of low discrepancy sequences to simulate underlying values.

The discrepancy of a set of points $P \subset [0,1]^s$ measures how evenly these points are distributed in the unit cube. The general measure of discrepancy is given by:

$$D_n(\mathcal{B}; P) := \sup_{B \in \mathcal{B}} \left| \frac{A(B; P)}{n} - \lambda_s(B) \right| \qquad (16.12)$$

where $A(B; P)$ is the number of points in P belonging to B, $\lambda_s(B)$ is the Lebesgue measure of the set B, $\mathcal{B}$ is a family of Lebesgue measurable subsets of $[0,1]^s$, and n is the number of elements in P.

The discrepancy of a set is the largest difference between the number of points in a subset and the measure of the subset. If we define $\mathcal{B}$ to be the family $\mathcal{J}$ of subintervals $\prod_{i=1}^{s}[0, u_i)$, then we get a special measure, the star-discrepancy:

$$D_n^*(P) := D_n(\mathcal{J}; P) \qquad (16.13)$$

16.2.2   Error bounds

For the star-discrepancy measure and reasonable assumption on the nature of the function that has to be integrated an upper bound on the error is given by the following theorem:

THEOREM 16.1 (Koksma-Hlawka) *If the function f is of finite variation $V(f)$ in the sense of Hardy and Krause, then the following equation holds for all sets of points $\{x_1, \ldots, x_n\} \subset I^s = [0,1]^s$*

$$\left| \frac{1}{n} \sum_{i=1}^{n} f(x_i) - \int_{I^s} f(u)du \right| \leq V(f) D_n^*(x_1, \ldots, x_n) \qquad (16.14)$$

A proof is given in Niederreiter (1992).

This means that the error is bounded from above by the product of the variation $V(f)$, which in our case is model and payoff dependent and the star-discrepancy of the sequence. The bound cannot be used for an automatic error estimation since the variation and the star-discrepancy cannot be computed easily. It has been shown though that sequences exist with a star-discrepancy of the order $\mathcal{O}(n^{-1}(\ln n)^s)$. All sequences with this asymptotic upper bound are called low-discrepancy sequences Niederreiter (1992).   One particular low-discrepancy sequence is the Halton sequence.

16.2.3   Construction of the Halton sequence

We start with the construction of the one-dimensional Halton sequence within the interval $[0,1]$. An element of this sequence is calculated by using the following equation:

$$x_i = \sum_{k=0}^{\infty} n_{k,i} p^{-k-1} \tag{16.15}$$

with $i > 0$, $p = 2$ and $n_{k,i}$ determined by the following equation:

$$i = \sum_{k=0}^{\infty} n_{k,i} p^k; \quad 0 \le n_{k,i} < p; \; n_{k,i} \in \mathbb{N} \tag{16.16}$$

Note that with the above equation $n_{k,i}$ is a function of i and takes values only in $\{0;1\}$. To illustrate the algorithm we calculate the first three points.

$i = 1$: $n_{0,1} = 1$, $n_{k,1} = 0$ for every $k > 0$

$i = 2$: $n_{1,2} = 1$, $n_{k,2} = 0$ for every $k \ne 1$

$i = 3$: $n_{0,3} = n_{1,3} = 1$, $n_{k,3} = 0$ for every $k > 1$

Therefore we get the sequence $1/2, 1/4, 3/4, 1/8, 5/8, ...$ The extension of this construction scheme to higher dimensions is straightforward. For every dimension $j = 1, \ldots, d$ we define x_i^j by

$$x_i^j = \sum_{k=0}^{\infty} n_{k,i}(j) p_j^{-k-1} \tag{16.17}$$

with p_j is the jth smallest prime number and $n_{k,i}(j)$ is calculated as follows:

$$i = \sum_{k=0}^{\infty} n_{k,i}(j) p_j^k; \quad 0 \leq n_{k,i}(j) < p_j; \; n_{k,i}(j) \in \mathbb{N} \; \forall j \qquad (16.18)$$

By using $p_1 = 2$, $p_2 = 3$ we get the following two-dimensional Halton sequence: $(1/2; 1/3), (1/4; 2/3), \dots$ In contrast to grid discretization schemes like i/n $i = 1, \dots, n$ low-discrepancy sequences fill the integration space in an incremental way avoiding the exponential growth of grid points of conventional schemes.

XploRe provides quantlets to generate pseudo random numbers and low discrepancy sequences. For the generation of the pseudo random numbers we use

```
erg = randomnumbers (seqnum,d,n)
     generates n pseudo random vectors of dimension d
```

where **seqnum** is the number of the random generator according to Table 16.1, **d** is the dimension of the random vector and **n** the number of vectors generated.

0	Park and Miller with Bays-Durham shuffle
1	L'Ecuyer with Bays-Durham shuffle
2	Knuth
3	generator from G. Marsaglia et al. Marsaglia (1993)
4	random number generator of your system
5	generator from ACM TOMS 17:98-111
6	multiply with carry gen. (Marsaglia) Marsaglia (1993)

Table 16.1. Random generator that can be used in XploRe

The generation of low discrepancy sequences is provided by

```
erg = lowdiscrepancy (seqnum,d,n)
     generates the first n low discrepancy sequence vectors of dimen-
     sion d
```

where **seqnum** is the number of the low discrepancy sequence according to Table 16.2.

0	Halton sequence
1	Sobol sequence
2	Faure sequence
3	Niederreiter sequence

Table 16.2.   Low-discrepancy sequences available in XploRe,
(Niederreiter, 1992) .

16.2.4   Experimental results

Figure 16.2 shows that two dimensional Halton points are much more equally
spaced than pseudo random points. This leads to a smaller error at least for
"smooth" functions.

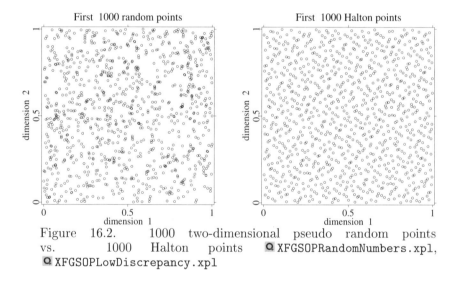

Figure   16.2.   1000   two-dimensional   pseudo   random   points
vs.   1000   Halton   points   ⧠ XFGSOPRandomNumbers.xpl,
⧠ XFGSOPLowDiscrepancy.xpl

The positive effect of using more evenly spread points for the simulation task
is shown in Figure 16.3. The points of a low-discrepancy sequence are designed
in order to fill the space evenly without any restrictions on the independence
of sequence points where as the pseudo random points are designed to show no
statistically significant deviation from the independence assumption. Because
of the construction of the low discrepancy sequences one cannot calculate an

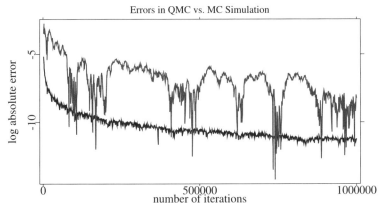

Figure 16.3. Absolute error of a random sequence and the Halton sequence for a put option

empirical standard deviation of the estimator like for Monte Carlo methods and derive an error approximation for the estimation. One possible way out of this dilemma is the randomization of the low-discrepancy sequences using pseudo random numbers i.e. to shift the original quasi random numbers with pseudo random numbers Tuffin (1996). If $x_1, \ldots, x_n$ are scalar elements of a low-discrepancy sequence X then we can define a new low discrepancy sequence

$$W(\epsilon) = \{y_1, \ldots, y_n\} \quad \text{with} \quad y_i = \begin{cases} x_i + \epsilon & x_i + \epsilon <= 1 \\ (x_i + \epsilon) - 1 & \text{otherwise} \end{cases} \quad (16.19)$$

for a uniformly distributed value ϵ. Then we can calculate an empirical standard deviation of the price estimates for different sequences $W(\epsilon)$ for independent values ϵ which can be used as a measure for the error. Experiments with payoff functions for European options show that this randomization technique reduces the convergence rate proportionally.

The advantage of the Quasi Monte Carlo simulation compared to the Monte Carlo simulation vanishes if the dimension increases. Especially the components with a high index number of the first elements in low-discrepancy sequences are not evenly distributed Niederreiter (1992). Figure 16.4 shows that the 49th and 50th component of the first 1000 Halton points are not evenly distributed. But the result for the first 10000 points of the sequence shows that the points become more evenly spread if the number of points increases.

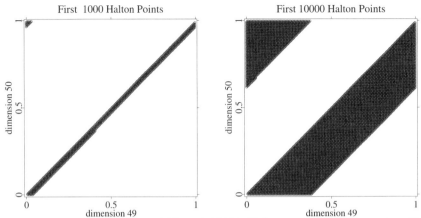

Figure 16.4. The first 1000 and 10000 Halton points of dimension 49 and 50 ⊛ XFGSOPLowDiscrepancy.xpl

However by using the Brownian Bridge path construction method we can limit the effect of the high dimensional components on a simulated underlying path and the corresponding path variable for the most common path dependent options, Morokoff (1996). This method start with an empty path with known start value and calculates at each step the underlying value for a time point with maximum time distance to all other time points with known underlying value until the whole path is computed. Experimental results show that we can still get a faster convergence of the QMC simulation for options up to 50 time points if we apply this path construction method.

16.3   Pricing options with simulation techniques - a guideline

In this section we would like to give a short guideline how to price exotic options with Monte Carlo and Quasi Monte Carlo simulation techniques within the framework described above. Furthermore we give some indications about the limits of these techniques.

16.3.1   Construction of the payoff function

As a first step we have to define the payoff function corresponding to our option product. Within the methods defined in the quantlib finance we have to consider three different cases.

One underlying + path independent

In this case the payoff function is called by the pricing routine with the simulated underlying value at maturity as the single argument. It calculates the corresponding payoff and returns this value. We have defined the payoff function for a put option with strike price 100 as an example for a one dimensional payoff function.

Several underlying + path independent

For options whose payoff depends on the underlying values of several assets at maturity, we have to define a payoff function on the vector of the underlying values at maturity. An example for such an option is an exchange option that permits to swap a defined share with the best performing share in a basket. Its payoff function is given by:

$$C_T((S_T^1, \ldots, S_T^5)) = max\{0, \alpha_i(S_T^i - K^i) + 55 - S_T^3 | i = 1, .., 5\}$$

One underlying + path dependent

The third category of option types that are captured are path dependent options on one underlying. The payoff function of these options depends on the underlying values at several fixed time points during the lifetime of the option. Payoff functions for these contracts are called with a vector of underlying values whose ith element is the underlying value at the time t_i which has to be specified in the model.

16.3.2   Integration of the payoff function in the simulation framework

After defining the payoff function in XploRe we can start to calculate a price estimate with the help of the appropriate simulation routine. In the one dimensional case we just have to call

```
erg = BlackScholesPathIndependent1D (s0,r,vola,dt,opt,
                                                itr,gen)
```
   MC estimation of the option price for a path independent option.

```
erg = BlackScholesPathIndependent1DQMC (s0,r,vola,dt,opt,
                                                  itr,gen)
```
   QMC estimation of the option price for a path independent option.

to get a price estimate and for the Monte Carlo case an empirical standard deviation with respect to a start price of s0, a continuous risk free interest rate of r, a volatility vola, a time to maturity of dt years, the payoff function opt, sample size itr and the random/low-discrepancy generator with number gen. Table 16.1 shows the random number generators and table 16.2 the low-discrepancy generators that can be used. An application of these routines for a Put option can be found in ⊙ XFGSOP1DPut.xpl.

Pricing path-dependent options is only slightly more complicated. Here we have to define the vector of time points for which underlying prices have to be generated. This vector replaces the time to maturity used to price path independent options. Then we can apply one of the following methods to compute a price estimate for the path dependent option

```
erg = BlackScholesPathDependent1D (s0,r,vola,times,opt,
                                               itr,gen)
```
   MC estimation of the option price for path-dependent options.

```
erg = BlackScholesPathDependent1DQMC (s0,r,vola,times,opt,
                                                 itr,gen)
```
   QMC estimation of the option price for path-dependent options, with:

with respect to the start price s0, the continuous risk free interest rate r, the volatility vola, the time scheme times, the payoff function opt, sample size itr and the random/low-discrepancy generator with number gen, as given in Tables 16.1 and 16.2. Using the above quantlets, we calculate the price of an Asian call option in ⊙ XFGSOP1DAsian.xpl.

In the case of multidimensional options we have to define a start price vector
and a covariance matrix instead of a single underlying price and volatility value.
Then we can call one of the multi-dimensional simulation routines:

```
erg = BlackScholesPathIndependentMD (s0,r,vola,dt,opt
                                                ,itr,gen)
        MC estimation of the option price in the multidimensional Black
        Scholes model

erg = BlackScholesPathIndependentMDQMC (s0,r,vola,dt,opt
                                                  ,itr,gen)
        QMC estimation of the option price in the multidimensional
        Black Scholes model
```

with respect to the m dimensional start price vector s0, the continuous risk free
interest rate r, the m×m covariance matrix vola, the time to maturity dt, the
payoff function opt, the number of iterations itr and the generator number
gen according to the generators in Tables 16.1 and 16.2. Both quantlets are
illustrated in **Q** XFGSOPMD.xpl.

If in addition a dividend is paid during the time to maturity, we can use the
following two quantlets to calculate the option prices.

```
erg = BlackScholesPathIndependentMDDiv (s0,r,div,vola
                                              ,dt,opt,itr,gen)
        MC estimation of the option price in the multidimensional Black
        Scholes model

erg = BlackScholesPathIndependentMDDivQMC (s0,r,div,vola
                                                ,dt,opt,itr,gen)
        QMC estimation of the option price in the multidimensional
        Black Scholes model
```

The additional argument div is a m dimensional vector of the continuously paid
dividends. An application of these functions for our basket option is provided
in **Q** XFGSOPMDDiv.xpl.

16.3.3 Restrictions for the payoff functions

Monte Carlo based option pricing methods are not applicable for all types of payoff functions. There is one theoretical, and some practical limitations for the method. Let us look at the theoretical limitation first.

In the derivation of the probabilistic error bounds we have to assume the existence of the payoff variance with respect to the risk neutral distribution. It follows that we are no longer able to derive the presented error bounds if this variance does not exist. However for most payoff functions occurring in practice and the Black Scholes model the difference between the payoff samples and the price can be bounded from above by a polynomial function in the difference between the underlying estimate and the start price for which the integral with respect to the risk neutral density exists. Consequently the variance of these payoff functions must be finite.

Much more important than the theoretical limitations are the practical limitations. In the first place Monte Carlo simulation relies on the quality of the pseudo random number generator used to generate the uniformly distributed samples. All generators used are widely tested, but it can't be guaranteed that the samples generated for a specific price estimation exhibit all assumed statistical properties. It is also important to know that all generators produce the same samples in a fixed length cycle. For example if we use the random number generator from Park and Miller with Bays-Durham shuffle, we will get the same samples after $\approx 10^8$ method invocations.

Another possible error source is the transformation function which converts the uniformly distributed random numbers in normally distributed number. The approximation to the inverse of the normal distribution used in our case has a maximum absolute error of 10^{-15} which is sufficiently good.

The most problematic cases for Monte Carlo based option pricing are options for which the probability of an occurrence of a strictly positive payoff is very small. Then we will get either price and variance estimates based on a few positive samples if we hit the payoff region or we get a zero payoff and variance if this improbable event does not occur. However in both cases we will get a very high relative error. More accurate results may be calculated by applying importance sampling to these options.

Bibliography

Bauer, H. (1991). *Wahrscheinlichkeitstheorie*, W. de Gruyter.

Bosch, K. (1993). *Elementare Einführung in die Wahrscheinlichkeitsrechnung*, Vieweg.

Boyle, P. P. (1977). Options: A monte carlo approach, *Journal of Financial Economics* **4**: 323–338.

Broadie, M., Glasserman, P., and Ha,Z. (2000) Pricing American Options by Simulation Using a Stochastic Mesh with Optimized Weights, *Probabilistic Constrained Optimization: Methodology and Applications*, S. Uryasev ed., Kluwer.

Marsaglia, George (1993) Monkey tests for random number generators, *Computers & Mathematics with Applications* **9**: 1-10.

Niederreiter, H. (1992). *Random number generation and Quasi Monte Carlo methods*, 1 edn, Capital City Press, Monpellier Vermont.

Joy, C.,Boyle, P., and Tan, K. S. (1996). Quasi monte carlo methods in numerical finance, *Management Science* **42**(6): 926–936.

Tuffin, Bruno (1996). On the use of low discrepancy sequences in Monte Carlo Methods, *Technical Report IRISA - Institut de Recherche en Informatique et Systemes Aleatoires* **1060**.

Morokoff, William J.,andCaflish, Russel E. (1996) Quasi-monte carlo simulation of random walks in finance, *In Monte Carlo and Quasi-Monte Carlo methods*, 340-352, University of Salzburg, Springer.

Malvin H. Kalos (1986) *Monte Carlo Methods*, Wiley

17 Nonparametric Estimators of GARCH Processes

Jürgen Franke, Harriet Holzberger and Marlene Müller

The generalized ARCH or GARCH model (Bollerslev, 1986) is quite popular as a basis for analyzing the risk of financial investments. Examples are the estimation of value-at-risk (VaR) or the expected shortfall from a time series of log returns. In practice, a GARCH process of order (1,1) often provides a reasonable description of the data. In the following, we restrict ourselves to that case.

We call $\{\varepsilon_t\}$ a (strong) GARCH (1,1) process if

$$
\begin{aligned}
\varepsilon_t &= \sigma_t Z_t \\
\sigma_t^2 &= \omega + \alpha\,\varepsilon_{t-1}^2 + \beta\,\sigma_{t-1}^2
\end{aligned}
\tag{17.1}
$$

with independent identically distributed innovations Z_t having mean 0 and variance 1. A special case is the integrated GARCH model of order (1,1) or IGARCH(1,1) model where $\alpha + \beta = 1$ and, frequently, $\omega = 0$ is assumed, i.e.

$$
\sigma_t^2 = \alpha\,\varepsilon_{t-1}^2 + (1-\alpha)\,\sigma_{t-1}^2.
$$

This model forms the basis for the J.P. Morgan RiskMetrics VaR analysis using exponential moving averages (Franke, Härdle and Hafner, 2001, Chapter 15). The general GARCH(1,1) process has finite variance $\sigma^2 = \omega/(1-\alpha-\beta)$ if $\alpha + \beta < 1$, and it is strictly stationary if $\mathrm{E}\{\log(\alpha\,Z_t^2 + \beta)\} < 0$. See Franke, Härdle and Hafner (2001, Chapter 12) for these and further properties of GARCH processes.

In spite of its popularity, the GARCH model has one drawback: Its symmetric dependence on past returns does not allow for including the leverage effect into the model, i.e. the frequently made observation that large negative returns of stock prices have a greater impact on volatility than large positive returns. Therefore, various parametric modifications like the exponential

GARCH (EGARCH) or the threshold GARCH (TGARCH) model have been proposed to account for possible asymmetric dependence of volatility on returns. The TGARCH model, for example, introduces an additional term into the volatility equation allowing for an increased effect of negative ε_{t-1} on σ_t^2:

$$\varepsilon_t = \sigma_t Z_t, \quad \sigma_t^2 = \omega + \alpha \varepsilon_{t-1}^2 + \alpha^- \varepsilon_{t-1}^2 \cdot \mathbf{1}(\varepsilon_{t-1} < 0) + \beta \sigma_{t-1}^2.$$

To develop an exploratory tool which allows to study the nonlinear dependence of squared volatility σ_t^2 on past returns and volatilities we introduce a nonparametric GARCH(1,1) model

$$
\begin{aligned}
\varepsilon_t &= \sigma_t Z_t \\
\sigma_t^2 &= g(\varepsilon_{t-1}, \sigma_{t-1}^2)
\end{aligned}
\tag{17.2}
$$

where the innovations Z_t are chosen as above. We consider a nonparametric estimator for the function g based on a particular form of local smoothing. Such an estimate may be used to decide if a particular parametric nonlinear GARCH model like the TGARCH is appropriate.

We remark that the volatility function g cannot be estimated by common kernel or local polynomial smoothers as the volatilities σ_t are not observed directly. Bühlmann and McNeil (1999) have considered an iterative algorithm. First, they fit a common parametric GARCH(1,1) model to the data from which they get sample volatilities $\widehat{\sigma}_t$ to replace the unobservable true volatilities. Then, they use a common bivariate kernel estimate to estimate g from ε_t and $\widehat{\sigma}_t^2$. Using this preliminary estimate for g they obtain new sample volatilities which are used for a further kernel estimate of g. This procedure is iterated several times until the estimate stabilizes.

Alternatively, one could try to fit a nonparametric ARCH model of high order to the data to get some first approximations $\widehat{\sigma}_t^2$ to σ_t^2 and then use a local linear estimate based on the approximate relation

$$\widehat{\sigma}_t^2 \approx g(\varepsilon_{t-1}, \widehat{\sigma}_{t-1}^2).$$

However, a complete nonparametric approach is not feasible as high-order nonparametric ARCH models based on $\sigma_t^2 = g(\varepsilon_{t-1}, \ldots, \varepsilon_{t-p})$ cannot be reliably estimated by local smoothers due to the sparseness of the data in high dimensions. Therefore, one would have to employ restrictions like additivity to the ARCH model, i.e. $\sigma_t^2 = g_1(\varepsilon_{t-1}) + \ldots + g_p(\varepsilon_{t-p})$, or even use a parametric ARCH model $\sigma_t^2 = \omega + \alpha_1 \varepsilon_{t-1}^2 + \ldots + \alpha_p \varepsilon_{t-p}^2$. The alternative we consider here is a direct approach to estimating g based on deconvolution kernel estimates which does not require prior estimates $\widehat{\sigma}_t^2$.

17.1 Deconvolution density and regression estimates

Deconvolution kernel estimates have been described and extensively discussed in the context of estimating a probability density from independent and identically distributed data (Carroll and Hall, 1988; Stefansky and Carroll, 1990). To explain the basic idea behind this type of estimates we consider the deconvolution problem first. Let $\xi_1, \ldots, \xi_N$ be independent and identically distributed real random variables with density $p_\xi(x)$ which we want to estimate. We do not, however, observe the ξ_k directly but only with additive errors $\eta_1, \ldots, \eta_N$. Let us assume that the η_k as well are independent and identically distributed with density $p_\eta(x)$ and independent of the ξ_k. Hence, the available data are

$$X_k = \xi_k + \eta_k , \quad k = 1, \ldots, N.$$

To be able to identify the distribution of the ξ_k from the errors η_k at all, we have to assume that $p_\eta(x)$ is known. The density of the observations X_k is just the convolution of p_ξ with p_η:

$$p_x(x) = p_\xi(x) \star p_\eta(x) .$$

We can therefore try to estimate $p_x(x)$ by a common kernel estimate and extract an estimate for $p_\xi(x)$ out of it. This kind of deconvolution operation is preferably performed in the frequency domain, i.e. after applying a Fourier transform. As the subsequent inverse Fourier transform includes already a smoothing part we can start with the empirical distribution of $X_1, \ldots, X_N$ instead of a smoothed version of it. In detail, we calculate the Fourier transform or characteristic function of the empirical law of $X_1, \ldots, X_N$, i.e. the sample characteristic function

$$\widehat{\phi}_x(\omega) = \frac{1}{N} \sum_{k=1}^{N} e^{i\omega X_k} .$$

Let

$$\phi_\eta(\omega) = \mathrm{E}(e^{i\omega \eta_k}) = \int_{-\infty}^{\infty} e^{i\omega u} p_\eta(u)\, du$$

denote the (known) characteristic function of the η_k. Furthermore, let K be a common kernel function, i.e. a nonnegative continuous function which is symmetric around 0 and integrates up to 1: $\int K(u)\, du = 1$, and let

$$\phi_K(\omega) = \int e^{i\omega u} K(u)\, du$$

be its Fourier transform. Then, the *deconvolution kernel density estimate* of $p_\xi(x)$ is defined as

$$\widehat{p}_h(x) = \frac{1}{2\pi} \int_{-\infty}^{\infty} e^{-i\omega x} \phi_K(\omega h) \frac{\widehat{\phi}_x(\omega)}{\phi_\eta(\omega)} \, d\omega \ .$$

The name of this estimate is explained by the fact that it may be written equivalently as a kernel density estimate

$$\widehat{p}_h(x) = \frac{1}{Nh} \sum_{k=1}^{N} K^h \left(\frac{x - X_k}{h} \right)$$

with deconvolution kernel

$$K^h(u) = \frac{1}{2\pi} \int_{-\infty}^{\infty} e^{-i\omega u} \frac{\phi_K(\omega)}{\phi_\eta(\omega/h)} \, d\omega$$

depending explicitly on the smoothing parameter h. Based on this kernel estimate for probability densities, Fan and Truong (1993) considered the analogous deconvolution kernel regression estimate defined as

$$\widehat{m}_h(x) = \frac{1}{Nh} \sum_{k=1}^{N} K^h \left(\frac{x - X_k}{h} \right) Y_k \, / \, \widehat{p}_h(x).$$

This Nadaraya-Watson-type estimate is consistent for the regression function $m(x)$ in an errors-in-variables regression model

$$Y_k = m(\xi_k) + W_k, \quad X_k = \xi_k + \eta_k, \quad k = 1, \ldots, N,$$

where $W_1, \ldots, W_N$ are independent identically distributed zero-mean random variables independent of the X_k, ξ_k, η_k which are chosen as above. The X_k, Y_k are observed, and the probability density of the η_k has to be known.

17.2 Nonparametric ARMA Estimates

GARCH processes are closely related to ARMA processes. If we square a GARCH(1,1) process $\{\varepsilon_t\}$ given by (17.1) then we get an ARMA(1,1) process

$$\varepsilon_t^2 = \omega + (\alpha + \beta) \varepsilon_{t-1}^2 - \beta \zeta_{t-1} + \zeta_t,$$

where $\zeta_t = \sigma_t^2(Z_t^2 - 1)$ is white noise, i.e. a sequence of pairwise uncorrelated random variables, with mean 0. Therefore, we study as an intermediate step towards GARCH processes the nonparametric estimation for ARMA models which is more closely related to the errors-in-variables regression of Fan and Truong (1993). A linear ARMA(1,1) model with non-vanishing mean ω is given by

$$X_{t+1} = \omega + a\, X_t + b\, e_t + e_{t+1}$$

with zero-mean white noise e_t. We consider the nonparametric generalization of this model

$$X_{t+1} = f(X_t, e_t) + e_{t+1} \qquad (17.3)$$

for some unknown function $f(x, u)$ which is monotone in the second argument u. Assume we have a sample $X_1, \ldots, X_{N+1}$ observed from (17.3). If f does not depend on the second argument, (17.3) reduces to a nonparametric autoregression of order 1

$$X_{t+1} = f(X_t) + e_{t+1}$$

and the autoregression function $f(x)$ may be estimated by common kernel estimates or local polynomials. There exists extensive literature about that type of estimation problem, and we refer to the review paper of Härdle, Lütkepohl and Chen (1997). In the general case of (17.3) we again have the problem of estimating a function of (partially) non-observable variables. As f depends also on the observable time series X_t, the basic idea of constructing a nonparametric estimate of $f(x, u)$ is to combine a common kernel smoothing in the first variable x with a deconvolution kernel smoothing in the second variable u. To define the estimate we have to introduce some notation and assumptions.

We assume that the innovations e_t have a known probability density p_e with distribution function $P_e(v) = \int_{-\infty}^v p_e(u)\, du$ and with Fourier transform $\phi_e(\omega) \neq 0$ for all ω and

$$|\phi_e(\omega)| \geq c \cdot |\omega|^{\beta_0} \exp(-|\omega|^\beta / \gamma) \quad \text{for} \quad |\omega| \longrightarrow \infty$$

for some constants $c, \beta, \gamma > 0$, β_0. The nonlinear ARMA process (17.3) has to be stationary and strongly mixing with exponentially decaying mixing coefficients. Let $p(x)$ denote the density of the stationary marginal density of X_t.

The smoothing kernel K^x in x-direction is a common kernel function with compact support $[-1, +1]$ satisfying $0 \leq K^x(u) \leq K^x(0)$ for all u. The kernel K which is used in the deconvolution part has a Fourier transform $\phi_K(\omega)$

which is symmetric around 0, has compact support $[-1, +1]$ and satisfies some smoothness conditions (Holzberger, 2001). We have chosen a kernel with the following Fourier transform:

$$
\begin{aligned}
\phi_K(u) &= 1 - u^2 && \text{for} \quad |u| \leq 0.5 \\
\phi_K(u) &= 0.75 - (|u| - 0.5) - (|u| - 0.5)^2 \\
&\quad -220\,(|u| - 0.5)^4 + 1136\,(|u| - 0.5)^5 \\
&\quad -1968\,(|u| - 0.5)^6 + 1152\,(|u| - 0.5)^7 && \text{for} \quad 0.5 \leq |u| \leq 1.
\end{aligned}
$$

For convenience, we use the smoothing kernel K^x to be proportional to that function: $K^x(u) \propto \phi_K(u)$. The kernel K^x is hence an Epanechnikov kernel with modified boundaries.

Let $b = C/N^{1/5}$ be the bandwidth for smoothing in x-direction, and let $h = A/\log(N)$ be the smoothing parameter for deconvolution in u-direction where $A > \pi/2$ and $C > 0$ are some constants. Then,

$$
\widehat{p}_b(x) = \frac{1}{(N+1)b} \sum_{t=1}^{N+1} K^x\left(\frac{x - X_t}{b}\right)
$$

is a common Rosenblatt–Parzen density estimate for the stationary density $p(x)$.

Let $q(u)$ denote the stationary density of the random variable $f(X_t, e_t)$, and let $q(u|x)$ be its conditional density given $X_t = x$. An estimate of the latter is given by

$$
\widehat{q}_{b,h}(u|x) = \frac{1}{Nhb} \sum_{t=1}^{N} K^h\left(\frac{u - X_{t+1}}{h}\right) K^x\left(\frac{x - X_t}{b}\right) \Big/ \widehat{p}_b(x) \qquad (17.4)
$$

where the deconvolution kernel K^h is

$$
K^h(u) = \frac{1}{2\pi} \int_{-\infty}^{\infty} e^{-i\omega u} \frac{\phi_K(\omega)}{\phi_e(\omega/h)}\, d\omega .
$$

In (17.4) we use a deconvolution smoothing in the direction of the second argument of $f(x, u)$ using only pairs of observations (X_t, X_{t+1}) for which $|x - X_t| \leq b$, i.e. $X_t \approx x$. By integration, we get the conditional distribution function of $f(X_t, e_t)$ given $X_t = x$

$$
Q(v|x) = \mathrm{P}(f(x, e_t) \leq v | X_t = x) = \int_{-\infty}^{v} q(u|x)\, du
$$

and its estimate

$$\widehat{Q}_{b,h}(v|x) = \int_{-a_N}^{v} \widehat{q}_{b,h}(u|x)du \Big/ \int_{-a_N}^{a_N} \widehat{q}_{b,h}(u|x)\, du$$

for some $a_N \sim N^{1/6}$ for $N \to \infty$. Due to technical reasons we have to cut off the density estimate in regions where it is still unreliable for given N. The particular choice of denominator guarantees that $\widehat{Q}_{b,h}(a_N|x) = 1$ in practice, since $Q(v|x)$ is a cumulative distribution function.

To estimate the unconditional density $q(u)$ of $f(X_t, e_t) = X_{t+1} - e_{t+1}$, we use a standard deconvolution density estimate with smoothing parameter $h^* = A^*/\log(N)$

$$\widehat{q}_{h^*}(u) = \frac{1}{Nh^*} \sum_{t=1}^{N} K_{h^*}\left(\frac{u - X_t}{h^*}\right).$$

Let $p_e(u|x)$ be the conditional density of e_t given $X_t = x$, and let $P_e(v|x) = \int_{-\infty}^{v} p_e(u|x)\, du$ be the corresponding conditional distribution function. An estimate of it is given as

$$\widehat{P}_{e,h^*}(v|x) = \int_{-a_N}^{v} \widehat{q}_{h^*}(x - u)\, p_e(u)du \Big/ \int_{-a_N}^{a_N} \widehat{q}_{h^*}(x - u)\, p_e(u)\, du$$

where again we truncate at $a_N \sim N^{1/6}$.

To obtain the ARMA function f, we can now compare $Q(v|x)$ and $P_e(v|x)$. In practice this means to relate $\widehat{Q}_{b,h}(v|x)$ and $\widehat{P}_{e,h^*}(v|x)$. The nonparametric estimate for the ARMA function $f(x,v)$ depending on smoothing parameters b, h and h^* is hence given by

$$\widehat{f}_{b,h,h^*}(x,v) = \widehat{Q}_{b,h}^{-1}(\widehat{P}_{e,h^*}(v|x)\,|x)$$

if $f(x,v)$ is increasing in the second argument, and

$$\widehat{f}_{b,h,h^*}(x,v) = \widehat{Q}_{b,h}^{-1}(1 - \widehat{P}_{e,h^*}(v|x)\,|x)$$

if $f(x,v)$ is a decreasing function of v for any x. $\widehat{Q}_{b,h}^{-1}(\cdot|x)$ denotes the inverse of the function $\widehat{Q}_{b,h}(\cdot|x)$ for fixed x. Holzberger (2001) has shown that $\widehat{f}_{b,h,h^*}(x,v)$ is a consistent estimate for $f(x,v)$ under suitable assumptions and has given upper bounds on the rates of bias and variance of the estimate. We remark that the assumption of monotonicity on f is not a strong restriction. In the application to GARCH processes which we have in mind it seems to be intuitively reasonable that the volatility of today is an increasing function of the volatility of yesterday which translates into an ARMA function f which is decreasing in the second argument.

Let us illustrate the steps for estimating a nonparametric ARMA process. First we generate time series data and plot X_{t+1} versus X_t.

```
library("times")
n=1000
x=genarma(0.7,0.7,normal(n))
```

🔍 XFGnpg01.xpl

The result is shown in Figure 17.1. The scatterplot in the right panel of Figure 17.1 defines the region where we can estimate the function $f(x, v)$.

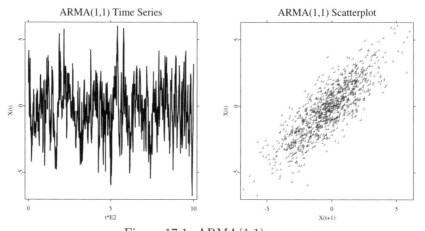

Figure 17.1. ARMA(1,1) process.

To compare the deconvolution density estimate with the density of $f(X_t, e_t)$ we use now our own routine (`myarma`) for generating ARMA(1,1) data from a known function (`f`):

```
proc(f)=f(x,e,c)
   f=c[1]+c[2]*x+c[3]*e
endp
```

```
proc(x,f)=myarma(n,c)
  x=matrix(n+1)-1
  f=x
  e=normal(n+1)
  t=1
  while (t<n+1)
    t=t+1
    f[t]=f(x[t-1],e[t-1],c)
    x[t]=f[t]+e[t]
  endo
  x=x[2:(n+1)]
  f=f[2:(n+1)]
endp

n=1000
{x,f}=myarma(n,0|0.7|0.7)

h=0.4
library("smoother")
dh=dcdenest(x,h)          // deconvolution estimate
fh=denest(f,3*h)          // kernel estimate
```

Q XFGnpg02.xpl

Figure 17.2 shows both density estimates. Note that the smoothing parameter
(bandwidth h) is different for both estimates since different kernel functions
are used.

---

f = nparmaest (x {,h {,g {,N {,R } } } })
      estimates a nonparametric ARMA process

The function **nparmaest** computes the function $f(x, v)$ for an ARMA process
according to the algorithm described above. Let us first consider an ARMA(1,1)

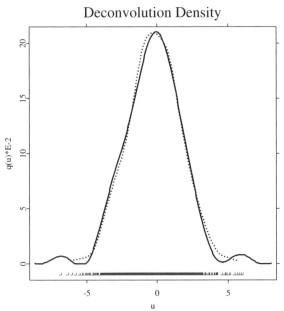

Figure 17.2. Deconvolution density estimate (solid) and kernel density estimate (dashed) of the known mean function of an ARMA(1,1) process.

with $f(x, v) = 0.3 + 0.6x + 1.6v$, i.e.

$$X_t = 0.3 + 0.6X_{t-1} + 1.6e_{t-1} + e_t.$$

Hence, we use `myarma` with `c=0.3|0.6|1.6` and call the estimation routine by

```
f=nparmaest(x)
```

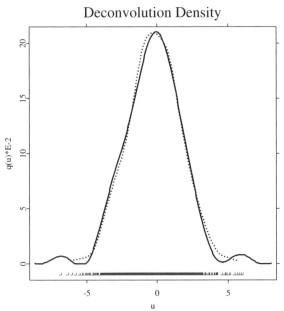 **Q** XFGnpg03.xpl

The optional parameters N and R are set to 50 and 250, respectively. N contains the grid sizes used for x and v. R is an additional grid size for internal computations. The resulting function is therefore computed on a grid of size N × N. For comparison, we also calculate the true function on the same grid. Figure 17.3 shows the resulting graphs. The bandwidths h (corresponding to h^*) for the one-dimensional deconvolution kernel estimator $\widehat{q}$ and g for the two-dimensional (corresponding to h and b) are chosen according to the rates derived in Holzberger (2001).

Linear ARMA(1,1)

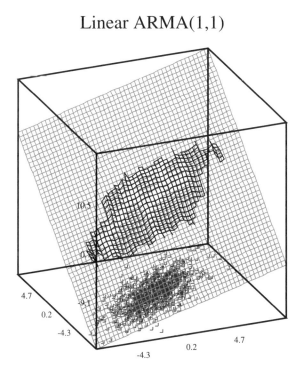

Figure 17.3. Nonparametric estimation of a (linear) ARMA process. True vs. estimated function and data.

As a second example consider an ARMA(1,1) with a truly nonlinear function $f(x, v) = -2.8 + 8F(6v)$, i.e.

$$X_t = -2.8 + 8F(6\,e_{t-1}) + e_t,$$

where F denotes the sigmoid function $F(u) = (1 + e^{-u})^{-1}$ In contrast to the previous example, this function is obviously not dependent on the first argument. The code above has to be modified by using

```
proc(f)=f(x,e,c)
```

```
   f=c[2]/(1+exp(-c[3]*e))+c[1]
endp
c=-2.8|8|6
```

Q XFGnpg04.xpl

The resulting graphs for this nonlinear function are shown in Figure 17.4. The estimated surface varies obviously only in the second dimension and follows the s-shaped underlying true function. However, the used sample size and the internal grid sizes of the estimation procedure do only allow for a rather imprecise reconstruction of the tails of the surface.

Nonlinear ARMA(1,1)

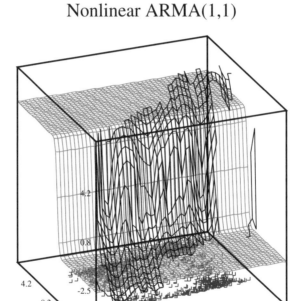

Figure 17.4. Nonparametric estimation of a (nonlinear) ARMA process. True vs. estimated function and data.

17.3   Nonparametric GARCH Estimates

In the following, we consider nonparametric GARCH(1,1) models which depend symmetrically on the last observation:

$$
\begin{aligned}
\varepsilon_t &= \sigma_t Z_t, \\
\sigma_t^2 &= g(\varepsilon_{t-1}^2, \sigma_{t-1}^2).
\end{aligned}
\tag{17.5}
$$

Here, g denotes a smooth unknown function and the innovations Z_t are chosen as in as in Section 17.2. This model covers the usual parametric GARCH(1,1) process (17.1) but does not allow for representing a leverage effect like the TGARCH(1,1) process. We show now how to transform (17.5) into an ARMA model. First, we define

$$
X_t = \log(\varepsilon_t^2), \quad e_t = \log(Z_t^2).
$$

By (17.5), we have now

$$
\begin{aligned}
X_{t+1} &= \log(\varepsilon_{t+1}^2) = \log \sigma_{t+1}^2 + e_{t+1} \\
&= \log g(\varepsilon_t^2, \sigma_t^2) + e_{t+1} \\
&= \log g_1(\log(\varepsilon_t^2), \log(\sigma_t^2)) + e_{t+1} \\
&= \log g_1(X_t, X_t - e_t) + e_{t+1} \\
&= f(X_t, e_t) + e_{t+1}
\end{aligned}
$$

with

$$
g_1(x, u) = g(e^x, e^u), \quad f(x, v) = \log g_1(x, x - v).
$$

Now, we can estimate the ARMA function $f(x, v)$ from the logarithmic squared data $X_t = \log(\varepsilon_t^2)$ as in Section 17.3 using the nonparametric ARMA estimate $\widehat{f}_{b,h,h^*}(x, v)$ of (17.5). Reverting the transformations, we get

$$
\widehat{g}_1(x, u) = \exp\{\widehat{f}_{b,h,h^*}(x, x - u)\}, \quad \widehat{g}_{b,h,h^*}(y, z) = \widehat{g}_1(\log y, \log z)
$$

or, combining both equations,

$$
\widehat{g}_{b,h,h^*}(y, z) = \exp\left\{\widehat{f}_{b,h,h^*}(\log y, \log(y/z))\right\}, \quad y, z > 0,
$$

as an estimate of the symmetric GARCH function $g(y, z)$.

We have to be aware, of course, that the density p_e used in the deconvolution part of estimating $f(x, v)$ is the probability density of the $e_t = \log Z_t^2$, i.e. if

$p_z(z)$ denotes the density of Z_t,

$$p_e(u) = \frac{1}{2}\left\{e^{u/2}p_z(e^{u/2}) + e^{-u/2}p_z(e^{-u/2})\right\}.$$

If ε_t is a common parametric GARCH(1,1) process of form (17.1), then $g(y,z) = \omega + \alpha y + \beta z$, and the corresponding ARMA function is $f(x,v) = \log(\omega + \alpha e^x + \beta e^{x-v})$. This is a decreasing function in v which seems to be a reasonable assumption in the general case too corresponding to the assumption that the present volatility is an increasing function of past volatilities.

As an example, we simulate a GARCH process from

```
proc(f)=gf(x,e,c)
  f=c[1]+c[2]*x+c[3]*e
endp

proc(e,s2)=mygarch(n,c)
  e=zeros(n+1)
  f=e
  s2=e
  z=normal(n+1)
  t=1
  while (t<n+1)
    t=t+1
    s2[t]=gf(e[t-1]^2,s2[t-1]^2,c)
    e[t]=sqrt(s2[t]).*z[t]
  endo
  e=e[2:(n+1)]
  s2=s2[2:(n+1)]
endp
```

```
f = npgarchest (x {,h {,g {,N {,R } } } } )
     estimates a nonparametric GARCH process
```

The function `npgarchest` computes the functions $f(x, v)$ and $g(y, z)$ for a GARCH process using the techniques described above.   Consider a GARCH(1,1) with

$$g(y, z) = 0.01 + 0.6\,y + 0.2\,z.$$

Hence, we use

```
n=1000
c=0.01|0.6|0.2
{e,s2}=mygarch(n,c)
```

and call the estimation routine by

```
g=npgarchest(e)
```

Q XFGnpg05.xpl

Figure 17.5 shows the resulting graph for the estimator of $f(x, v)$ together with the true function (decreasing in v) and the data (X_{t+1} versus X_t). As in the ARMA case, the estimated function shows the underlying structure only for a part of the range of the true function.

Finally, we remark how the the general case of nonparametric GARCH models could be estimated. Consider

$$
\begin{aligned}
\varepsilon_t &= \sigma_t Z_t && (17.6) \\
\sigma_t^2 &= g(\varepsilon_{t-1}, \sigma_{t-1}^2)
\end{aligned}
$$

where σ_t^2 may depend asymmetrically on ε_{t-1}. We write

$$g(x, z) = g^+(x^2, z)\,\mathbf{1}(x \geq 0) + g^-(x^2, z)\,\mathbf{1}(x < 0).$$

As g^+, g^- depend only on the squared arguments we can estimate them as before. Again, consider $X_t = \log(\varepsilon_t^2), e_t = \log(Z_t^2)$. Let N_+ be the number of all $t \leq N$ with $\varepsilon_t \geq 0$, and $N_- = N - N_+$. Then, we set

$$
\begin{aligned}
\widehat{p}_b^+(x) &= \frac{1}{N_+ b} \sum_{t=1}^{N} K^x(\frac{x - X_t}{b}) \mathbf{1}(\varepsilon_t \geq 0) \\
\widehat{q}_{b,h}^+(u|x) &= \frac{1}{N_+ h b} \sum_{t=1}^{N} K^h\left(\frac{u - X_{t+1}}{h}\right) K^x\left(\frac{x - X_t}{b}\right) \mathbf{1}(\varepsilon_t \geq 0) \,/\, \widehat{p}_b^+(x) \\
\widehat{q}_{h^*}^+(u) &= \frac{1}{N_+ h^*} \sum_{t=1}^{N} K^{h^*}\left(\frac{u - X_t}{h^*}\right) \mathbf{1}(\varepsilon_t \geq 0).
\end{aligned}
$$

Nonparametric GARCH(1,1)

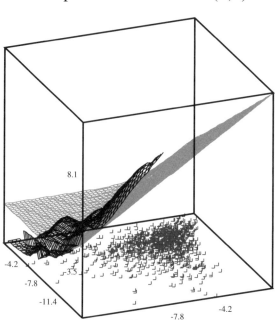

Figure 17.5. Nonparametric estimation of $f(x,v)$ for a (linear) GARCH process. True vs. estimated function, data $X_t = \log(\varepsilon_t^2)$.

$\widehat{Q}_{b,h}^+(v|x)$, $\widehat{P}_{e,h^*}^+(v|x)$ are defined as in Section 17.2 with $\widehat{q}_{b,h}^+, \widehat{p}_b^+$ replacing $\widehat{q}_{b,h}$ and $\widehat{p}_b$, and, using both estimates of conditional distribution functions we get an ARMA function estimate $\widehat{f}_{b,h,h^*}^+(x,v)$. Reversing the transformation from GARCH to ARMA, we get as the estimate of $g^+(x^2,z)$

$$\widehat{g}_{b,h,h^*}^+(x^2,z) = \exp\left\{\widehat{f}_{b,h,h^*}^+\left(\log x^2, \log(x^2/z)\right)\right\}.$$

The estimate for $g^-(x^2,z)$ is analogously defined

$$\widehat{g}_{b,h,h^*}^-(x^2,z) = \exp\left\{\widehat{f}_{b,h,h^*}^-\left(\log x^2, \log(x^2/z)\right)\right\}.$$

where, in the derivation of $\widehat{f}_{b,h,h^*}^-$, N_+ and $\mathbf{1}(\varepsilon_t \geq 0)$ are replaced by N_- and $\mathbf{1}(\varepsilon_t < 0)$.

Bibliography

Bollerslev, T.P. (1986). Generalized autoregressive conditional heteroscedasticity, *Journal of Econometrics* **31**: 307-327.

Bühlmann, P. and McNeil, A.J. (1999). *Nonparametric GARCH-models*, Manuscript, ETH Zürich, http://www.math.ethz.ch/~mcneil.

Carroll, R.J. and Hall, P. (1988). Optimal rates of convergence for deconvoluting a density, *J. Amer. Statist. Assoc.* **83**: 1184-1186.

Fan, J. and Truong, Y.K. (1993). Nonparametric regression with errors-in-variables, *Ann. Statist.* **19**: 1257-1272.

Franke, J., Härdle, W. and Hafner, Ch. (2001). *Statistik der Finanzmärkte*, Springer, ebook: http://www.quantlet.de.

Härdle, W., Lütkepohl, H. and Chen, R. (1997). A review of nonparametric time series analysis, *International Statistical Review* **65**: 49-72.

Holzberger, H. (2001). *Nonparametric Estimation of Nonlinear ARMA and GARCH-processes*, PhD Thesis, University of Kaiserslautern.

J.P. Morgan. RiskMetrics, http://www.jpmorgan.com.

Stefansky, L.A. and Carroll, R.J. (1990). Deconvoluting kernel density estimators, *Statistics* **21**: 169-184.

18 Net Based Spreadsheets in Quantitative Finance

Gökhan Aydınlı

18.1 Introduction

Modern risk management requires accurate, fast and flexible computing environments. To meet this demand a vast number of software packages evolved over the last decade, accompanying a huge variety of programming languages, interfaces, configuration and output possibilities. One solution especially designed for large scale explorative data analysis is XploRe, a procedural programming environment, equipped with a modern client/server architecture (Härdle et al. (1999) and Härdle et al. (2000)).

As far as flexibility in the sense of openness and accuracy is concerned XploRe has a lot to offer a risk analyst may wish. On the contrary its matrix oriented programming language (Fickel, 2001) might be seen as a drawback in respect to other computational approaches. In terms of learning curve effects and total cost of ownership an alternative solution seems desirable.

This chapter will present and demonstrate the net based spreadsheet solution MD*ReX designed for modern statistical and econometric analysis. We concentrate on examples of Value-at-risk (VaR) with copulas and means of quantifying implied volatilities presented in Chapter 2 and 6. All results will be shown in Microsoft Excel.

Recent research work suggests that the rationale for spreadsheet based statistical computing is manifold. Ours is to bring state-of-the-art quantitative methods to the fingertips of spreadsheet users. Throughout this chapter we will give a short introduction into our underlying technology, briefly explain the usage of the aforementioned spreadsheet solution and provide applications of this tool.

18.2   Client/Server based Statistical Computing

While the power of computing equipment increased exponentially, statistical algorithms yielded higher efficiency in terms of computing time and accuracy. Meanwhile the development of high capacity network architectures had another positive impact on this trend, especially the establishment of the world wide web. Consequently a vast number of researchers and programmers in computational statistics as well as institutions like commercial banks, insurers and corporations spent much effort to utilize this evolution for their field of research. An outcome has been the technological philosophy of *client/server* based statistical computing: meaning a decentralized combination of methods, users and providers of statistical knowledge.

Our understanding of client/server based statistical computing is such that there exists a formal relationship between user, provider and vendor of statistical methodology. An easy to grasp example is a telephone call. The caller (in our case the user demanding statistical methods and/or advice) calls (connects via TCP/IP enabled networks) someone (a high-performance server/vendor of statistical information and methods) who serves his call (the requested calculation is done/information is displayed in a HTML browser, etc.). This client/server understanding is an approach to gain scalability of computational tasks, resource shifting of processing power and decentralization of methods.

There are numerous ways of implementing client/server based statistics, among others Common Gateway Interfaces (CGI), JavaScript, Java Applets and Plug-Ins are the most commonly used techniques. The technology behind the XploRe client/server architecture is thoroughly explained in Kleinow and Lehmann (2002). While that solution is applet based the spreadsheet client presented here has an Add-in character. The MD*ReX-Client is a software tool, nested within an spreadsheet application. In both cases the communication technique relies on the protocol stack MD*CRYPT. For the spreadsheet solution the Java based MD*CRYPT has to be modified. As Microsoft does not support any Java natively for its Office suite, MD*CRYPT has been implemented as a dynamic link library to utilize its interface for Office applications like Excel. The technical aspects and the design philosophy of the MD*ReX-Client are discussed in detail in Aydınlı et al. (2002).

18.3 Why Spreadsheets?

Since their first appearance in the late 1970s spreadsheets gained a remarkable popularity in business as well as research and education. They are the most common software managers, researchers and traders utilize for data analysis, quantitative modelling and decision support.

Przasnyski and Seal (1996) find that most of the time series modeling done in the business world is accomplished using spreadsheets. Further research work suggests that those users have become so proficient with spreadsheets that they are reluctant to adopt other software solutions. Not even a higher suitability for specific applications is appealing then (Chan and Storey, 1996). An analysis of XploRe download profiles conducted in a data mining framework confirmed our perception of the statistical software market. A stunning majority of users are using Excel for statistical analysis (Sofyan and Werwatz, 2001).

A major difference between a spreadsheet application and statistical programming languages is the interaction model. This *"direct manipulation interaction model"* enables statistical computations e.g. by drag and drop (Neuwirth and Baier, 2001). In the cell based framework of spreadsheets the direct aspect of interaction means, that manipulations in one cell immediately effect the content of another cell. Of course this is only the case if the regarding cells are interconnected with appropriate cell functions and references. Especially in business applications the immediate visibility of numerical changes when cell values are modified, is an appreciated feature for decision making based on different scenarios.

Our approach is based on the philosophy to bring two ideals together: On the one hand an accurate and reliable statistical engine (which is represented by the XploRe Quantlet Server, *XQS*) and on the other a user friendly and intuitive Graphical User Interface like Excel. The numerical impreciseness of Excel has been discussed exhaustively in the literature. As a starting point the reader is referred to e.g. McCullough and Wilson (1999). The development of MD*ReX is guided by the principles of usability and flexibility. Hence we try to offer different modes of usage for varying user groups: a dialogue based and more "Windows" like appearance for the novice user of statistical software and a "raw" mode where the spreadsheet application merely functions as a data import wizard and scratch-pad for the advanced user.

18.4   Using MD*ReX

We will demonstrate the usage of MD*ReX in the context of quantitative financial modeling. In order to use MD*ReX a working installation of Excel 9.x is required. Furthermore the installation routine will setup a Java runtime environment and if needed a Virtual Java Machine. For more information please refer to `http://md-rex.com/`.

After successfully installing the client it can be used in two ways: for an on-demand usage MD*ReX can be accessed via the Start → Programs shortcut in Windows or if a permanent usage in Excel is requested, the Add-in can be installed from the Extras → Add-in Manager dialogue in Excel. The `rex.xla` file is located under

`%Systemroot%\%Program Files%\MDTech\ReX\ReX`.

In the latter case the client is available every time Excel is started. Anyway the client can be accessed via the Excel menu bar (Figure 18.1) and exposes its full functionality after clicking on the ReX menu item.

Figure 18.1. Excel and MD*ReX menus

In order to work with MD*ReX the user first has to connect herself to a running XploRe Quantlet Server. This can either be a local server, which by default is triggered if MD*ReX is started via the *Programs* shortcut, or any other XQS somewhere on the Internet. Evidently for the latter option a connection to the Internet is required. The *Connect* dialogue offers some pre-configured XQS'. After the connection has been successfully established the user can start right away to work with MD*ReX.

In contrast to XploRe, the user has the option to perform statistical analysis by using implemented dialogues e.g. the Time Series dialogue in Figure 18.3. Via this dialogue a researcher is able to conduct standard time series analysis techniques as well as e.g. more refined nonlinear approaches like ARCH tests based on neural networks. These interfaces encapsulate XploRe code while using the standard Excel GUI elements hence undue learning overhead is minimized. Alternatively one can directly write XploRe commands into the spreadsheet cells and then let these run either via the menu button or with the context menu, by right clicking the highlighted cell range (Figure 18.2). Furthermore it is now much easier to get data to the XploRe Quantlet Server. Simply marking an appropriate data range within Excel and clicking the *Put* button is enough to transfer any kind of numerical data to the server. We will show this in the next section. A further virtue of using a spreadsheet application is the commonly built-in database connectivity. Excel for example allows for various data retrieval mechanisms via the Open Database Connectivity (ODBC) standard, which is supported by most of the database systems available nowadays.

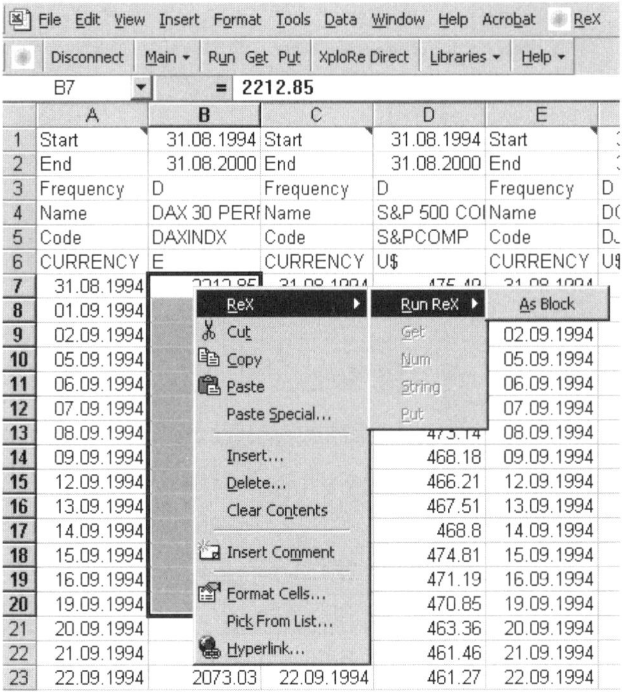

Figure 18.2. ReX Context Menu

18.5   Applications

In the following paragraph we want to show how MD*ReX might be used in order to analyze the VaR using copulas as described in Chapter 2 of this book. Subsequently we will demonstrate the analysis of implied volatility shown in Chapter 6. All examples are taken out of this book and have been accordingly modified. The aim is to make the reader aware of the need of this modification and give an idea how this client may be used for other fields of statistical research as well.

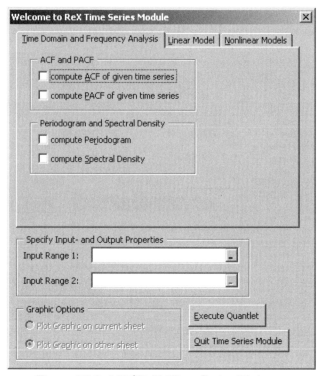

Figure 18.3. MD*ReX Time Series Dialogue

We have willingly omitted the demonstration of dialogues and menu bars as it is pretty straightforward to develop these kind of interfaces on your own. Some knowledge of the macro language Visual Basic for Applications (VBA) integrated into Excel and an understanding of the XploRe Quantlets is sufficient to create custom dialogues and menus for this client. Thus no further knowledge of the XploRe Quantlet syntax is required. An example is the aforementioned Time Series dialogue, Figure 18.3.

18.5.1   Value at Risk Calculations with Copulas

The quantification of the VaR of a portfolio of financial instruments has become a constituent part of risk management. Simplified the VaR is a quantile of the probability distribution of the value-loss of a portfolio (Chapter 2). Aggregating individual risk positions is one major concern for risk analysts. The $\mu - \sigma$ approach of portfolio management measures risk in terms of the variance, implying a "Gaussian world" (Bouyé et al., 2001). Traditional VaR methods are hence based on the normality assumption for the distribution of financial returns. Though empirical evidence suggests high probability of extreme returns (*"Fat tails"*) and more mass around the center of the distribution (*leptokurtosis*), violating the principles of the Gaussian world (Rachev, 2001).

In conjunction with the methodology of VaR these problems seem to be tractable with copulas. In a multivariate model setup a copula function is used to couple joint distributions to their marginal distributions. The copula approach has two major issues, substituting the dependency structure, i.e. the correlations and substituting the marginal distribution assumption, i.e. relaxation of the Gaussian distribution assumption. With MD*ReX the user is now enabled to conduct copula based VaR calculation with Excel, making use of Excel's powerful graphical capabilities and its intuitive interface.

The steps necessary are as follows:

1. Get the according Quantlets into Excel,

2. run them from there,

3. obtain the result,

4. create a plot of the result.

The first step is rather trivial: copy and paste the example Quantlet
Q XFGrexcopula1.xpl from any text editor or browser into an Excel worksheet.

Next mark the range containing the Quantlet and apply the *Run* command. Then switch to any empty cell of the worksheet and click *Get* to receive the numerical output `rexcuv`. Generating a tree-dimensional Excel graph from this output one obtains an illustration as displayed in Figure 18.4. The according Quantlets are **Q** `XFGrexcopula1.xpl`, **Q** `XFGrexcopula2.xpl`, **Q** `XFGrexcopula3.xpl` and **Q** `XFGrexcopula4.xpl`. They literally work the same way as the **Q** `XFGaccvar1.xpl` Quantlet.

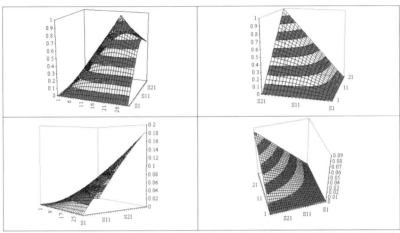

Figure 18.4. Copulas: $C_4(u,v)$ for $\theta = 2$ and $N = 30$ (upper left), $C_5(u,v)$ for $\theta = 3$ and $N = 21$ (upper right), $C_6(u,v)$ for $\theta = 4$ and $N = 30$ (lower left), $C_7(u,v)$ for $\theta = 5$ and $N = 30$ (lower right)

Of course the steps 1-4 could easily be wrapped into a VBA macro with suitable dialogues. This is exactly what we refer to as the change from the raw mode of MD*ReX into the "Windows" like embedded mode. Embedded here means that XploRe commands (quantlets) are integrated into the macro language of Excel.

The Monte Carlo simulations are obtained correspondingly and are depicted in Figure 18.5. The according Quantlet is **Q** `XFGrexmccopula.xpl`. This Quantlet again is functioning analogous to **Q** `XFGaccvar2.xpl`. The graphical output then is constructed along same lines: paste the corresponding results `z11` through `z22` in cell areas and let Excel draw a scatter-plot.

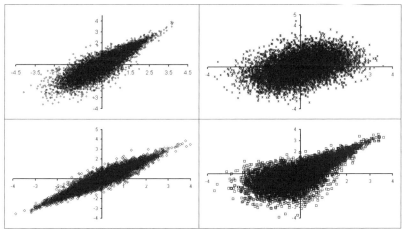

Figure 18.5. Monte Carlo Simulations for $N = 10000$ and $\sigma_1 = 1$, $\sigma_2 = 1$, $\theta = 3$

18.5.2 Implied Volatility Measures

A basic risk measure in finance is *volatility*, which can be applied to a single asset or a bunch of financial assets (i.e. a portfolio). Whereas the *historic volatility* simply measures past price movements the *implied volatility* represents a market perception of uncertainty. Implied volatility is a contemporaneous risk measure which is obtained by reversely solving an option pricing model as the Black-Scholes model for the volatility. The implied volatility can only be quantified if there are options traded which have the asset or assets as an underlying (for example a stock index). The examples here are again taken out of Chapter 6. The underlying data are `VolaSurf02011997.xls`, `VolaSurf03011997.xls` and `volsurfdata2`. The data has been kindly provided by MD*BASE. `volsurfdata2` ships with any distribution of XploRe. In our case the reader has the choice of either importing the data into Excel via the data import utility or simply running the command `data=read("volsurfdata2.dat")`. For the other two data sets utilizing the *Put* button is the easiest way to transfer the data to an XQS. Any of these alternatives have the same effect, whereas the former is a good example of how the MD*ReX client exploits the various data retrieval methods of Excel.

The Quantlet **Q** `XFGReXiv.xpl` returns the data matrix for the implied volatility surfaces shown in Figure 18.6 through 18.8. Evidently the Quantlet has to

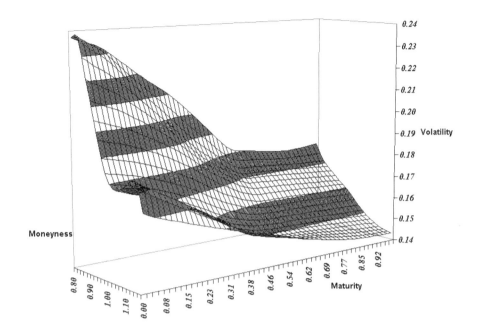

Figure 18.6. DAX30 Implied Volatility, 02.01.1997

be modified for the appropriate data set. In contrast to the above examples where Quantlets could be adopted without any further modification, in this case we need some redesign of the XploRe code. This is achieved with suitable reshape operations of the output matrices. The graphical output is then obtained by arranging the two output vectors x2 and y2 and the output matrix z1.

The advantage of measuring implied volatilities is obviously an expressive visualization. Especially the well known volatility smile and the corresponding time structure can be excellently illustrated in a movable cubic space. Furthermore this approach will enable real-time calculation of implied volatilities in future applications. Excel can be used as a data retrieval front end for real-time market data providers as Datastream or Bloomberg. It is imaginable then to analyze tick-data which are fed online into such an spreadsheet system to evaluate contemporaneous volatility surfaces.

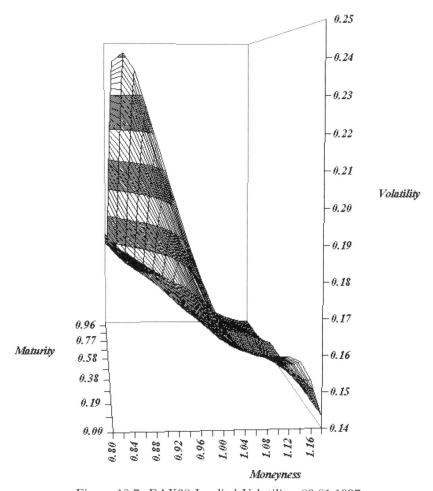

Figure 18.7. DAX30 Implied Volatility, 03.01.1997

Bibliography

Aydınlı, G., Härdle, W., Kleinow, T. and Sofyan, H.(2002). *ReX: Linking XploRe to Excel*, forthcoming Computational Statistics Special Issue, Springer Verlag, Heidelberg.

Bouyé, E., Durrleman, V., Nikeghbali, A., Riboulet, G. and Roncalli, T.(2000).

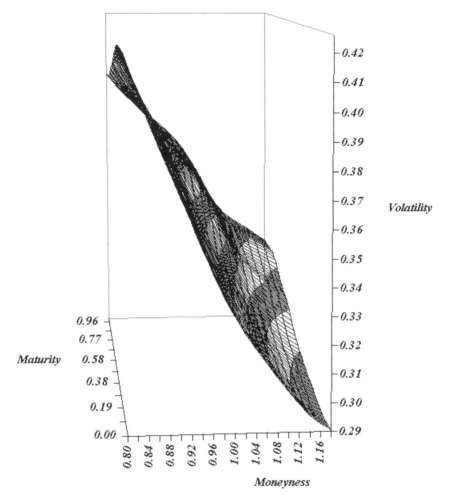

Figure 18.8. DAX30 Implied Volatility

Copulas for Finance, A Reading Guide and some Applications, unpublished manuscript, Financial Econometrics Research Centre, City University Business School, London, 2000.

Chan, Y.E. and Storey, V.C. (1996). *The use of spreadsheets in organizations: determinants and consequences*, Information & Management, Vol. 31, pp. 119-134.

Fickel, N. (2001). *Book Review: XploRe - Learning Guide*, Allgemeines Statistisches Archiv, Vol. 85/1, p. 93.

Härdle, W., Klinke, S. and Müller, M. (1999). *XploRe Learning Guide*, Springer Verlag, Heidelberg.

Härdle, W., Hlavka, Z. and Klinke, S. (2000). *XploRe Application Guide*, Springer Verlag, Heidelberg.

Kleinow, T. and Lehmann, H. (2002). *Client/Server based Statistical Computing*, forthcoming in Computational Statistics Special Issue, Springer Verlag, Heidelberg.

McCullough, B.D. and Wilson, B. (1999). *On the Accuracy of Statistical Procedures in Microsoft Excel*, Computational Statistics & Data Analysis, Vol. 31, p. 27-37.

Neuwirth, E. and Baier, T. (2001). *Embedding R in Standard Software, and the other way round*, DSC 2001 Proceedings of the 2nd International Workshop on Distributed Statistical Computing.

Przasnyski, L.L. and Seal, K.C. (1996). *Spreadsheets and OR/MS models: an end-user perspective*, Interfaces, Vol. 26, pp. 92-104.

Rachev, S. (2001). *Company Overview*, Bravo Consulting, http://www.bravo-group.com/inside/bravo-consulting_company-overview.pdf.

Ragsdale, C.T. and Plane, D.R. (2000). *On modeling time series data using spreadsheets*, The International Journal of Management Science, Vol. 28, pp. 215-221.

Sofyan, H. and Werwatz, A. (2001). *Analysing XploRe Download Profiles with Intelligent Miner*, Computational Statistics, Vol. 16, pp. 465-479.

Index

Printing: Druckhaus Berlin-Mitte
Binding: Buchbinderei Stein & Lehmann, Berlin

www.mdtech.de

www.springer.de

This

W. Härdle, T. Kleinow and G. Stahl:
"Applied Quantitative Finance"
ISBN 3-540-43460-7

can be downloaded from

www.xplore-stat.de

Please use the licence key

AQF-DE-6050-8749